THE ROAD TO MIDDLE-EARTH

THE ROAD TO MIDDLE-EARTH

T. A. SHIPPEY

Boston

HOUGHTON MIFFLIN COMPANY

1983

First American Edition 1983

Copyright © 1982 by T. A. Shippey

Library of Congress Cataloging in Publication Data
Shippey, T. A.
The road to Middle-earth.
Includes bibliographical references and index.
1. Tolkien, J. R. R. (John Ronald Reuel), 1892-1973.
Lord of the rings. I. Title.
PR6039.O32L6375   1983   823'.912   83-108
ISBN 0-395-33973-1

Printed in the United States of America

S 10 9 8 7 6 5 4 3 2 1

Dedicated to the memory of
John Ernest Kjelgaard
lost at sea, *HMS Beverley*
11 April 1943

CONTENTS

ACKNOWLEDGEMENTS AND ABBREVIATIONS

I have had several clear warnings as to the dangers of writing this book, not least from Professor Tolkien himself: who, on reading a very short and early draft of it twelve years ago, replied kindly, but with the hint that he would like to 'talk more' with me 'about "design" as it appears or may be found in a large finished work, and the actual events or experiences as seen or felt by the waking mind in the course of actual composition'. Evidently he felt that I had found 'design' too readily, and become, as critics do, too faithful to my own scheme. Some years before, his Valedictory Address to the University of Oxford (now printed in *Memoriam Essays*) had made clear his low opinion of literary 'research'; while his letters bear witness to a particular suspicion of source-studies. This book continues to talk about design, and to indicate sources, and to that extent goes against the wishes of its subject, or rather its subject's creator. However I may hope that, warned early, and educated at all times under a plan Professor Tolkien had approved (and in most cases himself had followed), I have not become as 'bewildered' as many. My first acknowledgement must then be to Professor Tolkien himself, for a prompt and salutary tip.

This book could further not have been written without the immense assistance of Mr Humphrey Carpenter's three works, *J. R. R. Tolkien: a Biography*, *The Inklings*, and the *Letters of J. R. R. Tolkien*, edited by Mr Carpenter with the assistance of Christopher Tolkien. They have provided a frame for my inquiries, and I have referred to them continually. Both Mr Carpenter and Mr Tolkien have furthermore read many hundreds of pages of type-script and have corrected many errors, both factual and of interpretation, thoughtfully and magnanimously. Those that remain are my responsibility alone, as is the general trend of this book's argument, which no adviser, perhaps, could satisfactorily modify. I am much indebted also to Mr Rayner Unwin for encouragement without pressure over too long a period; and to Mrs Pam Armitage for typing repeated drafts with exemplary care.

Friends and colleagues past and present have provided me with much additional information, in particular John Bourne, Lesley Burnett, Janet and Malcolm Godden, Tony Green, Constance Hieatt, David Masson and Rory McTurk; while Tolkienists both within and without the Tolkien Society have put me straight on details. I must thank especially Rhona

Beare and Jessica Yates for many long letters and contributions, as also Charles Noad and Gary Kuris. Some of these debts are acknowledged more fully in text and notes.

Cornell University Press have kindly permitted me to reproduce here the substance of my chapter 'Creation from Philology in *The Lord of the Rings*', from *J. R. R. Tolkien, Scholar and Story-Teller: Essays in Memoriam*, edited by Mary Salu and Robert T. Farrell, copyright © 1979 by Cornell University; and I have also to thank Tolkien's literary executors for permission to translate the four poems in Appendix B. They and Messrs George Allen & Unwin have further allowed me to quote freely from all Tolkien's published works. Thanks are due to the Oxford University Press for permission to quote from the *Oxford English Dictionary*, and indeed the most courteous deed of all is that of Mr Robert Burchfield, the Dictionary's General Editor, who has given such permission in spite of all the shafts which Tolkien and I have levelled at the work of his predecessors. It should not need me to say that, whatever additions one can make to it, the *OED* remains the most useful work any English critic can possess.

When it comes to citation of ancient texts (as in this book it often does) I have not given full references in academic style. Partly this is because they would be useless to the general reader. More forcefully, one can say that there is no subject for which 'standard editions' are less relevant than the works of Tolkien. He knew *Beowulf*, and the *Anglo-Saxon Poetic Records*, and the *Elder Edda*, and *Pearl* and *Sir Gawain* and Saxo Grammaticus, a good deal better than most of their editors, even when, as happened occasionally, his earlier self *was* the editor. It may be taken, then, that 'standard editions' have been referred to, and some are cited in Appendix A to this work, but quotations rest on the authority of the original manuscripts, and have sometimes been emended to what I think are the most 'Tolkienian' forms. With Old English and Old Norse I have used marks of vowel-length similar to those in *The Lord of the Rings*, though I have not introduced them to *The Hobbit* nor to much-mentioned Old English names such as Beowulf (Béowulf). All translations, unless separately acknowledged, are my own.

Abbreviations used in the text and notes are as follows (all works mentioned being by Tolkien himself, unless otherwise stated):

'AW'	'*Ancrene Wisse* and *Hali Meiðhad*', *Essays and Studies* vol. 14 (1929), pp. 104–26.
Biography	*J. R. R. Tolkien: a Biography*, by Humphrey Carpenter (London: George Allen & Unwin, 1977).
'EW'	'English and Welsh', in *Angles and Britons: O'Donnell Lectures* (Cardiff: University of Wales Press, 1963), pp. 1–41.
Giles	*Farmer Giles of Ham* (London: George Allen & Unwin, 1949).

'Guide' 'Guide to the Names in *The Lord of the Rings*' in *A Tolkien Compass*, edited by Jared Lobdell (La Salle, Illinois: Open Court, 1975), pp. 153–201.

Hobbit *The Hobbit: or There and Back Again* (3rd ed., London: George Allen & Unwin, 1966).

'Homecoming' 'The Homecoming of Beorhtnoth Beorhthelm's Son', *Essays and Studies* N.S. vol. 6 (1953), pp. 1–18.

Inklings *The Inklings: C. S. Lewis, J. R. R. Tolkien, Charles Williams and their friends*, by Humphrey Carpenter (London: George Allen & Unwin, 1978).

'Leaf' 'Leaf by Niggle', see *TL* below.

Letters *Letters of J. R. R. Tolkien*, edited by Humphrey Carpenter with the assistance of Christopher Tolkien (London: George Allen & Unwin, 1981).

LOTR *The Lord of the Rings* (three vols, London: George Allen & Unwin, 2nd ed., 1966). Cited by volume and page, or by book and chapter.

Memoriam Essays *J. R. R. Tolkien, Scholar and Story-Teller: Essays in Memoriam*, edited by Mary Salu and Robert T. Farrell (Ithaca and London: Cornell University Press, 1979).

'Monsters' 'Beowulf: the Monsters and the Critics', *Proceedings of the British Academy* vol. 22 (1936), pp. 245–95.

OED *The Oxford English Dictionary* (13 vols, Oxford: Clarendon Press, 1933). Note that this is a re-issue of *The New English Dictionary on Historical Principles*, issued in 10 volumes, 1884–1928.

'OES' 'The Oxford English School', *The Oxford Magazine* vol. 48, no. 21, 29 May 1930, pp. 778–82.

'OFS' 'On Fairy-Stories', see *TL* below.

Pictures *Pictures by J. R. R. Tolkien*, with Foreword and Notes by Christopher Tolkien (London: George Allen & Unwin, 1979).

'Preface' Preface to *Beowulf and the Finnesburg Fragment: a Translation into Modern English* by J. R. Clark Hall, revised by C. L. Wrenn (London: George Allen & Unwin, 1940).

Road *The Road Goes Ever On: a Song Cycle*, poems by J. R. R. Tolkien set to music by Donald Swann (London: George Allen & Unwin, 1968).

S *The Silmarillion*, by J. R. R. Tolkien, edited by Christopher Tolkien (London: George Allen & Unwin, 1977).

SGGK *Sir Gawain and the Green Knight*, edited by J. R. R. Tolkien and E. V. Gordon (Oxford: Clarendon Press, 1925).

SGPO *Sir Gawain and the Green Knight, Pearl and Sir Orfeo*, translated by J. R. R. Tolkien, edited and with a preface by Christopher Tolkien (London: George Allen & Unwin, 1975).

Smith	*Smith of Wootton Major* (London: George Allen & Unwin, 1967).
Songs	*Songs for the Philologists*, by J. R. R. Tolkien, E. V. Gordon and others (privately printed at the Dept. of English, University College, London, 1936).
TB	*The Adventures of Tom Bombadil and other verses from The Red Book* (London: George Allen & Unwin, 1962).
TL	*Tree and Leaf* (London: George Allen & Unwin, 1964). This contains both 'Leaf by Niggle' and 'On Fairy-Stories', first published in 1945 and 1947 respectively. References to both are by page in this volume.
UT	*Unfinished Tales of Numenor and Middle-earth*, by J. R. R. Tolkien, edited by Christopher Tolkien (London: George Allen & Unwin, 1981).
YWES	Chapters on 'Philology, General Works' in *The Year's Work in English Studies*, vols 4–6 for 1923–5. Cited by volume number and page.

For fuller bibliographical details, especially of Tolkien's many separately-printed poems and learned articles, one should consult the list of his published writings in *Biography*, pp. 268–75.

Chapter 1

'LIT. AND LANG.'

Old Antipathies

'This is not a work that many adults will read right through more than once.' With these words the anonymous reviewer for the *Times Literary Supplement* (25 November 1955) summed up his judgement of J. R. R. Tolkien's *The Lord of the Rings*. It must have seemed a pretty safe prophecy at the time, for of course very few adults (or children) read anything right through more than once, still less anything as long as *The Lord of the Rings*. However it could not have been more wrong. This did not stop critics continuing to say the same thing. Six years later, after the three separate volumes had gone through eight or nine hardback impressions each, Philip Toynbee in the *Observer* (6 August 1961) voiced delight at the way sales, he thought, were dropping. Most of Professor Tolkien's more ardent supporters, he declared, were beginning to 'sell out their shares' in him, so that 'today these books have passed into a merciful oblivion'. Five years afterwards the authorised American paperback edition of *The Lord of the Rings* was moving rapidly past its first million copies, starting a wave which has never receded even to the more-than-respectable levels of 1961.

The point is not that reviewers make mistakes (something which happens too often to deserve comment). It is that they should insist so perversely in making statements not about literary merit, where their opinions could rest undisprovable, but about popular appeal, where they can be shown up beyond all possibility of doubt. Matters are not much better with those critics who have been able to bring themselves to recognise the fact that some people *do* like Tolkien. Why was this 'balderdash' so popular, Edmund Wilson asked himself, in *The Nation* (14 April 1956). Well, he concluded, it was because 'certain people – especially, perhaps, in Britain – have a life-long appetite for juvenile trash'. Some twenty-five years before the same critic had delivered a little homily on the subject of intolerant responses to new fictions, in his book *Axel's Castle*:

it is well to remember the mysteriousness of the states with which we respond to the stimulus of works of literature and the primarily suggestive character of the language in which these works are written, on any occasion when we may be tempted to characterise as 'nonsense', 'balderdash' or 'gibberish' some new and outlandish-looking piece of writing to which we do not happen to respond. If other persons say they do respond, and derive from doing so pleasure or profit, we must take them at their word.[1]

A good rule, one must admit! But Mr Wilson had evidently forgotten it by the time he came to read *The Lord of the Rings*: or perhaps every time he said 'we' in the passage just quoted, he really meant 'you'.

Very similar play is made with pronouns in C. N. Manlove's *Modern Fantasy* (1975), a book dedicated to the thesis that no work of modern fantasy has remained 'true to its original vision', but one which like Edmund Wilson's review does at least confront the problem of Tolkienian popularity – of course much more evident in 1975 than 1956. Dr Manlove also thinks that the whole thing might be mere national aberration, though *he* prefers to blame the United States and 'the perennial American longing for roots'. Or could it all be due to mere length?

> Doubtless there is such a thing as the sheer number of pages the reader has had to turn that can add poignancy to the story – one almost feels this is the case as we come to the great close of Malory's epic. But not with Tolkien's book, for we have never been very much involved anyway.[2]

Who are 'we'? Readers of *Modern Fantasy*? Readers of *The Lord of the Rings*? There is no sensible answer to the question. For all the display of scholarly reflection this is, just like the bits from Messrs Toynbee and Wilson and the *TLS* reviewer, once more the criticism of blank denial. People won't like *The Lord of the Rings*, they don't like *The Lord of the Rings*, they've stopped liking *The Lord of the Rings*. Matter closed.

In an exasperated kind of way Tolkien would, I think, have been particularly delighted to read Dr Manlove's essay. He had run into criticism like that before, indeed it is a major theme of his tauntingly-titled British Academy lecture of 1936, '*Beowulf*: the Monsters and the Critics'. The critics he had in mind were critics of *Beowulf*, but they were saying pretty much the same thing: *Beowulf* didn't work, it was intrinsically silly, and 'we' weren't involved with it. 'Correct and sober taste', Tolkien wrote (p. 257), 'may refuse to admit that there can be an interest for *us* – the proud *we* that includes all intelligent living people – in ogres and dragons; we then perceive its puzzlement in face of the odd fact that it has derived great pleasure from a poem that is actually about these unfashionable creatures.' Tolkien had not, in 1936, realised how quickly 'correct and sober taste' could stamp 'puzzlement' out, and 'pleasure' along with it. However, for the rest he might just as well have been writing about responses to *The Lord of the Rings*. No doubt he would have felt honoured, in a way, to find himself as well as the *Beowulf*-poet driving critics to take refuge in threadbare and hopeless 'we's'.

The similarities between responses to *Beowulf* (as analysed by Tolkien) and to *The Lord of the Rings* do not end there. If one looks at Tolkien's remarks about the *Beowulf* critics, one can see that the thing he found worst about them was their monoglottery: they seemed able to read only one language, and even if they knew a bit of French or some other modern tongue they were quite incapable of reading ancient texts, ancient English texts, with anything like the degree of detailed verbal insight that was required. They relied on translations and summaries, they did not pay close attention to particular words. 'This is an age of potted criticism and pre-digested literary opinion', Tolkien wrote in 1940 in apologetic Preface to a translation of *Beowulf* which he hoped would only be used as a crib; 'in the making of these cheap substitutes for food translations unfortunately are too often used' (p. x). Now this could hardly be said about *The Lord of the Rings*, which is after all mostly in modern English. Or could it? Were people really paying close attention to words, Tolkien must have wondered as he read through the reviews? Or were they just skipping through for the plot again?

His irritation surfaced in the 1966 Foreword to the second edition of *The Lord of the Rings*, where he wrote, rather cattily:

> Some who have read the book, or at any rate have reviewed it, have found it boring, absurd, or contemptible; and I have no cause to complain, since I have similar opinions of their works, or of the kinds of writing that they evidently prefer. (*LOTR*, I, 6)

Probably this was, strictly speaking, unfair. All the reviewers I have come across do seem to have read the book right through with no more than a normal run of first-reading miscomprehensions. However it is a surprising fact that Edmund Wilson, who declared that he had not only read the book but had read the whole thousand pages out loud to his seven-year-old daughter, nevertheless managed consistently to spell the name of a central character wrong: 'Gandalph', for 'Gandalf'. Edwin Muir in the *Observer* preferred 'Gandolf'. This may seem purely trivial; but Tolkien would not have looked at it that way. He knew that 'ph' for 'f' was a learned spelling, introduced sporadically into English from Latin from about the fourteenth century, mostly in words of Greek origin like 'physics' or 'philosophy'. It is not used for native words like 'foot' or 'fire'. Now in the rather similar linguistic correspondences of Middle-earth (they are laid out in Appendices E and F of *The Lord of the Rings*, for those who haven't already noticed) it is clear that 'Gandalf' belongs to the latter set rather than the former. 'Gandalph' would accordingly have seemed to Tolkien as intrinsically ludicrous as 'phat' or 'phool', or come to that 'elph' or 'dwarph'. He could hardly have conceived of the state of mind that would regard such variations as meaningless, or beneath notice. As for 'Gandolf', that is an Italian miscomprehension, familiar from Browning's poem 'The Bishop Orders His Tomb', but wildly inappropriate to a work which does its best to avoid Latinisms.

No compromise is possible between what one might call 'the Gandalph-mentality' and Tolkien's. Perhaps this is why *The Lord of the Rings* (and to a lesser extent Tolkien's other writings as well) makes so many literary critics avert their eyes, get names wrong, write about things that aren't there and miss the most obvious points of success. Tolkien thought this instinctive antipathy was an ancient one: people who couldn't stand his books hadn't been able to bear *Beowulf*, or *Pearl*, or Chaucer, or *Sir Gawain*, or *Sir Orfeo* either. For millennia they had been trying to impose their views on a recalcitrant succession of authors, who had fortunately taken no notice. In the rather steely Preface to their edition of *Sir Gawain and the Green Knight* (in which the word 'criticism' is conspicuously shunned), Tolkien and his colleague E. V. Gordon declared that they wanted to help people read the poem 'with an appreciation as far as possible of the sort which its author may be supposed to have desired' (p. v). Doing the same job for Tolkien ought to be easier, since he is so much more our contemporary than the *Gawain*-poet; on the other hand Tolkien's mind was one of unmatchable subtlety, not without a streak of deliberate guile. However nothing is to be gained by applying to it the criteria of 'correct and sober taste', of the great but one-sided traditions of later English literature, of those 'higher literary aspirations' so haughtily opposed by Anthony Burgess to 'allegories with animals or fairies' (*Observer*, 26 November 1978). These lead only to the conclusion that there is nothing to be said and no phenomenon to consider. Still, something made Tolkien different, gave him the power so markedly to provoke these twin reactions of popular appeal and critical rage.

The Nature of Philology

Whatever it was, it almost self-evidently had something to do with his job. For most of his active life Tolkien taught Old English, Middle English, the history of the English language; in doing so he was competing with teachers of English literature for time, funds and students, on the whole a thankless task since for all that Tolkien could do the current was setting firmly away from him and from his subjects. Tolkien was by all accounts as capable of keeping up a grudge as the next man, and his minor writings often show it. The anthology of *Songs for the Philologists* which he and E. V. Gordon compiled and had privately printed in 1936 contains at least two poems by Tolkien attacking teachers of 'Lit.'; one of them, titled variously 'Two Little Schemes' and 'Lit. and Lang.', the worst he ever wrote; so bad indeed that it makes me think (or hope) that something must have gone wrong with it *en route* between poet and printer. Meanwhile he was from the start of his learned career barely able to use the word 'literature' at all without putting inverted commas round it to show he couldn't take it seriously. Thus his famous article on *'Ancrene Wisse* and *Hali Meiðhad'*,† published in 1929, opens with the remark that: 'The *Ancrene Wisse* has already developed a "literature", and it is very possible that nothing I can say about it will be either new or illuminating to the industrious or leisured that have kept up with it. I have not' ('AW', p. 104). There are variants on the same innuendo at the start of the *Beowulf* lecture of 1936 and in the *Sir Gawain* Preface of 1925. Of course there is a reason (of characteristic deviousness) for this repeated Tolkienian joke, and one which can easily be extracted from the pages of the *Oxford English Dictionary*, on which Tolkien had himself worked in youth. There one can find that the meaning which Tolkien foisted on to 'literature' is indeed recognised, under heading 3b: 'The body of books and writings that treat of a particular subject'. But why should Tolkien insist on using *that* one when heading 3a is less narrow and much more generally pertinent: 'Literature' meaning 'literary productions as a whole ... Now also, in a more restricted sense, applied to writing which has claim to consideration on the ground of beauty of form or emotional effect'? The sting for Tolkien lay in the illustrative quotations which form the backbone of the definition, of which the sixth reads 'The full glory of the new literature broke in England with Edmund Spenser', i.e. in 1579. The true mordancy of that opinion may not appear till later. It is enough to note that if you took the *OED* seriously you could argue (a) that the valueless accumulation of books about *Beowulf* and the *Ancrene Wisse* and *Sir Gawain* were all 'literature', under heading 3b, but (b) the original and creative works themselves, all very much pre-1579, were not, under 3a. Naturally no one would be stupid enough to put forward such a proposition seriously and in so many words. Still, Tolkien did not think these semantic tangles entirely fortuitous; the *OED* might not mirror truth but it did represent orthodox learned opinion. It was typical of him to note the confusion and the slur it implied, to use the one to avenge the other – 'literature' was 'books about books', the dead Latin 'letter' opposed to the ancient English spirit.

Yet what this obsessive playing with words shows, better than anything, is that beneath the fog and fury of academic politics, Tolkien realised that all discussions of 'language' and 'literature' were irretrievably poisoned

† The letter 'ð' here is used in several Old English, Middle English and Old Norse quotations throughout this book. Like the other (runic) letter retained almost into the modern era, 'þ', it stands for 'th'. Thus Meiðhad=Meith-had=Maid(en)hood. The work mentioned is a treatise on 'Holy Virginity'.

by the very terms they were bound to use. When he was not simply playing for his side, he accepted that 'lang.' was just as foolish a rallying-cry as 'lit.'. In his manifesto of 1930, 'The Oxford English School', he even suggested that both terms should be scrapped in favour of 'A' and 'B'. The same article makes it clear that he thought both 'linguistic' and 'literary' approaches too narrow for a full response to works of art, especially early works of art, and that furthermore what was needed was not some tame compromise between them (which is all most Schools of English usually manage to provide), but something as it were at right angles to both. This third dimension was the 'philological' one: it was from this that he trained himself to see things, from this too that he wrote his works of fiction. 'Philology' is indeed the only proper guide to a view of Middle-earth 'of the sort which its author may be supposed to have desired'. It is not Tolkien's fault that over the last hundred years 'philology', as a term and as a discipline, has been getting itself into even worse tangles than 'English literature'.

Dictionary definitions are, symptomatically, unhelpful. The *OED*, though conceived and created by philologists and borne along by the subject's nineteenth-century prestige, has almost nothing useful to offer. 'Philology', it suggests, is: '1. Love of learning and literature; the study of literature in a wide sense, including grammar, literary criticism and interpretation . . . polite learning. Now *rare* in *general* sense.' Under 2 it offers 'love of talk, speech or argument' (this is an offensive sense in which philology is mere logic-chopping, the opposite of true philosophy); while 3 recovers any ground abandoned in 1 by saying it is 'The study of the structure and development of language; the science of language; linguistics. (Really one branch of sense 1.)' So 'philology' is 'lang.' and 'lit.' too, all very charitable but too vague to be any use. The *Deutsches Wörterbuch* set in motion by Jacob Grimm (himself perhaps the greatest of all philologists and responsible in true philological style for both 'Grimm's Law of Consonants' and *Grimms' Fairy Tales*) could do little better, defining *philologie* with similar inclusiveness as 'the learned study of the (especially Classical) languages and literatures'. The illustrative quotation from Grimm's own work is more interesting in its declaration that 'none among all the sciences is prouder, nobler, more disputatious than philology, or less merciful to error'; this at least indicates the expectations the study had aroused. Still, if you didn't know what 'philology' was already, the Grimm definition would not enlighten you.

The matter is not cleared up by Holger Pedersen's assertion of 1924 that philology is 'a study whose task is the interpretation of the literary monuments in which the spiritual life of a given period has found expression'[3] (for this leaves you wondering why 'spiritual' has been put in and 'language' for once left out); nor by Leonard Bloomfield's aside a year later, when, proposing the foundation of a Linguistic Society for America, he explicitly rejected the term 'philological' and noted that while British scholars tended to use it to mean 'linguistic', Americans would prefer to keep the latter term and to revere philology rather more from a distance as 'that noblest of sciences . . . the study of national culture . . . something much greater than a misfit combination of language plus literature'.[4] Anyway some Britons were very far removed from his position. John Churton Collins, nineteenth-century man of letters and candidate for an Oxford Chair, had written in 1891 (it was part of his campaign to keep men like Joseph Wright, Tolkien's tutor, *out* of any prospective English School at Oxford):

> it [i.e. philology] too often induces or confirms that peculiar woodenness and opacity, that singular coarseness of feeling and purblindness of moral and intellectual vision, which has in all ages been the characteristic of mere philologists . . . [it] too often resembles that rustic who, after listening for several hours to Cicero's most brilliant conversation, noticed nothing and remembered nothing but the wart on the great orator's nose.[5]

Opinions such as this clung on a long time in England. Tolkien wrote in 1924 ' "Philology" is in some quarters treated as though it were one of the things that the late war was fought to end' (*YWES* 4, p. 37). When I first read this I took it to be a joke. However just three years before the British Board of Education had printed a Report on *The Teaching of English in England* which declared, among much else, that philology ought not to be taught to undergraduates, that it was a 'German-made' science, and (this comes in a footnote on p. 286) that by contributing to German arrogance it had led in a direct way to the outbreak of World War I.

Philology was 'the noblest of sciences'; it was literary; it was linguistic; it was German; it was Classical; it was different in America; it was about warts on noses; it was 'the special burden of the Northern tongues' (Tolkien speaking); also 'the special advantage they possess as a discipline' (Tolkien once again). This begins to sound like the Babel of conflicting voices which Tolkien guyed so fiercely in his lecture on *Beowulf*, except that in this case the final universal chorus of all voices 'it is worth studying!' would clearly be somewhat ragged. If no single answer to the question 'what is philology?' can be found, at least few authorities would dissent from the view that the redefinition of philology – the moment when it stopped being used in the *OED*'s vaguest senses of 'love of talk' or 'love of learning' – came in 1786 when Sir William Jones informed the Bengal Society in Calcutta that Sanskrit resembled Greek and Latin too strongly for this to be the result of chance, but that all three, together with Germanic and Celtic, must have 'sprung from some common source which, perhaps, no longer exists'.[6]

Obviously this thought must have crossed many minds before 1786, for even between English and Latin, say, there are enough similarities – one, two, three, *unus, duo, tres* – to make one think there may be some sort of a connection. But until the turn of the eighteenth century such speculations had foundered immediately on the great reefs of dissimilarity surrounding the occasional identical rocks. After all the main thing anyone knew about languages was that they were so different they had to be learnt one at a time. The great alteration Jones and his successors brought to the problem was the idea of looking not for chance resemblances – which had already been used to 'prove' relationships all over the map – but for regular change. *Bad* in modern Persian had the same sound and sense as 'bad' in English (remarked A. E. Pott in 1833), but that was just coincidence. On the other hand *xvāhar* in Persian was originally the same word as *xo* in Ossetic, and both were related to English 'sister'; furthermore the intermediate stages could be inferred and on occasion recovered.[7] Like many mental revolutions, this linguistic one depended on being counterintuitive. It was also to an intense degree *comparative*, using many languages to explain and corroborate each other; and, since different stages of the same language could be used comparatively, by nature overwhelmingly historical. 'Philology unfolds the genesis of those laws of speech which grammar contemplates as a finished result', says a citation in the *OED*, dated 1852. Its author did not mean 'philology' in any of the senses quoted from the *OED* on p. 6 above; he meant *comparative* philology, the science inspired by Sir William and carried on through many inheritors to Professor Tolkien himself. One may remark that the confidence with which 'genesis' is approached was characteristic of the time.

By 1852, indeed, 'the new philology' had many triumphs to look back on, with several yet to come: one might pick out the prize-winning essay of Rasmus Rask in 1814, on Old Icelandic, and on the relationship of Scandinavian languages to Slavic, Celtic, Finnish and Classical ones; the enormous 'Comparative Grammar' or *Vergleichende Grammatik* of Franz Bopp in 1833–49, which covered Sanskrit, Zend, Armenian, Greek, Latin, Lithuanian, Old Slavic, Gothic and German; the *Deutsche Grammatik* (1819) of Jacob Grimm, and all their many successors.[8] The point which all these works brandished was the intensely *systematic* nature of discovery, expressed as time went on increasingly by the word 'laws' (see *OED* citation above), and on the analogy of physics or chemistry by the association of laws with discoverers: Grimm's Law, Verner's Law, Kuhn's Law, Thomsen's Law, etc. There was and still is something insidiously fascinating about the relationships these laws uncover, in such detail and such profusion. Latin *pisces* is the same word as Old English *fisc*, observed Jacob Grimm, or indeed modern English 'fish'; *pes* is the same as 'foot' and *pellis* as 'fell' (the old word for 'skin'). What about *porcus* and 'pig',

though, where the p/f alternation breaks down? Well, there is an Old
English word *fearh* which corresponds properly, noted Grimm, its modern
descendant being 'farrow', again an old or dialectal word for a 'birth' of
piglets. The mill of comparisons will not work on basic or standard or
literary languages alone, but demands ever-increasing grist from older or
localised or sub-standard forms. The reward it offers is first an increasing
sense that everything *can* be worked out, given time and material, second
an exciting tension between the modern meanings of words – words
everyone has known all their lives – and what appear as the ancient
meanings. 'Daughter' in modern Hindustani comes out as *beti*; yet there
is a connection between the two languages in the word *dudh*, 'milk'. In
ancient days, it seems, a word like Sanskrit *duhitar* meant 'the little
milker'; but the job was so often given to daughters that task and relationship became fused. It 'opens before our eyes a little idyll of the poetical
and pastoral life of the early Aryans', enthused Max Müller,[9] whose
lectures on comparative philology bowled over not only (or not even) the
learned world in the 1860s and after, but also London's high society.
Comparison was the rage: it didn't tell you only about words, it told you
about people.

But somewhere towards the end of the nineteenth century things had
begun to go wrong. As is obvious from all that Tolkien ever said about
literature and about philology, he felt that he had taken over (perhaps
unfairly, but possibly not) a losing position in the academic game from his
predecessors. Why – he could hardly have helped wondering – was that?
Why had philology so ignominiously belied its promise?

Probably the short answer is that the essence of comparative philology
was slog. There is something wistful in Tolkien's astonished praise of the
'dull stodges' of Leeds University (*Biography*, p. 104), in his insistence
that at Leeds anyway 'Philology is making headway . . . and there is no
trace of the press-gang!' (*Letters*, p. 11). For matters were different
elsewhere. No science, Jacob Grimm had said of philology, was 'prouder,
nobler, more disputatious, *or less merciful to error*' (my italics). All its
practitioners accepted, to a degree now incredible, a philosophy of rigid
accuracy, total coverage, utter right and utter wrong: in 1919 the old and
massively distinguished Eduard Sievers happily put his reputation on the
line when he offered to dissect a text provided unseen by Hans Lietzmann,
and to show from linguistic evidence how many authors had composed it
(he had already done the same thing to the Epistles of Paul). He got
Lietzmann's specimen totally wrong. But no one said the idea of the test
itself was unfair.[10] Further down the scale, the discoveries of Grimm and
his successors as far as Ferdinand de Saussure (now famous for inventing
'structuralism' but before that a student of *Ablaut*) were communicated
increasingly to students as facts, systems of facts, systems divorced from
the texts they had been found in. We must have philology within English

Studies, wrote F. York Powell the Icelandicist in 1887, 'or goodbye to accuracy'.[11] The claim was false – you can be accurate about other things besides sound-shifts – but after seventy years of unbroken progress for the subject it was also damningly unambitious. Looking back many years later, R. W. Chambers (the man who turned down the Chair of Anglo-Saxon which eventually went to Tolkien in 1925) summed up success and failure by observing that in 1828 'the comparative philologist was like Ulysses', but 'Scoffers may say that my parallel is all too true – that students of comparative language, like [Dante's] Ulysses, found only the mountain of Purgatory – Grimm's Law, Verner's Law, Grassmann's Law – rising in successive terraces of horror – and then were overwhelmed . . .'[12] Scoffers said exactly that; their viewpoint became dominant; comparative philology seen as 'hypothetical sound-shiftings in the primeval German forests'[13] went into a decline nearly as precipitate as its rise.

This is why 'philology' has first the old vague sense of 'love of learning'; then the new nineteenth century one of 'study of texts leading to comparative study of language leading to comprehension of its evolution'; and in the twentieth century the specialised meaning, within departments of English Studies, of 'anti-literary science kept up by pedants (like Professor Tolkien) which ought to be stopped as soon as possible'. But these interesting semantic changes leave something out: the 'spiritual life' waved at by Holger Pedersen, the 'national culture' saluted by Leonard Bloomfield – or, to put it another way, the *Grimms' Fairy Tales*.

Lost Romances

For philology, after the Rask–Bopp–Grimm breakthrough, had moved in other directions beside the phonological and morphological. The mill of historical comparison called increasingly for fresh material, and one natural effect, besides the study of language in general, was the study of languages in particular. Scholars became much more interested in unread texts; they also became spectacularly better at reading them, at producing dictionaries of stone-dead languages. As Tolkien noted himself ('Preface', p. xii), the word *hós(e)* in *Beowulf* was never found anywhere else in Old English, so that one would have to guess at its meaning from context, were it not for the fact that philology proved it was the 'same' word as Old High German *hansa*, as in 'Hanseatic League', with the meaning 'retinue', or possibly 'band of people connected by mutual oaths'. The dead languages furnished comparative material; the comparative material illuminated dead languages. Men learnt to read Hittite, recognised as an Indo-European language in the 1920s (with marked effect on Old Testament studies), Tokharian (another Indo-European language once spoken by steppe-nomads but now represented mostly by texts preserved accidentally in an oasis in Turkestan), more recently to decipher 'Linear B' (an exploration of Cretan archaeology which would have been impossible in a pre-Bopp era). Much obscurer discoveries were made. A whole nation was theorised to lie behind the tiny fragment of Kottish, a language spoken when it was investigated by only five people. Holger Pedersen said of their relatives the Yenisei that they seem to be 'the last remnants of a powerful folk who, with the Thibetan empire as their southern neighbour, ruled over a great part of Siberia, but were at length compelled to submit to the Turks'.[14] Yet of their rule no traces remain other than linguistic ones. The romance of these investigations can still be felt. It is a large-scale analogue of Müller's remarks on *duhitar*, of the awareness that some forms even of modern language took you back to the Stone Age (as in English 'hammer', cognate with Old Slavic *kamy*, 'stone'). The romance became stronger, perversely, the closer it got to home.

Thus Old English itself looked very strikingly different after the philologists got hold of it – and it was they who insisted on calling it Old English instead of Anglo-Saxon to mark what they saw as an essential continuity. The story of Gothic, however, was even more dramatic. Some awareness of this language had been around from an early period. People knew that such texts as the Uppsala *Codex Argenteus* were *in* Gothic, that the Goths were an East Germanic tribe who had overrun parts of the Roman Empire from about AD 376, that they had been converted to literacy and Christianity, and become linguistically extinct some time round the eighth century. Philology shattered this picture. For one thing Gothic became suddenly more than comprehensible, it became vital: it was the earliest Germanic language recorded, Germanic was the area of most philologists' main interest (they were mostly Germans), and Gothic exhibited, in ways that Old English and Old High German did not, stages in the history of all the Germanic languages inferable from but not recorded in its cousins. So, modern English says 'old' but 'elder', Old English (in its Early West Saxon form) *eald* but *ieldra*, both say (more or less) 'to heal' but 'hale (and hearty)'. For these Gothic offers respectively *altheis*, *althiza*, *háiljan*, *háils*. The common element deduced is that when an *-i-* or *-j-* followed *a* or *ái* in *old* Old English (this goes back to the time before Englishmen had learnt to write) speakers began to change the earlier vowel into *e*, *æ* – with similar changes affecting other vowels. Where there is a succeeding *-i-* in Gothic there is a change of vowel in Old (and often still in modern) English; not otherwise.

This phenomenon, known as 'i-mutation', became one of the most familiar horrors of university philology, but there is in it something both mysterious and satisfactory: a whole series of things which people said, and still *say*, without in the least knowing why, turn out to have one very old but clear, 100 per cent predictable reason. It is almost like genetics. No wonder that Grimm said Gothic was a 'perfect' language, Tolkien ('EW',

p. 38) that it took him by storm. A further stage in the developing romance of 'Gothia' was the thought that the Goths might *not* be extinct. At some time in the 1560s one Ogier van Busbecq, a Fleming then acting as ambassador in Istanbul, had heard some foreigners whose speech sounded familiar. He recorded a list of words from them and printed it in 1589. They proved to be Gothic, nearly a thousand years out of place. Their interest aroused several centuries later, scholars could for a while entertain the hope that a living Gothic was still somewhere in existence, as a kind of Abominable Snowman of language. Alas, it wasn't. But at least it became clearer how Gothic *had* survived, in the remote Crimea, and it became possible to piece together once again the history of a vanished people.

It is not too much to say that this language and this people haunted Tolkien all his life. As is noted by Christopher Tolkien (*UT*, p. 311), the names of the leaders of the Rohirrim before the dynasty of Eorl are not Old English, like everything else in the Riders' culture, but Gothic, e.g. Vidugavia, Vidumavi, Marhwini, etc. (see *LOTR* III, 326). They function there to suggest language behind language and age behind age, a phenomenon philologists so often detected. On a larger scale the Battle of the Pelennor Fields closely follows the account, in Jordanes' *Gothic History*, of the Battle of the Catalaunian Plains, in which also the civilisation of the West was preserved from the 'Easterlings', and in which the Gothic king Theodorid was trampled by his own victorious cavalry with much the same mixture of grief and glory as Tolkien's Théoden. Perhaps the most revealing remark, however, comes in a letter from Tolkien to his son Christopher after the latter had read a paper on the heroes of northern legend. In this he praised his son's paper for the light it shed on men and on history, but added:

> All the same, I suddenly realized that I am a *pure* philologist. I like history, and am moved by it, but its finest moments for me are those in which it throws light on words and names! Several people (and I agree) spoke to me of the art with which you made the beady-eyed Attila on his couch almost vividly present. Yet oddly, I find the thing that thrills my nerves is the one you mentioned casually: *atta, attila*. Without those syllables the whole great drama both of history and legend loses savour for me. (*Letters*, p. 264)

The point is that Attila, though a Hun, an enemy of the Goths under Theodorid, and a byword for bloody ferocity, nevertheless does not appear to bear a barbarian name. 'Attila' is the diminutive form of the Gothic word for 'father', *atta*: it means 'little father', or even 'dad', and it suggests very strongly the presence of many Goths in Attila's conquering armies who found loot and success much more attractive than any questions of saving the West, Rome or civilisation! As with *duhitar*, 'little milker', or *kamy* as a cognate for 'hammer', the word tells the story. Tolkien went on in his letter to say that in his mind that was exactly how *The Lord of the Rings* grew and worked. He had not constructed a design. Instead he had tried 'to create a situation in which a common greeting would be *elen síla lúmenn' omentielmo'*. Literary critics might not believe him, but philologists (if any were left) ought to know better.

Atta, Attila: what's in a name? One answer is, a total revaluation of history. It is instructive to look at older and newer editions of Edward Gibbon's *Decline and Fall of the Roman Empire* (first published 1776–88). Gibbon knew the Goths from many Roman and Greek historians, including Jordanes, but these were his only sources of information and he could not imagine another one. 'The memory of past events', he remarked with classically-educated superciliousness, 'cannot long be preserved, in the frequent and remote emigrations of illiterate Barbarians' (chapter 26). As for the great Gothic king of the fourth century, he said, 'The name of Hermanric is almost buried in oblivion'. It did not stay buried. 'Hermanric' turned up in recognisable form in *Beowulf* (not printed till 1815) as *Eormenric*. The same name and man, with little stories attached, appeared also in the Old English poems *Deor* and *Widsith*. As *Ermenrich* he survived into the Middle High German romances of *Dietrichs Flucht, Alpharts Tod*, and many others. Most powerfully, *Jǫrmunrekkr* turned out to be a most prominent character in the Old Norse poems of the *Elder Edda*, which had lain unnoticed in an Icelandic farmhouse till the 1640s, and not been published in full till Rasmus Rask did the job in 1818. The 'illiterate Barbarians' were not as forgetful as Gibbon thought. They could at least remember names, and even if these had been affected by sound-changes in the same way as other words, no archaic poet produced anything as false as Gibbon's '(H)ermanric'. From the joint evidence of old poems in English, Norse and German one could in fact deduce that the king's name, though never recorded in Gothic, must have been *Airmanareiks*.

And, as with 'Attila', there is a thrill of old passion lurking in the name, buried though this may be in editors' footnotes and the inferences of scholarly works. The tales of Ermanaric's death vary. He committed suicide (round AD 375) for fear of the Huns, says an early Roman source. Jordanes tells a more complicated story of treachery, punishment and revenge. The Old Norse poems, more grisly and more personal, insist that Ermanaric was attacked by his brothers-in-law for murdering their sister, and was left after their death under a hail of Gothic stones – for on them no weapon would bite – to survive as a *heimnár* or 'living corpse', a trunk with both arms and legs cut off. This last tale seems totally unlikely. But it does preserve some agreement over names and incidents with Jordanes: maybe something peculiar and tragic *did* take place during the collapse of the Gothic Empire in the fourth century. To the philologist who compared these versions there was a further charm in guessing what strange chains of transmission and quirks of national bias had transformed king into villain. Had the defeated Goths cast him as a scapegoat? Had he been made a wife-murderer to gloss over the feelings of those Goths who changed sides and joined the 'Easterlings', calling the Hunnish king their 'little father'? Had Crimean Goths sung lays of Ermanaric to Norsemen of the Varangian Guard in the courts of the Greek emperor? Tolkien followed these inquiries closely, buying for instance the volumes of Hermann Schneider's *Germanische Heldensage* as they came out 1928–34,† and claiming in 1930 ('OES', pp. 779–80) that Gothic was being studied under his direction not only for sound-laws but 'as a main source of the poetic inspiration of ancient England and the North'. As he said in the letter quoted above, the legends of heroes had a fascination in themselves; they were also part of 'a rational and exacting discipline'.

Philology illuminated the Dark Ages. Certainly, when it comes to Gothic chieftains, J. B. Bury's revised edition of Gibbon (in 1896) proceeds with a new caution! But the essential point – it is a point which Tolkien's academic predecessors had signally failed to grasp, with consequent ruin for their subject – lies in the immense stretch of the philological imagination. At one extreme scholars were drawing conclusions from the very *letters* of a language: they had little hesitation in ascribing texts to Gothic or Lombardic authors, to West Saxons or Kentishmen or Northumbrians, on the evidence of sound-changes recorded in spelling. At the other extreme they were prepared to pronounce categorically on the existence or otherwise of nations and empires on the basis of poetic tradition or linguistic spread. They found information, and romance, in songs and fragments everywhere. The *Lex Burgundionum* of King Gundobad opened, as had been known for centuries, with a list of royal ancestors, Gibica, Gundomar, Gislaharius, Gundaharius. It took philology to equate nos. 1, 3 and 4 with the Gifica, Gíslhere and Gúthhere of Old English poems, nos. 1 and 4 with the Gibeche and Gunther of the Germans' epic, the *Nibelungenlied*. Simultaneously it became apparent that the epic had a kernel of truth: the Huns *had* wiped out a Burgundian king and army in the 430s (as Gibbon had vaguely noted), some of the names *were* authentic, there had been a continuing tradition of poetry from fifth to twelfth centuries, even if it had all vanished and never been written down. Sidonius Apollinaris, bishop of Clermont, indeed mentioned the Burgundians' songs with distaste in a sixth-century lyric. 'The learned and eloquent Sidonius', Gibbon calls him. 'How gladly would we now give all his verses for ten lines of the songs in which these "long-haired seven-foot high, onion-eating barbarians" celebrated, it may be, the openhandedness of Gibica, or perhaps told how, in that last terrible battle, their fathers had fallen fighting round Gundahari', wrote R. W. Chambers

† His signed copies are in the Taylorian Library at Oxford.

more sourly.[15] The change of viewpoint marks an enormous if temporary shift of poetic and literary interest from Classical to native. It also shows how philology could seem, to some, the 'noblest of sciences', the key to 'spiritual life', certainly 'something much greater than a misfit combination of language plus literature'.

'Asterisk-Reality'

Nevertheless Sidonius's poems *had* survived, and the Burgundian epics hadn't. There was an image forming in many men's minds of the days when an enormous Germanic empire had stretched from the Baltic to the Black Sea, only to go down before the Huns and disperse into settlements everywhere from Sweden to Spain – but the image remained tantalisingly on the edge of sight. 'The ill-grace of fate has saved hardly anything . . . of the poetry possessed by the eighth, seventh and earlier centuries', lamented Jacob Grimm and his brother Wilhelm.[16] 'It grieves me to say it,' said Axel Olrik, 'the old *Biarkamál*, the most beloved and most honoured of songs in all the North, is not known to us in the form it had.'[17] 'Alas for the lost lore, the annals and old poets', wrote Tolkien, referring indeed to Virgil but by analogy to the sources of *Beowulf*.[18] Gudbrand Vigfusson and F. York Powell, editing the *Corpus Poeticum Boreale*, the whole poetry of the North, in the 1880s, might look back on past ages and see the 'field of Northern scholarship' as 'a vast plain, filled with dry bones', up and down which there walked 'a company of men, doing their best to set these bones in order, skull by skull, thigh by thigh, with no hope or thought of the breath that was to shake this plain with the awakening of the immortal dead'.[19] But though philology did come and breathe life into the dry bones of old poems, filling history with the reverberations of forgotten battles and empires, still there was a point beyond which it could not go; old languages could be understood, old stories edited and annotated, but living speakers could not be found. Nor were the poems left usually the poems most ardently desired.

That is why the characteristic activity of the philologist came, in the end, to be 'reconstruction'. This might be no more than verbal. From the circumstance that English and German both change the vowel of 'man' in the plural to 'men' or *Männer*, you could infer that Primitive Germanic, of which not one word has ever been recorded, would have said **maniz*, producing as usual 'i-mutation'. The * is the sign of the reconstructed form, proposed by August Schleicher in the 1860s and used widely ever since. On a higher level you might reconstruct a language. Schleicher indeed wrote a little fable in 'Indo-European', that 'common source' for Sanskrit, Latin and Greek which Sir William Jones had suggested. *Avis, jasmin varna na ā ast, dadarka akvams*, it began, 'A sheep, which had no wool on it, saw a horse...' Schleicher's colleagues were not much impressed, and indeed the researchers of Verner, Brugmann and de Saussure in the 1870s prompted H. Hirt to offer a corrected version of it some years later; no language changed as quickly in the 1870s as Primitive Indo-European, ran the philological joke.[20] But the method itself was not seriously questioned, only the answer reached. In between these two extremes an editor might find himself rewriting a poem. *Eorl sceal on éos boge, worod sceal getrume rídan*, says the Old English poem *Maxims I*, 'earl shall on horse's back, warband (*worod*) ride in a body'. Most warbands in Old English history marched on their feet; and anyway *worod* fails to keep up the poetic alliteration. *Éored* is the proper word here, say the editors, and it means 'a troop of cavalry', being related to the word *eoh*, 'horse', cp. Latin *equus*. It's true that the word is used by itself only twice elsewhere in Old English, and only once correctly – the word and idea must have become unfamiliar. But that is no deterrent. The post-philological editor can assume he knows more, indeed knows better than the native speaker or scribe, if not the original poet – another reason, be it said, for beliefs like Tolkien's, that he had a cultivated sympathy with the authors of *Beowulf* or *Sir Gawain* or *The Reeve's Tale* which even the poet's contemporaries had not and which would certainly never be reached by straight 'literary criticism'.

Examples could be multiplied almost indefinitely: it is impossible to avoid mentioning the fact that the very core and kernel of *Beowulf*-criticism in the last hundred years has been the story of 'the fall of the house of the Scyldings', which, as it happens, neither the poet nor any *other* ancient writer ever got round to explaining, but which was 'reconstructed' in great and (to my mind) totally convincing detail by a succession of scholars up to R. W. Chambers. But the vital points to grasp are these:

(1) The thousands of pages of 'dry as dust' theorems about language-change, sound-shifts and *ablaut*-gradations were, in the minds of most philologists, an essential and natural basis for the far more exciting speculations about the wide plains of 'Gothia' and the hidden, secret trade-routes across the primitive forests of the North, *Myrkviðr inn ókunni*, 'the pathless Mirkwood' itself. You could not have, you would never have *got* the one without the other.

(2) In spite of the subject's apparent schizophrenia and the determination of its practitioners to make nothing easy, philology was, for a time, the cutting edge of all the 'soft' or 'behavioural' sciences, literature, history, sociology and anthropology at once. That is why it attracted such a following and why Jacob Grimm, for instance, could hope to sell his dictionary, the *Wörterbuch der deutschen Sprache*, to a mass-audience as something designed for entertainment.

(3) In this entire process the thing which was perhaps eroded most of all was the philologists' sense of a line between imagination and reality. The

whole of their science conditioned them to the acceptance of what one might call '*-' or 'asterisk-reality', that which no longer existed but could with 100 per cent certainty be inferred.

(4) In a sense, the non-existence of the most desired objects of study created a romance of its own. If we had the lost Gothic 'Ermanaric-lays' we might think little of them, but find them lame, crude or brutal; quite likely, the very first version of the *Nibelungenlied* (composed in the ashes of the Burgundian kingdom) was just an attempt by the poet to cheer himself up. But the fact that these things do not exist, hover forever on the fringe of sight, makes them more tantalising and the references to them more thrilling. There is a book by R. M. Wilson called *The Lost Literature of Medieval England*, which Tolkien must often have read – see note [11] to p. 127 below. *The Lost Literature of Dark-Age Europe*, however, would be a title almost too painful for words. Still, it would cover plenty of material. The best lines about King Arthur are not the long explicit descriptions of the later medieval romances, but those in the almost deliberately uninformative Welsh triads, e.g. from the Black Book of Carmarthen:

> Bet y March, bet y Guythur,
> bet y Gugaun   Cledyfrut;
> anoeth bid   bet y Arthur

> 'There is a grave for March, a grave for Gwythur,
> a grave for Gwgawn Red-sword;
> the world's wonder a grave for Arthur.'[21]

As for Old English, my guess is that the most stirring lines to Tolkien must have come, not even from *Beowulf*, but from the fragment *Waldere*, where an unknown speaker reminds the hero that his sword was given by Theodoric to Widia 'because Wayland's child let him out of captivity, hurried him out of the hands of the monsters'. Somewhere in the Dark Ages, this seems to suggest, there must have been a legend, a story of how the Gothic king *Thiudoreiks was stolen away to the land of giants, to be rescued after long adventures by his faithful retainers Widia and Hildebrand. Why did the giants take him, where and how did they live, what were their relations with humanity? Once upon a time many people must have known the answers: the story survives in a decadent form in the medieval German romances of *Das Eckenlied*, *Sigenot*, *Laurin* and others, while there is an intensely irritating scrap of a Middle English poem on the subject tucked into a dull sermon on humility:

> Summe sende ylues, and summe sende nadderes:
> summe sende nikeres, the bi den watere wunien.
> Nister man nenne, bute Ildebrand onne.

'Some sent elves, and some sent serpents,
some sent sea-monsters, that live by the water.
No one knew any of them, but Hildebrand alone.'[22]

What must it have been like in Old English – a poem not about monsters
erupting on humanity, as in *Beowulf*, but about men going into the heart
of the monsterworld, for adventures in the 'Ettenmoors' themselves! But
fate had snatched that prospect (almost) into utter oblivion.

The wilderness of dragons, the shrewedness of apes

Probably the most disheartening conclusion to be drawn from this brief
review of intellectual history is that the history of English studies in
British and American universities has been forever marred by incomprehension and missed opportunities. Professor D. J. Palmer has shown how
the birth of the Oxford English School in particular was accompanied by
desperate struggles between language and literature, philologists and
critics, ending not in mutual illumination but in a compromise demarcation
of interests.[23] Quite possibly the philologists were most to blame in this.
Peter Ganz, Professor of German at Oxford, has pointed out that Jacob
Grimm's chief intellectual defect was a refusal to generalise.[24] Indeed as
he neared the end of his *Teutonic Mythology* (four volumes in the translation
of J. S. Stallybrass, and 1887 pages) Grimm wrote a Preface referring to
himself as a gleaner, whose observations he left to 'him who, standing on
my shoulders, shall hereafter get into full swing the harvesting of this
great field'.[25] But actually there was no field left to harvest; while few
would relish the thought of spending a lifetime putting someone else's
observations in order, without the fun of first collecting them! So the
impetus of philology ran out in a series of Primers and Readers and
Grammars, endless academic brickmaking without any sign of an architect.
No wonder the early critics got annoyed. On the other hand they showed
little magnanimity, or even curiosity, once they got control.

The overt result for the young Tolkien must have been that, when he
returned from World War I to Oxford University in 1919, he found
himself once again in a battle being fought by two sides from deep
entrenchments, and one whose stalemates were as unlikely to be broken
as the greater ones of Ypres or the Somme by frontal offensives. Still,
both sides kept trying them. Tolkien did his best to make peace. His
1930 'manifesto' led at least to the elimination of some academic 'No
Man's Land', during the syllabus campaign of 1951 he even emerged
from his trench to fraternise with the enemy (till C. S. Lewis stopped
him, see *Inklings*, pp. 229–30). But a covert result may have been that he
gave up hope, at least from time to time, of penetrating other people's

vested interests and making them understand the appeal of the subjects he would have liked to teach. His jokes on the subject get wryer, his gestures of rapprochement – 'the boundary line between linguistic and literary history is as imaginary as the equator – a certain heat is observable, perhaps, as either is approached' (*YWES* 6, p. 59) or 'the "pure philologist who cannot do literature"... is as rare as the unicorn' ('OES', p. 782) – these become more perfunctory and finally disappear. What was possibly a natural bent towards reserve became more pronounced; it is hard to escape the feeling that in some of the interviews given after celebrity had arrived Tolkien was still liable to give easy or unnoticedly ambiguous answers to save the trouble of explaining something which he knew had proved incomprehensible many times before. *The Hobbit* and *The Lord of the Rings* had made his point, whether it had been intellectually apprehended or not; and the hostile or even malignant reaction it evoked from so many on the 'lit.' side was only what he might have expected.

Indeed, to go back to the animus *The Lord of the Rings* created: it is striking that next to the books' sheer success the thing that irritated reviewers most was their author's obstinate insistence on talking about language as if it might be a subject of interest. 'The invention of languages is the foundation', Tolkien had said. 'The "stories" were made rather to provide a world for the languages than the reverse' (*Letters*, p. 219). 'Invention' of course comes from Latin *invenire*, 'to find'; its older sense, as Tolkien knew perfectly well, was 'discovery'. If one were to say of nineteenth-century philology that 'the discovery of languages was *its* foundation', one would be stating literal truth; as often, probably, Tolkien was playing with words, juxtaposing the languages he had made up out of his own head with those that others had found or 'reconstructed' all over the world, so aligning himself yet again with his professional inheritance. Meanwhile the second sentence, though no doubt personally true again, might almost have been said of Ermanaric or Theodoric or the nineteenth-century vision of a 'historical' King Arthur. An element of generalisation underlay the particular application to Tolkien's own case.

This remained completely unperceived by his critics. 'He has explained that he began it to amuse himself, as a philological game', translated Edmund Wilson. 'An overgrown fairy story, a philological curiosity – that is, then, what *The Lord of the Rings* really is.' Philology, you note, is peculiar but not serious. Lin Carter (who prepared for his commentary on Tolkien by looking up 'philology' in 'the dictionary', to little profit – maybe it was the wrong dictionary) professed the same opinion even more blankly, if kindly, by claiming that Tolkien was really interested in 'the eternal verities of human nature', and that the appendices of *The Lord of the Rings* needed to be seen that way and not just as 'the outgrowth of a don's scholarly hobbies'. The idea could be right, but the notion of 'scholarly hobbies' is singularly naïve. Neil D. Isaacs, also writing in

Tolkien's defence, took the blunder on by asserting that 'Tolkien's own off-hand remarks about the importance of philology to the creative conception of the trilogy need not be taken too seriously', and R. J. Reilly put the tin lid on the whole discussion by saying, in attempted refutation of Edmund Wilson, that *The Lord of the Rings* can't have been a philological game because it's too serious, and therefore, seemingly, cannot possibly be philology. 'No one ever exposed the nerves and fibres of his being in order to make up a language; it is not only insane but unnecessary.'[26]

Like the reviewers quoted at the start of this chapter, Mr Reilly here makes a factual statement about humanity which is factually wrong. The aberration he talks about may not be common, but is not unprecedented. August Schleicher exposed the nerves and fibres of *his* being to make up Primitive Indo-European, and had them shredded for his trouble. Willy Krogmann, of the University of Hamburg, not only came to the conclusion that the Old High German *Hildebrandslied* (the oldest German heroic poem) must originally have been composed in Lombardic, a West Germanic language surviving outside '*-reality' only in a handful of names, but also reconstructed the language and rewrote the poem, publishing his new edition as late as 1959. No one, as far as I know, went so far as to reconstruct the Burgundian Nibelung-story, the first Ostrogothic Ermanaric-lay, or the Danish *Ur-Beowulf*; but such thoughts were in many minds. The only extant Gothic poem is by Tolkien, 'Bagme Bloma', in *Songs for the Philologists*. The drives towards creativity do not all emanate from the little area already mapped by 'literary' criticism. Awareness of this fact should have aroused a certain humility, or anyway caution, in Tolkienian commentators.

As it is, some of Tolkien's earliest writings seem to carry a certain foreboding truth. It has already been remarked that he tended to open learned articles with attacks on, or ripostes to, the 'literature' or the 'criticism' of his particular subject, whether this was Chaucer or the *Ancrene Wisse* or translators of *Beowulf*. Probably the sharpest and most revealing instance comes in the British Academy lecture on 'The Monsters and the Critics', as Tolkien moves on from the melancholy state of *Beowulf* criticism as a whole to the remarks of W. P. Ker and then of R. W. Chambers – philologists whom Tolkien respected but who he thought had given too much away to the other side. 'In this conflict between plighted troth and the duty of revenge', wrote Chambers, of a subject the *Beowulf*-poet had neglected for the sake of monsters, 'we have a situation which the old heroic poets loved, and would not have sold for a wilderness of dragons.' 'A wilderness of dragons!' exploded Tolkien, repeating the phrase and grasping instantly its deliberate syntactic ambiguity (between phrases like 'a field of cows' and phrases like 'a pride of lions'):

There is a sting in this Shylockian plural, the sharper for coming from a critic, who deserves the title of the poet's best friend. It is in the tradition of the Book of St. Albans, from which the poet might retort upon his critics: 'Yea, a desserte of lapwynges, a shrewednes of apes, a raffull of knaues, and a gagle of gees.' ('Monsters', p. 252)

Geese, knaves, apes, lapwings: these formed Tolkien's image of the literary critic, and they are emblematic respectively of silliness, fraud, mindless imitation and (see Horatio in *Hamlet* V ii) immaturity. But there is a multiple barb on the second phrase, the 'shrewednes of apes'. For 'shrewednes', like most words, has changed its meaning, and as with 'literature' Tolkien thought the changes themselves significant. Nowadays it means (*OED* again) 'Sagacity or keenness of mental perception or discrimination; sagacity in practical affairs.' Once upon a time it meant 'maliciousness', with particular reference to feminine scolding or nagging. No doubt the transit came via such phrases as 'a shrewd blow', first a blow which was meant to hurt, then one that did hurt, then one that was accurately directed, and so on. In all these senses Tolkien's remark was 'shrewd' itself. It creates a vivid if exaggerated picture of the merits and demerits of the literary profession seen *en bloc*: undeniably clever, active, dexterous (so exemplifying 'shrewdness' in the modern sense), but also bitter, negative and far too fond of 'back-seat driving' (see 'shrewed' in the old sense) – overall, too, apish, derivative, cut off from the full range of human interests. It would be a pity for his claim to ring true. But the history of reactions to Tolkien has tended to uphold it. One can sum up by saying that whether the hostile criticism directed at *The Lord of the Rings* was right or wrong – an issue still to be judged – it was demonstrably compulsive, rooted only just beneath the surface in ancient dogma and dispute.

Chapter 2

PHILOLOGICAL INQUIRIES

Roads and Butterflies

The Grimms and Tolkien prove that philological approaches to poetry did not have to exclude everything that would now be called 'literary'. Still, their attitudes were sharply distinct from those now normal among literary critics. For one thing philologists were much more likely than critics to brood on the sense, the form, the other recorded uses (or unrecorded uses) of single words. They were not, on the whole, less likely to respect the original author's intentions, but their training *did* make them prone to consider not only what a word was doing in its immediate contexts, but also its roots, its analogues in other languages, its descendants in modern languages, and all the processes of cultural change that might be hinted at by its history. It might be said that to Tolkien a word was not like a brick, a single delimitable unit but like the top of a stalactite, interesting in itself but more so as part of something growing. It might also be said that he thought there was in this process something super-human, certainly super-any-one-particular-human, for no one knew how words *would* change, even if he knew how they *had*. In one of his last published poems, a tribute in Old English to W. H. Auden, with facing-page modern English translation, Tolkien begins by calling Auden a *wōðbora*, and ends by promising him lasting praise from the *searopancle*.[1] The first noun is translated 'one [who] has poetry in him', the second as 'the word-lovers'. 'Word-lovers' is, however, etymologically parallel with 'philologists', while the first element of *wōð-bora* is also the word recorded in the god-name Woden, or Óthinn, and in the archaic adjective 'wood', meaning 'crazy'; it refers to the mystic rage of bard or shaman or (as we now say) berserker. Poets and philologists, Tolkien felt, were the ones to appreciate *that*.

An associated difference was that philologists were more likely than critics to believe in what one might call 'the reality of history'. One good reason for this was that they tended to work with manuscripts rather than printed books, and the former are much more instructive than the latter. In some cases they have been physically written by the original poet or author; in others they have been corrected by him; in others they all too clearly have not, with incomprehension so thick on the page that one can visualise the author's baffled rage were he ever to guess (as Chaucer did, occasionally) what had happened or was going to. The sense that ghosts cluster in old libraries is very strong. Another reason for the feeling of intimate involvement with history, though, lies in the philologists' awareness of the shaping of present by past – the stalactites of words again, but also the creation of nation-states by language-separation (e.g. Dutch and German), the growth of national myth from forgotten history (as with the Finnish *Kalevala*), but perhaps as much as anything the fastening down of landscape to popular consciousness by the habit of naming places. Less than thirty miles from Tolkien's study stands the prehistoric barrow known as 'Wayland's Smithy'. Its name is more than a thousand years old; perhaps it was in the mind of King Alfred (born at Wantage seven miles off) when he interjected into his translation of Boethius the outcry: *Hwæt synt nú þæs foreméran ond þæs wisan goldsmiðes bán Wélondes?* 'What now are the bones of Wayland, the goldsmith pre-eminently wise?' Alfred might also have thought of Wayland as the father of Widia, who in the lost poems released Theodoric from the power of the monsters; maybe he had heard them sung. But though the poems had gone, and the monsters with them, and 'Wayland' no longer meant anything at all to English people, the name survived down the centuries and carried with it a hint of what once had been. Such chains of association littered the landscape for Tolkien; they did not have to be confined to books. When he said that 'History often resembles "Myth" ', or when Wilhelm Grimm refused to segregate 'Myth' from 'Heroic Legend', both had entirely prosaic reasons for doing so.[2] They knew that legend often became a matter of everyday.

Something like these two awarenesses, of continuing history and continuing linguistic change, can be inferred (admittedly with the aid of vast quantities of hindsight) from the first thing Tolkien ever published, bar a few lines in school and college magazines: the poem 'Goblin Feet' in *Oxford Poetry 1915*.[3] This begins:

> I am off down the road
> Where the fairy lanterns glowed
> And the little pretty flittermice are flying:
> A slender band of grey
> It runs creepily away
> And the hedges and the grasses are a-sighing.
> The air is full of wings
> And of blundering beetle-things
> That warn you with their whirring and their humming.
> O! I hear the tiny horns
> Of enchanted leprechauns
> And the padding feet of many gnomes a-coming.

This is, admittedly, not very good. Indeed one can imagine the response to it of the literary 'side', full of armèd vision, not to mention critical temper. 'Why', it might ask, 'do we have the past tense in line 2 and the present everywhere else? Does this mean the "fairy lanterns" have gone out and the "I-narrator" is pursuing them? Or could it be that the author is stuck for a rhyme to "road"? As for "*a*-sighing" and "*a*-coming", these look like scansion devices, mere padding. But in any case there is nothing in nature to suggest that the hedges and the grasses *were* "sighing" at all, while the "creepiness" of the road is just something the poet has decided to project on to the landscape from himself. That's why we don't *believe* the "I-narrator" when he says he hears "tiny horns"! And what about "enchanted leprechauns"? Does that mean they've *been* enchanted by someone else; or that they're enchant*ing*; or are all leprechauns enchanted, i.e. magic, i.e. not-real? The poet gives himself away. This is an evasive poem, a self-indulgent one. "Off down the road" indeed! Road to nowhere!'

So the critical indictment might run, and it is hard to counter. Readers of *The Lord of the Rings* will have noted further the as yet undiscriminating use of 'fairy', 'gnome' and later 'goblin', not to mention the quite cross-cultural use of 'leprechauns' and the insistence (later to be most strongly abjured) on the little, the tiny, the insect-like. Still, there are hints of hope in the poem after all, and better questions to be asked than those which have been.

What is this 'road', for instance, the 'slender band of grey', the 'crooked fairy lane'? It clearly is not a tarmac one; on another level it is to be a recurring Tolkienian image:

> The Road goes ever on and on
> Down from the door where it began . . .

And oddly, G. B. Smith – Tolkien's school and college friend, killed the following year in Flanders, to have his poems posthumously published with a foreword by Tolkien – had addressed himself to the same theme in a poem four pages earlier in the *Oxford Poetry* collection:

> This is the road the Romans made,
> 　　This track half lost in the green hills,
> Or fading in a forest glade
> 　　'Mid violets and daffodils.
>
> The years have fallen like dead leaves
> 　　Unwept, uncounted and unstayed
> (Such as the autumn tempest thieves)
> 　　Since first this road the Romans made.[4]

Now this theme of time is intensely Tolkienian (if one may be permitted to put it that way round). The last sight of Lórien in *The Fellowship of the Ring*, published thirty-nine years later, is of Galadriel singing *Ai! laurië lantar lassi súrinen!* 'Ah! like gold fall the leaves in the wind! And numberless as the wings of trees are the years . . .' (*LOTR* I, 394, and see also Fangorn's song, II, 72). In this case the hope which G. B. Smith expressed in his final letter to Tolkien before death – 'May God bless you, my dear John Ronald, and may you say the things I have tried to say long after I am not there to say them' – appears against all probability to have been fulfilled (*Biography*, p. 86). However the clue to follow, for the moment, is 'the road the Romans made'.

It may seem perverse to seek to identify this road, but on the other hand it isn't very hard. There are only two Roman roads near Oxford, and the better-preserved is the old highway from Bath to Towcester, still visible as a straight line across the map but dwindled along much of its Oxford stretch to a footpath. It is now called 'Akeman Street', like 'Wayland's Smithy' a name of some fascination for philologists. It implies for one thing an old and massive population change. No town in Roman Britain had a more simply descriptive name than Aquae Sulis, 'the waters of Sul', and so prominent were its mineral springs with the Roman spa around them that even the Anglo-Saxons began to call it *æt baðum*, 'at the baths', and later Bath. One of them wrote a poem about the site, now called *The Ruin*. However they also called the town *Acemannesceaster*, 'Akeman's chester' or 'Akeman's (fortified) town'. That is why the Bath–Towcester road acquired the name 'Akeman Street'; the people who called it that knew it went to Bath, but had forgotten that Bath was ever Aquae Sulis; they were invaders, of a lower cultural level than the Romans, and soon they ceased to use the road for anything like the traffic it had once carried. Its name and its decline in status from highway to footpath bear witness to the oblivion that can fall on a civilisation. But what was the reaction of these invaders to the historical monuments they could hardly help seeing in their new land, the stone roads, the villas, the great ruins which they (as in *The Ruin*) called vaguely the *eald enta geweorc*, 'the old work of giants'? Place-names again give suggestive clues.

About nine miles north-west of Oxford and half a mile from Akeman Street across the river Evenlode stands a villa, excavated in 1865 and once the property of some Romano-British noble. It is distinguished by the remains of a fourth-century tessellated pavement in different colours. The village nearby is called Fawler. To most people, including its inhabitants, this name now means nothing. But once it was *Fauflor*, a spelling recorded in 1205, and before that, in Old English, *fág flór*, 'the coloured floor, the painted floor'. There can be little doubt that the village was called after the pavement; so the pavement was still visible when the invaders came. Why, then, did they not occupy the villa, but chose to live instead on an undeveloped site a few furlongs off? No one can tell, but perhaps they were afraid. A further twist in the story is that there is another *fág flór* in Anglo-Saxon record, in the great hall of *Beowulf*, haunted by Grendel the maneater:

> on fágne flór féond treddode,
> éode yrremód; him of éagum stód
> ligge gelícost léoht unfæger.

'The fiend stepped on to the painted floor, angrily he paced; from his eyes there stood an ugly light, like fire.'

So wrote the poet, in one of his classic passages of 'Gothic' suggestion. Could *Beowulf* have been sung in Fawler? What would its inhabitants have thought? Tolkien knew *Beowulf*, of course, virtually by heart, and he knew what 'Fawler' meant, for he hailed the etymology with delight in his 1926 review of the *Introduction to the Survey of Place-Names*; such work, he pointed out, is fired by 'love of the land of England', by 'the allurement of the riddle of the past', it leads to 'the recapturing of fitful and tantalising glimpses in the dark' (*YWES* 5, p. 64). He was interested in the names of roads, too, for he had argued the year before that 'Watling Street' was an old name for the Milky Way, 'an old mythological term that was first applied to the *eald enta geweorc* [i.e. the Roman road from Dover to Chester] after the English invasion' (*YWES* 4, p. 21). Nor did he forget Bath and *The Ruin*. Legolas's 'lament of the stones' on page 297 of *The Fellowship of the Ring* is an adaptation of part of the poem. At some stage of his life Tolkien must certainly have noted all the strange implications and suggestions of 'Akeman Street'.

Did he know them in 1915, and share them with his friend G. B. Smith? Is the quest for Fairyland in 'Goblin Feet' a kind of translation of the quest for the romantic realities of history? Probably the answer to both questions is 'No'. However, disentangling fact from inference as carefully as possible, one can say first that Tolkien and Smith evidently shared a feeling for the ancient roads, the 'old straight tracks' and 'crooked lanes' of England; second that Smith even in 1915 appreciated the sadness of the relationship between what these are and what they were; third that before many years were out it would be certain that Tolkien appreciated the same thing much more fully, with a wealth of reference to history and poetry and present-day reality. Even in 1915, one might say, a road, a *real* road, could possess a 'creepiness' for him which was based on some factual knowledge, not entirely self-generated. Philology would reinforce this. But already one image in his poem drew on some historical force.

Further, Tolkien was already thinking of words as 'stalactites'. 'Flitter-mice' in line 3 is not normal English. According to the *OED* it was introduced in the sixteenth century by analogy with German *Fledermaus*, for 'bat'. However 'bat' is not recorded in Old English, and it is possible that some ancestor of 'flittermouse', e.g. *fleðer-mús, was natural to English all along, but never got written down. There is an apparently similar puzzle over 'rabbit' (for which see pp. 52–4 below), which Tolkien at least signals awareness of in the second stanza by using the odd term 'coney-rabbits'. Finally 'honey-flies' in line 30 is elsewhere unrecorded. From context one would think he meant 'butterflies'. Perhaps he was aware, though, of the unexpected scatalogical sense of that innocent-looking word in Old English – a language which has had many rudenesses pruned by educated usage. He could have found out by looking 'butterfly' up in the *OED*, and at least it had occurred to him to wonder *why* butterflies were always and for no apparent reason so called. These verbal creations admittedly do not add much to the overall effect of 'Goblin Feet', but they exemplify an attempt to combine philological insight with poetry. Both roads and words hint at the early complexity of Tolkien's inner life, its unusual combination of emotion with inquiry.

Survivals in the West

Such hints, of course, fizzle out immediately. *The Silmarillion* had begun its sixty-year gestation by 1914,[5] but in 1915 Tolkien went off to the war in which G. B. Smith was to die. On demobilisation he was preoccupied with the problem of earning a living, first in Oxford with the *OED*, then in the English Department at Leeds University, finally, with secure status and no lure of further advancement, back in Oxford again in 1925. He published nothing (bar the note to Smith's posthumous collection of poems) for five years after 'Goblin Feet', and a good deal of his subsequent work was written for simple motives – money, or to keep his name in front of the people who counted, who made appointments 'with tenure'. Much of his inner life *did* find its way into the twenty or thirty poems contributed to various periodicals or collections between 1920 and 1937; Tolkien's habit of thriftily rewriting them and using them in *The Hobbit* or *The Lord of the Rings* or *The Adventures of Tom Bombadil* shows how important some of them were to him.[6] Still, it is fair to say that these remain by themselves thin, or uncertain. The brew that was to become his fiction needed a good deal of thickening yet; and this could only come from the interaction of poetry with philology.

From this point of view one of Tolkien's most revealing pre-Hobbit pieces is his almost unread comment on 'The Name "Nodens" ' for the Society of Antiquaries in 1932.[7] This virtually repeats the story of 'Fawler'. In 1928 excavations on a site near Lydney in the west of England had revealed a temple devoted to some kind of mystery cult and still flourishing in the fourth century, i.e. well after the introduction of Christianity to England. The temple was eventually abandoned as a result of the barbarian and also non-Christian English, who however had their own cults. As with the villa at Fawler the Lydney temple fell into disuse – but not completely into oblivion. The iron-mines not far away were remembered: and whether because of them or from a continuing superstitious respect for the site, it was given a new Anglo-Saxon name, persisting to modern times – Dwarf's Hill. The Society of Antiquaries made no comment on all this, but in the story and the place-name one can hear the echo of a hopeless resistance from the Darkest of Dark Ages, pagan to Christian, pagan to pagan, Welsh to English, all ending in forgetfulness with even the memory of the resisters blurred, till recovered by archaeology – and by philology. For Tolkien's job was to comment on the name 'Nodens' found in an inscription on the site, and he did it with immense thoroughness.

His conclusion was that the name meant 'snarer' or 'hunter', from an Indo-European root surviving in English only in the archaic phrase 'good neat's leather'. More interesting was his tracing of the descent of Nodens from god to Irish hero (*Núadu Argat-lam*, 'Silverhand'), then to Welsh hero (*Lludd Llaw Ereint*, also 'Silverhand'), finally to Shakespearean hero – King Lear. Even Cordelia, Tolkien noted, was derived from the semi-divine *Creiddylad*, of whom was told a version of the story of 'the Everlasting Battle', which interested Tolkien in other ways. Shakespeare can naturally have known nothing about 'Nodens', or about *Beowulf* (a poem in which some have seen the first dim stirrings of 'Hamlet the Dane'). That did not mean that the old stories were not in some way working through him, present even in his much-altered version. Like 'Akeman Street' and 'Wayland's Smithy', Tolkien might have concluded, even *King Lear* could bear witness to a sort of English, or British, continuity.

And one could say the same of Old King Cole. Tolkien never actually rewrote *his* saga in epic verse (though one can now see why he remarked casually of Milton, 'Monsters', p. 254, that he 'might have done worse' than recount 'the story of Jack and the Beanstalk in noble verse' – it would have been a monster-poem, like the lost 'Rescue of Theodoric'). Still, he would certainly have recognised the 'merry old soul' as a figure similar in ultimate origin and final 'vulgarisation' to King Arthur or King Lear.[8] This interest in the descent of fables probably explains why Tolkien did try his hand at two 'Man in the Moon' poems, 'The Man in the Moon came down too soon' (which appeared first in 1923 and was collected in *The Adventures of Tom Bombadil* thirty-nine years after), and 'The Cat and the Fiddle: A Nursery Rhyme Undone and its Scandalous Secret Unlocked' (also out first in 1923 but to achieve far wider circulation as sung by Frodo in Book 1, chapter 9 of *The Fellowship of the Ring*, 'At the Sign of the Prancing Pony'). No one would call either of these serious poems. But what they do is to provide a narrative and semi-rational frame for the string of totally irrational non-sequiturs which we now call 'nursery rhymes'. How could 'the cow jump over the moon'? Well, it might if the

Moon were a kind of vehicle parked on the village green while its driver had a drink. How could the Man in the Moon have 'come by the south And burnt his mouth With eating cold plum porridge'? Well, it doesn't seem very likely, but perhaps it points to an ancient story of earthly disillusionment. If one assumes a long tradition of 'idle children' repeating 'thoughtless tales' in increasing confusion, one might think that poems like Tolkien's were the remote ancestors of the modern rhymes. They are 'asterisk-poems', reconstructed like the attributes of Nodens. They also contain, at least in their early versions, hints of mythological significance – the Man in the Moon who fails to drive his chariot while mortals panic and his white horses champ their silver bits and the Sun comes up to overtake him is not totally unlike the Greek myth of Phaethon, who drove the horses of the Sun too close to Earth and scorched it. Finally, the reason why Tolkien picked 'the Man in the Moon' for treatment rather than 'Old King Cole' or 'Little Bo-Peep' is, no doubt, that he knew of the existence of a similar 'Man in the Moon' poem, in Middle English and from a time and place in which he took particular interest.

This is the lyric from Harley Manuscript no. 2253, now known generally as 'The Man in the Moon'.[9] It is perhaps the best medieval English lyric surviving, and certainly one of the hardest, prompting many learned articles and interpretations. However three points about it are clear, and all gave it especial charm for Tolkien. In the first place it is extremely bizarre; it is presented as a speech by an English villager *about* the Man in the Moon, asking why he doesn't come down or move. It also has a very sharp and professional eye for English landscape; the villager concludes that the Man in the Moon is so stiff because he has been caught stealing thorns and carrying them home to mend his hedges with (an old image of the Moon's markings is of a man with a lamp, a dog, and a thorn-bush, see Starveling in *A Midsummer Night's Dream* V i). Finally, for all the poem's thick dialect and involvement with peasant life, it is full of self-confidence. 'Never mind if the hayward has caught you pinching thorns', calls the narrator to the Man in the Moon, 'we'll deal with that. We'll ask him home':

> 'Drynke to hym deorly of fol god bous,
> Ant oure dame douse shal sitten hym by.
> When that he is dronke ase a dreynt mous,
> Thenne we schule borewe the wed ate bayly.'

> 'We'll drink to him like friends in excellent booze,
> and our sweet lady will sit right next to him.
> When he's as drunk as a drowned mouse,
> we'll go to the bailiff and redeem your pledge.'

And without this evidence, clearly, the indictment will be quashed! It all sounds a most plausible way to work, and one which casts an unexpected light on the downtrodden serfs of medieval England – not as downtrodden as all that, obviously. Their good-natured resourcefulness seems to be an element in the make-up of Tolkien's hobbits. More significantly, the poem makes one wonder about the unofficial elements of early literary culture. Were there other 'Man in the Moon' poems? Was there a whole genre of sophisticated play on folk-belief? There *could* have been. Tolkien's 1923 poems attempt to revive it, or invent it, fitting into the gaps between modern doggerel and medieval lyric, creating something that might have existed and would, if it had, account for the jumble and litter of later periods – very like Gothic and 'i-mutation'.

One sees that the thing which attracted Tolkien most was darkness: the blank spaces, much bigger than most people realise, on the literary and historical map, especially those after the Romans left in AD 419, or after Harold died at Hastings in 1066. The post-Roman era produced 'King Arthur', to whose cycle King Lear and King Cole and the rest became eventual tributaries. Tolkien knew this tradition well and used it for *Farmer Giles of Ham* (published 1949, but written much earlier), the opening paragraphs of which play jokingly with the first few lines of *Sir Gawain*. However he also knew that whatever the author of *Sir Gawain* thought, the Arthurian tradition was originally non-English, indeed dedicated to the overthrow of England; its commemoration in English verse was merely a final consequence of the stamping-out of native culture after Hastings, a literary 'defoliation' which had also led to the meaninglessness of English names like 'Fawler' and the near-total loss of all Old English heroic tradition, apart from *Beowulf*. What, then, had happened to England and the English during those 'Norman centuries' when, it might be said, 'language' and 'literature' had first and lastingly separated?

Tolkien had been interested in that question for some time. Not much was known about Early Middle English, and indeed several of its major texts remain without satisfactory editions today. However, one important work was evidently the *Ancrene Wisse*, a 'guide for anchoresses (or female hermits)', existing in several manuscripts from different times and places, but one of few Middle English works to be translated *into* French rather than out of it. With this were associated several other texts with a 'feminist' bias, the tract on virginity *Hali Meiðhad*, the saints' lives *Seinte Juliene*, *Seinte Marherete*, *Seinte Katherine*, the little allegory *Sawles Warde*. All looked similar in dialect, and in sophistication of phrase; on the other hand their subject-matter meant they were unlikely ever to take the 'literature' side by storm. What *could* be said about them?

Tolkien began with a review of F. J. Furnivall's edition of *Hali Meiðhad*, in 1923; he went on to make 'Some Contributions to Middle English Lexicography' in *Review of English Studies* (1925), most of them drawn from *Ancrene Wisse*, and some of them incidentally interesting, like the remark that *medi wið wicchen* must mean, not 'meddle with witches' but 'bribe, purchase the service of witches', apparently a known practice to the author of the 'Rule'. In 'The Devil's Coach-Horses' in the same periodical that year he spent enormous effort on the single word *eaueres* from *Hali Meiðhad*, arguing that it did not mean 'boars' as the *OED* had said, but 'heavy horses, draft horses'. Philologically this was interesting as showing a Germanic root *abra-z, meaning 'work' and connected with Latin *opus*. Mythologically it was interesting too as showing an image of the devil galloping away not on fire-breathing steeds, but on 'heavy old dobbins' – a contemptuous barnyard image of evil. All very well, but still, some would have said, distinctly peripheral.

The breakthrough came with Tolkien's article for *Essays and Studies* (1929), '*Ancrene Wisse* and *Hali Meiðhad*', the most perfect though not the best-known of his academic pieces. This rested in classic philological style on an observation of the utmost tininess. In Old English a distinction was regularly made between verbs like *hé hiereð, hie hierað* 'he hears, they hear', and *hé lócað, hie lóciað* 'he looks, they look'. An -*að* ending could be singular or plural, depending on what sort of a verb it was attached to. This clear but to outsiders utterly unmemorable distinction was, after Hastings, rapidly dropped. Two manuscripts, however, one of *Ancrene Wisse*, the other of its five associated texts, not only preserved the distinction but went on to make another *new* one, between verbs within the *lócian* class: they distinguished e.g. between *ha polieð*, 'they endure', O.E. *hie poliað*, and *ha fondið*, 'they inquire', O.E. *hie fondiað*. The distinction had a sound phonological basis and was not the result of mere whim. Furthermore the two manuscripts could not have been by the same man for they were in different handwriting. Evidently – I summarise the chain of logic – they were the product of a 'school'; so were the works themselves, composed in the same dialect by another man or men; and this 'school' was one that operated in English, and in an English descended without interruption from Old English, owing words certainly to the Norse and the French but not affected by the confusion their invasions had caused. To put it Tolkien's way:

There is an English older than Dan Michel's and richer, as regular in spelling as Orm's [these are two other relatively consistent writers of Middle English] but less queer; one that has preserved something of its former cultivation. It is not a language long relegated to the 'uplands' struggling once more for expression in apologetic emulation of its betters or out of compassion for the lewd, but rather one that has never fallen back into 'lewdness', and has contrived in troublous times to maintain the air of a gentleman, if a country gentleman. It has traditions and some acquaintance with the pen, but it is also in close touch with a good living speech – a soil somewhere in England. ('AW', p. 106)

It is in short a language which had defied conquest and the Conqueror.

There are several signs here of Tolkien's underlying preoccupations. One is the power of philology: the regularity and rigour of its observations can resurrect from the dead a society long since vanished of which no other trace remains than the nature of dialect forms in a few old manuscripts. These observations are incontestable. They are also suggestive, permitting us to make informed guesses at, say, the level of independence of western shires in the twelfth century and the nature of their race-relations. They pleased Tolkien further because their implication was so clearly patriotic, that there had been an England beyond England even in the days when anyone who was anyone spoke French. In that way they also corroborated the impression of self-confidence made by the 'Man in the Moon' poem, itself an example of what Tolkien in that article (p. 116) called 'the westerly lyric, whose little world lay between Wirral and the Wye'. As for the *Ancrene Wisse* itself, Tolkien had little doubt that the 'soil somewhere in England' to which it should be ascribed was Hereford-shire, a decision confirmed by later research. All in all the picture these inquiries gave was of a far-West shire, cut off from and undisturbed by foreigners, adhering to the English traditions elsewhere in ruins. If only such a civilisation had endured to be the ancestor of ours! Tolkien, with his family connections in and nostalgic memories of Worcestershire, the next most-western county to Hereford and like it a storehouse of Old English tradition, felt the pull of this 'might have been' strongly and personally. In a revealing passage at the end of the article (p. 122), he noted a few exceptions to his general rule and remarked:

> Personally I have no doubt that if we could call the scribes of A and B before us and silently point to these forms, they would thank us, pick up a pen, and immediately substitute the *-in* forms, as certainly as one of the present day would emend a minor aberration from spelling or accidence, if it was pointed to.

The ghosts would be gentlemen, scholars, Englishmen too. Tolkien felt at home with them.

This sentiment may have been misguided: if we really *had* the 'lays' on which *Beowulf* was based we might not think much of them, and if we had to deal with the scribes of *Ancrene Wisse* we might find them difficult people. There is a streak of wishful thinking in Tolkien's remark near the end of this article that if his argument was sound, English in the west at that time must have been 'at once more alive, and more traditional and organized as a written form, than anywhere else'. He was used to having 'traditional' literature viewed as dead: it was nice to think of a time when tradition was rated higher than modern fashion. Still, it is hard to say his sentiment was wrong. It was based on rational argument, and the whole theory integrated (as theories should) many thousands of separate facts which had been needing explanation already. With hindsight one can see that this philological vision of ancient Herefordshire was a strong component of Tolkien's later conception of the hobbits' 'Shire', also cut-off, dimly remembering former empires, but effectively turned in on itself to preserve an idealised 'English' way of life. But 'the Shire' is fiction, and philology fact. The questions which begin to show themselves in Tolkien's work from about this time on are: how far did he distinguish the two states? And how much of his later success was caused by reluctance to admit a distinction?

Connections are exemplified in Tolkien's article *'Sigelwara land'*, published in two parts in *Medium Aevum* 1932 and 1934. Typically this considers a single Old English word, *Sigelware*, and typically corrects that briskly to *Sigelhearwan*. What were these? Literate Anglo-Saxons used the word to translate *Æthiops*, 'Ethiopian', but, Tolkien argued, the word must have been older than English knowledge of Latin, let alone Ethiopians, and must have had some other and earlier referent. Pursuing *sigel* and *hearwa* separately through many examples and analogues, he emerged with two thoughts and an image: (1) that *sigel* meant originally both 'sun' and 'jewel', (2) that *hearwa* was related to Latin *carbo*, 'soot', (3) that when an Anglo-Saxon of the pre-literate Dark Age said *sigelhearwan*, what he had in mind was 'rather the sons of Múspell [the Norse fire-giant] than of Ham, the ancestors of the Silhearwan with red-hot eyes that emitted sparks, with faces black as soot'. What was the point of the speculation, admittedly 'guess-work', admittedly 'inconclusive'? It offers some glimpses of a lost mythology, suggested Tolkien with academic caution, something 'which has coloured the verse-treatment of Scripture and determined the diction of poems'.[10] A good deal less boringly, one might say, it had helped to naturalise the 'Balrog' in the traditions of the North, and it had helped to create (or corroborate) the image of the *silmaril*, that fusion of 'sun' and 'jewel' in physical form. Tolkien was already thinking along these lines. His scholarly rigour was not 'put-on', but it was no longer only being directed to academic, un-creative ends.

Allegories, Potatoes, Fantasy and Glamour

One may now see in rather a different light the four minor prose works written by Tolkien in the late 1930s and early 1940s, those years in which *The Hobbit* came to term and *The Lord of the Rings* began to get under way – the years, one may say, when Tolkien turned away from pursuing his trade and began instead to use it. He knew he was doing this, as one can see from the little allegory 'Leaf by Niggle' (published 1945, but written *c.* 1943). Since Tolkien said in later years that he 'cordially disliked' allegory, it is perhaps worth repeating that 'Leaf by Niggle' *is* one, and that you can prove it. The story's first words are, 'There was once a little man called Niggle, who had a long journey to make', and to any Anglo-Saxonist this is bound to recall the Old Northumbrian poem known as *Bede's Death-Song*, memorable (a) for being in Old Northumbrian, (b) for being so clearly the true, last words of the Venerable Bede, England's greatest churchman, all of whose other works are in Latin. This goes: 'Before that compelled journey (*néidfáerae*) no man is wiser than he needs to be, in considering, before his departure, what will be judged to his soul after his deathday, good or evil.' Obviously someone should have said this to Niggle! But the lines also give a good and ancient reason for carrying out the basic operation of allegory, which is to start making equations.

Thus journey=death. Niggle the painter further=Tolkien the writer. One can see as much from the accusation of being 'just idle', softened later to being 'the sort of painter who can paint leaves better than trees', or to being unable to organise his time; Tolkien was sensitive to accusations of laziness, but it is clear enough that he was a perfectionist, and also easily distracted.[11] Niggle's 'leaf'=*The Hobbit*, his 'Tree'=*The Lord of the Rings*, the 'country' that opens from it=Middle-earth, and the 'other pictures . . . tacked on to the edges of his great picture'=the poems and other works which Tolkien kept on fitting into his own greater one. Meanwhile the garden which Niggle does not keep up looks ominously like Tolkien's professorial duties; the visitors who hinted 'that he might get a visit from an Inspector' remind one of that discourteous colleague of Tolkien's, who even *after The Lord of the Rings* came out snapped ungraciously 'He ought to have been teaching!'[12] One can go on making these equations, and one is *supposed* to; the essence of an allegory, Tolkien thought, was that it should be 'just', i.e. that all the bits should fit exactly together, compelling assent (and amusement) by their minuteness. If one realises that, there is a certain bite in the place where Niggle does his painting. He keeps his great canvas 'in the tall shed that had been built for it out in his garden (on a plot where once he had grown potatoes)'. Niggle sacrificed potatoes to paint. What did Tolkien sacrifice to *The Lord of the Rings*? The real answer is, articles like those on *Ancrene Wisse* and the *Sigelware*; after 1940 (when he was only 48) Tolkien wrote only five more, and two of these were collaborations and two others not entirely academic in style. Still, Tolkien never went over to despising the advancement of learning. It is Niggle's expressed gratitude for Parish's 'excellent potatoes' which persuades the First Voice to let him out of the Workhouse (=Purgatory). One could say that the whole tale expresses both Tolkien's self-accusation and self-justification, and that its solution in Heaven lies in Niggle and Parish, the creative and the practical aspects of Tolkien himself, learning to work together – though what they work on, you notice, is very definitely Niggle's Tree and Country, not Parish's potatoes at all.

Tolkien was giving up the academic *cursus honorum* in the late 1930s, and he knew it. How did he justify this to himself, and how far could he reconcile the claims of 'potatoes' and 'Trees' (=scholarship and fantasy)? These questions underlie, often unsuspectedly, the three critical works roughly contemporary with 'Leaf by Niggle', i.e. *'Beowulf*: the Monsters and the Critics' (published 1936), 'On Fairy-Stories' (first version 1939), and the 'Preface' to C. L. Wrenn's revision of the Clark Hall translation of *Beowulf* (1940). None of these contains very much philology in the narrow sense of sound-changes or verb-paradigms, and they have accordingly been fallen on gratefully by commentators who never wanted to learn any. However, philology still remains their essential guts; while they lead forward to fantasy they also look back to and rest always on an intensely rigorous study of 'the word'.

So, to take the last piece first, the 'Clark Hall' introduction has only one main point to make, and that is that words mean more than their dictionary entries. What happens if you look up *Sigelware* in the standard Old English dictionary of J. Bosworth and T. N. Toller? It says 'the Ethiopians', and that's all. What of *éacen*, a word in *Beowulf*? The dictionary says 'Increased, great, vast, powerful'. To 'the enquirer into ancient beliefs', wrote Tolkien, only the first was right, for *éacen* meant not 'large' but 'enlarged' and denoted a supernatural addition of power. As for runes, Bosworth–Toller translated the Beowulfian phrase *onband beadurúne* (meaninglessly) as 'unbound the war-secret', while Clark Hall tried 'gave vent to secret thoughts of strife'. 'It means "unbound a battle rune"', declared Tolkien. 'What exactly is implied is not clear. The expression has an antique air, as if it had descended from an older time to our poet: a suggestion lingers of the spells by which men of wizardry could stir up storms in a clear sky' (pp. xiii–xiv). Fanciful, the shades of Bosworth and Toller might have said. If the facts point *to* fantasy, Tolkien could have retorted, fantasy is what we must have! The 'Preface' is in a wider sense a protest against translating *Beowulf* only into polite modern English, a plea for listening to the vision contained, not in plots, but in words – words like *flæsc-homa, bán-hús, hreðer-loca, ellor-sið* ('flesh-raiment', 'bone-house', 'heart-prison', 'elsewhere-journey'). The poet who used these words, Tolkien wrote, did not see the world like us, but:

> saw in his thought the brave men of old walking under the vault of heaven upon the island earth (*middangeard*) beleaguered by the Shoreless Seas (*gársecg*) and the outer darkness, enduring with stern courage the brief days of life (*læne líf*), until the hour of fate (*metodsceaft*), when all things should perish, *léoht ond líf samod* [light and life together]. (p. xxvii)

He 'did not say all this fully or explicitly'. Nevertheless, the insistence ran, *it was there*. You didn't need a mythological handbook of Old English if you paid attention to the words; like place-names or Roman roads or Gothic vowels, they carried quite enough information all by themselves.

The same insistence on 'the reality of language' permeates the British Academy lecture of 1936. There, however, it is further intertwined with beliefs about 'the reality of history' – rather curious beliefs which Tolkien does not seem to have wanted to express directly. The general flow of the lecture is in fact extremely sinuous, causing great trouble to the many later Beowulfians who have tried to paraphrase it; it abounds in asides, in hilarious images like the Babel of conflicting critics and the 'jabberwocks of historical and antiquarian research', in wildernesses of dragons and shrewdnesses of apes. However a vital point about it, never directly stated or defended, is Tolkien's conviction that he knew exactly when and under what circumstances the poem was written. '*At a given point*', he says (his italics, p. 262), there was a fusion, reflected in the poem; at this 'precise point' (p. 269) an imagination was kindled. Since there is no unquestioned evidence at all for the date and place when *Beowulf* was composed (it could be anywhere from Tyne to Severn, from AD 650 to 1000), one wonders what Tolkien meant. But the nearest he approaches to an answer is via allegory once more, in his little story of the man and the tower, on pp. 248–9.

This runs as follows:

> A man inherited a field in which was an accumulation of old stone, part of an older hall. Of the old stone some had already been used in building the house in which he actually lived, not far from the old house of his fathers. Of the rest he took some and built a tower. But his friends coming perceived at once (without troubling to climb the steps) that these stones had formerly belonged to a more ancient building. So they pushed the tower over, with no little labour, in order to look for hidden carvings ... They all said 'This tower is most interesting.' But they also said (after pushing it over): 'What a muddle it is in!' And even the man's own descendants, who might have been expected to consider what he had been about, were heard to murmur: 'He is such an odd fellow! Imagine using these old stones just to build a nonsensical tower! Why did not he restore the old tower? He had no sense of proportion.' But from the top of that tower the man had been able to look out upon the sea.

Now, as with 'Leaf by Niggle', everything in his story can be 'equated'. 'The man'=the *Beowulf*-poet. The 'friends' looking for hidden carvings= the *Beowulf*-scholars trying to reconstruct history. The 'tower' with its view on the sea=*Beowulf* itself, with its non-scholarly impulse towards pure poetry. More difficult are 'the accumulation of old stone', the 'older hall' (also 'the old house of his fathers'), and 'the house in which he actually lived'. From this one can deduce that Tolkien thought that there had been older poems than *Beowulf*, pagan ones, in the time of the Christian past already abandoned; they are the 'older hall'. However debris from them remained available, poetic formulas and indeed stray pagan concepts like the *Sigelware*; that is the 'accumulation of old stone'. Some indeed of this was used for Biblical poems like *Exodus*, in which the *Sigelware* figure, part of the new civilisation of Christian Northumbria (or Mercia); that is 'the house' in which the man 'actually lived'. Rejected bits were nevertheless used by the poet to build his poem or 'tower'; and *they* are pre-eminently the monsters, the dragon, the *eotenas* and *ylfe*, 'elves' and 'giants', words once common but used either not at all or very rarely in the rest of Old English literature.

The gist of this is that no one, friends or descendants or maybe even contemporaries, had understood *Beowulf but Tolkien*. The work had always been something personal, even freakish, and it took someone with the same instincts to explain it. Sympathy furthermore depended on being a descendant, on living in the same country and beneath the same sky, on speaking the same language – being 'native to that tongue and land'. This is not the terminology of strict scholarship, though that does not prove the opinion wrong. What it does prove is that Tolkien felt more than continuity with the *Beowulf*-poet, he felt a virtual identity of motive and of technique.† Nowhere was the identity stronger than over 'the monsters and the critics', the latter deeply antipathetic to both of them – as Tolkien thought he had proved – the former deeply interesting. But what did the dragon, for instance, mean to the *Beowulf*-poet? For him, Tolkien argued, dragons might have been very close to the edge of reality; certainly the poet's pagan ancestors could have thought of dragons as things they might one day have to face. Equally certainly dragons had to the poet not yet become allegorical, as they would to his descendants – the dragon as Leviathan, the devil, 'that old serpent underground', etc. Yet even to the poet a dragon could not be mere matter-of-fact. He was indeed phenomenally lucky in his freedom to balance exactly between 'dragon-as-simple-beast' and 'dragon-as-just-allegory', between pagan and Christian worlds, on a pinpoint of literary artifice and mythic suggestion. One sees why Tolkien insisted on a 'precise' kindling point of imagination, a 'given point' of 'fusion', a 'pregnant moment of poise'. Knowing exactly when the poem was written was part of knowing its exact literary mode, and that literary mode was the one he himself wanted! But the circumstances

† The tower looking out over the sea, for instance, is a strong and private image of Tolkien's own for what he desired in literature. The 1920 poem 'The Happy Mariners' begins 'I know a window in a western tower/That opens on celestial seas...' In *The Lord of the Rings* (I, 16), the hobbits believe that you can see the sea from the top of the tallest elvish tower on the Tower Hills; but none of them has ever tried to climb it.

of the modern literary world made things much harder for him than for his mighty predecessor and kindred spirit.

'A dragon is no idle fancy', wrote Tolkien. 'Whatever may be his origins, in fact or invention, the dragon in legend is a potent creation of men's imagination, richer in significance than his barrow is in gold. Even to-day (despite the critics) you may find men . . . who have yet been caught by the fascination of the worm' (pp. 257–8). This last sentence is true mainly of Tolkien, whose 1923 poem 'Iumonna Gold Galdre Bewunden' is about a dragon-hoard and self-evidently *Beowulf*-derived. The one before is no doubt true as regards 'significance', but smacks of special pleading; Tolkien didn't want dragons to be symbolic, he wanted them to have a claw still planted on *fact* (as well as 'invention'). What did he mean by 'no idle fancy'? The truth of it is, I think, that Tolkien was very used to scrutinising old texts and drawing from them surprising but rational conclusions about history and language and ancient belief. In the process he developed very strongly a sort of tracker-dog instinct for validity, one which enabled him to say that such and such a word, like *éacen* or *beadurún* or *hearwa* or *éored*, was true, even if unrecorded, meaning by 'true' a genuine fragment of older civilisation consistent with the others. All his instincts told him that dragons were like that – widespread in Northern legend, found in related languages from Italy to Iceland, deeply embedded in ancient story. Could this mean nothing? He was bound to answer 'No', and hardly deterred by the thought that 'intelligent living people' would disagree with him. After all, what did they know about butterflies, let alone dragons! Still, though dragons, and Balrogs, and Shires, and silmarils were all taking shape in his mind as fiction, and were all simultaneously related to philological fact, he had not at this stage evolved a theory to connect the two. Possibly he never quite managed to make the link.

He had a determined try in 'On Fairy-Stories' three years later. However this is Tolkien's least successful if most discussed piece of argumentative prose. The main reason for its comparative failure, almost certainly, is its lack of a philological core or kernel; Tolkien was talking to, later writing for, an unspecialised audience, and there is some sign that he tried to 'talk down' to them. Repeatedly he plays the trick of pretending that fairies are real – they tell 'human stories' instead of 'fairy stories', they put on plays for men 'according to abundant records', and so on. This comes perilously close to whimsy, the pretence that something not true *is* true to create an air of comic innocence. However, beneath this, and beneath the very strong sense that Tolkien is 'counterpunching' to a whole string of modern theories which he did not like (fairies were small, only children liked fairies, Thórr was a nature-myth, etc. etc.), it is just about possible to make out the bones of an argument, or rather of a conviction.

The conviction is that fantasy is not entirely made up. Tolkien was not prepared to say this in so many words to other people, to sceptics, maybe not to himself. That is why he continually equivocated with words like 'invention' and 'no idle fancy', and also why a good deal of 'On Fairy-Stories' is a plea for the power of literary art; this is dignified with the form 'Sub-Creation', and to it are ascribed the continuing power of *Grimms' Fairy-Tales*, the (partial) success of *Macbeth*, the very existence of 'fantasy' as an art-form. Bobbing continually above the surface of these rational and literary opinions, however, are other, more puzzling statements. By 'fantasy' Tolkien declared (with a long haggle over the inadequacies of the *OED* and S. T. Coleridge), he meant first 'the Sub-creative Art in itself', but second 'a quality of strangeness and wonder in the Expression, derived from the Image'. The last phrase is the critical one, for it implies that the 'Image' was there before anyone derived any expression from it at all. The same implication lurks in Tolkien's own autobiographical statement, *à propos* of dragons, that 'Fantasy, the making or glimpsing of Otherworlds, was the heart of the desire of Faërie.' Making up dragons is Art; 'glimpsing' them and the worlds they come from is not. Tolkien would not let 'fantasy' mean either the one (rational) or the other (mystic) activity, but kept hinting it was both. He does so particularly, through the whole of the essay, with the idea of 'elves': these, he insists, may be (1) 'creations of Man's mind', which is what nearly everybody thinks, or (2) true, i.e. they 'really exist independently of our tales about them'. But (3) the essence of their activity even as 'creations of Man's mind' is that they are also creators, supreme illusionists, capable of luring mortals away, by their beauty, to the 'elf-hills' from which they will dazedly emerge centuries later, unaware of the passage of time. They form an image, a true image, of the 'elvish craft' of fantasy itself; stories about them are man-made fantasies about independent fantasts.

There is a strong sense of circularity in all these statements, as if Tolkien was hovering around some central point on which he dared not or could not land, and it is easy to dismiss that central point as mere personal delusion. We are back, indeed, with 'creepiness', that quality that 'Goblin Feet', in one view, thrusts subjectively on to something in reality perfectly ordinary; but which, in another view, stems from something still perfectly real and rational but which Tolkien was much better at detecting than most others. It seems to me that this 'real centre' was philological, and that Tolkien could not express it in ordinary literary terms. He came closest to it, in 'On Fairy-Stories', when he brushed past the edges of single words, especially *spell* and *evangelium*. These two words are related, historically, for the Old English translation of Greek *evangelion*, 'good news', was *gód spell*, 'the good story', now 'Gospel'. *Spell* continued to mean, however, 'a story, something said in formal style', eventually 'a formula of power', a *magic* spell. The word embodies much of what Tolkien meant by 'fantasy', i.e. something unnaturally powerful (magic spell), something literary (a story), something in essence true (Gospel). At the very end of his essay he asserts that the Gospels have the 'supremely convincing tone' of Primary Art, of truth – a quality he would also like to assert, but could never hope to prove, of elves and dragons.

There is a better word, though, buried in Tolkien's remarks, which I can only conclude he decided not to discuss as being too complicated for a non-philological piece; he would have done better to focus on it. This is 'glamour'. Actually Tolkien may also have been too revolted by the semantic poisonings of modernity to want to discuss the word, for now in common parlance it means overwhelmingly the aura of female sexual attraction, or to be more exact female sexual attraction *at a distance* – a showbiz word, an advertiser's word, false and meretricious, taking a part in such nasty compounds as 'glamour-girl', 'glamour-puss' and even 'glamour-pants'. The 1972 Supplement to the *OED* concedes the point and adds the coinages 'glamourize', 'glammed-up', and even 'glam' (a word Tolkien would have especially hated as showing that the old word used in dialect and in *Sir Gawain* for 'mirth, merriment', *glam, glaum*, was so dead as to be no competitor). The main G volume, published in 1897, however tells a story not much happier. 'Glamour', it alleges, is a made-up word, 'introduced into the literary language by Sir Walter Scott'. What it means is 'Magic, enchantment, spell; esp. in the phrase *to cast the glamour over one*'; from this sense has evolved the idea of 'A magical or fictitious beauty . . . a delusive or alluring charm', and so, pretty obviously, the cardboard senses of today. Tolkien would have been more interested in the quotation cited from Scott, which says 'This species of witchcraft is well known in Scotland as the glamour, or *deceptio visus*, and was supposed to be a special attribute of the race of Gipsies.' What he knew, and what the *OED* didn't, was that exactly this phenomenon was at the centre of Snorri Sturluson's *Prose Edda*, which begins with the *Gylfaginning* or 'Delusion of Gilfi', and includes within that the highly prominent and amusing tale of the delusion of Thórr by *sjónhverfing*='aversion of the sight'=*deceptio visus*='glamour'. 'Glamour' was then well exemplified in Norse tradition and never mind the gypsies.

Further, the word was evidently by origin a corruption of 'grammar', and paralleled in sense by 'gramarye'='Occult learning, magic, necromancy', says the *OED*, 'Revived in literary use by Scott.' Cambridge University had indeed preserved for centuries the office of 'Master of Glomerye', whose job it was to teach the younger undergraduates Latin. Tolkien must have been amused at the thought of a University official combining instruction in language – his own job – with classes in magic and spell-binding – his own desire. He wrote of the parson in *Farmer Giles of Ham* (a figure underrated by critics, but having some of the good as well as the bad points of the professional philologist), 'he was a grammarian, and could doubtless see further into the future than most'. But once again Tolkien knew more than the *OED*. The first citation it gives under 'gramarye' in the 'magic' sense is from the ballad of *King Estmere*, 'My mother was a westerne woman, And learned in gramarye'. How right that a 'western' woman should know grammar, like the sages of Herefordshire! How pleasing if the study should turn out to have a few practical advantages. But besides, the vital facts about *King Estmere*, as Tolkien could have observed from a glance at the introduction to the poem in F. J. Child's famous collection of *English and Scottish Popular Ballads* (1882–98), were that its closest analogues came from Faroese and Danish (which once again related 'glamour' to the ancient traditions of the North); and that the philologist Sophus Bugge had gone so far as to relate it to the Old Norse *Hervarar saga*. This itself is possibly the most romantically traditional of all the Norse 'sagas of old times'; it contains fragments with a claim to being the oldest heroic poetry of the North; and it was edited and translated in 1960 by Tolkien's son Christopher, under the title *The Saga of King Heidrek the Wise*.

> Þess galt hon gedda
> fyrir Grafár ósi,
> er Heiðrekr var veginn
> undir Harvaða fjǫllum.

So writes the forgotten poet: 'The pike has paid/by the pools of Grafá/for Heidrek's slaying/under Harvad-fells.' But, Christopher Tolkien comments, 'the view is not challenged . . . that *Harvaða* is the same name in origin as "Carpathians". Since this name in its Germanic form is found nowhere else at all, and must be a relic of extremely ancient tradition, one can hardly conclude otherwise than that these few lines are a fragment of a lost poem . . . that preserved names at least going back to poetry sung in the halls of Germanic peoples in central or south-eastern Europe.' One could hardly have a more romantically suggestive comment, or a more rigorously philological one, for as Christopher Tolkien footnotes, 'The stem *karpat-* was regularly transformed into *xarfaþ-* by the operation of the Germanic Consonant Shift (Grimm's Law).'[13] 'Glamour', 'gramarye', grammar, philology – these were on several levels much the same thing.

One can see now why Tolkien used the same word for both the characteristic literary quality of *Beowulf*, a 'glamour of Poesis' ('Monsters', p. 248), and for the characteristic but maybe not literary quality of 'fairy-stories', the 'glamour of Elfland' ('On Fairy-Stories', p. 13). He did not know quite *what* he was detecting, but he was in no doubt that he felt something consistent in many stories and poems which could not all be the work of the same man. It might after all only be the result of age and distance, the 'elvish hone of antiquity', or we might think the distorting glass of philology; it might point to some great lost truth in the areas of utter historical darkness of which he was so conscious; it might be a memory, or a prophecy, of Paradise, as in 'Leaf by Niggle'; or, again as in 'Leaf by Niggle', it might be mankind's one chance to create a vision of Paradise which would be true in the future if never in the past. Tolkien's theories on all this never coalesced. Still, we can say that the quality he evidently valued more than anything in literature was that shimmer of suggestion which never quite becomes clear sight but always hints at something deeper further on, a quality shared by *Beowulf*, *Hervarar saga*, 'Fawler', 'The Man in the Moon', 'Wayland's Smithy', and so much else. This was 'glamour', the opposite one may say of 'shrewdness' – for as the one had climbed into favour the other had been debased, in simultaneous proof of the superiority of ancient over modern world views. If Tolkien took 'glamour' too seriously, translating it into an entirely personal concept of fantasy, he had at any rate precedent and reason. As Jacob Grimm wrote (it is quoted under the definition of *philology* in the *Deutsches Wörterbuch*):

> You can divide all philologists into these groups, those who study words only for the sake of the things, or those who study things only for the sake of the words.

Grimm had no doubt that the former class was superior, the latter falling away into pedantry and dictionaries. Of that former class Tolkien was the pre-eminent example.

Chapter 3

THE BOURGEOIS BURGLAR

The word and the thing. elves and dwarves

Sigelhearwan, Nodens, Fawler, fancy, glamour: stripped of its layers of scholarly guardedness, the essence of Tolkien's belief was that 'the word authenticates the thing'. This was a belief grounded on philology. Tolkien thought, indeed he knew, that he could distinguish many words and word-forms into two classes, one 'old-traditional-genuine', the other 'new-unhistorical-mistaken'. From this he went on to form the opinion, less certain but still highly plausible, that the first group was not only more correct but also more interesting than the second; it had compelled assent over the millennia, it had a definite 'inner consistency', whether or not that was the 'inner consistency of reality' or merely of Secondary Art.

These beliefs go a long way towards explaining Tolkien's sudden displays of scrupulosity. In 1954 he was 'infuriated' to find that the printers of the first edition of *The Lord of the Rings* had gone through it, with the best will in the world and in conformity with standard English practice, changing 'dwarves' to 'dwarfs', 'dwarvish' to 'dwarfish', 'elven' to 'elfin', and so on. Considering the hundreds of changes involved (and the cost of proof correction) many authors might have let the matter ride; but Tolkien had all the original forms restored (see *Biography*, p. 217). In 1961 Puffin Books did much the same thing to a reprint of *The Hobbit*, and Tolkien complained to his publishers (*Letters*, p. 236) at greater length. His point was that even in modern English many old words ending in -f can still be told from new ones by their plural forms: old words (or at least old words of one particular class in Old English) behave like 'hoof' or 'loaf' and become 'hooves', 'loaves', while new ones (unaffected by sound-changes in the Old English period) simply add -s, as in 'proofs', 'tiffs', 'rebuffs'. Writing 'dwarfs' was then, to Tolkien's acute and trained sensibility, the equivalent of denying the word its age and its roots. Much the same reasoning had led Jacob Grimm, many years before, to leave the word *Elfen* out of his dictionary altogether, as an English import, replacing it with the native form *Elben* (which no one actually used any more) – his argument is repeated almost verbatim in the advice to German translators in Tolkien's 'Guide to the Names in *The Lord of the Rings*', p. 164. Even more than 'dwarfs' Tolkien disliked the word 'elfin', since this was a personal and pseudo-medieval coinage by Edmund Spenser – the poet hailed by the *OED*'s citations as the dawn of modern literature, and also the man whose first poem, *The Shepheardes Calender* of 1579, was ornamented by the most offensive gloss that Tolkien probably ever encountered. In quick succession this declared that for all its age 'that rancke opinion of Elfes' [*sic*] should be rooted 'oute of mens hearts', as being a mistaken form of the Italian faction the 'Guelfes', and in any case a Papistical notion spread by 'bald Friers and knauish shauelings'.[1] Tolkien would not have known whether to be offended most as philologist, as patriot, or as Roman Catholic! All round, the gloss no doubt confirmed him in the belief that modern and erroneous spellings went with stupid and self-opinionated people.

Belief was reinforced further by the history of the word 'fairy'. The *OED*, true to form, said that this was the word that should be used: 'In mod. literature, *elf* is a mere synonym of FAIRY, which has to a great extent superseded it even in dialects.' But whether this particular fact was true or not, Tolkien knew that much else of the *OED*'s information on such points was wrong. Its first citation for 'fairy' in its present sense is from John Gower, 1393, 'And as he were a fairie'; but as Tolkien remarked in 'On Fairy-Stories' (p. 14), what Gower really wrote was 'as he were *of* faierie', 'as if he had come from (the land of) Faërie'. Just above the *OED* cites the earlier poem of *Sir Orfeo* as evidence for the belief that 'the fairy' could be a collective noun, 'the fairy-folk': 'Awey with the fayré sche was ynome', i.e. presumably 'she was taken away by the fairy-people'. Tolkien made no overt remark on the matter, but his translation of *Sir Orfeo*, published in 1975, has the line correctly translated, 'By magic was she from them caught'. 'Fayré' in that context means 'glamour', the *deceptio visus* of the inhabitants of Fairyland. The gist of these observations for Tolkien must have been that 'fairy' in its modern sense was a newer word than the *OED* realised; that it was furthermore a foreign word derived from French *fée*; and had been throughout its history a source of delusion and error for English people, ending in the compound words 'fairy-tale' and 'fairy-story' which as Tolkien observed in 'On Fairy-Stories' were badly defined, uninformed, and associated with literary works (like Drayton's *Nymphidia*) bereft of the slightest trace of sub-creation or any other respectable literary art.

Good writing began with right words. Tolkien accordingly schooled himself to drop forms like 'elfin', 'dwarfish', 'fairy',' gnome', and eventually 'goblin', though he had used all of them in early works up to and including *The Hobbit*.[2] More importantly he began to work out their replacements, and to ponder what concepts lay behind the words and uses which he recognised as linguistically authentic. This activity of recreation – creation from philology – lies at the heart of Tolkien's 'invention' (though maybe not of his 'inspiration'); it was an activity which he kept up throughout his life, and one which is relatively easy to trace, or to 'reconstruct'.

Thus there can be little doubt what Tolkien thought of the 'elves' of English and Germanic tradition. He knew to begin with that Old English *ælf* was the ancestor of the modern word, was cognate with Old Norse *álfr*, Old High German *alp*, and for that matter, had it survived, Gothic **albs*. It was used in *Beowulf*, where the descendants of Cain include *eotenas ond ylfe ond orcnéas*, 'ettens and elves and demon-corpses', and in *Sir Gawain and the Green Knight*, where the seven-foot green giant with his monstrous axe is described nervously by bystanders as an *aluisch mon* or uncanny creature. The wide distribution of the word in space and time proves that belief in such creatures, whatever they were, was once both normal and immemorially old, going back to the times when the ancestors of Englishmen and Germans and Norwegians still spoke the same tongue. Yet what did the belief involve? Considering concept rather than word, Tolkien must soon have come to the conclusion that all linguistically authentic accounts of the elves, from whichever country they came, agreed on one thing: that the elves were in several ways paradoxical.

For one thing, people did not know where to place them between the polarities of good and evil. They were the descendants of Cain, the primal murderer, said the *Beowulf*-poet. They weren't as bad as *that*, imply the characters in *Sir Gawain* – actually the green giant plays fair and even lets Sir Gawain off – but they were certainly very frightening. It was wrong to offer sacrifice to them (*álfa-blót*) concurred all post-Christian Icelanders. On the other hand it might have seemed a good idea to propitiate them; if you didn't, Anglo-Saxons perhaps reminded each other, you might get *wæterælfádl*, the 'water-elf disease', maybe dropsy, or *ælfsogoða*, lunacy. There was a widespread belief in 'elf-shot', associated on the one hand with the flint arrows of prehistoric man and on the other with the metaphorical arrows of diabolic temptation. The consensus of these references is fear.

Simultaneous with that, though, is allure. *Ælfscýne* is an approbatory Anglo-Saxon adjective for a woman, 'elf-beautiful'. *Fríð sem álfkona*, said the Icelanders, 'fair as an elf-woman'. The standing and much-repeated story about the elves stresses their mesmeric charm. It may be 'True Thomas' on Huntly bank who sees 'the queen of fair Elfland', or a young woman who hears the elf-horn blowing, but either way the immediate reaction is of desire. True Thomas disregards all warnings to make off with the elf-queen, does not return to earth for seven years, and (in Walter Scott's version) leaves immediately again as soon as he is called. The medieval romance of *Sir Launfal* ends with the same glad desertion. For women to run off with elves was regarded with more suspicion. 'Lady Isabel' in the Scottish ballad saves her maidenhood and her life from the treacherous elf-knight she herself has summoned, and at the start of *The Wife of Bath's Tale* Chaucer makes a series of jokes about elves and friars, the burden of which is that the latter are sexually more rapacious than the former, though the former had a bad reputation with young women as well. The allure and the danger are mixed. Indeed a common variant of the 'young man/elf-queen' story ends with him in despair, not at having been seduced but at being deserted. It is the memory of former happiness, the 'disillusionment' of loss of 'glamour', which leaves Keats's character 'Alone and palely loitering'.

Now one can see very easily how such an apparent discrepancy of fear and attraction might in sober reality arise. Beauty is itself dangerous: this is what Sam Gamgee tries to explain to Faramir in *The Two Towers*, when interrogated on the nature of Galadriel, the elf-queen herself. 'I don't know about *perilous*' says Sam (p. 288), replying to Faramir's highly accurate remark that she must be 'perilously fair':

'It strikes me that folk takes their peril with them into Lórien, and finds it there because they've brought it. But perhaps you could call her perilous, because she's so strong in herself. You, you could dash yourself to pieces on her, like a ship on a rock; or drownd yourself, like a hobbit in a river. But neither rock nor river would be to blame.'

One could say the same of Sir Launfal's lady, or True Thomas's. One can also see how the rejected wives and fiancées, or husbands and fathers of people under elvish allure would concoct a very different story! Before long they would have the *ylfe* in exactly the same category as Cain – or Moloch. But this would be a second-hand opinion, and a prejudiced one (like those of Boromir, or Éomer and the Riders, *LOTR* I 352 or II 35).

It is in fact the strong point of Tolkien's 're-creations' that they take in all available evidence, trying to explain both good and bad sides of popular story; the sense of inquiry, prejudice, hearsay and conflicting opinion often gives the elves (and other races) depth. In Lothlórien we can see Tolkien exploiting, for instance, variant ideas about the elves and time. Most stories agreed that humans returning from Elf-land were temporally confused. Usually they thought time outside had speeded up: three nights in Elf-land might be three years outside, or a century. But sometimes they thought it had stood still. When the elf-maid sings in the Danish ballad of 'Elverhøj', or 'Elf-hill':

> Striden strøm den stiltes derved,
> som førre var van at rinde;
> de liden smaafiske, i floden svam,
> de legte med deres finne.

'The swift stream then stood still, that before had been running; the little fish that swam in it played their fins in time.'[3]

Did the discrepancy disprove the stories? Tolkien thought it pointed rather to what C. S. Lewis called the 'unexpectedness' of reality,[4] and paused to explain the phenomenon in *The Fellowship of the Ring*, pp. 404–5. There Sam thinks that their stay in Lothlórien, the 'elf-hill' itself, might have been three nights, but 'never a whole month. Anyone would think that time did not count in there!' Frodo agrees, but Legolas says that from an elvish viewpoint things are more complicated than that:

> 'For the Elves the world moves, and it moves both very swift and very slow. Swift, because they themselves change little, and all else fleets by: it is a grief to them. Slow, because they do not count the running years, not for themselves. The passing seasons are but ripples ever repeated in the long long stream.'

His remarks harmonise the motifs of 'The Night that Lasted a Year' and 'The Stream that Stood Still'. They are in a way redundant to the mere action, the plot of *The Lord of the Rings*. Yet they, and many other incidental turns, explanations, allusions,† help to keep up a sense of mixed strangeness and familiarity, of reason operating round a mysterious centre. This feeling Tolkien himself acquired from long pondering on literary and philological cruxes; it explains why he laid such stress on 'consistency' and 'tone'.

To cut matters short, one can remark that Tolkien went through much the same process with the 'dwarves'. This is also an old word, cf. Old English *dweorh*, Old Norse *dvergr*, Old High German *twerg*, Gothic **dvairgs* etc. It seems to have cohabited with the word for 'elf' over long periods, causing a sequence of confusions over 'light-elves' (=elves), 'black-elves' (=? dwarves), and 'dark-elves' (=?), which Tolkien never forgot and eventually brought to prominence in the story of Eöl in *The Silmarillion*. More interesting is some slight sense in various sources that men dealt with dwarves in a way they could not with elves, on an equal basis marred often by hostility. The seven dwarves help Snow-White in the familiar fairy-tale (from the Grimms' collection), but in 'Snow-White and Rose-Red' (also from Grimm) the dwarf combines great wealth with sullen ingratitude. The association with gold and mining is strong, as in the site of 'Dwarf's Hill', see p. 28 above; so are the stories of broken

† There are too many of these to fit into an argument: one might note, though, that the skill of Tolkien's elves in archery goes back to 'elf-shot'; that their association with the sea and their taking of Frodo is very like the passing of Arthur in (and only in) the account of Laȝamon, a twelfth-century Worcestershire poet whom Tolkien regarded as the last preserver of Old English tradition; that the gifts of Galadriel correspond to stories preserved in English and Scandinavian *family* traditions such as that of 'the Luck of Edenhall' or the one recorded in Sigrid Undset's novel *Kristin Lavransdatter*, part 2, ch. 6; that 'elvishness' is a quality recognised in men several times in *The Lord of the Rings*, but also ascribed to himself by the poet Geoffrey Chaucer. Tolkien makes no use, however, of the very common 'changeling' belief.

bargains, as when the Norse god Loki refuses to pay a dwarf the head he
has lost, with Portia-like quibbles, or when Loki again strips the dwarf
Andvari of all his wealth, even the last little (fatal) ring that Andvari
pleads for.[5] *Inter uos nemo loquitur, nisi corde doloso*, says the dwarf in the
eleventh-century German poem *Ruodlieb*, with hostile truth: 'among you
(men) no one speaks except with a deceitful heart. That is why you will
never come to long life...' Both the longevity of dwarves and their
tendency to get into disputes over payment are remembered on several
occasions in *The Hobbit*. Their 'under-the-mountain' setting there is
traditional too. The great Old Norse poem on world's end, the *Vǫluspá*,
links them with stone: *stynia dvergar fyr steindurom*, 'the dwarves groan
before their stone-doors'. Snorri Sturluson (a kind of Northern Laȝamon)
says that they 'quickened in the earth... like maggots', while his Icelandic
countrymen long called echoes *dvergmál*, 'dwarf-talk'. The correspondence
between such separated works as Snorri's *Prose Edda* (thirteenth-century
Icelandic) and the Grimms' *Kindermärchen* (nineteenth-century German)
is indeed in this matter surprisingly, even provocatively strong, and Tolkien
was not the first to see it; the Grimms themselves observed that such
things were a proof of some 'original unity', *des ursprünglichen Zusammen-
hangs*.[6] *Zusammenhang*: a 'hanging together'. That is very much what
Tolkien thought of all these tales, and the phenomenon remains no matter
what interpretation one puts on it.

However, both with elves and with dwarves there is one further factor
to which Tolkien gave great weight; and that is literary art. No matter
how many cross-references he could find and use, it looks as if he gave
greatest weight and longest consideration to single poems, tales, phrases,
images, using these as the centre of his portrayals of whole races or species.
Naturally it is a speculative business to identify these, but I would suggest
that the 'master-text' for Tolkien's portrayal of the elves is the description
of the hunting king in *Sir Orfeo*; and for the dwarves is the account of the
Hjaðningavíg, the 'Everlasting Battle', in Snorri's *Edda*. These give further
the 'master-qualities' of, respectively, evasiveness and revenge.

To take the simpler one first, the story of the 'Everlasting Battle' is as
follows: once upon a time there was a king called Högni, whose daughter
was Hildr. She, however, was abducted in his absence (some versions say
seduced by a master-harper) by a pirate king called Hethinn. Högni
pursued them and caught up at the island of Hoy in the Orkneys. Here
Hildr tried to make a reconciliation, warning her father that Hethinn was
ready to fight. Högni 'answered his daughter curtly'. As the two sides
draw up to each other, though, Hethinn makes a better and more courteous
offer. But Högni refuses, saying: 'Too late have you made this offer of
coming to terms, for now I have drawn Dáinsleif which the dwarves made,
which must kill a man every time it is drawn, and never turns in the stroke,
and no wound heals where it makes a scratch.' Unintimidated by words

(like most Vikings) Hethinn shouts back that he calls any sword good that serves its master, and the battle is on. Every day the men fight, every night Hildr wakes them by witchcraft, so it will go to Doomsday.[7]

This story is one, evidently, of remorseless pride flaring only in taciturnity; its centre is Högni's decision to fight rather than look for a moment as if he could be bought; the 'objective correlative' of pride and decision is the sword Dáinsleif, the 'heirloom of Dáin', which the dwarves made and which knows no mercy. The sword Tyrfing in the *Heidrek's saga* edited by Christopher Tolkien is virtually identical – dwarf-made, cursed, remorseless, leading to murder between close relatives and the final lament, 'It will never be forgotten; the Norns' doom is evil'. These qualities, it seems, are those which Tolkien chose and developed for his dwarves. Thorin and Company act out of revenge as well as greed in *The Hobbit*, the long and painful vengeance of Thráin for Thrór is the centre of what we are told of the dwarves in Appendix A of *The Lord of the Rings*, Dáin Ironfoot himself incarnates in Tolkien's Middle-earth the whole tough, fair, bitter, somehow unlucky character of the dwarvish race.[8] It is not too much to say that the 'inspiration' of their portrayal as opposed to the more laborious element of 'invention', springs directly from Snorri and the *Hjaðningavíg* and 'Dáinsleif which the dwarves made'. To use Tolkien's phrase, this was a 'fusion-point of imagination', once met never forgotten.

As for the elves, their fusion or kindling-point would seem to be some twenty or thirty lines from the centre of the medieval poem of *Sir Orfeo*, itself a striking example of the alchemies of art. In origin this is only the classical story of Orpheus and Eurydice, but the fourteenth-century poet (or maybe some forgotten predecessor) has made two radical changes to it: one, the land of the dead has become elf-land, from which the elf-king comes to seize Dame Heurodis; two, Sir Orfeo, unlike his classical model, is successful in his quest and bears his wife away, overcoming the elf-king by the mingled powers of music and honour. The poem's most famous and original passage is the image of the elves in the wilderness, seen again and again by Orfeo as he wanders mad and naked, looking for his wife, but never certainly identified as hallucinations, phantoms, or real creatures on the other side of some transparent barrier which Orfeo cannot break through. To quote Tolkien's translation:

> There often by him would he see,
> when noon was hot on leaf and tree,
> the king of Faerie with his rout
> came hunting in the woods about
> with blowing far and crying dim,
> and barking hounds that were with him;
> yet never a beast they took nor slew,
> and where they went he never knew . . .

(SGPO, pp. 129–30)

Many hints from this took root in Tolkien's mind: the shadow-army with its echoing horns which was to follow Aragorn from the 'paths of the dead', the 'dim blowing of horns' as a 'great hunt' goes past the silent dwarves in Mirkwood in *The Hobbit*, and in *The Hobbit* again the image of the fierce, proud, impulsive, honourable elf-king who imprisons Thorin but will take no advantage in the end even of Bilbo. Stronger than anything, though, is the association of the elves with the wilderness – an idea corroborated to Tolkien by the many Anglo-Saxon compounds such as 'wood-elf', 'water-elf', 'sea-elf' and so on – and with the music of the harp, the instrument by which Sir Orfeo wins back his wife. It may even have seemed significant to Tolkien that in *Sir Orfeo* the elves freed and rewarded their harper-enemy for his skill, while in some versions of the *Hjaðningavíg* the dwarvish weapon Dáinsleif condemns Hjarrandi (the Northern Orpheus) not just to death but to death everlastingly repeated. A whole conflict of temperament between two species is summed up in the detail, and a conflict of style. However the further one traces Tolkien's debt to ancient texts and fragments, in this matter, the more one realises how easy it was for him to feel that a consistency and a sense lay beneath the chaotic ruin of the old poetry of the North – if only someone would dig it out. To quote Shakespeare's observations on another Enchanted Wood which sensible people can make nothing of (in *A Midsummer Night's Dream* V i):

> But all the story of the night told over,
> And all their minds transfigured so together,
> More witnesseth than fancy's images,
> And grows to something of great constancy;
> But howsoever, strange and admirable.

I do not suppose Tolkien would have liked the down-grading of 'fancy', nor the comedy of Peaseblossom, Cobweb, Moth and Mustardseed. Bully Bottom, though, has a Tolkienish bravura; and Hippolyta's feeling that 'there must have been *something* in it' was his own.

Creative anachronisms

It was by similar processes of 'reconstruction' that Tolkien arrived at his 'orcs' and 'wargs', later his 'ents' and 'woses'.† None of the foregoing,

† 'Orcs' go back to the *orcnéas*, the 'demon-corpses' of the *Beowulf*-poet, and to another Old English word *orcþyrs*, 'orc-giant'. 'Wargs' are a linguistic cross between Old Norse *vargr* and Old English *wearh*, two words showing a shift of meaning from 'wolf' to 'human outlaw'. For the 'ents' see below, p. 100. The 'woses' are perhaps primarily an apology for *Sir Gawain* line 721, where *wodwos* is offered as a plural, though historically a singular derived from Old English *wudu-wása*. It would not have escaped Tolkien, though, that his office at Leeds University (like

however, offers any help at all with 'hobbits'. If 'the word authenticates the thing', they are not authentic, for 'hobbit' is in no sense an ancient word. Nor indeed does their genesis seem to have had any element of 'invention' in it; it was pure 'inspiration', without any trace of thought at all. The moment of the word's arrival has in fact been recorded by Tolkien, and subsequently by Humphrey Carpenter:

> It was on a summer's day, and he was sitting by the window in the study at Northmoor Road, laboriously marking School Certificate exam papers. Years later he recalled: 'One of the candidates had mercifully left one of the pages with no writing on it (which is the best thing that can possibly happen to an examiner) and I wrote on it: "*In a hole in the ground there lived a hobbit.*" Names always generate a story in my mind. Eventually I thought I'd better find out what hobbits were like. But that's only the beginning.' (*Biography*, p. 172)

The incident seems a perfect example of the creative unconsciousness: the boring job, the state. of combined surface concentration and deeper lack of interest, the sudden relaxation which allows a message to force its way through from some unknown area of pressure. It is reminiscent of the flashes of insight which solve scientists' problems in dreams (like von Kékulé the chemist and the snake with its tail in its mouth). But what has philology to do with an event so mysterious and so personal?

Tolkien had no opinion to offer himself. In a letter in the *Observer* (20 February 1938), he answered speculation by saying 'I do not remember anything about the name and inception of the hero', and denied (without total certainty) that the word 'hobbit' could have come from prior reading in African exploration or fairy-tale, as had been suggested. He thought that earlier writers' hobbits, if they existed, were probably 'accidental homophones', i.e. the name was the same but the thing was not. Much later, in a letter he seems never to have posted (*Letters*, pp. 379–87), he observed that though he could often remember acquiring names this process played little part in the construction of stories. It is somehow typical that the *OED* should have claimed (*Times*, 31 May 1977) to have identified Tolkien's 'source' and 'inspiration' in J. Hardy's edition of *The Denham Tracts*, Vol. II (1895), which declares that 'The whole earth was overrun with ghosts, boggles ... hobbits, hobgoblins'. The word 'hobbit' is there, but in a run of distinctly insubstantial creatures which hardly correspond to Tolkien's almost pig-headedly solid and earthbound race. Words are not things: the name 'hobbit' may seem to be for the researcher, a dead-end.

mine) stood just off 'Woodhouse Lane', which crosses 'Woodhouse Moor' and 'Woodhouse Ridge'. These names may preserve, in mistaken modern spelling, old belief in 'the wild men of the woods' lurking in the hills above the Aire. See further Tolkien's notes on 'Orc' and 'Woses' in 'Guide'.

Even dead-ends have their uses, though (see p. 55 below). This particular one prompts several thoughts. One is that although Tolkien accepted the word as coming from outside, not being rooted in antiquity at all, he nevertheless did not rest until he had worked out an acceptable etymology for it. 'In a hole in the ground there lived a hobbit' is of course the first sentence of *The Hobbit*. Not quite the last sentence, but on the last page of the last appendix of *The Lord of the Rings*, is the note on the word 'hobbit' which gives its derivation, viz. from Old English **hol-bytla*, 'hole-dweller' or 'hole-builder'. *Holbytla* is an 'asterisk word'. It was never recorded, but nevertheless could, is even on the whole likely to have existed, like **dvairgs*. Furthermore it makes the magic sentence of inspiration into a tautology: 'In a hole in the ground there lived a hole-liver . . .' What else would you expect? The implication is that the inspiration was a memory of something that could in reality have existed, and that anyway conformed to the inflexible rules of linguistic history: as a word 'hobbit' was more like 'dwarves' than 'elfin'.

The next point is that Tolkien did admit one possible source in Sinclair Lewis's novel *Babbitt* (1922), the story of the near-disgrace and abortive self-discovery of a complacent American businessman; to this theme the journey and the nature of Bilbo Baggins show some correspondence. But the source that Tolkien emphatically rejected is the word 'rabbit', of which so many critics have been reminded. 'Calling Bilbo a "nassty little rabbit" was a piece of vulgar trollery', he wrote, 'just as "descendant of rats" was a piece of dwarfish [*sic*] malice' (*Observer*, 20 February 1938). 'Certainly not rabbit' he affirmed later. Internal evidence runs against him here, however, for it is not only the trolls who think simultaneously of Bilbo and rabbits. Bilbo makes the comparison himself in chapter 6 of *The Hobbit*, when he sees the eagle sharpening its beak and begins 'to think of being torn up for supper like a rabbit'. Three pages later the same thought occurs to the eagle, 'You need not be frightened like a rabbit, even if you look rather like one.' Thorin shakes Bilbo 'like a rabbit' in chapter 16, and much earlier Beorn – admittedly a rude and insensitive character – pokes Mr Baggins in the waistcoat and observes 'little bunny is getting nice and fat again' (p. 141). He is in a sense repaying the insult Bilbo offered earlier (p. 125), when he thought Beorn's 'skin-changing' meant he was 'a furrier, a man that calls rabbits conies, when he doesn't turn their skins into squirrels'. But the multiplicity of names gives a further clue to Tolkien's real thoughts, incubating since 1915 and the neologism 'coney-rabbits' in 'Goblin Feet'.

The fact is that 'rabbit' is a peculiar word. The *OED* can find no 'ultimate etymology' for it, nor trace it back in English before 1398. 'Coney' or 'cunny' is little better, going back to 1302, while 'bunny' is a pet-name used originally for squirrels, as it happens, and not recorded till the seventeenth century. The words for 'rabbit' differ in several

European languages (French *lapin*, German *kaninchen*), and there is no Old English or Old Norse word for it at all. These facts are unusual: 'hare' for instance is paralleled by Old English *hara*, German *hase*, Old Norse *heri*, and so on, while the same could be said for 'weasel' or 'otter' or 'mouse' or 'brock' or most other familiar mammals of Northern Europe. The reason, of course, is that rabbits are immigrants. They appeared in England only round the thirteenth century, as imported creatures bred for fur, but escaped to the wild like mink or coypu. *Yet they have been assimilated.* The point is this: not one person in a thousand realises that rabbits (no Old English source) are in any historical way distinct from mice (O.E. *mýs*) or weasels (O.E. *weselas*), while the word is accepted by all as familiar, native, English. The creature has further established itself irreversibly in the folk-imagination, along with wise owls (O.E. *úlan*) and sly foxes (O.E. *fuhsas*). But if an Anglo-Saxon or Norseman had seen one he would have thought it alien if not bizarre. Rabbits prove that novelties can be introduced into a language and then *made to fit* – of course as long as one exhibits due regard to deep structures of language and thought. 'If a foreign word falls by chance into the stream of a language', wrote Jacob Grimm, 'it is rolled around till it takes on that language's colour, and in spite of its foreign nature comes to look like a native one.'[9]

Now this situation of anachronism-cum-familiarity certainly has *something* to do with hobbits. The first time that Bilbo Baggins appears in close focus he is 'standing at his door after breakfast smoking an enormous long wooden pipe'. Smoking later appears as not just *a* characteristic of hobbits, but virtually *the* characteristic, 'the one art that we can certainly claim to be our own invention', declares Meriadoc Brandybuck (*LOTR* I, 17). But what are they smoking besides pipes? '*Pipeweed, or leaf*', declares the *Lord of the Rings* Prologue firmly. Why not say 'tobacco', since the plant is 'a variety probably of *Nicotiana*'? Because the word would sound wrong. It is an import from some unknown Caribbean language via Spanish, reaching English only after the discovery of America, sometime in the sixteenth century. The words it resembles most are 'potato' and 'tomato', also referring to new objects from America, eagerly adopted in England and naturalised with great speed, but marked off as foreign by their very phonetic structure. 'Pipeweed' shows Tolkien's wish to accept a common feature of English modernity, which he knew could not exist in the ancient world of elves or trolls, and whose anachronism would instantly be betrayed by a word with the foreign feel of 'tobacco'. Actually Bilbo *does* use 'tobacco' on page 12 of *The Hobbit*, and Gandalf mentions 'tomatoes' not much later. *In the first edition.* The third changes 'cold chicken and tomatoes' to 'cold chicken and pickles',[10] and after that the foreign fruit is excluded. 'Potatoes' stay in, being indeed the speciality of Gaffer Gamgee, but his son Sam has a habit of assimilating the word to the more native-sounding 'taters' – Tolkien notes elsewhere that the word was borrowed into colloquial Welsh from colloquial English as *tatws*, in which form it sounds much less distinctive ('EW', p. 34). But in fact the scene in which Sam discusses 'taters' with Gollum (*LOTR* II, 261–3) is a little cluster of anachronisms: hobbits, eating rabbits (Sam calls them 'coneys'), wishing for potatoes ('taters') but out of tobacco ('pipeweed'). One day, offers Sam to Gollum, he might cook him something better – 'fried fish and chips'. Nothing could now be more distinctively English! Not much would be *less* distinctive Old English. The hobbits, though, are on our side of many cultural boundaries.

That, then, is their association with rabbits. One can see why Tolkien denied the obvious connection between the two: he did not want hobbits classified as small, furry creatures, vaguely 'cute' just as fairies were vaguely 'pretty'. On the other hand both insinuated themselves, rabbits into the homely company of fox and goose and hen, hobbits into the fantastic but equally verbally authenticated set of elves and dwarves and orcs and ettens. One might go so far as to say that the absence of rabbits from ancient legend made them not an 'asterisk word' but an 'asterisk thing' – maybe they were there but nobody noticed. That is exactly the ecological niche Tolkien selected for hobbits, 'an *unobtrusive* but *very ancient* people' (*LOTR* I, 10, my italics). It is not likely that this role was devised for them before the arrival of the inspired 'In a hole-in the ground there lived a hobbit', any more than the etymology from *holbytla*. Still, the amazing thing about that sentence, looking back, is the readiness with which it responded to development. The first half of it helped to anchor hobbits in history, via *holbytlan*, the second to characterise them in fiction, via the anachronisms associated with the rabbit-analogy. Such complexity could be the result of prior unconscious cogitation or later artistic effort. Either way, 'hobbit' as word and concept threw out its anchors into Old and modern English at once: 'grammarye' at work once more.

Breaking Contact

This preamble makes it easier to say what Tolkien was doing in *The Hobbit*. Like Walter Scott or William Morris before him, he felt the perilous charm of the archaic world of the North, recovered from bits and scraps by generations of inquiry. He wanted to tell a story about it simply, one feels, because there were hardly any complete ones left; *Beowulf* or *The saga of King Heidrek* stimulated the imagination but did not satisfy it. Accordingly he created a sort of 'asterisk-world' for the Norse *Elder Edda*. The dwarf-names of 'Thorin and Company', as well as Gandalf's, come from a section of the Eddic poem *Vǫluspá*, often known as the *Dvergatal* or 'Dwarves' Roster'. This is not much regarded now, and has been called a 'rigmarole', a meaningless list; *The Hobbit* implies, though, that that meaningless list is the last faded memento of something once great and important, an Odyssey of the dwarves. As for the landscape through which Gandalf, Thorin and the rest move, that too is an Eddic one; 'the pathless Mirkwood' is mentioned in several poems, while 'the Misty Mountains' come from the poem *Skírnismál*, where Freyr's page, sent to abduct the giant's daughter, says grimly to his horse:

> 'Myrct er úti, mál qveð ec ocr fara
> úrig fiǫll yfir
> þyrsa þióð yfir;
> báðir við komomc, eða ocr báða tecr
> sá inn ámátki iǫtunn.'

'The mirk is outside, I call it our business to fare over the misty mountains, over the tribes of orcs (*þyrs=orc*, see note to p. 50 above); we will both come back, or else he will take us both, he the mighty giant.'

All that Tolkien has done, in a way, is to make place-names out of adjectives, to turn words into things.

But there is one very evident obstacle to recreating the ancient world of heroic legend for modern readers, and that lies in the nature of heroes. These are not acceptable any more, and tend very strongly to be treated with irony: the modern view of *Beowulf* is John Gardner's novel *Grendel* (1971). Tolkien did not want to be ironic about heroes, and yet he could not eliminate modern reactions. His response to the difficulty is Bilbo Baggins, the hobbit, the anachronism, a character whose initial role at least is very strongly that of mediator. He represents and often voices modern opinions, modern incapacities: he has no impulses towards revenge or self-conscious heroism, cannot 'hoot twice like a barn-owl and once like a screech owl' as the dwarves suggest, knows almost nothing about Wilderland and cannot even skin a rabbit, being used to having his meat 'delivered by the butcher all ready to cook'. Yet he has a place in the ancient world too, and there is a hint that (just like us) all his efforts cannot keep him entirely separate from the past.

His name, thus, is Baggins, and he lives in Bag End. This latter name had personal and homely associations for Tolkien (see *Biography*, p. 176). But it is also a literal translation of the phrase one sees often yet stuck up at the end of little English roads: *cul-de-sac*. *Cul-de-sacs* are at once funny and infuriating. They belong to no language, since the French call such a thing an *impasse* and the English a 'dead-end'. The word has its origins in snobbery, the faint residual feeling that English words, ever since the Norman Conquest, have been 'low' and that French ones, or even *Frenchified* ones, would be better. *Cul-de-sac* is accordingly a peculiarly ridiculous piece of English class-feeling – and Bag End a defiantly English reaction to it. As for Mr Baggins, one thing he is more partial to than another is his tea, which he has at four o'clock. But over much of the country 'tea', indeed anything eaten between meals but especially afternoon tea 'in a substantial form' as the *OED* says, is called 'baggins'. The *OED* prefers the 'politer' form 'bagging', but Tolkien knew that people who used words like that were almost certain to drop the terminal -g (another post-Conquest confusion anyway). He would have found the term glossed under *bæggin, bægginz* in W. E. Haigh's *Glossary of the Dialect of the Huddersfield District* (London: Oxford University Press), for which he had written an appreciative prologue in 1928. Mr Baggins, then, is at the start of *The Hobbit* full of nonsense, like modern English society as perceived by Tolkien: he takes pride in being 'prosy', pooh-poohs anything out of the ordinary, and is almost aggressively *middle* middle-class in being more respectable than the Tooks though rather 'well-to-do' than 'rich'. If he went much further in this direction he would end up like his cousins the 'Sackville-Bagginses' – they, of course, have severed their connection with Bag End by calling it *cul-de-sac(k)* and tagging on the French suffix *-ville*! Yet Bilbo's heart is in the right place (also like modern English society as perceived by Tolkien). He likes flowers; he is proud of his ancestor the Bullroarer; if not quite 'as fierce as a dragon in a pinch' he is at any rate no coward; and like his name he is ample, generous, substantial, if undeniably plain and old-fashioned. He has therefore not entirely lost his passport into the ancient world, and can function in it as our representative, without heroic pretensions but also without cynical ironies. He is admittedly a *bourgeois*. That is why Gandalf turns him into a Burglar. Both words come from the same root (*burh*='town' or 'stockaded house'), and while they are eternal opposites they are opposites on the same level. By the end of *The Hobbit*, though, Bilbo as burglar has progressed so far as to rub shoulders with heroes, even to be (just) considerable as one himself.†

The early moves of *The Hobbit* depend very much on this tension between ancient and modern reactions. It begins almost as satire on modern institutions, with Mr Baggins's language particularly taking some shrewd knocks: the more familiar it seems the more fossilised it is. Thus Bilbo's 'Good Morning' is no longer a wish offered to another person, but either that, or an objective statement, or a subjective statement, or all of them together, or even a gesture of hostility. ' "What a lot of things you do use *Good morning* for!" said Gandalf. "Now you mean that you want to get rid of me, and that it won't be good till I move off." ' His 'not at

† I do not know the origin of the personal name 'Bilbo', but can record that on one occasion I found myself using Ordnance Survey map no. 161, of S. Herefordshire, to locate churches of similar date to *Ancrene Wisse* and preserving fragments of the early Anglo-Norse style of stonework. As I did this my eye moved west from Kilpeck to Wormbridge to Abbey Dore to a hill called 'Great Bilbo'. The *Place-Name Survey* has not done Herefordshire yet, and I have no explanation for the name; maybe Tolkien had one of his own.

all' means 'yes', his 'my dear sir' means nothing, and when he says 'I beg your pardon' he no longer has any sense that he is asking for anything or that 'pardon' might be a valuable thing to receive. Against this the dwarves' ceremonious style of salutation – 'At your service!' 'At yours and your family's!' 'May his beard grow ever longer!' 'May the hair on his toes never fall out!' – may seem pompous and indeed be insincere, but at any rate it is *about* something, not just semantically empty. Similarly Bilbo, trying to be business-like, flees to abstractions, only to have the narrator expose them: ' "Also I should like to know about risks, out-of-pocket expenses, time required and remuneration, and so forth" – by which he meant: "What am I going to get out of it? And am I going to come back alive?" ' Thorin, though long-winded enough, does not talk about calculations, but about *things*†: the dwarf-song which opens their conclave centres on the misty mountains cold and grim, on harps, necklaces, twisted wire, pale enchanted long-forgotten gold. No wonder the hobbit feels 'the love of beautiful things made by hands and by cunning and magic moving through him, a fierce and a jealous love, the desire of the hearts of dwarves'. In the first clash between ancient and modern 'ancient' wins easily; in an entirely proper sense (*res*='thing') it seems much realer.

In any case the narrator has his thumb firmly on the balance. His voice is very prominent throughout *The Hobbit* (as it is not in *The Lord of the Rings*), and as has been said it provides 'a very firm moral framework by which to judge'[11] – elves are good, goblins bad, dwarves, eagles, dragons, men and Beorn all in different ways in between. Besides building up morality, though, it more interestingly tears down expectation. The narrator's favourite phrase is 'of course', but this usually introduces something unexplained or unpredictable: 'That, of course, is the way to talk to dragons', or 'He knew, of course, that the riddle game was sacred', or 'It was often said . . . that long ago one of the Took ancestors must have taken a fairy wife. That was, of course, absurd'. Sometimes these and similar remarks introduce information. More often they create a sense that more information exists round the edges of the story, and that events are going according to rules only just hinted at, but rules just the same. Adjectives like 'the *famous* Belladonna Took' or 'the great Thorin Oakenshield *himself*' imply a depth of history, statements like 'no spider has ever liked being called Attercop' one of experience. The frequent remarks about legendary creatures of the 'Trolls' purses are the mischief' kind furthermore blur ordinary experience into the magical, while the question 'what would you do, if an uninvited dwarf came and hung his things up

† The contract he finally does deliver on p. 38 is typically more practical than Bilbo at his most business-like had thought. It covers profits, delivery, travelling expenses, but also defrayal of funeral expenses 'by us or our representatives, if occasion arises and the matter is not otherwise arranged for'. This means 'you or all of us may die, and also be eaten'.

in your hall?' is very much in the style of 'have you stopped beating your wife?' The child reader senses, perhaps, the sportiveness of all this, and delights in it; the adult, as he goes along, finds himself succumbing to the ancient principle that 'redundancy is truth' – the more *unnecessary* details are put in the more lifelike we take fiction to be. The underlying point, though, is that the narrator is there cumulatively to express a whole attitude to the archaic-heroic setting: casual, matter-of-fact, even unimpressed, but accordingly lulling. He gets the landscape, the characters and the 'rules' through the modern barriers of disbelief and even, potentially, of contempt.

The way *The Hobbit* works in fact shows up well in any comparison of Chapter 2, 'Roast Mutton', with its analogue in the Grimms' folk-tale of 'The Brave Little Tailor'. In this latter a tailor (the trade was synonymous with feebleness, as in Shakespeare's *Henry IV Part II* III ii) kills seven flies at a blow, and is so emboldened that he starts a career of violence and monster-killing. He bluffs his way through a contest of strength with one giant, and frightens off a whole gang of them: 'each of them had a roast sheep in his hand and was eating it'. Sent by the king to catch two more, he hides up a tree and throws stones at them till they quarrel and kill each other: 'they tore up trees in their agony and defended themselves', he says airily when he shows the bodies, 'but all that does no good when a chap like me comes along who can kill seven with one blow!' Bilbo starts off very much as a 'little grocer', but he never shows anything like the 'little tailor's' resource or effrontery; an omni-competent character would destroy any modern story's action. Instead he is presented very much as a reader-surrogate, driven on by shame to try to be 'The Master Thief' (like the character in Asbjörnsen and Moe's Norse folk-tale) but hampered by utter ignorance of the rules of the game. He is caught by one 'fact' which neither he nor the reader could have predicted – trolls' purses talk – and saved by two more: wizards can ventriloquise, and 'trolls, as you probably know, must be underground before dawn, or they go back to the stuff of the mountains they are made of, and never move again'. 'As you probably know' is here the final blow in Tolkien's strategy of 'counter-realism'. Nobody knows that; indeed it isn't true; in a traditional tale no narrator could get away with so shamelessly exploiting the gap between his world and his listener's, because of course there wouldn't *be* one! However in *The Hobbit* the combined assurance of Gandalf, the narrator, the trolls and the dwarves outweighs the ignorance of Bilbo, and the reader. As it happens the belief about being underground before dawn is as traditional as belief in trolls and dwarves at all, going back to the *Elder Edda* and the end of the *Alvíssmál*, where Alvíss the dwarf is kept talking till daylight by Thórr, and so turned to stone.†

† There is a further weak analogue in Grimms' tale no. 195, 'The Grave-Mound', and a much stronger one in C. S. Lewis's *That Hideous Strength* (London: Bodley Head, 1945), end of chapter 16. There, though, the tale is given a moral significance, a little like Tolkien explaining 'elf-time' in Lothlórien.

Inventive resource is very strong in *The Hobbit*, over words and races and characters and events. The book's *distinguishing* characteristic, though, is its sense that all these things come from somewhere outside and beyond the author, forming a *Zusammenhang* as solid as everyday's and on occasion no more irrational.

The Ring as 'Equalizer'

This 'illusion of historical truth and perspective' is, of course, as Tolkien himself said of *Beowulf*, 'largely a product of art' ('Monsters', p. 247). And sometimes the art ran out. Tolkien himself admitted (*Observer*, 20 February 1938) that twice he got stuck. He did not say where, leaving that for later researchers to make fools of themselves over, but it may be argued that the first few chapters of *The Hobbit* consist mostly of disengagement and playing down the readers' collective sense of doubt. As late as the start of chapter 4 the company is halted again (for the third time), and there is a sense of the author groping for intellectual justification. In the mountain-storm Bilbo looks out and sees that 'across the valley the stone-giants were out, and were hurling rocks at one another for a game, and catching them, and tossing them down into the darkness where they smashed among the trees far below'. Giants never enter the Tolkien universe again – Gandalf accepts their existence for a second in chapter 7 – and the passage is a failure of tone; it reads like an old interpretation of giants as 'nature-myth', i.e. as personifications of the avalanche like Thórr and his hammer personifying thunder and lightning. This is too allegorical for Middle-earth. But the story takes off very shortly afterwards, with the capture by the goblins (incidentally still too close to munitions workers as the trolls were to labourers), the escape, the goblin runners pursuing 'swift as weasels in the dark', and Bilbo's forcible detachment from the dwarves. Crawling along the tunnel hours later 'his hand met what felt like a tiny ring of cold metal lying on the floor of the tunnel. It was a turning point in his career', comments Tolkien, 'but he did not know it.' A turning-point in Tolkien's career too, for from this came most of his subsequent inspiration – Gollum, Sauron, eventually *The Lord of the Rings* itself.

But no more than Bilbo did Tolkien realise this at the time. As he testified later (*LOTR* I, 5), glimpses in *The Hobbit* 'had arisen unbidden of things higher or deeper or darker than its surface: Durin, Moria, Gandalf, the Necromancer, the Ring'. The ring changed its significance even between editions of *The Hobbit*. In the first matters were relatively straightforward: Bilbo found the ring, met Gollum, they agreed to hold a riddle-contest, the stakes being Bilbo's life against Gollum's 'precious'. Bilbo won, but since by accident he'd acquired Gollum's 'precious' already he asked to be shown the way out instead. The sequence works, it excuses Bilbo of any charge of theft (he'd won the ring fair and square) – but as anyone familiar with the Ring in its later manifestations will see, the amazing thing is Gollum's readiness to *bet* his 'precious', bear the loss of it, and then offer to show the way out as a *douceur*. 'I don't know how many times Gollum begged Bilbo's pardon. He kept on saying: "We are ssorry; we didn't mean to cheat, we meant to give it our only pressent, if it won the competition" ' (*Hobbit* first edition, p. 92). In the second and third editions his last words are 'Thief! Thief! Thief! Baggins! We hates it, we hates it for ever!' Furthermore the charge is arguably true, since in *this* version the deal was Bilbo's life against any nominated service, such as showing the way out. In both versions Bilbo gets the ring and the exit, but in the latter one it is his claim to the *ring* which is shaky.

Now, Tolkien integrated this second thought into his story marvellously well, even keeping the first version as an excuse Bilbo had told with uncharacteristic dishonesty to put his claim to the 'precious' beyond doubt. However it is the first thought one should keep in mind while considering the genesis of *The Hobbit*. And here the obvious point, surely, is that the ring is just a prop: a stage-prop, like the marvellous devices common in fairy-tales or legends (there is a wish-fulfilling ring in the Grimms' 'The King of the Golden Mountain', and a cloak of invisibility), but also a prop for Bilbo's status with the dwarves. It is a kind of 'Equalizer'. After acquiring it Bilbo remains in most ways as out of touch with Wilderland as before: he cannot dress meat or dodge wargs, and when in chapter 15 Balin asks if he can make out the bird's speech he has to reply 'Not very well' – the narrator, still maximising the distance between him and every-day Middle-earth normality, adds '(as a matter of fact, he could make nothing of it at all)'. He cannot even tell when crows are being insulting. But the ring makes up for this. Before he had it he was essentially a package to be carried, his name as a 'burglar' nothing but an embarrassment even to himself. With the ring he can take an active part. He uses it straight away to get past the dwarves' look-out and raise his prestige – they 'looked at him with quite a new respect' – and then to save his companions first from the spiders and second from the elvish dungeons. The problem after *that* is in a way to maintain his status without simply reducing it to the accident of owning a magic ring. Tolkien takes some trouble over this, observing in the wood-elves' dungeon that 'One invisible ring was a fine thing, but it was not much good among fourteen' – so that credit for that escape is Bilbo's – and after the fight with the spiders that 'knowing the truth about the vanishing did not lessen [the dwarves'] opinion of Bilbo at all; for they saw that he had some wits, as well as luck and a magic ring – and all three were useful possessions.' There is something provocative in this last statement, for it seems to deny that owning a magic ring *could* be an accident. Still, the very arguability of Bilbo's status shows how the ring changed *The Hobbit*: it brought a new possibility of action which would be simultaneously 'heroic' and credible, it developed the opposition of ancient and modern motifs into something like a dialogue.

The main subject of that dialogue is courage. Few modern readers of *Beowulf*, or the *Elder Edda*, or the Icelandic 'family sagas', can escape a certain feeling of inadequacy as they contemplate whole sequences of characters who appear, in a casual and quite lifelike way, not to know what fear is. How would we manage in such a society? With our culture's characteristic 'softness, worldliness, and timidity',[12] would we be fit for anything but slavery? To this self-doubt Bilbo Baggins makes a sober but relatively optimistic response. *His* style of courage shows up when he is in the dark and alone. He faces fear first in the escape from Gollum, when he takes a 'leap in the dark' rather than kill a defenceless enemy (this comes only in the second edition). A more significant scene is when he faces the giant spider and kills it 'all alone by himself in the dark without the help of the wizard or the dwarves or of anyone else'. A third is as he creeps down the tunnel to his first sight of Smaug, but stops as he hears dragon-snoring ahead. Tolkien lays great stress on this:

> Going on from there was the bravest thing he ever did. The tremendous things that happened afterwards were nothing compared to it. He fought the real battle in that tunnel alone, before he ever saw the vast danger that lay in wait. At any rate after a short halt go on he did . . . (pp. 226–7)

Such scenes remind us that even Samuel Colt's 'Equalizer' did not make all men heroes: it only made them all the same size. They also provide a behaviour-model which is not quite beyond emulation (no one can fight a dragon, but everyone can fight fear). Mainly they place in a kindly light that style of courage – cold courage, 'moral courage', two o'clock in the morning courage – which our age is most prepared to venerate.

They further expose the dwarves to something like the satire turned on Mr Baggins's modernisms at the start of the story. Thorin Oakenshield, for all his heroic name, sends Bilbo down the tunnel, and the rest do little but look embarrassed. The narrator insists (p. 225) that 'they would all have done their best to get him out of trouble . . . as they did in the case of the trolls', but he may not carry entire conviction. When he escaped from the goblins Bilbo had just decided he had to go back into the tunnels and look for his friends when he found his friends deciding just the opposite about him! 'If we have got to go back into those abominable tunnels to look for him, then drat him', is their last word. Maybe Gandalf would have talked them round. But before this begins to sound like treason against the images of the ancient North (the 'great contribution' of whose early literature, Tolkien had said, was 'the theory of courage', 'Monsters',

p. 262), it needs to be said that *The Hobbit*'s dialogue contains many voices. There is something splendid in the narrator's reversion to laconicism at the end, when he says (as a matter of course) that since Thorin is dead Fili and Kili are too; they 'had fallen defending him with shield and body, for he was their mother's elder brother', a motif immemorially old. Much can be said too for Thorin Oakenshield, while for some considerable stretch of the story, say chapters 6 to 8, one can see Tolkien exploring with delight that surly, illiberal independence often the distinguishing mark of Old Norse heroes. Gandalf's own reaction to being treed is just to kill as many enemies as possible; the rescuing eagles are, the narrator says euphemistically, 'not kindly birds'; there is a fine scene of sullen insolence between Thorin and the elf-king; but the centre of the whole sequence is Beorn.

He is in a way the least invented character in the book. His name is an Old English heroic word for 'man', which meant originally 'bear', so that naturally enough he is a were-bear, who changes shape, or 'skin' as Gandalf calls it, every night. He has a very close analogue in Bǫthvarr Bjarki (='little bear'), a hero from the Norse *Saga of Hrólfr Kraki*, and another in Beowulf himself, whose name is commonly explained as Beowulf='bees' wolf'=honey-eater=bear, and who breaks swords, rips off arms and cracks ribs with ursine power and clumsiness. Beorn keeps bees too; is surly in disposition; not to be trusted after dark; and 'appalling when he is angry', a description not altogether different from being 'kind enough if humoured'. The dwarves and Bilbo see both sides of him, but perceive them as one. On their second morning they find him in a good mood, telling 'funny stories' and apologising for having doubted their word – it has been confirmed by two prisoners:

> 'What did you do with the goblin and the Warg?' asked Bilbo suddenly.
> 'Come and see!' said Beorn, and they followed round the house. A goblin's head was stuck outside the gate and a warg-skin was nailed to a tree just beyond. Beorn was a fierce enemy. But now he was their friend ... (pp. 142–3)

'The heart is hard, though the body be soft', said Tolkien of fairy-tale readers. But actually in context Beorn's ferocity is attractive. It goes with his rudeness and his jollity, all projections of that inner self-confidence which as Tolkien knew lay at the core of the 'theory of courage'. 'What do you believe in?' ask whole sequences of kings to Icelandic wanderers in sagas. '*Ek trúi á sjálfan mik*', runs the traditional response, 'I believe in myself'. Killer-Glúmr, an axeman like Beorn, widens this to believing in his axe and his moneybag and his storehouse as well. Both characters have the air of men who have 'been into' a crisis of existentialism – and straight out the other side, leaving the crisis sadly tattered.

The solitary conquest of fear: the fierce denial of it. These two conceptions, one modern, one archaic, circle round each other most of the way through *The Hobbit*. It would be wrong to say they are ever resolved, but they do at least reach climaxes of anachronism and clash of style near the end; first in the death of Smaug, then around the Battle of the Five Armies.

To take these in order, it may be said that killing Smaug is the basic problem of *The Hobbit*, and not just for the dwarves. Tolkien had few models to work from: Beowulf killed his dragon in plain fight, but without surviving, Sigurthr killed Fáfnir in the *Edda* by stratagem and via the notorious draconic 'soft underbelly', Víðarr at Ragnarǫk is to slay the *Miðgarðsormr* (or 'Middle-earth Worm') by putting foot on lower jaw and hand on upper and tearing the beast apart. This last is implausible for men or hobbits, Beowulf's case is depressing, and Sigurthr's frankly too obvious to be interesting: Tolkien thought of something like it to begin with, but if the dwarves are well up on 'stabs and jabs and undercuts' then probably Smaug would be too. In the end he had to use a variant on 'soft underbellies', but to it he adds a notion as anachronistic to old-style 'heroism' as are Bilbo's decisions in the dark. This new element is 'discipline'.

Like 'glamour', 'discipline' is a much-altered word. Its earliest English meaning, in the *Ancrene Wisse*, is 'flogging'; the lady anchorites, says its author, must well tame their flesh *mid herde disciplines*. Later on the word comes to mean teaching or training, especially military training or drill; by the eighteenth century it covered the whole complex business of priming, loading, cocking, presenting and firing the 'Brown Bess' infantry muskets to the beat of drum, a ritual which if carried out perfectly left British redcoats invulnerable to direct assault (as at Culloden), but when bungled left them, as an *OED* citation says, 'fit only for the contempt and slaughter of their enemies' (as at Falkirk the year before). In Tolkien's day the word had come to signify the most prized of all British imperial qualities, a specialised cold-bloodedness and readiness to take punishment which the *OED* finds itself unable to define. Its classic case was perhaps the wreck of the *Birkenhead* troopship on 25th February 1852, when 500 soldiers found themselves on a sinking ship with inadequate lifeboats in a shark-infested sea. They were drawn up on deck, maintaining, says the *Annual Register* for 1852, 'perfect discipline', and told eventually to jump overboard and make for the few boats which had been launched. But the ship's captain begged them not to, as the boats with the women in would inevitably be swamped. ' "Not more than three" ', he reported, ' "made the attempt." Under this heroic obedience to discipline the whole mass were engulphed in the waves by the sinking of the ship.'[13] The event became a part of British mystique, as did the quality. Lord Kitchener asked Tolkien's army of 1916 to show 'discipline and steadiness under fire', with typical attention to passivity. Nothing like this can be seen in early Northern literature; the analogue to the *Birkenhead* disaster in *The saga of Eirik the Red* has indeed a Norseman giving up his place in a life-boat, but he does it with characteristic personal bravura (and rudeness).[14] Nevertheless Tolkien had been taught to value discipline, and it solved his problem over Smaug.

It is Bard the Bowman who kills Smaug, heroically enough with a lost arrow saved as a family heirloom for generations. Before that, though, Bard has figured as a nameless participant in a crowd scene about the giving and taking of orders. He has the trumpets blown, the warriors armed, the pots filled with water and the bridge to the land thrown down; it is this last precaution which daunts Smaug for a moment as he sweeps in over the cold fire-quenching lake. Then the dragon is faced with 'a hail of dark arrows' from platoons of bowmen, urged on by 'the grim-voiced man (Bard was his name), who ran to and fro cheering on the archers and urging the Master to order them to fight to the last arrow'. Fighting to the last *round* is of course the traditional phrase; being a 'discipline' concept it post-dates musketry. But Tolkien has here transferred the ethic of Waterloo or Albuera back to ancient days. He does it again as the dragon shatters the town and the townspeople break for *their* lifeboats: 'But there was still a company of archers that held their ground among the burning houses. Their captain was Bard . . .' The phrase 'hold one's ground' is not even recorded by the *OED* till 1856, though there is a parallel in the Old English poem *Maldon*, where the English are exhorted to 'hold their stead' (which they don't). Not that holding their ground does these particular archers any good, or Smaug any harm; he is killed by the last arrow, the one particular arrow shot heroically by Bard. Still, the whole pressure of the scene is towards modern coolness and preparation, not ancient 'berserk' fury (a 'berserk' being a 'bear-shirt', a man like Beorn). It is discipline that does for Smaug: discipline and that element of 'complacency' (*OED* 1650) which lets Smaug neglect his armour and so betray himself successively to hobbit, thrush and man.

The death of Smaug, like Bilbo in the dark, lets us see courage in a modern way. Their obverse is the Battle of the Five Armies (where Bilbo disappears from sight and heroic displays come from Thorin, Fili, Kili, Dain and especially Beorn), and the unusually complex scene of debate before it in chapter 15. Here Bard and Thorin oppose each other, and do so in highly un-childlike and ratiocinative style. To summarise Bard's proposition to Thorin, he says in essence: (1) I have killed the dragon, so I deserve a reward, (2) I am also the heir of Girion lord of Dale, and much of Smaug's treasure was his, so I should have it back, (3) Smaug's destruction of Laketown has left destitute the people who helped the dwarves, and they deserve repayment, especially as the dragon-attack was the dwarves' fault (or actually Bilbo's). To these points – split up in the original by heavy rhetorical questions – Thorin replies in the same mode, though not the same order. He ignores (1), perhaps out of pride, rejects (2), on the ground that Girion is dead and so can have no claim, and half-accepts (3); in dwarvish style he agrees to pay a fair price for earlier assistance, but refuses compensation for the dragon-attack since that was Smaug's business not his own. Finally he refuses to parley under threat and asks a rhetorical question himself: 'It is in my mind to ask what share of their inheritance you would have paid to our kindred, had you found the hoard unguarded and us slain'.

The laborious legalism of this is straight out of Icelandic saga: one thinks of the hero of *The Saga of Hrafnkell* ticking off the appropriate compensations for the murders he has committed, the hamstringing he has suffered, loss of goods during feud and even the natural increase of animals during periods of confiscation – all co-existing, of course, with an ethic of ruthless violence. It is clear that Tolkien was all but enchanted by that ethical and literary style. The whole scene is presented very much for our admiration, and when later on Dain and the dwarves of the Iron Hills appear, their stilted ceremoniousness – 'But who are you that sit in the plain as foes before defended walls?' – rings much more powerfully than the narrator's modernistic translation: 'You have no business here. We are going on, so make way or we shall fight you!' Nevertheless between these two moments another scene has intervened, marked by the greatest cluster of anachronisms since chapter 1: Bilbo's delivery of the Arkenstone to Bard, the Elvenking and Gandalf.

Bilbo has all along been (nearly) immune to the paraphernalia of heroism. He would like to see himself in a 'looking-glass' when Thorin outfits him with *mithril* armour, but fears he looks 'rather absurd', especially when he thinks of his neighbours on The Hill back home. He also listens with dismay and disapproval to the proud speeches of Bard and Thorin, and takes his own steps to break heroic deadlock.

> 'Really you know', Bilbo was saying in his best business manner, 'things are impossible. Personally I am tired of the whole affair. I wish I was back in the West in my own home, where folk are more reasonable. But I have an interest in this matter – one fourteenth share, to be precise, according to a letter, which fortunately I believe I have kept.' He drew from a pocket in his old jacket (which he still wore over his mail), crumpled and much folded, Thorin's letter that had been put under the clock on his mantelpiece in May!
>
> 'A share in the *profits*, mind you,' he went on. 'I am aware of that. Personally I am only too ready to consider all your claims carefully, and deduct what is right from the total before putting in my own claim.' (p. 282)

This speech and speaker could hardly be less like the ones that surround it. Bilbo's behaviour is solidly anachronistic, for he is wearing a jacket, relying on a written contract, drawing a careful distinction between gain and profit, and proposing a compromise which would see Bard's claim as running expenses (almost tax-deductible). Where Bard and Thorin used archaic words ('Hail!', 'foes', 'hoard', 'kindred', 'slain'), he uses modern ones: 'profit', never used in English till 1604, and then only in Aberdeen, 'deduct', recorded in 1524 but then indistinguishable from 'subtract' and not given its commercial sense till much later, 'total', not used as here till 1557, 'claim', 'interest', 'affair', 'matter', all French or Latin imports not adopted fully into English till well after the Norman Conquest. It is fair to say that no character from epic or saga could even begin to think or talk like Bilbo. But what is the effect here of this final sharp juxtaposition between Bard and Bilbo, 'hero' and 'businessman'?

It does continue *The Hobbit*'s strong vein of comedy. It also leads to a sort of 'eucatastrophe', to use Tolkien's own term, as Mr Baggins and the sympathetic reader with him find themselves and the modern code of humility and compromise regarded with gratifying wonder by the Elven-king and Gandalf himself. Still, the comedy is not all one way, for Bilbo remains faintly ridiculous; no one should see *The Hobbit* as a straight progression from satire against the modern world to satire against the ancient one. What chapter 16 and the scenes around it do most powerfully, perhaps, is to enforce a plea for tolerance across an enormous gap of times and attitudes and ethical styles. On the one hand there is Bilbo Baggins, with his virtue of 'moral courage' or readiness 'to encounter odium, disapproval, or contempt rather than depart from what he deems the right course' (first recorded 1822); his corresponding vice is 'self-distrust' (1789). On the other we have Beorn, Thorin, Dain, whose virtue can only be described by such a non-English noun as the Old Norse *drengskapr* – magnanimity, the awareness of being a warrior and so on one's dignity, the quality Dain shows in ratifying Thorin's agreement even though Thorin is dead – and whose vice is a kind of selfish materialism. Neither side is better than the other, or has any right to criticise. The contrast is one of styles, not of good and bad. Accordingly, though throughout *The Hobbit* there have been scenes where the pretensions of one have been exposed by the other (Bilbo sneering at Thorin's elevated language, p. 224, Gloin cutting Bilbo very short at p. 27), by the end even the two *linguistic* styles have become invulnerable to each other's ironies:

> 'Good-bye and good luck, wherever you fare!' said Balin at last. 'If ever you visit us again, when our halls are made fair once more, then the feast shall indeed be splendid!'
> 'If ever you are passing my way,' said Bilbo, 'don't wait to knock! Tea is at four; but any of you are welcome at any time!'
> (p. 305)

There is not much in common between the language of these two speakers; nevertheless it is perfectly clear that they are saying the same thing. Going on from his beliefs in 'the reality of language' and 'the reality of history', Tolkien was perhaps beginning to arrive at a third: 'the reality of human nature'.

The bewilderment of Smaug

This is a slippery and a dangerous concept. If there is one thing which twentieth-century anthropology has proved, it is that people are different, and that even matters which appear entirely natural or instinctive are so enmeshed in nets of custom as to make it impossible to detect 'human universals'. There is no sign that Tolkien took any notice of modern anthropology, but then he hardly needed to. Ancient texts would provide him with any number of examples of how what is now considered natural might be in another age unthinkable, or vice versa. People's behaviour all too evidently changes. But isn't there something underneath the nets of custom that remains the same? Something that would link modern Englishmen with their Anglo-Saxon ancestors just as philology sees, beneath a thousand years of change, essential continuity between the language of *Beowulf* and that of today?

Tolkien must have been brooding on this question for many years. In 1923 he published in *The Gryphon* (the magazine of Leeds's Yorkshire College) a poem called 'Iumonna Gold Galdre Bewunden', the first version of what was to become in 1970 'The Hoard'. The first title is better, though, for it means 'the gold of ancient men, wound round with magic', it is line 3052 of *Beowulf*, and it points to a notorious difficulty in that poem over the hero's motives. When he went to fight *his* dragon he appeared to do so for the best of reasons, i.e. to protect his people. On the other hand he also showed a keen interest in the treasure, which the dragon was only trying to guard, having been provoked by the theft of a cup by a passing runaway (or 'burglar'). At one point indeed, in a violently-disputed passage, the poet seems to say that there was a curse on the gold, so that the man who plundered it 'should be guilty of sin, be shut up in devil's haunts, bound in hell-bands and tormented grievously. Yet by no means too eagerly had Beowulf before gazed upon its owner's treasure of gold with the curse on it.'[15] Was Beowulf guilty or not? Did the curse punish him or not? Certainly the hoard he wins brings death to him and disaster to his people. Maybe this is also a punishment for the spark of avarice the poet is hinting at. But then maybe the dragon-curse is *itself* avarice. So Tolkien suggested in the 1923 poem, tracing in successive stanzas the transmission of a treasure from elf to dwarf to dragon to hero and ending with the picture of an old and miserly king overthrown by his rivals and leaving his gold to oblivion. All the characters in it are the same: they begin with vitality, mirth and courage, they end in age, wealth and squalor. Their decline is caused by gold. Could their progress also be a kind of analogue of human history, beginning in heroic endeavour and ending in 'commercialism', 'materialism', 'industrialism', that whole series of distinctively modern concepts which nevertheless centre if not on gold, on that 'idolatry of artefacts' which C. S. Lewis called, in evident agreement with Tolkien, the 'great corporate sin of our own civilisation'?[16] If one does think that for a moment, there is a further corollary: just as old miser grew out of young hero eager for treasure, so the 'great corporate sin' of modernity must have had some ancient origin. This sinful continuity between ancient and modern must have been on Tolkien's mind as he finished *The Hobbit*.

There is in the final chapters a continuum of greed. Least reprehensible is the Elvenking's: he likes artefacts, but for their beauty, and is satisfied in the end with the emeralds of Girion. Bard is more modern in tone, but is let off as well since his motives are so clearly constructive. Bilbo too, with his ethic of being 'well-to-do' rather than vulgarly 'rich', is relatively immune. The dwarves, though, have very strong feelings about treasure, especially their 'pale enchanted gold' or *gold galdre bewunden*; they even put 'a great many spells' over the trolls' hoard, just in case. As soon as they come within range of Smaug's treasure *its* spell starts to work on them. They send Bilbo down the tunnel; they rejoice prematurely; on first sight of the treasure they have to be dragged away from it by Bilbo, 'not without many a backward glance of longing'. Finally Thorin himself is obsessively determined to give nothing to Bard or elves or Lakemen, and when forced to disgorge by Bilbo's theft of the Arkenstone, thinks against normal dwarvish behaviour-patterns of breaking his word. 'So strong was the bewilderment of the treasure upon him, he was pondering whether by the help of Dain he might not recapture the Arkenstone and withhold the share of the reward.'

'Bewilderment' is a good word there. In modern parlance it means 'mental confusion', which is fair enough as a description of Thorin's state – he has no idea how he will reach his ends, or what these ends are, only that parting with treasure is not among them. The modern sense however arises from the physical one of being 'lost in the wild', and Thorin is that too, being stuck in the centre of the Desolation of Smaug with plenty of gold but little to eat; he could end up as literally 'bewildered' as the Master of Laketown who, fleeing with his city's share of the treasure, 'died of starvation in the waste'. There is even a third sense of the word to remind us of the visible, tactile source of the treasure's power, the quality that makes the dwarves run their fingers through it: it means 'a tangled or labyrinthine condition of objects', says the *OED*, quoting (1884) 'What a bewilderment of light and color met her eyes.' When one thinks of the dim images of gold and jewels and 'silver red-stained in the ruddy light' which is Bilbo's first glimpse of the hoard, one sees that this sense for 'the bewilderment of the treasure' is appropriate too.

Thorin's 'bewilderment' is physical and mental and moral as well. The 'dragon-sickness' which he and the Master of Laketown catch is also simultaneously magical and moral. At the bottom of it there lies an old superstition which says that dragons are actually misers who have in greed and despair walled themselves up alive, 'lain down on their gold' as sagas say. Naturally the gold on which they have brooded (see *Hobbit*, p. 276) exudes a miasma of avarice. Yet one has the sense of an external force meeting an internal weakness, especially strong in the artefact-worshipping dwarves, and in the Master whose mind was given 'to trades and tolls, to cargoes and gold', who despises old songs and speaks on occasion (p. 267) with a distinctive post-Industrial Revolution modernity. This is in fact a complex and successful presentation of the motives behind a real historical change; one might usefully compare the scene at the end of Kurt Vonnegut's *Player Piano* (1952), where the revolutionaries against the Automated State turn obsessively, with their first success, to tinkering with machines. Both books are making the same sort of (not very liberal) point: things, metal things, are genuinely fun to play with, but it's very hard to stop the fun from getting out of hand, though only in the twentieth century have we become really aware of that. Hence the 'continuum of greed' from Elvenking to Master. Hence, too, the brooding from 1923 on the word *galdor*. Besides 'spell' and 'bewilderment' it also means 'poetry'; you could say that the 'enchantment' of the treasure is a kind of wicked equivalent of 'glamour'.

There is however another character in this continuum, indeed at one end of it, and that is Smaug. His name is another 'asterisk word', being the past tense *smaug* of a Germanic verb *smugan*, 'to squeeze through a hole', as Tolkien said in his 1938 *Observer* letter; also the Old Norse equivalent of an Old English magic word found in a spell *wið sméogan wyrme*, 'against the penetrating worm'. But he has a mental sense as well as a physical one, since O.E. *sméagan* also means 'to inquire into' and in adjectival form 'subtle, crafty'. All round it is appropriate that Smaug should have the most sophisticated intelligence in *The Hobbit*.

Bilbo's conversation with him is indeed a brilliant stroke. Like so much in the book it has a model in an Eddic poem, the *Fáfnismál*, in which Sigurthr and Fáfnir talk while the dragon dies of the wound the hero has given him. Like Bilbo, Sigurthr refuses to tell the dragon his name but replies riddlingly (for fear of being cursed); like Smaug, Fáfnir sows dissension between partners by remarking on the greed that gold excites; the dissension actually breaks out when eating the dragon's heart helps Sigurthr to understand bird-talk (another prominent *Hobbit* motif). Nevertheless the *Fáfnismál* once again did not offer Tolkien enough. It drifted off into mere exchange of information, it contained as Tolkien said of *Beowulf* too much '*draconitas*' and not enough '*draco*', not enough of the 'real worm, with a bestial life and thought of his own'.[17] Tolkien therefore set himself to repair this gap, and did so once more by introducing a strong dose of anachronistic modernity.

Thus the most remarkable thing about Smaug is his oddly circumlocutory mode of speech. He speaks in fact with the characteristic aggressive politeness of the British upper class, in which irritation and authority are in direct proportion to apparent deference or uncertainty. 'You have nice manners for a thief and a liar' are his opening words to Bilbo (their degree of irony unclear). 'You seem familiar with my name, but I don't seem to remember smelling you before. Who are you and where do you come from, may I ask?' He might be a testy colonel approached by a stranger in a railway carriage; why has Bilbo not been introduced? At the same time the 'bestial life' of the worm keeps intruding, as he remarks on Bilbo's smell and boasts parenthetically 'I know the smell (and taste) of dwarf – none better', or when he rolls over, 'absurdly pleased' like a clumsy spaniel, to show the hobbit his armoured belly. One result is a frequent and vivid sense of paradox, which the ancient world, innocent of scientific rationalism, could hardly have developed: Smaug has both wings and weight, as we are reminded when he leaves his lair and '*float[s] heavy and slow* in the dark like a monstrous crow' (my italics); and in the cold reptilian belly he keeps hot fire, which peeps out from under his eyelids when he pretends to sleep and flashes 'like scarlet lightning' when he is amused. The paradoxes, the oscillations between animal and intelligent behaviour, the contrast between creaky politeness of speech and plain gloating over murder, all help to give Smaug his dominant characteristic of 'wiliness', and what the narrator calls with utter modernity (the noun dates in this sense from 1847) his 'overwhelming personality'.

All this gives great plausibility to another unexpected datum which the narrator springs on us, i.e. 'the effect that dragon-talk has on the inexperienced', the 'dragon-spell' which keeps prompting Bilbo to run out and confess. No ancient text contains any such motif, but as Smaug oozes confidentially on – 'I will give you one piece of advice . . . I suppose you got a fair price. Come now, did you? . . . Well, that's just like them . . . I don't know if it has occurred to you . . . Bless me! Had you never thought of the catch?' – he assumes the 'old experienced' end of the polarity so strongly that it is no surprise for Bilbo to find himself pressed towards the 'young innocent' one. Yet the combined magico-moral effect (is it 'spell' or is it 'personality'?) reminds one also of the 'dragon-sickness' that Smaug and his treasure between them seem practically and magically to generate. The character of Smaug is part of a *Zusammenhang*: nothing could be more archaic or fantastic than a dragon brooding on its gold, and yet the strong sense of familiarity in this one's speech puts it back into the 'continuum of greed', makes it just dimly possible that dragon-motivations could on their different scale have some affinity with human ones – even real historical human ones.

If one followed this line of reasoning too far *The Hobbit* could appear suddenly as a *roman à thèse*, or even an allegory, in which Bilbo Baggins as Modern Man embarks on his Pilgrim's Progress (or Regress) into Fantasy, only to find that at the very heart of his monsterworld there is none other than an embodiment of his own worst nature, Greed or even Capitalism itself, skulking on its gold like a fiercer Miss Havisham. The moral would be that all *bourgeois* must turn Burglar, or something of the sort. Of course such a reading would only be a joke. Still, if by no stretch of the imagination an allegory, *The Hobbit* does begin to show by its conclusion some flickers of the 'large symbolism' Tolkien saw in *Beowulf* and tried more positively to reproduce in *The Lord of the Rings*. In its last scene, the conversation between Gandalf, Bilbo and Balin, the wizard is allowed to make the point that metaphors can 'after a fashion' be true, that romance and reality are differences of presentation not of fact. The logic of what he says is that if the matter behind old songs can contain someone as prosaic as Bilbo then maybe even the prosaic events of today will sometime be the matter of old songs. There is accordingly a reality, and a continuity, in human nature, even dwarf-hobbit-human nature.

Yet the reason why this hint should not be taken further is obvious enough. Most of *The Hobbit* suggests strongly that Tolkien did not work from ideas, but from words, names, consistencies and contradictions in folk-tales, things as localised as the dissatisfaction with *Fáfnismál* which produced Smaug, the brooding over the riddle-contests of *Vafðrúðnismál* or *The Saga of King Heidrek* which led (somehow) to Gollum. The two most powerful fragments of all ancient poetry for Tolkien at this time, I cannot help thinking, were the two similar bits from *Beowulf* and *Sir Gawain* which imply there are whole worlds the narrator simply cannot get round to. The Old English poet hints at the 'wide journeys' which Sigemund the dragon-slayer made, 'the wicked deeds and battles which the children of men' (but maybe not of monsters) 'never knew clearly'. His medieval successor says of Sir Gawain six centuries later that he would never even have reached his main adventure 'Had he not been stalwart and staunch and steadfast in God', so many were his clashes with worms and wolves, with wood-trolls 'and with ogres that hounded him from the heights of the fells'. In exactly the same spirit we are told that even going home Bilbo 'had many hardships and adventures before he got back', since 'The Wild was still the Wild, and there were many other things in it in those days besides the goblins'. Some of them have been half-glimpsed already: eyes in the darkness, 'old castles with an evil look', 'startled ears' responding to the news of the death of Smaug. But in essence the plot of *The Hobbit* is a tour through darknesses, with no more connection between Gollum and the eagles and Beorn and the spiders

than that of one-after-another. The true end of *The Hobbit*, as opposed to
the last scene of chaos and tidying-up,† is the regretful farewell to the
Wild just before, as archaic Took cedes to Edwardian Baggins:

> They came to that high point at morning, and looking backwards
> they saw a white sun shining over the outstretched lands. There behind
> lay Mirkwood, blue in the distance, and darkly green at the nearer edge
> even in spring. There far away was the Lonely Mountain on the edge
> of eyesight. On its highest peak snow yet unmelted was gleaming pale.
> 'So comes snow after fire, and even dragons have their ending!' said
> Bilbo, and he turned his back on the adventure. (p. 307)

Adventure in Middle-earth embodies a modern meaning, but does not
exist to propagate it. Insofar as the two worlds are related it is because
the 'inner consistency' of Secondary Art must necessarily (in order to be
consistent) be the same as that of Primary Art or truth.

† Even this, I suspect, has a philological root. In the 1928 introduction he wrote
to W. E. Haigh's *Glossary of the Dialect of the Huddersfield District*, mentioned
above in connection with 'Baggins', Tolkien had said that it was important to
observe 'the changes in sense that take place when words of more "learned" origin
are adopted and put to everyday use in dialect (see *keęnsil, okshęn, inséns*)'. But
okshęn in Huddersfield dialect meant not 'auction' but 'mess'. 'Shu'z nout but ę
slut; ęr eęs ęz ę feęr okshęn', quoted Mr Haigh, or for non-natives, 'She's nothing
but a slut; her house is a fair auction'. When he gets home Mr Baggins finds his
house a 'fair auction' in both senses. Not only are they selling his goods, they are
failing to wipe their feet on the mat! The word has become a 'fusion-point' of
outraged respectability.

Chapter 4

A CARTOGRAPHIC PLOT

Maps and names

Seventeen years went by between the publication of *The Hobbit* and that of *The Fellowship of the Ring*. It is true that in the interim a World War was fought, and Tolkien's family grew up, while Tolkien himself was committed to many professorial duties which, as he later insisted, he did not neglect. Nevertheless the main reason for the long hiatus was the pace of Tolkien's own creative processes. He remained absorbed in Middle-earth, to it indeed he dedicated his 'years of authority' as a scholar; but he found the composition, one might even say the secretion, of *The Lord of the Rings* a matter which had to be allowed to obey its own laws. Something of what was going on in his head is revealed by one of the major differences between *The Hobbit* and *The Lord of the Rings*: their use of maps and names.

In *The Hobbit* names are astonishingly rare. There are of course the twelve dwarves, all taken from the *Dvergatal* poem, and apprehended I suspect by most readers as a homogeneous unit broken only by Fili and Kili, who are young, Bombur, who is fat, Balin, who is kindly, and Thorin, who is boss. There are few elf-names, and none of those which do occur – Bladorthin, Dorwinion, Girion, Galion, Moria, Esgaroth – is at all prominent in the story. The Elvenking remains anonymous in *The Hobbit* and is identified as Thranduil only in *The Lord of the Rings* I, 253. The only hobbit-surnames given are Baggins, Took and Sackville-Baggins (this last to prove an anomaly in Middle-earth and a failure of tone), with 'Messrs Grubb, Grubb and Burrowes' the auctioneers at the very end. Elrond, Azog, Radagast, the ravens' onomatopoeic Roäc and Carc – these all but complete *The Hobbit*'s list. A common practice for Tolkien at this stage was simply to make names out of capital letters. Thus Bilbo lives in a tunnel which goes 'not quite straight into the side of the hill – The Hill, as all the people for many miles round called it'. The stream at the foot of The Hill is called The Water, the hobbits' town on The Water is called Hobbiton (near Bywater), and so on into Wilderland, where we find the Misty Mountains, the Long Lake, the Lonely Mountain, a river called Running and a valley called Dale. Even 'Gandalf' is actually a name of this type. It also comes from the *Dvergatal*, where it is near Thráinn, Thorinn and Thrór, but Tolkien evidently regarded it with some suspicion since it contained the element -*álfr*, while it was his opinion that elves and dwarves cohabited only in the pages of the *OED*. So what was 'Gandalf' doing in a dwarves' roster, and anyway what was a 'gand-'? If Tolkien looked in the *Icelandic Dictionary* of R. Cleasby and Gudbrand Vigfusson he would have found the opinions that the meaning of *gandr* was 'somewhat dubious' but probably '*anything enchanted* or *an object used by sorcerers*', while *gandálfr* was either 'a wizard' or maybe a 'bewitched demon'. He concluded, clearly, that *gandr* meant 'staff' (the common property of wizards as one can tell even from Shakespeare's Prospero or Milton's Comus). Accordingly when Gandalf first appears 'All that the unsuspecting Bilbo saw that morning was *an old man with a staff*' (my italics). He turns out not to be an elf, but by the end of *The Lord of the Rings* it is clear he comes from Elvenhome. 'Gandalf' is in fact from the beginning not a name but a description, as with Beorn, Gollum, the Necromancer, and other people, places and things in *The Hobbit*.

Since *The Silmarillion*, with its developed nomenclature, was already in existence, it would be wrong to say that Tolkien in the 1930s was not interested in names. It does look, though, as if he was not sure how to bring them into fiction, especially if they were English names. Yet the point had caught his attention. Once *The Hobbit* was finished he focused on the problem with sudden clarity – as one can see from *Farmer Giles of Ham*, not published till 1949, but composed apparently in the period 1935–8, i.e. overlapping with the final production of *The Hobbit* (see *Biography*, pp. 165–6). This throws many interesting sidelights on Tolkien's fictional development. For one thing it is the only one of his stories set unmistakably in England, and while its history is that of nursery-rhyme† its geography is remarkably clear. Ham is now Thame, a town in Buckinghamshire twelve miles east of Oxford. Worminghall is four miles away and Oakley, which had its parson eaten, five. The capital of the Middle Kingdom, 'some twenty leagues distant from Ham', sounds like Tamworth, the historical capital of the Mercian kings, sixty-eight miles from Thame as the crow flies (a league, NB, is three miles). Farthingho in Northamptonshire, where once 'an outpost against the Middle Kingdom was maintained', is on a direct line between those two places about a third of the way from Thame – proof of the 'Little Kingdom's' lack of territorial

---

† At the bridge Chrysophlax the dragon sticks his claw into the King's white horse and roars 'There are knights lying cold in the mountain-pass, and soon there will be more in the river. *All the King's horses and all the King's men!*' (my italics). There is also passing reference to (Old) King Coel, and to King Lear, who was responsible for the 'partition under Locrin, Camber and Albanac'. The world of the imagined 'editor' is that of the 'Brutus books', or fake history of Britain accepted as true in medieval times (and later). He treats the author of *Sir Gawain and the Green Knight* as a 'historian', paraphrasing his 'Where . . . oft boþe blysse and blunder/Ful skete hat3 skyfted synne' as, p. 7, 'the years were filled with swift alternations of war and peace, of mirth and woe'.

ambition. Wales, where the giants live, and the (Pennine) mountains where the dragons live are on this parochial scale suitably far off. And when Farmer Giles refuses to listen to tales about the folk 'North over the hills and far away, beyond the Standing Stones and all', he means Warwickshire, probably, whose boundary with Oxfordshire runs by the Rollright Stones.

All in all it is extremely unfair of the imagined 'editor' of *Farmer Giles* to criticise its imagined 'author' for feeble geography; that 'author', like Tolkien, 'lived himself in the lands of the Little Kingdom' and knew what he was writing about. But what is the point of this sudden precision? Evidently, Tolkien wanted to recreate a timeless and idealised England (or rather Britain) in which the place and the people remained the same regardless of politics. The story of *Farmer Giles* is therefore largely the triumph of native over foreign (for in Giles's court 'the vulgar tongue came into fashion, and none of his speeches were in the Book-latin'), as simultaneously of worth over fashion and of heroic song and popular lay over pompous pernickety rationalistic scholarship. In all these ways *Farmer Giles* continues the vein of the 'Man in the Moon' poems and of *The Hobbit* – as it does also in its jibing at the *OED* with its arrogantly 'civilised' definition of 'blunderbuss'.[1] However at the same time the story can be seen as one of the several works Tolkien wrote around this time with reference to his own switch from academicism to creativity (see pp. 33–42 above). Is *Farmer Giles*, like 'Leaf by Niggle', an allegory?

The main reason for thinking so is Giles's supporter the parson, a 'grammarian', note, who 'could no doubt see further into the future than most men'. His vital act is to remind Giles to take a long rope with him when he goes to hunt the dragon. Without that rope, one may say, there would have been no treasure, no tame dragon, no Thame, no Little Kingdom. Moreover the parson is also in a sense responsible for Tailbiter, Giles's sword. He guesses what the sword is while Giles and the Miller are still arguing, confirms the guess when it will not go into its scabbard with a dragon near, and in spite of his patter about 'epigraphical signs' and archaic characters does actually read the runes on the sword and declare its identity as Tailbiter (or as he prefers to call it, Caudimordax). By doing all this the parson puts heart into Giles. All round he deserves a lot of the credit – certainly much more than Augustus Bonifacius Ambrosius Aurelianus Antoninus, the proud tyrant who sent Giles the sword, though only because to him plain heavy things were out of fashion. It is very nearly irresistible to conclude that in his mixture of learning, bluff and sense the parson represents an idealised (Christian) philologist; in which case the proud tyrant of the Middle Kingdom who discards his most trenchant blade looks very like literary criticism taking no notice of historical language study! One could go on: Farmer Giles would be the creative instinct, the rope (like Tailbiter) philological science, the dragon the ancient world of the Northern imagination brooding on its treasure of lost lays, the Little Kingdom the fictional space which Tolkien hoped to carve out, make independent and inhabit. Of course such an allegory would be a joke;[2] but a joke in Tolkienian style, an optimistic counter-part to 'Leaf by Niggle' a few years later.

In the whole story linguistic humour is paramount, from the gloomy proverbs of 'Sunny Sam' and his pigheaded misprision of Hilarius and Felix – 'Ominous names . . . I don't like the sound of them' – to Giles's own determined native errors of grammar. The real errors, though, Tolkien ends by remarking, come from later and more 'learned' history. Thus Thame should be Tame, 'for Thame with an *h* is a folly without warrant'. In actuality, of course, the whole story that Tolkien tells to account for the names of Thame and Worminghall is based on nothing, is mere fiction. Still, even in actuality Thame-with-an-h *remains* a folly without warrant, part of the wave of Book-latinisms which have given us T*h*ames and T*h*omas and cou*l*d and de*b*t and dou*b*t and half the other non-sounded, unhistorical, un-English inserted letters that plague our spelling to this day. Tolkien would have liked them not to exist. He deplored the feeble modern understanding of English names, English places, English culture. In *Farmer Giles of Ham* one can see him brooding over problems of re-creation and of continuity – for names and places remain whatever people think about them. Though he joked about them, Thame and Worminghall are a long step on from The Hill and The Water. Farthingho set Tolkien thinking about the Farthings of 'The Shire'.

The further development into *The Lord of the Rings* is obvious. Where *The Hobbit* had some forty or fifty rather perfunctory names, the indices of *The Lord of the Rings* list over 600 names of 'Persons, Beasts and Monsters', almost as many places, with a couple of hundred unclassifiable but named objects for good measure. In the same way Thror's Map and the map of Wilderland in *The Hobbit*, which added nothing to the story but decoration and a 'Here be tygers' feel of quaintness, have ceded to the foldout map of Middle-earth in the first edition of *The Fellowship of the Ring*, the even more detailed map of the Marches of Gondor and Mordor in *The Return of the King*, the map of the Shire at the end of the 'Prologue', the still further elaborated map issued as a poster by Pauline Baynes in 1970. All these are full of details never used in the text. The characters of *The Lord of the Rings* furthermore have a strong tendency to talk like maps, historical ones at that. At I, 397 Aragorn begins 'You are looking now south-west across the north plains of the Riddermark . . . Ere long we shall come to the mouth of the Limlight that runs down from Fangorn to join the Great River.' A little before Celeborn had been tracing the course of Anduin 'to the tall island of the Tindrock, that we call Tol Brandir', where it falls 'over the cataracts of Rauros down into the Nindalf, the Wetwang as it is called in your tongue. That is a wide region of sluggish fen . . . There the Entwash flows in . . . About that stream, on this side of the Great River, lies Rohan. On the further side are the bleak hills of the Emyn Muil.' The flow of knowledge, and of names, seems irrepressible, and the habit is shared by Gimli, Gandalf, Fangorn, even Meriadoc. Why such elaboration?

The answer, oddly, lies as far back as *The Hobbit*. There Bilbo on one occasion screwed up his courage to ask *why* something was called 'The Carrock'. Because it *was*, replied Gandalf nastily (p. 125).

'He called it the Carrock, because carrock is his word for it. He calls things like that carrocks, and this one is *the* Carrock because it is the only one near his home and he knows it well.'

This is unhelpful, and not even true, since *carrecc* is Old Welsh for 'rock', preserved in several modern names like Crickhowell in Brecon (or Crick-hollow in the Buckland). However Gandalf has put his finger on one point about names, which is that they are arbitrary, even if they were not so in the beginning. Once upon a time all names were like 'Gandalf' or 'the Hill': thus (the) Frogmorton meant 'the town in the marshy land where the frogs are' (see 'Guide', p. 185), Tolkien was *der tollkühne* or 'the foolhardy one', Suffield, Tolkien's mother's name, '(the one from the) south field', and so on. However, *that is not how names are now perceived*. In the modern world we take them as labels, as things accordingly in a very close one-to-one relationship with whatever they label. To use a pompous phrase, they are 'isomorphic with reality'. And that means they are extraordinarily useful to fantasy, weighing it down as they do with repeated implicit assurances of the existence of the things they label, and of course of their nature and history too.

Tolkien's new equation of fantasy with reality comes over most strongly in his map, account and history of 'the Shire', an extended 'Little Kingdom', one might say, transplanted to Middle-earth. The easiest way to describe it is to say that the Shire is 'calqued' on England, 'calquing' being a linguistic term to mean that process in which the elements of a compound word are translated bit by bit to make a new word in another language, as in French *haut-parleur* from 'loudspeaker' (*parler haut*='speak loudly'), or Irish *each-chumhacht* from 'horsepower' (*each*='horse', like *eoh*, *equus* on p. 16 above). The point about calques is that the derivative does not sound anything like its original: nevertheless it betrays influence at every point. Thus historically the Shire is like/unlike England, the hobbits like/unlike English people. Hobbits live in the Shire as the English live in England, but like the English they come from somewhere else, indeed from the Angle (in Europe between Flensburg Fjord and the Schlei, in Middle-earth between Hoarwell and Loudwater). Both groups have forgotten this fact. Both emigrated in three tribes, Angles, Saxons and Jutes or Stoors, Harfoots and Fallohides, all since then largely mingled.

The English were led by two brothers, Hengest and Horsa, i.e. 'stallion' and 'horse', the hobbits by Marcho and Blanco, cp. Old English *marh, 'horse', blanca (only in Beowulf) 'white horse'.[3] All four founded realms which evolved into uncharacteristic peace: there was no battle in the Shire between the Greenfields, 1147, and the Battle of Bywater, 1419, an interval of 272 years very like the 270 between publication of The Return of the King and the last battle fought on English soil, Sedgemoor, 1685. Organisationally too the Shire, with its mayors, musters, moots and Shirriffs, is an old-fashioned and idealised England, while the hobbits, in their plainness, greediness, frequent embarrassments, distrust of 'outsiders'† and most of all in their deceptive ability to endure rough handling form an easily recognisable if again old-fashioned self-image of the English. The calquing is most evident, however, on the map.

Here all that need be said is that Tolkien took most of his Shire-names from his own near surroundings. They sound funny but they ring true. Thus 'Nobottle' in the Northfarthing makes us think of glass containers, hardly plausible as features of the landscape, but the name comes from Old English néowe, 'new', +botl, 'house' (as in bytla, cp. 'hobbit'). There is a Nobottle in Northamptonshire thirty-five miles from Oxford (and not far from Farthingstone). It means much the same as Newbury, also a town in England twenty-five miles south of Oxford and also a place in the Shire, or rather in the Buckland. Buckland itself is an Oxfordshire place-name, common all over England since it has the rather dull etymology of bócland, land 'booked' to the Church by charter, and so different from folcland or 'folkland' which was inalienable. That derivation was impossible in Middle-earth, so Tolkien constructed the more satisfactory one that the Buckland was where the Buck family lived, was indeed a 'folkland' centred on Bucklebury like the 'Tookland' centred on Tuckborough. As for 'Took', that too appears a faintly comic name in modern English (people prefer to respell it 'Tooke'), but it is only the ordinary Northern pronunciation of the very common 'Tuck'. Five minutes with the Oxford Dictionary of Place-Names, E. Ekwall's English River Names or P. H. Reaney's Dictionary of British Surnames will provide explanations for most hobbitic names of any sort, and the same is true, on a more learned scale, of the rest of Middle-earth. Thus Celeborn's 'Wetwang' is also a place in Yorkshire, the Riders' 'Dunharrow' has evident English parallels, the rivers Gladden, Silverlode, Limlight, etc., all have English roots or analogues, and so on outwards. The work that went into all these is immense. It also seems

† 'Outsiders' lead to one of Tolkien's weakest jokes. In early English a 'bounder' was someone who set boundaries, and so kept out 'outsiders'. However in the slang of his youth a 'bounder' was, OED post-1889, 'A person who by his behaviour places himself outside the pale of well-bred society', i.e. an 'outsider'. Hence the joke in LOTR I, 121. It seems that Tolkien had not decided early on how funny the hobbits were to be. Some of the parodic element of The Hobbit persists for a couple of chapters: 'eleventy-first', 'tweens', 'mathoms', etc.

largely wasted, since for all the characters' efforts half the names never get into the plot! Still, Tolkien certainly thought, and very probably he thought rightly, that all this effort was *not* wasted. The maps and the names give Middle-earth that air of solidity and extent both in space and time which its successors so conspicuously lack. They mark an ambition much increased from *The Hobbit*'s opening scenes of parody and close of detached appreciation. They also quite simply provided grist for Tolkien's creative mill – one which like the mills of God ground slow but ground (in the end) exceeding small.

Getting started

In a footnote to the 'Epilogue' of 'On Fairy-Stories', Tolkien noted, or confessed, that though every fantasy-writer aims at truth 'it is seldom that the "inspiration" is so strong and lasting that it leavens all the lump, and does not leave much that is mere uninspired "invention".' One might think that authors start off with a flash of 'inspiration' and as it dies away keep things going with 'invention'. In Tolkien's case I think it more likely that he worked the other way round: he got started on relatively laborious 'inventions', and found as the story gathered way that the inevitable complications of these brought him 'inspiration'. Thus *The Hobbit* does not quite take off till Bilbo finds the ring, and even then the sense of events gaining continuity is not strong till the company reaches Mirkwood, on the other side of the house of Beorn. The same is true of *The Lord of the Rings*.

It is for one thing remarkable that Frodo has to be dug out of no less than *five* 'Homely Houses' before his quest is properly launched: first Bag End, then the little house at Crickhollow with its redundant guardian Fredegar Bolger, then the house of Tom Bombadil, then the *Prancing Pony*, and finally Rivendell with its 'last Homely House east of the Sea'. Each of these locations has of course its images and encounters to present, and some of them (like the meeting with Strider) turn out to be vital. Nevertheless there is a sense that the zest of the story goes not into the dangers but the recoveries – hot baths at Crickhollow, song and dancing at Bree, Goldberry's water that seems like wine, and Butterbur's 'small and cosy room' with its 'hot soup, cold meats, a blackberry tart, new loaves, slab of butter, and half a ripe cheese'. And this is to take no account of meals *en passant*, like Gildor Inglorion's pastoral elvish banquet and Farmer Maggot's 'mighty dish of bacon and mushrooms'! Meanwhile the Black Riders, for all their snuffling and deadly cries, are not the menace they later become, for though they may only be waiting for a better chance, as Aragorn insists, they could have saved themselves trouble several times in the Shire, in Bree and on Weathertop by pressing their attacks home.

It seems likely that, as at the start of *The Hobbit*, Tolkien found the transit from familiar Shire to archaic Wilderland an inhibiting one. He said himself that when he first reached the *Prancing Pony* he had no more idea than the hobbits who Strider was, while in the first draft his place was filled by a kind of hero-hobbit called 'Trotter' (*Biography*, p. 188). Tolkien broke through in *The Hobbit* with the trolls and then the ring. In *The Lord of the Rings* his invention came, to begin with, from a sort of self-plagiarism.

The hobbits' first three real encounters are with the Willow-man and Tom Bombadil in the Old Forest, and with the Barrow-wight on the Downs outside. All three could almost be omitted without disturbing the rest of the plot. Willow-man is a forerunner of the Ents, or rather the Huorns, but Bombadil never comes back into the story at all: the Council of Elrond considers him for a moment, Gandalf stops for a chat when all serious work is over. The Barrow-wight does a little more in providing the sword that Merry uses on the chief-Ringwraith in Book V, a sword specifically designed for use against the Witch-king of Angmar, which is what that Nazgûl turns out to be. Still, that is a by-product. All three of these characters furthermore go a long way back in Tolkien's mind, as far back as hobbits, probably, further than the Shire or the Ring; they are all in the poem 'The Adventures of Tom Bombadil', printed in the *Oxford Magazine* in 1934 (just as the song Frodo sings in the *Prancing Pony* is a revision from 1923). Tolkien was raiding his own larder, and one can in the end see why.

It is admittedly not so easy in the beginning. The thing we would like to know about Tom Bombadil is what he *is*, but this is never asked or answered directly. In chapter 7 Frodo raises the courage to ask instead *who* he is, only to receive the answers, from Goldberry, (1) 'He is', (2) 'He is, as you have seen him', (3) 'He is the Master of wood, water and hill', and from Tom himself (4) 'Don't you know my name yet? That's the only answer.' He seems in fact to be a *lusus naturae*, a one-member category; the hobbits are doubtful whether he can be called a man, though he looks like one apart from his size, which is intermediate between man and hobbit. More revealing is his main attribute, fearlessness, present in *The Lord of the Rings* but even clearer in the 1934 poem (and in its rewritten form as lead-poem of *The Adventures of Tom Bombadil* in 1962). The action of that is simply four clashes between Tom and potentially hostile creatures, Goldberry, 'the Riverwoman's daughter', who pulls him into the river, Willow-man, who catches him in a crack, the Badgerfolk who drag him down their tunnel, and finally as Tom goes home the Barrow-wight behind the door:

> 'You've forgotten Barrow-wight dwelling in the old mound
> up there a-top the hill with the ring of stones round.

He's got loose to-night: under the earth he'll take you!
Poor Tom Bombadil, pale and cold he'll make you!'

But Tom reacts only with simple imperatives: 'You let me out again . . . You show me out at once . . . Go back to grassy mound, on your stony pillow/lay down your bony head, like Old Man Willow.' And once the threats have been dismissed Tom goes further, going back to seize Goldberry from her nameless mother 'in her deep weedy pool', taking her back to his house to be married. Their wedding-night is undisturbed by the hags and bogles murmuring outside, and the poem ends with Goldberry combing her hair and Tom chopping sticks of willow. As Goldberry says to Frodo, Tom is 'the Master'. What he *is* may not be known, but what he *does* is dominate.

Tom's other major quality is naturalness. Even his language has something unpremeditated about it. A lot of what he says is nonsense, the first thing indeed that the hobbits notice, even before they see him. When it is not 'hey dol! merry dol!' and the like, it tends to be strongly assertive or onomastic, mere lists of names and qualities. From time to time it breaks through to being 'perhaps a strange language unknown to the hobbits, an ancient language whose words were mainly those of wonder and delight'. But though they may not know the language, the hobbits understand it, as they understand Goldberry's rain-song without recognising the words; and when Tom names something (as he does with the hobbits' ponies) the name sticks – the animals respond to nothing else the rest of their lives. There is an ancient myth in this feature, that of the 'true language', the tongue in which there is a thing for each word and a word for each thing, and in which signifier then naturally has power over signified – language 'isomorphic with reality' once again.[4] It is this which seems to give Tom his power. He is the great singer; indeed he does not yet seem to have discovered, or sunk into, prose. Much of what he says is printed by Tolkien as verse, but almost all of what he says can be *read* as verse, falling into strongly-marked two-stress phrases, with or without rhyme and alliteration, usually with feminine or unstressed endings; see for instance his last 'prose' speech, 'Tóm will give you góod advice,/tíll this day is óver/(áfter that your ówn luck/must gó with you and gúide you)/: fóur miles alóng the road/you'll cóme upon a víllage,/Brée under Brée-hill,/with dóors looking wéstward.' The scansion-system (more complicated than I have marked) is a little like that of the Old English verse Tolkien was later to reproduce in the songs of Rohan, but more like that of much Old English 'prose', over whose claim to being 'verse' editors still hesitate. The point is though that while we appreciate it as rhythmical (unlike prose), we also do not mark it as premeditated or artificial (unlike verse). The hobbits fall into song themselves, 'as if it was easier and more natural than talking'.

Tom Bombadil, then, is fearless. In some way he antedates the corruptions of Art. According to Elrond he is 'Iarwain Ben-adar . . . oldest and fatherless'. Like Adam, also fatherless, 'whatsoever [he] called every living creature, that was the name thereof'. Unlike the descendants of Adam he does not suffer from the curse of Babel; everybody understands his language by instinct. It is odd, though, that Tom shares the adjective 'oldest' with another being in *The Lord of the Rings*, Fangorn the Ent, whom Gandalf calls 'the oldest living thing that still walks beneath the Sun' (II, 102). An inconsistency? It need not be so, if one accepts that Tom is not living – as the Nazgûl and the Barrow-wight are not dead. Unlike even the oldest living creatures he has no date of birth, but seems to have been there since before the Elves awoke, a part of Creation, an exhalation of the world. There are hints in old poems of such an idea. The Old English poem *Genesis B*, originally written in Old Saxon, at one point calls Adam *selfsceafte guma*, which could be translated calquishly as 'self-shaped man'. Modern translations prefer to say 'self-doomed' or something of the sort, while the Bosworth-Toller *Dictionary* prefers 'a man by spontaneous generation'. Adam of course *wasn't* spontaneously generated. But Tolkien may have wondered what the thing behind such a word could be. He must have also reflected on the strange Green Knight who comes to challenge Sir Gawain in the poem he had edited in 1925, like Tom Bombadil unflappable, a *lusus naturae* in size and colour, conveying to many critics a sense of identification with the wild wintry landscape from which he appears, called by the poet in respectful but uncertain style *an aghlich mayster*, 'a terrible Master'. The green man, the uncreated man, the man grown by 'spontaneous generation' . . . From what? Obviously, from the land. Tom Bombadil is a *genius loci*. But the *locus* of which he is the *genius* is not the barren land of the Green Knight's Pennine moors, but the river and willow country of the English midlands, or of the Thames Valley. He represents, as Tolkien said himself, 'the spirit of the (vanishing) Oxford and Berkshire countryside' (*Letters*, p. 26).

It is interesting that Tom's adversary from 1934 on is Willow-man. By *The Fellowship of the Ring* both have become attached to the River Withywindle, 'withy' of course being no more than the local word for 'willow', while 'windle' is O.E. *windol, 'winding brook'. There is a Withybrook north of Oxford, in Warwickshire, while Windsor in Berkshire to the south could be derived from *windolsora, 'the landing-place on the winding stream', in this case the Thames. As for the sudden striking description of the Withywindle in chapter 6, with its drowsy late-afternoon sunshine and through it winding lazily 'a dark river of brown water, bordered with ancient willows, arched over with willows, blocked with fallen willows, and flecked with thousands of faded willow-leaves', it would not do badly as a description of the stream that runs down to join the Thames at Oxford, the Cherwell – a 'very apt name', says Ekwall's *English River-*

Names, meaning probably 'the winding river'. The hobbits, to be brief, have got outside the Shire but not outside the boundaries of 'the Little Kingdom'. Tom is the spirit of pretty much their own land, and so like them in being slow, lavish, unbeautiful, but only stupid-seeming. Willowman is a narrower variant of the same idea, and Goldberry another in being 'the River-daughter', at first sight 'enthroned in the midst of a pool', with rippling hair and reed-green gown and flag-lilies round her waist and feet. Barrow-wight too springs from landscape, for barely fifteen miles from Oxford begins the greatest concentration of barrows in the country, where the green Berkshire downs rise from the plain. 'Wayland's Smithy' and the others must have called to Tolkien's mind the many Icelandic tales of the dwellers in the mounds, the *haugbúar* or 'hogboys' of dialect story. As for 'Bree on Bree-hill', it shows its conception in its name. Three miles from Worminghall and ten from Oxford the town of Brill sits on its hummock, betraying in its name a tale of ancient conquest.[5] 'Bree' *means* 'hill' in Welsh and Brill (from 'bree-hill') is therefore in a way nonsense, exactly parallel with Chetwode (or 'woodwood') in Berkshire close by, exactly opposite to the 'capitalised' names of The Hill, The Water or The Carrock. Tolkien borrowed the name for its faint Celtic 'style', to make subliminally the point that hobbits were immigrants too, that their land had had a history before them. But for their first hundred-odd pages the hobbits seem to be wandering through a very closely localised landscape, one even narrower than their own travels; and that landscape and the beings attached to it are in a way the heroes. They force themselves into the story. But while they slow its pace, appear strictly redundant, almost eliminate the plot centred on the Ring, they also do the same job as the maps and the names: they suggest very strongly a world which is more than imagined, whose supernatural qualities are close to entirely natural ones, one which has moreover been 'worn down', like ours, by time and by the process of lands and languages and people all growing up together over millennia. In sober daylight no linguist would care to admit that places exhale their own names any more than English counties exude Tom Bombadils. Many people however feel that names fit; and that places have a character of their own. On this not entirely irrational opinion much of Middle-earth is based.

What has just been argued naturally says little about the story in *The Fellowship of the Ring* chapters 1–10, except perhaps that it was not the author's overriding interest. Still, much could be said about that too. Probably an analysis of the fantasy in those chapters would do well to start with the things that are *not* old in Tolkien's imagination and do *not* appear to fit. It is a great moment for instance when Merry wakes from the wight's spell and remembers only a death not his own. 'The men of Carn Dûm came on us at night, and we were worsted. Ah! The spear in my heart!' He seems to have taken on the personality of the body in the barrow, but that warrior can hardly be the wight, for Bombadil remembers the dead lords and ladies with affection. So what did the wight intend, and what is it itself, human ghost or alien 'shadow' or sediment of death attaching itself to gold like the dragon-spell of avarice in *The Hobbit*? The uncertainty and the glimpses of an alien world that defies understanding (white robes, wriggling hand, sword across neck), these offer the special thrill of fantasy beyond study. However that thrill is also related to the sense of solidity already mentioned. Without the feeling that he is at once independent, *sui generis*, and also related to a larger pattern that can take in the Ring and Farmer Maggot and the elves and the Dark Lord, even Bombadil would be a lesser creation.

Stars, shadows, cellar-doors: patterns of language and of history

The basis of Tolkien's invention is unexpectedly earthbound and factual. However he was also good at peripheral suggestion. ' "Strider" I am', says Aragorn, 'to one fat man who lives within a day's march of foes that would freeze his heart, or lay his little town in ruin, if he were not guarded ceaselessly.' He does not say what the 'foes' are – wood-orcs? trolls? killer-Huorns? ettens from the high fells? – but the idea of glimpsed shapes in the sunless woods remains. In the same style Gandalf declares that 'Far, far below the deepest delving of the Dwarves, the world is gnawed by nameless things', but does not particularise. The 'things' include Durin's Bane, the Balrog (maybe the same as the creature that replies to Pippin's stone with faint knockings, but maybe not), and such beings as Shelob, Gollum, the 'fell voices' and maniac laughter of the elementals like mad Bombadils who haunt the Dimrill Stair. Sometimes a veil is lifted for a moment, as when Gandalf tells the story of Gollum and takes Frodo back for a moment to Sméagol and Déagol and their quiet empty world of pools and irises and little boats made of reeds. However more often stories are not told. Aragorn does not explain 'the cats of queen Beruthiel' (I, 325), he cuts off the tale of Gil-galad just before Frodo gets to the word 'Mordor' (I, 203), he offers only a selection from Beren and Tinúviel (I, 203–5). Gandalf says similarly that if he were to tell Frodo all the story of the Ring 'we should still be sitting here when Spring had passed into Winter', and of Sauron's loss of the Ring 'That is a chapter of ancient history which it might be good to recall ... One day, perhaps, I will tell you all the tale.' *Might* and *perhaps* are the operative words. It is a mistake to think these matters are settled by Appendices (even if some of them eventually are). Their job in context is to whet the appetite and provide perspective: they do this, perhaps, less powerfully as history than as 'myth'.

The centre of Gandalf's account in 'The Shadow of the Past' is thus the little verse about the rings, which acts as epigraph to the whole work and also as final confirmation of the nature of the Ring itself. It concludes:

> One Ring to rule them all, One Ring to find them,
> One Ring to bring them all, and in the darkness bind them
> In the land of Mordor where the Shadows lie.

The last line is a kind of internal refrain for the verse. It is echoed oddly in the snatch of song that Sam repeats a hundred and forty pages later, about Gil-galad, which ends:

> But long ago he rode away
> and where he dwelleth none can say;
> for into darkness fell his star
> in Mordor where the shadows are.

The stanza is yet *another* pause on the brink of a story, but it acts also as a corroboration. What is the relationship between the one poem and the other? Nobody says, but there must be some relationship, some body of lore that has acted as stimulus for both; and this is not Gandalf's property alone, but something (once) widely dispersed in Middle-earth.

Bits of it keep turning up. Gildor and the other elves appear at I, 88 singing a 'hymn' to Elbereth which ends 'We still remember, we who dwell/In this far land beneath the trees,/Thy starlight on the Western Seas.' The implication is that the elves are exiles, themselves living in shadow though not in Mordor, looking up to a starlight from which they are now excluded. Bombadil evokes the same image of loss when he says sixty pages later 'Few now remember them, yet still some go wandering, sons of forgotten kings walking in loneliness, guarding from evil things folk that are heedless', and his words stir in the hobbits 'a vision as it were of a great expanse of years behind them, like a vast shadowy plain over which there strode shapes of Men, tall and grim with bright swords, and last came one with a star on his brow'. We realise eventually that this last is Strider, or rather Elessar 'the Elfstone'; but Bombadil's words just before are paralleled by Bilbo's gnomic and descriptive rhyme, heard before anything of Strider's lineage is revealed:

> All that is gold does not glitter,
> Not all those who wander are lost . . .

The echoes run off in many directions, but through them run the words 'remember', 'wander', 'dwell', most of all 'star' and 'shadow'. From all these references, together with others like Aragorn's song of Beren and Tinúviel with its heavy but elusive use of 'stars in shadow', 'trembling starlight', 'shadowy hair', one could further construct a kind of repeated pattern, allegedly historical, in which stars and shadows are always at strife, the latter nearer and more powerful, the former persisting in memory and in resistance.[6] Probably no reader actually does this, but all readers nevertheless perceive something, to be confirmed, reinforced, but not supplanted later on by fuller accounts from Gandalf and Elrond, from Galadriel's song at I, 388–9, from the Appendices, eventually from *The Silmarillion*. Few readers also can fail to have resonances struck from their own familiar myths: the 'sons of Martha' story, maybe, in the grim unthanked indispensable Rangers, the Harrowing of Hell in Bilbo's 'A light from the shadows shall spring', Icarus or Prometheus or Balder Dead in the fall of Gil-galad. All these remain unfocused but not unfelt. Without extensive explanations they set the characters in a moral world as well as a geographical one, both of them like but not the same as our own.

'Gil-galad', then, has a function rather analogous to 'Nobottle'. Both offer the assurance that there is more to Middle-earth than can immediately be communicated. Among the many differences between the two names, though, is the fact that 'Gil-galad' is clearly something from an unfamiliar language; the effect of languages in Tolkien's world, as might be expected, is as great as those of maps or of myths. As might also be expected, Tolkien used them in an extremely peculiar, idiosyncratic and daring way, which takes no account at all of predictable reader-reaction. The 'myth of stars and shadows', for instance, is repeated in entirely characteristic style in a song sung in Rivendell (I, 250): 'O Elbereth who lit the stars . . . I will sing to you after having looked into far lands from here in tree-tangled Middle-earth . . .' However no reader of *The Lord of the Rings* can actually know that, since it is sung in the elvish language Sindarin and not offered in translation till p. 64 of *The Road Goes Ever On*, the song-cycle published in 1968.[7] As they stand in *The Fellowship of the Ring* they are nonsense-syllables: *A Elbereth Gilthoniel . . . Na-chaered palan-díriel o galadhremmin ennorath, Fanuilos, le linnathon*. What could any reader be expected to make of that?

Tolkien of course had an answer to the question, a private theory. It had been on his mind since 1926, when in his 'General Philology' chapter for *The Year's Work in English Studies* vol. 5 he had hinted there might be such a science as *Lautphonetik*, translatable as 'a phonology of sounds'. But all phonology is about sounds. Tolkien seems to have meant 'an aesthetics of sounds', a science that would explain why certain sounds or combinations of sounds produced different effects from others. Thirty years later he came back to the same idea in his last major learned work, the O'Donnell lecture on 'English and Welsh' given in Oxford in 1954 just after *The Fellowship of the Ring* came out. It is a discursive piece which covers many points, but one of them is a considered though not scientific attempt to say what makes a language beautiful. There is a pleasure, insisted Tolkien, 'in the phonetic elements of a language and in the style of their patterns'. More pleasure may come from 'the association of these word-forms with meanings', but that is a separate stage. Tolkien said that he had only needed to see a vocabulary-list of Gothic for his heart to be taken by storm. The same was true of Finnish; and all along something of the sort had flashed on him at the sight of Welsh names on English coal-trucks, or such simple inscriptions as *adeiladwyd 1887* on Welsh chapels.

What kind of pleasure was this? At the age of 62 Tolkien felt no urge to found a new branch of learning, and fell back on the word 'style': the pleasure comes from 'fitness . . . to a whole style', is felt in 'the reception (or imagination) of a word-form which is felt to have a certain style'. One feature of the Welsh 'style' might be 'the fondness for nasal consonants . . . and the frequency with which word-patterns are made with the soft and less sonorous *w* and the voiced spirants *f* and *dd* contrasted with the nasals: *nant, meddiant, afon, llawenydd, cenfigen, gwanwyn, gwenyn, crafanc*, to set down a few at random' (p. 40). The word and the theory were also in Tolkien's head when he wrote Appendix F to *The Lord of the Rings* and declared that he had used names like Bree, Combe, Archet and Chetwood because they contained non-English elements and he needed words to sound 'queer', to imitate 'a style that we should perhaps vaguely feel to be "Celtic" '. This was Tolkien's major linguistic heresy. He thought that people could feel history in words, could recognise language 'styles', could extract sense (of sorts) from sound alone, could moreover make aesthetic judgements based on phonology. He said the sound of 'cellar door' was more beautiful than the sound of 'beautiful'. He clearly believed that *untranslated* elvish would do a job that English could not.

Could he have been right? Tolkien's heresy was against the belief that language is only in a very limited way onomatopoeic, that we just happen from long habit to think 'pig' sounds piggish, while Danes (presumably) think *pige* sounds girlish. It was like him to think, Bombadil-style, that beneath all this there might be a 'true language', one 'isomorphic with reality', and that in any case there might often be a close connection between thing-signified, person-signifying, and language-signified-in, especially if the person who spoke the language lived on the thing. Legolas puts this view strongly in *The Two Towers* when he listens to Aragorn singing in Rohirric, a language he does not know, and then remarks (II, 112), 'That, I guess, is the language of the Rohirrim . . . for it is like to this land itself, rich and rolling in part, and else hard and stern as the mountains. But I cannot guess what it means, save that it is laden with the sadness of Mortal Men.' He is right, but his is only one of many correct appraisals in the trilogy. The hobbits hear Gildor and the elves singing, and even the ones who know no Quenya find that 'the sound blending with the melody seemed to shape itself in their thought into words which they only partly understood' (I, 88). The dirge of Gléowine for Théoden has the same effect at III, 254. Gandalf uses the Black Speech of Mordor in Rivendell at I, 267 and his voice turns 'menacing, powerful, harsh as stone', so that the elves cover their ears and Elrond rebukes him, not for what he says but for the language he says it in. Conversely Merry 'felt his heart leap' at the songs of the Muster of Rohan (III, 65); and when Gimli sings of Durin Sam Gamgee – not a learned character – responds simply and directly to the ring of elvish and dwarvish names. ' "I like that!" said Sam. "I should like to learn it. *In Moria, in Khazad-dûm!*" ' Obviously his response is a model one.

One can see from all this why Tolkien made the seemingly wild assertion, in 1955, that to him his work was 'largely an essay in linguistic esthetic' (*Letters*, p. 220). One can also see that he was convinced his heresy had worked, for at the end of his remarks on 'the Welsh linguistic style' in 'English and Welsh' he brought forward *The Lord of the Rings* not as fiction but as evidence, declaring: 'the names of persons and places in this story were mainly composed on patterns deliberately modelled on those of Welsh (closely similar but not identical). This element in the tale has given perhaps more pleasure to more readers than anything else in it.' 'Mainly' is a bit of an exaggeration; the Welsh-modelled names in Middle-earth are only those of Gondor and of Elvish, or more accurately of Sindarin, and these are precisely the most doubtful cases. Many English readers, however, accustomed to the linguistic map of England with its varying Anglo-Saxon, Old Norse and Welsh components, might in all sobriety be able to say 'Garstang sounds northern' or 'Tolpuddle sounds West Country', and be able to go on from there to cope with the varying styles of the Shire, the Riddermark and the dwarves. There must be much more doubt over how many readers grasp first-hand that the Rivendell song at I, 250 is in Sindarin but Galadriel's at I, 394 in Quenya, and that these two languages are furthermore related. Still, it would be as wrong to say that readers understand nothing of alien songs as to say they understand everything. As with place-names, landscapes, mythic fragments, 'feel' or 'style' is enough, however much it escapes a cerebral focus.

Tolkien's linguistic map of Middle-earth furthermore shows exception-ally well the relation in his mind between 'inspiration' and 'invention'. One could argue that much of what he decided was forced on him: mere 'invention' to get out of difficulty. Thus it was inevitable that the story should be in modern English, and from the start of *The Hobbit* it was clear that the Bagginses at least were English by temperament and turn of phrase. Now Tolkien knew (none better) that logically this was impossible. He was committed then to a fiction in which 'hobbitic' was an *analogue* of English, was in fact a 'stylistically' neutral variant of a Common Speech. What then of dwarvish? Dwarf-names were already there in *The Hobbit*, and were in Old Norse, a language whose relationship to modern English was to Tolkien all but tangible. The dwarves then must have spoken a language analogous to the Common Speech in exactly the same way as Old Norse is to modern English; and since that was hardly likely in the case of two totally different species (men and hobbits are not really different species, see I, 11), Tolkien found himself committed also to the notion that the dwarves spoke human languages and used human names for convenience, but had a secret language and secret names of their own, the latter not even to be carved on tombs (a belief which he no doubt enjoyed because of its corroboration in the Grimms' 'Rumpelstiltskin'). Having fitted in English and Norse, Old English could not be far behind: hence the Riders with their entirely Old English terminology, their names which are often Old English nouns capitalised (like Théoden King, a phrase of exactly the same type as Bree-hill),[8] the sense the characters occasionally indicate that 'hobbitic' is a worn-down variant of Rohirric in which words are changed but sound (II, 163) 'not unfitting'. But by this stage 'invention' has stopped and 'inspiration' taken over. In the conversation between Pippin, Merry and Théoden outside Isengard Tolkien is no longer trying to explain old inconsistencies from *The Hobbit*, but writing ever deeper into a world with a life of its own.

This led him, indeed, into yet further inconsistencies, or rather disingenuousnesses. Tolkien was obliged to pretend to be a 'translator'. He developed the pose with predictable rigour, feigning not only a text to translate but behind it a whole manuscript tradition, from Bilbo's diary to the Red Book of Westmarch to the Thain's Book of Minas Tirith to the copy of the scribe Findegil. As time went on he also felt obliged to stress the autonomy of Middle-earth – the fact that he was only translating analogously, not writing down the names and places as they really had been, etc. Thus of the Riddermark and its relation to Old English he said eventually 'This linguistic procedure [i.e. translating Rohirric into Old English] does not imply that the Rohirrim closely resembled the ancient English otherwise, in culture or art, in weapons or modes of warfare, except in a general way due to their circumstances...' (III, 414). But this claim is totally untrue. With one admitted exception, the Riders of Rohan resemble the Anglo-Saxons down to minute details. The fact is that the ancient languages came first. Tolkien did not draw them into a fiction he had already written because there they might be useful, though that is what he pretended. He wrote the fiction to present the languages, and he did that because he loved them and thought them intrinsically beautiful. Maps, names and languages came before plot. Elaborating them was in a sense Tolkien's way of building up enough steam to get rolling; but they had also in a sense provided the motive to want to. They were 'inspiration' and 'invention' at once, or perhaps more accurately, by turns.

'The Council of Elrond'

The gist of what has been said in this chapter is that *The Lord of the Rings* possesses unusual cultural depth. 'Culture' is not a word Tolkien used much; it changed meaning sharply during his lifetime, and not in a direction he approved. Still, one can see a deep understanding of its modern meaning of 'the whole complex of learned behaviour . . . the material possessions, the language and other symbolism, of some body of people' in chapter 2 of Book II of *The Fellowship of the Ring*. This marks a jump-off point for the characters, whose objective is disclosed within it. It was also I suspect a jump-off point for Tolkien, since after that he was no longer writing his way through landscapes he had travelled before. It is therefore perhaps not surprising that as with the house of Beorn in *The Hobbit* 'The Council of Elrond' should provide a sudden introduction to archaic and heroic worlds confronting and overwhelming modern, practical ones. The later work is, however, many degrees more complex than its earlier analogue, being indeed an interweaving of at least six major voices besides minor ones and reported ones; as well as telling a complex tale in complex fashion what all these voices do is present, in our language, a violent 'culture-clash'.

This comes out most in the speeches and scripts impacted *inside* Gandalf's monologue of pages 269–78, the fifth and longest from a major speaker (the others coming from Glóin, Elrond, Boromir, Aragorn, Legolas). Within that monologue Gaffer Gamgee functions as a kind of base-line of normality – and, concomitantly, of emptiness. 'I had words with old Gamgee', Gandalf reports, 'Many words and few to the point':

> ' "I can't abide changes," said he, "not at my time of life, and least of all changes for the worst." "Changes for the worst," he repeated many times.
> ' "Worst is a bad word," I said to him, "and I hope you do not live to see it." '

It is indeed a bad word, especially when all the Gaffer has to complain about is the Sackville-Bagginses; Denethor uses it as well, much later (III, 87), but again with ominous effect. As for 'abide', as used by Gaffer Gamgee it has almost no semantic content at all; in context it means 'bear, tolerate, put up with', but in that sense is simply untrue. The Gaffer *can* abide changes; he just has. He means only that he doesn't like them. But there is a moral for him in the history of the word, which has the frequent early sense of 'to await the issue of, to wait (stoically) for, to live to see'. In this last sense the Gaffer *could* 'abide' changes, and he does. Right at the end he moralises, stubborn as ever, 'It's an ill wind as blows nobody any good, *as I always say*' (my italics), 'And All's well as ends Better' (III, 302). At least he has learnt to eschew superlatives. But his language in Gandalf's monologue conveys an unwelcome reminder of psychological unpreparedness.

His son Sam re-establishes the hobbits slightly with his terminal comment, 'A nice pickle we have landed ourselves in, Mr Frodo', for though he is as obtuse as his father – Sam got himself into trouble, but Frodo did not – this blindness does co-exist with a thoughtless courage, a relish for gloom, and a refusal to see Doomsday as more than a 'pickle', all adding up to the notorious Anglo-hobbitic inability to know when they're beaten. However there is another modern voice in Gandalf's monologue to act as vehicle for cultural contrast: this is Saruman's. He has hardly been mentioned before, and the question whether he is good or bad is more difficult to decide than with most. But when he is introduced by Gandalf, we know what to think very soon; the message is conveyed by style and lexis. Saruman talks like a politician. 'We can bide our time', he says, using a fossilised phrase:

'we can keep our thoughts in our hearts, deploring maybe evils done by the way, but approving the high and ultimate purpose: Knowledge, Rule, Order, all things that we have so far striven in vain to accomplish, hindered rather than helped by our weak or idle friends. There need not be, there would not be, any real change in our designs, only in our means.' (I, 272–3)

What Saruman says encapsulates many of the things the modern world has learnt to dread most: the ditching of allies, the subordination of means to ends, the 'conscious acceptance of guilt in the necessary murder'. But the way he puts it is significant too. No other character in Middle-earth has Saruman's trick of balancing phrases against each other so that incompatibles are resolved, and none comes out with words as empty as 'deploring', 'ultimate', worst of all, 'real'. What is a 'real change'? The *OED*'s three columns of definition offer nothing appropriate; the word has got below dictionary level. As we all know, 'real' is now a word like 'sincere' or 'genuine', a word whose meaning its speaker asks you to take for granted, a politician's word, an advertiser's word. 'Real change' shows Saruman up with even greater economy than 'changes for the worst' does Gaffer Gamgee.

By contrast with these familiar styles and voices several of the other participants in the Council come over as archaic, blunt, clear-sighted. Gandalf himself uses an older vocabulary than usual, as if to authenticate himself, and Elrond's speech (256–8), as is only suitable for one so old, is full of old-fashioned inversions of syntax and words like 'weregild', 'esquire', 'shards'. Its burden is to state the Northern 'theory of courage', as Tolkien called it in his British Academy lecture, whose central thesis is that even ultimate defeat does not turn right into wrong.† Elrond has

† For all its age this was evidently still a vital belief for Tolkien, and for other Inklings too. In C. S. Lewis's most Tolkienian work *That Hideous Strength* (1945), Mark Studdock for all his failings reinvents it spontaneously at the end of chapter 15, section IV. The book also contains some fine Saruman-style speeches.

seen 'many defeats, and many fruitless victories', and in a way he has even given up hope, at least for his adopted people the elves (see I, 282 and further III, 315); but this does not make him change his mind or look for easy options.

The heroic note is struck most firmly, however, by the dwarf Glóin, or rather by his report of the dialogue between Sauron's messenger and that exemplar of stubbornness King Dáin. The messenger offers 'great reward and lasting friendship' in return for information about hobbits, or for the Ring. If Dáin refuses, he says:

' "... things will not seem so well."
'At that his breath came like the hiss of snakes, and all who stood by shuddered, but Dáin said: "I say neither yea nor nay. I must consider this message and what it means under its fair cloak."
' "Consider well, but not too long," said he.
' "The time of my thought is my own to spend," answered Dáin.
' "For the present," said he, and rode into the darkness.'

We get exchanges like this several times in *The Lord of the Rings*, mostly involving dwarves: Elrond and Gimli swap grim proverbs in the next chapter, Théoden King silences Merry in similarly abrupt style in Book V chapter 2, and Appendix A offers several dwarvish dialogues around the battle of Azanulbizar. Their unifying feature is delight in the contrast between passionate interior and polite or rational expression; the weakness of the latter is an index of the strength of the former. Thus the messenger's 'things will not seem so well' works as violent threat; 'not too long' means 'extremely rapidly'. In reply Dáin's 'fair cloak' implies 'foul body' and the obscure metaphor of spending the 'time of my thought' indicates refusal to negotiate under threat. Both participants seek to project a cool, ironic self-control. If Elrond's recommendation was courage, and Gandalf's hope, Dáin's contribution to the ethical mix of the Council is a kind of unyielding scepticism. This virtue is no longer much practised, swept away by the tide of salesmanship, winning friends and influencing people, the belief that all aggression is dissolved by smiles. We no longer even have a name for it – except perhaps that people who call their tea their 'baggins' might recognise it in their approving use of 'bloody-mindedness' (not recorded by the *OED*). Whatever it is, it comes over in Dáin's speech as a force: words imply ethics, and the ethics of the spokesmen of Middle-earth fit together, beneath surface variation. None of them but Saruman pays any attention to expediency, practicality, *Realpolitik*, 'political realism'.

Any one of the counsellors in this chapter would bear similar analysis. Gandalf's account of Isildur makes a point through its combination of ancient words and endings ('glede', 'fadeth', 'loseth', etc.) with sudden recall of the words of Bilbo and Gollum. 'It is precious to me, though I buy it with great pain'; the 'reality of human nature' persists. More subtly Aragorn and Boromir strike sparks off each other through their ways of speech as well as their claims, Aragorn's language deceptively modern, even easy-going on occasion, but with greater range than Boromir's slightly wooden magniloquence. There is even significance in Aragorn letting his rival have the last word in their debate, with a clause which is perfectly in line with modern speech – 'we will put it to the test one day' – but also relates easily to the vaunts of ancient heroes, like Ælfwine's *nú mæg cunnian hwá céne sý* in *The Battle of Maldon*, 'now who is bold can be put to the test'. Still, the overriding points are these: the 'information content' of 'The Council of Elrond' is very high, much higher than can be recorded by analyses like this; much of that information is carried by linguistic mode; nevertheless most readers assimilate the greater part of it; in the process they gain an image of the 'life-styles' of Middle-earth the solider for its occasional contrasts with modernity. Language variation gives Tolkien a thorough and economical way of dramatising ethical debate.

The horses of the Mark

This virtue is easily missed by critics or reviewers skimming through for the plot; and perhaps we have now reached one reason for the enormous difference of opinion between Tolkien's admirers and his detractors. The whole of *The Lord of the Rings* is on its larger scale like 'The Council of Elrond'. Through both there runs a narrative thread, but just as the single chapter relies for a great part of its effect on the relishing of stylistic variation, so the work as a whole depends very largely on *tableaux*: separate images of places, peoples, societies, all in some way furthering the story, but sometimes (as with Bombadil or Willow-man) not furthering it very much, there mostly or largely for their own sake. Someone not prepared to read slowly enough – Tolkien thought his books were best read aloud – might paradoxically write off the story as 'slow' or 'nerveless'; and there would be a basis of truth for the observation *as long as it confined itself to the story*. But this is a poor way to appreciate the whole.

Any one of Tolkien's *tableaux* would stand analysis, and the obvious one to choose is perhaps Gondor. However I prefer to start with the Riders of Rohan, not the first children of Tolkien's imagination but the ones he regarded with most affection and also in a sense the most central. In creating them Tolkien was once again playing with his own background and his home in 'the Little Kingdom'. Thus 'Rohan' is only the Gondorian word for the Riders' country; they themselves call it 'the Mark'. Now there is no English county called 'the Mark', but the Anglo-Saxon kingdom which included both Tolkien's home-town Birmingham and his *alma mater* Oxford was 'Mercia' – a Latinism now adopted by historians mainly because the native term was never recorded. However the West Saxons called their neighbours the *Mierce*, clearly a derivation (by 'i-mutation') from *Mearc*; the 'Mercians' ' own pronunciation of that would certainly have been the 'Mark', and that was no doubt once the everyday term for central England. As for the 'white horse on the green field' which is the emblem of the Mark, you can see it cut into the chalk fifteen miles from Tolkien's study, two miles from 'Wayland's Smithy' and just about on the borders of 'Mercia' and Wessex, as if to mark the kingdom's end. All the Riders' names and language are Old English, as many have noted;† but they were homely to Tolkien in an even deeper sense than that.

As has already been remarked, though, the Riders according to Tolkien did not resemble the 'ancient English . . . except in a general way due to their circumstances: a simpler and more primitive people living in contact with a higher and more venerable culture, and occupying lands that had once been part of its domain'. Tolkien was stretching the truth a long way in asserting that, to say the least! But there is one obvious difference between the people of Rohan and the 'ancient English', and that is horses. The Rohirrim call themselves the Éothéod (Old English *eoh*='horse'+*þéod*='people'); this translates into Common Speech as 'the Riders'; Rohan itself is Sindarin for 'horse-country'. Prominent Riders call themselves after horses (Éomund, Éomer, Éowyn), and their most important title after 'King' is 'marshall', borrowed into English from French but going back to an unrecorded Germanic *marho-skalkoz*, 'horse-servant' (and cp. the name of the hobbits' Hengest). The Rohirrim are nothing if not cavalry. By contrast the Anglo-Saxons' reluctance to have anything militarily to do with horses is notorious. *The Battle of Maldon* begins, significantly enough, with the horses being sent to the rear. Hastings was lost, along with Anglo-Saxon independence, largely because the English heavy infantry could not (quite) hold off the combination of archers and mounted knights. The *Anglo-Saxon Chronicle* entry for 1055 remarks sourly that at Hereford 'before a spear was thrown the English fled, because they had been made to fight on horseback'. How then can Anglo-Saxons and Rohirrim ever, culturally, be equated?

A part of the answer is that the Rohirrim are not to be equated with the Anglo-Saxons of history, but with those of poetry, or legend. The chapter 'The King of the Golden Hall' is straightforwardly calqued on *Beowulf*. When Legolas says of Meduseld, 'The light of it shines far over the land', he is translating line 311 of *Beowulf*, *lixte se léoma ofer landa fela*.

† Not many have noted that they are not in the 'standard' or 'classical' West Saxon dialect of Old English but in what is thought to have been its Mercian parallel: so Saruman, Hasufel, Herugrim for 'standard' Searuman, Heasufel, Heorugrim, and cp. *Mearc* and *Marc*. In *Letters* p. 65 Tolkien threatens to speak nothing but 'Old Mercian'.

'Meduseld' is indeed a Beowulfian word (line 3065) for 'hall'. More importantly the poem and the chapter agree, down to minute detail, on the procedure for approaching kings. In *Beowulf* the hero is stopped first by a coastguard, then by a doorward, and only after two challenges is allowed to approach the Danish King; he and his men have to 'pile arms' outside as well. Tolkien follows this dignified, step-by-step ceremonial progress exactly. Thus in 'The King of the Golden Hall' Gandalf, Aragorn, Legolas and Gimli are checked first by the guards at the gates of Edoras (='enclosures'), and then by the doorward of Meduseld, Háma. He too insists on the ceremony of piling arms, though Tolkien's characters object more than Beowulf does, largely because he is a volunteer and in any case fights by choice bare-handed. There is a crisis over Gandalf's staff, indeed, and Háma broods, reflecting rightly that 'The staff in the hand of a wizard may be more than a prop for age'; he settles his doubts with the maxim 'Yet in doubt a man of worth will trust to his own wisdom. I believe you are friends and folk of honour, who have no evil purpose. You may go in.' In saying so he echoes the maxim of the coastguard of *Beowulf* (lines 287–92), 'a sharp shield-warrior must know how to tell good from bad in every case, from words as well as deeds. I hear [from your words] that this warband is friendly . . . I will guide you.'

The point is not, though, that Tolkien is once more writing a 'calqued' narrative, but that he is taking advantage of a modern expansive style to spell out things that would have been obvious to Anglo-Saxons – in particular, the truths that freedom is not a prerogative of democracies, and that in free societies orders give way to discretion. Háma takes a risk with Gandalf; so does the coastguard with Beowulf. So does Éomer with Aragorn, letting him go free and lending him horses. He is under arrest when Aragorn re-appears, and Théoden notes Háma's dereliction of duty too. Still, the nice thing about the Riders, one might say, is that though 'a stern people, loyal to their lord', they wear duty and loyalty lightly. Háma and Éomer make their own decisions, and even the suspicious gate-ward wishes Gandalf luck. 'I was only obeying orders', we can see, would *not* be accepted as an excuse in the Riddermark. Nor would it in *Beowulf*. The wisdom of ancient epic is translated by Tolkien into a whole sequence of doubts, decisions, sayings, rituals.

One could go further and say that the Riders spring from poetry not history in that the whole of their culture is based on *song*. Almost the first thing Gandalf and the others see, nearing Meduseld, are the mounds covered in *simbelmynë* either side of the way. *Simbelmynë* is a little white flower, but also means 'ever-mind', 'ever-memory', 'forget-me-not'. Like the barrows it stands for the preservation of the memory of ancient deeds and heroes in the expanse of years. The Riders are fascinated by memorial verse and oblivion, by deaths and by epitaphs. They show it in their list of kingly pedigrees, from Théoden back to Eorl the Young, in the suicidal urges of Éomer and Éowyn to do 'deeds of song',[9] in the song that Aragorn sings to set the tone of the culture he is visiting:

'Where now the horse and the rider? Where is the horn that was blowing?
Where is the helm and the hauberk, and the bright hair flowing? . . .'

Most of all it comes over in the alliterative dirges made for Théoden by Gléowine, for the dead of Pelennor by an anonymous 'maker', even in the rhyming couplet made for the horse Snowmane. These preserve the sonority, the sadness, the feeling for violent opposites ('death' and 'day', 'lords' and 'lowly', 'halls' and 'pastures') integrated in the Riders' language and culture. Their visual correlatives, one might say, are the spears planted in burial-mounds by Fangorn and at the Fords of Isen; or perhaps the spears are the men and the mounds are poems, for Éomer says of one burial, 'when their spears have rotted and rusted, long still may their mounds stand and guard the Fords of Isen!' The men die and their weapons rust. But their memory remains, passes into *simbelmynë*, 'evermind', the oral heritage of the race.

One should see at this point how far Tolkien's imagination surpasses that of most fantasy-writers. Proud barbarians are ten a penny in modern fantasy. Hardly one of their creators grasps the fact that barbarians are sensitive too: that a heroic way of life preoccupies men with death and with the feeble, much-prized resistances to death which their cultures can offer. Of course Tolkien drew his knowledge from Old English, from that literature whose greatest monument is not an epic but the 'dirge' of *Beowulf*; 'The King of the Golden Hall' echoes that poem as closely as Aragorn's song above echoes the Old English *Wanderer*. However Tolkien was trying to go beyond translation to 'reconstruction'. And this is what explains the horses. The feeling of Anglo-Saxon poetry for these was markedly different from that of Anglo-Saxon history. Thus the retainers of *Beowulf* joyfully race their *mearas* back from the monsters' lake as they sing their praise songs; the ancient gnomic poem *Maxims I* observes enthusiastically that 'a good man will keep in mind a good, well-broken horse, familiar, well-tried, and round-hoofed'; it has already been noted that the same poem declared that 'an earl goes on the arched back of a war-horse, a mounted troop (*éored*) must ride in a body', only for a historical Anglo-Saxon scribe to rewrite *éored* foolishly as *worod* or '(foot) body guard'. Tolkien may have known that the confusing Anglo-Saxon words for colour were once words for the colour of horses' coats, like Hasufel='grey coat', suggesting an early society as observant of horses as modern African tribes of cows.[10] Maybe the infantry-fixation of historical periods was the result of living on an island. Maybe the Anglo-Saxons *before they migrated to England* were different. What would have happened had they turned East, not West, to the German plains and the steppes beyond?

In creating the Riddermark Tolkien thought of his own 'Mercia'. He also certainly remembered the great lost romance of 'Gothia' (see pp. 11–15 above), of the close kin of the English turning to disaster and oblivion on the plains of Russia. No doubt he knew the dim tradition that the word 'Goths' itself meant 'Horse-folk'.[11] This is what adds 'reconstruction' to 'calquing' and produces fantasy, a people and a culture that never were, but that press closer and closer to the edge of might-have-been. The Riders gain life from their mixture of homely, almost hobbitic familiarity with a strong dash of something completely alien. Éomer is a nice young man, but there is a streak of nomad ferocity in the way he and his men taunt Aragorn and company with their narrowing circle of horses and Éomer's silent advance 'until the point of his spear was within a foot of Aragorn's breast'. They behave like mail-shirted Red Indians. And like a Middle-earth Deerslayer Aragorn 'did not stir', recognising the nomad appreciation of impassivity. A certain craziness shows itself in the Rohirric psychology at other points, as Éowyn rides in search of death and Éomer, sure he is doomed to die, laughs out loud for joy. The Dunlendings have heard that the Riders 'burned their prisoners alive'. Tolkien denies it, but there is something in his description that keeps the image alive.

For all this there is, once more, a visual correlative, and it is the first flash of individuality Éomer is given; he is (II, 34) 'taller than all the rest; from his helm as a crest a white horsetail flowed'. A horsetail plume is the traditional prerogative of the Huns and the Tartars and the steppe-folk, a most un-English decoration, at least by tradition.† Yet it comes to prominence several times. Across the chaotic battlefield of Pelennor it is 'the white crest of Éomer' that Merry picks out from the 'great front of the Rohirrim', and when Théoden charges at last, opposing hornblast and poetry to horror and despair, behind him come his knights and his banner, 'white horse upon a field of green', and Éomer, 'the white horsetail on his helm floating in his speed'. As it happens, there is a word for both Éomer's decoration and the Riders' collective quality, but it is not an English word: it is *panache*, the crest on the knight's helmet, but also the virtue of sudden onset, the dash that sweeps away resistance. This is exactly the opposite of English 'doggedness', and is a virtue traditionally regarded with massive suspicion by English generals. However *panache* in both the abstract and concrete senses help to define the Riders, to present them as simultaneously English and alien, to offer a glimpse of the way land shapes people. Théoden's kindly interest in herbs and hobbits (they would have had him smoking a pipe, given time) co-exists with his peremptory decisions and sudden furies. It is a strange mixture but not an

† The Assistant Curator of the Household Cavalry Museum, Mr C. W. Frearson, informs me that the now-familiar white horsetail plumes of the Life Guards are an innovation brought in by Prince Albert in 1842. The Prince was copying a Prussian style itself copied from Russian regiments.

implausible one. There must have been people like that once, if we only knew.

The edges of the Mark

The Mark works on a system of contrasts and similarities. This is rationally based and even has a sort of historical integrity; but as with place-names and elvish songs no one can tell how much of the author's system is apprehended unconsciously by the un-studious reader. The evidence suggests, though, that it is quite a lot: that the difference between Tolkien and Robert E. Howard, say, or E. R. Eddison or James Branch Cabell, lies precisely in his intense and brooding systematisation, never analytically presented but always deliberately nurtured (if not deliberately conceived). The planning behind Tolkien's cultural *tableaux* shows in the further set of contrasts and similarities round the Mark – contrasts which work, it should be noted, both inside the story (i.e. contrasts between Rohan and Gondor, Rohan and the Shire, Éomer and Gimli, etc.) and outside it (i.e. the running inevitable comparison of all those societies and the real one, the one we ourselves live in). Tolkien obviously worked at these just as he worked at the stylistic clashes of 'The Council of Elrond', and for the same reason, to provide cultural solidity.

Thus there are three scenes at least where the men of the Mark are opposed to the men of Gondor. These are the two 'meetings in the wilderness', of Éomer and his men with Aragorn, Legolas and Gimli (II, 32–42), and of Faramir and his men with Frodo and Sam (II, 265–91); the two set-piece 'building descriptions' of Meduseld (II, 116) and the great hall of Minas Tirith (III, 26); the longer comparisons of the dotage, cure and death of Théoden with the corruption, relapse and suicide of Denethor – two old men who have both lost their sons. All these characterise cultures as much as people. To take the first one first, there are all manner of similarities between Éomer's position and Faramir's, for both men come upon lonely trespassers, both have orders to detain such people, both would gain something by doing so, whether Narsil or the Ring, and both in the end make their own minds up, let the strangers go and offer them assistance. Yet in the end difference is perhaps more prominent than likeness.

Éomer for one thing is compulsively truculent. It *is* compulsive, for when his men move away he becomes much easier, but he takes little care to be polite. A large part of the reason is ignorance, signalled by almost his first speech, 'Are you elvish folk?' The answer that one of them is surprises him, for 'elvish' to him as to the *Gawain*-poet just means 'uncanny'. Éomer and his men are sceptics, about the Golden Wood, about elves, about halflings; they are also in a way superstitious (a combination Tolkien thought common enough), for Éomer says Saruman is 'dwimmercrafty', using an old word for 'nightmare' or 'illusion' to say that wizards are 'skinturners' like Beorn, which as far as we know they are not. By contrast Faramir comes over as wiser, deeper, older; but this is a function of his society not himself. He keeps using the post-Anglo-Saxon word 'courtesy', which like 'civilisation' or 'urbanity' implies a post-nomadic and settled state of culture. Frodo's courteous speech is one reason why Faramir recognises in him 'an elvish air', the word used this time in a sense exactly opposite to Éomer's disapprobation. Faramir is patient, too, and though both he and Éomer assert strongly their hatred of lies it is fair to say that Faramir allows himself a relatively oblique approach to truth. He asks fewer direct questions; he hides the fact that he knows Boromir is dead; he lets Sam change the subject when they get too close to Isildur's Bane and the Ring. He smiles, as well. While the Gondorians are dignified and even say a kind of 'grace', they are not as much *on* their dignity as the Riders, or as stiffly ceremonious as Shire-hobbits. Faramir is self-assured, in a word, and he explains why in his account of the Kings and Stewards and Northmen, the High and Middle peoples. Both he and Éomer think Boromir was nearer the Middle than the High, but Éomer thinks that is all to the good while Faramir does not. The two contrasted scenes are making a very strong assertion about cultural evolution.

The balance is redressed, maybe, by Théoden and Denethor. If one looks at their houses the latter's is the greater achievement, but it is lifeless. 'No hangings or storied webs, nor any things of woven stuff or of wood, were to be seen in that long solemn hall; but between the pillars there stood a silent company of tall images graven in cold stone.' In this sentence the word that stands out is 'web', for it is Old English, the normal Anglo-Saxon word for 'tapestry' (cp. the name 'Webster'). The criticism of life-lessness is one a Rider might have made. By contrast the corresponding scene in Meduseld is dominated by the *fág flór*, the floor 'paved with stones of many hues', and by the sunlit image of the young man on the white horse, blowing a great horn, with yellow hair flying and the horse's red nostrils displayed as it smells 'battle afar'. Yet the bravura of the Riders' culture is also complemented by one odd word, the 'louver' in the roof that lets the smoke out and the sunbeams in. This is a late word, French-derived, not recorded till 1393. If the Anglo-Saxons had such things they called them something else. One might say that the Riders have learnt from Gondor, but not vice versa. If that is too much to build on two words, one can certainly say that the behaviour of Denethor, indeed the very self-assuredness he shares with his son, points to the weaknesses of civilised cultures: over-subtlety, selfishness, abandonment of the 'theory of courage', a calculation that turns suicidal. Gandalf can cure Théoden; but Denethor almost makes me use the word 'neurotic' (first recorded in the modern sense five years before Tolkien was born).

Such ramifications are almost inexhaustible, but their core is history –

real history, but history philological-style, not in the footprints of Edward Gibbon. That is why it was said earlier that the Riders were in a sense central. Whether one thinks of them as Anglo-Saxons or as Goths, they represent the bit that Tolkien knew best. Against them Gondor is a kind of Rome, also a kind of mythical Wales of the sort that bred King Coel and King Arthur and King Lear. On their southern border are the 'Woses', an Old English word and an Anglo-Saxon bogey, surviving mis-understood into *Sir Gawain* like the word 'elvish' and enjoying a last flicker of life in the common English name 'Woodhouse' (see note on pp. 50–1 above). To the North are the Ents, another Old English word which had interested Tolkien since he first wrote on Roman roads in 1924, and identified them with the *orþanc enta geweorc*, the 'skilful work of ents' of the poem *Maxims II*. Anglo-Saxons believed in ents, as in woses. What were they? Clearly they were very large, great builders, and clearly they didn't exist any more. From such hints Tolkien created his fable of a race running down to extinction.

However the point that should be taken by now is not just that Tolkien worked by 'reconstruction' or from the premise that poetry is in essence true; rather it is that his continual play with calques and cruxes gave *The Lord of the Rings* a dinosaur-like vitality which cannot be conveyed in any synopsis, but reveals itself in so many thousands of details that only the most biased critical mind could miss them all. It is not a paradox to say further that this decentralised life is also at the same time 'nuggety', tending always to focus on names and words and the things or realities which lie behind them. The first Rohirric place-name we hear is 'Eastemnet', followed soon by 'Westemnet'. An 'emnet' is a thing in Middle-earth, also a place in Norfolk, also an asterisk-word, *emnmæþ* for 'steppe' or 'prairie', also the green grass which the Riders use as a touchstone for reality. Everything Tolkien wrote was based on fusions like that, on 'woses' and 'emnets' and *éoreds*, on 'elvish' or *orthanc* or *panaches*.

'Magyk natureel'

Like a goldfish in a weedy pool, the theme that flashes from much of Tolkien's work is that of the identity of man and nature, of namer and named. It was probably his strongest belief, stronger even than his Catholicism (though of course he hoped the two were at some level reconciled). It was what drove Tolkien to write; he created Middle-earth before he had a plot to put in it, and at every delay or failure of 'inspiration' he went back to the map and to the landscape, for Bombadil and the Shire, the Mark and the ents. Through all his work moreover there runs an obsessive interest in plants and scenery, pipeweed and *athelas*, the crown of stonecrop round the overthrown king's head in Ithilien, the staffs of *lebethron*-wood with a 'virtue' on them of finding and returning, given by Faramir to Sam and Frodo, the holly-tree outside Moria that marks the frontier of 'Hollin' as the White Horse of Uffington shows the boundary of the Mark, and over all the closely visualised images of dells and dingles and Wellinghalls, hollow trees and clumps of bracken and bramble-coverts for the hobbits to creep into. The *simbelmynë*, as has been said, is a kind of symbol for the Riders, and the *mallorn* does the same for Galadriel's elves. The hobbits are only just separable from the Shire, and Tom Bombadil not at all from the Withywindle. Fangorn is a name for both character and forest, and as character he voices more strongly than anybody else the identity of name and namer and thing. 'Real names tell you the story of the things they belong to in my language', he says, but it seems unlikely that anyone but an ent could learn Old Entish. With Bombadil the identity of name and thing gives the namer a kind of magic. With the hobbits much the same effect is created by simple harmony. They don't in fact practise magic, says the 'Prologue', but the impression that they do is derived from 'close friendship with the earth'. Earth and magic and non-human species are all in differing proportions very closely combined. The voices that explain this to us, Fangorn's and the narrator's, are authoritative and indeed, especially Fangorn, 'professorial'. They admit no denial.

There is a sense, even, in which the non-human characters of *The Lord of the Rings are* natural objects: a tenuous sense but one deeply ingrained. On his first appearance Fangorn is seen by Pippin and Merry but categorised as 'one old stump of a tree with only two bent branches left: it looked almost like the figure of some gnarled old man, standing there, blinking in the morning light' (II, 65). Gandalf a little later speaks of his struggle with the Balrog and asks himself how it would have seemed to outside observers; just thunder and lightning, he replies. 'Thunder, they heard, and lightning, they said, smote upon Celebdil, and leaped back broken into tongues of fire. Is not that enough?' (II, 105). As for the elves and Elrond and Gandalf, how would they have seemed to mortal senses? Near the end Tolkien replies:

> If any wanderer had chanced to pass, little would he have seen or heard, and it would have seemed to him only that he saw grey figures, carved in stone, memorials of forgotten things now lost in unpeopled lands. For they did not move or speak with mouth, looking from mind to mind; and only their shining eyes stirred and kindled as their thoughts went to and fro. (III, 263)

At the end they fade into the stones and the shadows.

'Fade', or 'turn'? The future fate of the elves is often mentioned in *The Lord of the Rings* but never becomes quite clear. Some will leave

Middle-earth, some will stay. Those who stay, says Galadriel, will 'dwindle to a rustic folk of dell and cave, slowly to forget and to be forgotten'. 'Dwindle' could have a demographic meaning; there could be fewer of them. It could be physical too, looking forward to the 'tiny elves' of Shakespeare, and even moral, making one think of the detached, cruel, soulless elves of Scottish and Danish tradition. The best fate for the elves who stay, perhaps, would be to turn into landscape. There is a local legend of that kind attached to the Rollright Stones on the north edge of Oxfordshire, mentioned for a moment in *Farmer Giles of Ham*. These, says the story,[12] were once an old king and his men. Challenged by a witch to take seven strides over the hill and look into the valley below, the king found his view blocked by a barrow and the witch's curse fulfilled:

> 'Rise up, stick, and stand still, stone,
> For king of England thou shalt be none.
> Thou and thy men hoar stones shall be
> And I myself an eldern-tree.'

The stones are still there, mysterious and by tradition uncountable. And though it may seem hard-hearted to wish for people to be petrified, it does assure them a kind of existence, a kind of integrity with the land they come from.

It's hard to say, declares Sam Gamgee of the elves of Lothlórien, 'Whether they've made the land, or the land's made them' (I, 376). And his perceptions are often deep, even if his education has been neglected. His further explanation may be taken to refer to *The Lord of the Rings* as well as to Lothlórien: 'Nothing seems to be going on,' he says, 'and nobody seems to want it to. If there's any magic about, it's right down deep, where I can't lay my hands on it, in a manner of speaking.' Yes, agrees Frodo, complementing Sam's style as often with his own. Still, 'You can see and feel it everywhere'.

Chapter 5

INTERLACEMENTS AND THE RING

A problem in corruption

Lothlórien has won many hearts, and even the most censorious of Tolkien's critics have accordingly been ready to grant him the ability to create nice settings. 'What is outstanding, though, is the scenery', declared the kindly reviewer for the *Bath and West Evening Chronicle* (7 December 1974). However good scenery is not one of the major virtues on the critical scale; many published opinions throw it in as a sop, a makeweight to balance what they see as much more serious flaws deep in the heart of the Tolkienian 'fable', in the essential story of *The Lord of the Rings*. The characters, it is often alleged, are flat; there is not enough awareness of sexuality; good and evil are presented as absolutes, without a proper sense of inner conflict within individuals; there is something incoherent in the 'main pattern' of the story, which prevents one from reading it as 'a connected allegory with a clear message for the modern world'. Most of all, *The Lord of the Rings* is felt not to be true to 'the fundamental character of reality', not to mirror 'an adult experience of the world', not to portray 'an emotional truth about humanity'. Professor Mark Roberts, speaking from the centre of the critical consensus, declared: 'It doesn't issue from an understanding of reality which is not to be denied, it is not moulded by some controlling vision of things which is at the same time its *raison d'être*.' The archaism of the settings, in short, goes along with an escapism of intention, a deliberate turning away from real life and from present-day experience.[1]

Now it is evident that some of these statements have gone beyond compromise. When people start appealing to 'truth', 'experience' and 'reality', still more to 'the fundamental character of reality', they imply very strongly that they know what these things *are*, an insight not likely to be shaken by argument. Probably at the bottom of the confrontation between *The Lord of the Rings* and its critics there lies some total disagreement over the nature of the universe, a disagreement surfacing in strong, instinctive, mutual antipathy. Nothing will cure this. However it ought to be possible to bring the reasons for it out into the light, and by doing so to show that whatever may be said of Tolkien's view of reality, it was neither escapist nor thoughtless. A sensible place to begin this endeavour is with the mainspring of the story's action, the Ring (here capitalised to distinguish it from the relatively insignificant stage-prop or 'Equalizer' of *The Hobbit*).

The most evident fact to note about the Ring is that it is in conception strikingly anachronistic, totally modern. In the vital chapter 'The Shadow of the Past' Gandalf says a great deal about it, but his information boils down to three basic data: (1) the Ring is immensely powerful, in right or wrong hands; (2) it is dangerous and ultimately fatal to all its possessors – in a sense there *are* no right hands; (3) it cannot simply be left unused or put aside, but must be destroyed, something which can happen only in the place of its origin, Orodruin, Mount Doom. 'There is only one way', he says to Frodo, and it is essential to the story that this should be accepted as true: the Ring *cannot* be kept, it has power over *everybody*, it *has* to be destroyed. Spread over sixteen pages (I, 56–71) these remarks function as part of a story, but as soon as they are put together it is a dull mind which does not reflect, 'Power corrupts, and absolute power corrupts absolutely'. That maxim, one could say, is the core of *The Lord of the Rings*, and it is reinforced from the start by all that Gandalf says about the way Ring-bearers *fade*, regardless of all their 'strength' or 'good purpose', and further by his violent refusal to take the Ring himself:

> 'Do not tempt me! For I do not wish to become like the Dark Lord himself. Yet the way of the Ring to my heart is by pity, pity for weakness and the desire of strength to do good. Do not tempt me! I dare not take it, not even to keep it safe, unused. The wish to wield it would be too great for my strength . . .' (I, 71).

His renunciation makes sense in an age which has seen many pigs become farmers; no reviewer has ever balked at this basic opening move of Tolkien's.

Yet the opinion that 'power corrupts' is a distinctively modern one. Lord Acton gave it expression for the first time in 1887, in a letter which Tolkien might have been interested enough to read – it is in a strongly anti-Papal context.[2] William Pitt had said something similar a hundred years before, 'Unlimited power is apt to corrupt the minds of those who possess it', but before that the idea does not seem to have been attractive. It might even have been thought perverse. Lord Acton's actual words were: 'Power tends to corrupt and absolute power corrupts absolutely. Great men are almost always bad men . . .', and with this latter opinion no medieval chronicler, romancer or hagiographer would have been likely to concur. There is as it happens an Anglo-Saxon proverb analogous to Lord Acton's, but still significantly different. What *it* says is *Man dep swá hé byþ þonne hé mót swá hé wile*, 'Man does as he is when he may do as he wishes', or more colloquially 'you show what you're like when you can do what you like'.[3] This is certainly cynical about the ill-effects of power, but what it implies is 'power *exposes*', not 'power corrupts'. The idea that a person once genuinely good could be made bad merely by the removal of restraints is not yet present. Tolkien is certain to have felt the modernity of his primary statement about the Ring. One has to wonder then why he made it and how he related it to the archaic world of his plot. Does Lord Acton's Victorian proverb, in Middle-earth, ring true?

There is at least a plausible argument to say that it does not. Thus Gandalf says at the start that the Ring will 'possess' and 'devour' any creature who uses it, while Elrond later goes further and says 'The very desire of it corrupts the heart' (I, 281). As has been said, these are essential data for the story, and some of the time they seem to be confirmed. Gollum, for instance, is presented throughout as very nearly enslaved to the Ring, with only fleeting traces of free will left, and those dependent on keeping away from it. Much higher up the moral scale Boromir bears out Elrond's words. He never touches the Ring, but desire to have it still makes him turn to violence. Obviously his original motive is patriotism and love of Gondor, but when this leads him to exalt 'strength to defend ourselves, strength in a just cause', our modern experience of dictators immediately tells us that matters would not stay there. Kind as he is, one can imagine Boromir as a Ringwraith; his never-quite-stated opinion that 'the end justifies the means' adds a credible perspective to corruption. The same could be said of his father Denethor, to whom Gandalf again makes the point that even unhandled the Ring can be dangerous: 'if you had received this thing, it would have overthrown you. Were it buried beneath the roots of Mindolluin, still it would burn your mind away.' With examples like these, it is easy to go further and accept, for the purposes of the story, that even Gandalf's good intentions would not resist the Ring, and that Galadriel too does right to refuse it at I, 381. While the Ring stays a veiled menace, one may conclude, it works perfectly well.

The problem comes from the apparent immunity of so many other characters. Frodo, after all, is in contact with the Ring nearly all the time, but shows little sign of being corrupted. He goes through great labours to get rid of it. Furthermore when he *does* give way and claim it for his own, he loses it almost immediately to Gollum, who bites off Ring and finger with it. Gandalf had said much earlier that 'Already you too, Frodo, cannot easily let it go, nor will to damage it. And I could not "make" you – except by force, which would break your mind.' But in the Sammath Naur we have force being used very strongly, in the shape of Gollum's teeth; yet Frodo's mind remains unaffected. Anyway, what about Sam, who takes the Ring but hands it back with only momentary delay, Pippin and Merry, who show no desire for it at all, Aragorn, Legolas and Gimli, who display the same indifference without the excuse of ignorance, and Boromir's brother Faramir, who realises the Ring is in his power but refuses to take it, with no more sign of mental turmoil than a 'strange smile' and a glint in the eye? One sees the beginnings of a serious criticism of the very basis of *The Lord of the Rings* here: the author appears to have presented a set of rules and then observed them only partially, reserving as it were the right to exceptions and miracles. This is what has made some people think that in this work the distinction between good and bad is simply arbitrary, residing not in the nature of the characters but in the needs of the plot.[4]

Actually all the doubts just mentioned can be cleared up by the use of one word, though it is a word never used in *The Lord of the Rings*. The Ring is 'addictive'. All readers probably assimilate Gollum early on to the now-familiar image of a 'drug-addict', craving desperately for a 'fix' even though he knows it will kill him. For the same reason they understand why Gandalf tells Frodo not to use the Ring (use always causes addiction); why Sam, Bilbo and Frodo nevertheless survive their use of it (addiction in early stages is curable); why Boromir succumbs to the Ring without handling it (use has to be preceded by desire); and why Faramir can shrug it off (a wise person is capable of stifling the desire to become addicted, though no wisdom will stifle addiction once contracted). As for the scene in the Sammath Naur, it is even more Providential than it looks. What Gandalf said to Frodo at the start, we should realise, was that he might be able to give the Ring away or destroy it, though only with a struggle; he could not however be made to *want* to do so (except by some kind of dangerous thought-control). In the end Frodo does want to destroy the Ring but has not the strength. Gollum is accordingly necessary after all – a striking irony. Extending the parallel with heroin one may say that addicts *can* be cured by the use of external force, and often they have to be, though their co-operation certainly helps. To expect them to break their syringes and throw away their drugs by will-power alone, though, is to confuse an addiction, which is physical, with a habit, which is moral. In this aspect of the Ring as in others Tolkien is totally consistent.

He is, however, once again being distinctively modern. The phrase 'drug addict' is not recorded by the *OED* till 1920; probably the concept was created by the synthesis of heroin in 1898. As for the term 'addictive', by some oversight the full *OED* has never recognised its existence at all. Still, during Tolkien's lifetime the words and the realities behind them became more and more familiar, bringing with them, one should note, entirely new ideas about the nature and limitations of human will. As with 'power corrupting', Tolkien was during the 1930s and 1940s reacting quite evidently to the issues of his time. These deliberate modernities should clear him of any charge of merely insulated 'ivory tower' escapism. They ought to suggest also that he thought more deeply than his critics have ever recognised about just those issues he is commonly alleged to ignore: the processes of temptation, the complex nature of good and evil, the relationship between reality and our fallible perception of it. Nothing can prevent people from saying that the answers he gave were not 'adult' or 'fundamental', but it should be obvious that such adjectives are as culture-biased as Saruman's 'real': by themselves they express only the prejudices of the user. Tolkien was, in short, trying to make Middle-earth say something, as well as conducting his readers on a tour of it. Decision on whether the message is right or wrong should at least come after working out what the message *is*. But proper understanding of that, as often, depends on comparing ancient things and modern ones, checking old texts against new understandings, and against timeless realities.

Views of evil: Boethian and Manichaean

A good way to understand *The Lord of the Rings* in its full complexity is to see it as an attempt to reconcile two views of evil, both old, both authoritative, both living, each seemingly contradicted by the other. One of these is in essence the orthodox Christian one, expounded by St Augustine and then by Catholic and Protestant teaching alike, but finding its clearest expression in a book which does not mention Christ at all: Boethius's *De Consolatione Philosophiae*, a short tract written c. AD 522–5 by a Roman senator shortly before his execution by *Thiudoreiks (or Theodoric), king of the Goths. This says that there is no such thing as evil: 'evil is nothing', is the absence of good, is possibly even an unappreciated good – *Omnem bonam prorsus esse fortunam*, wrote Boethius, 'all fortune is certainly good'. Corollaries of this belief are, that evil cannot itself create, that it was not in itself created (but sprang from a voluntary exercise of free will by Satan, Adam and Eve, to separate themselves from God), that it will in the long run be annulled or eliminated, as the Fall of Man was redressed by the Incarnation and Death of Christ. Views like these are strongly present in *The Lord of the Rings*. Even in Mordor Frodo asserts that 'the Shadow . . . can only mock, it cannot make: not real new things of its own' (III, 190), and Fangorn has already corroborated him, 'Trolls are only counterfeits, made by the Enemy in the Great Darkness, in mockery of Ents, as Orcs were of Elves' (II, 89). What the difference is between a real thing and a 'counterfeit', one cannot tell, but anyway the idea of perversion as opposed to creation comes over. It goes with Elrond's firm statement even earlier that 'nothing is evil in the beginning. Even Sauron was not so' (I, 281). On these ultimate points Tolkien was not prepared to compromise.

Still, there is an alternative tradition in Western thought, one which has never become 'official' but which nevertheless arises spontaneously from experience. This says that while it may be all very well to make philosophical statements about evil, evil nevertheless *is* real, and not merely an absence; and what's more it can be resisted, and what's more still *not* resisting it (in the belief that one day Omnipotence will cure all ills) is a dereliction of duty. The danger of this opinion is that it tends towards Manichaeanism, the heresy which says that Good and Evil are equal and opposite and the universe is a battlefield; however the Inklings may have had a certain tolerance for that (see C. S. Lewis's *Mere Christianity*, Book 2, section 2). Furthermore one can imagine statements about the nature of evil which would go past Boethius but stop short of Manichaeus. Tolkien perhaps found such opinions in a work he knew well, King Alfred the Great's personal translation of Boethius into Old English.

This is a remarkable book, mainly because while King Alfred showed a decent regard for the philosopher he was translating, he was not too modest to add bits of his own. He had moreover, unlike Boethius, had the experience of seeing what Viking pirates did to his defenceless subjects; and again unlike Boethius had taken such drastic measures against evil as hanging Viking prisoners, and rebellious monks, and in all probability cutting the throats of any wounded pirates so unlucky as to be left on the battlefield. All this did not stop Alfred from being a Christian king; indeed some of his recorded behaviour seems almost Quixotically forgiving. Nevertheless his career reveals the strong point of a 'heroic' view of evil, the weak point of a Boethian one: if you regard evil as something internal, to be pitied, more harmful to the malefactor than the victim, you may be philosophically consistent but you may also be exposing others to sacrifices to which they have not consented (like being murdered by Viking ravagers or, as *The Lord of the Rings* was being written, being herded into gas-chambers). In the 1930s and 1940s Boethius was especially hard to believe. Still, his view could not just be set aside.

Tolkien's way of presenting this philosophical duality was through the Ring. It seems in several ways inconsistent. For one thing it is notoriously elastic, and not entirely passive. It 'betrayed' Isildur to the arrows of the orcs; it 'abandoned' Gollum, says Gandalf, in response to the 'dark thought from Mirkwood' of its master; it all but betrays Frodo in the *Prancing Pony* when it slips on to his finger and proves his invisibility to the spies for the Nazgûl then present. 'Perhaps it had tried to reveal itself in response to some wish or command that was felt in the room', thinks Frodo, and he is clearly right. For all that it remains an object which cannot move itself or save itself from destruction. It has to work through the agency of its possessors, and especially by picking out the weak points of their characters – possessiveness in Bilbo, fear in Frodo, patriotism in Boromir, pity in Gandalf. When Frodo passes it to Gandalf so that its identity can be confirmed, 'It felt suddenly very heavy, as if *either it or Frodo himself* was in some way reluctant for Gandalf to touch it' (I, 58, my italics). Maybe the Ring is magically conscious of Gandalf's power: maybe, though, Frodo is already afraid that he will lose it. These two possible views of the Ring are kept up throughout the three volumes: sentient creature, or psychic amplifier. They correspond respectively to the 'heroic' view of evil as something external to be resisted and the Boethian opinion that evil is essentially internal, psychological, negative.

The point is repeated in several scenes of temptation. Frodo puts on the Ring six times during *The Lord of the Rings*: once in the house of Tom Bombadil (which does not seem to count), once by accident in the *Prancing Pony*, once on Weathertop, twice on Amon Hen, once in the final scene in the Sammath Naur. On several other occasions he feels an urge to, most strongly in the valley below Minas Morgul, as the Ringwraith leads out his army. Four of these scenes at least are highly significant. Thus on Amon Hen Frodo puts on the Ring, contrary to Gandalf's injunction, simply to escape from Boromir, and the narrator ratifies his decision: 'There was only one thing to do'. He keeps it on, though, goes to the summit of Amon Hen and sits on the Seat of Seeing. There the Eye of Sauron becomes aware of him and leaps towards him like a searchlight:

Very soon it would nail him down, know just exactly where he was. Amon Lhaw it touched. It glanced upon Tol Brandir – he threw himself from the seat, crouching, covering his head with his grey hood.

He heard himself crying out: *Never, Never!* Or was it: *Verily I come, I come to you?* He could not tell. Then as a flash from some other point of power there came to his mind another thought: *Take it off! Take it off! Fool, take it off! Take off the Ring!*

The two powers strove in him. For a moment, perfectly balanced between their piercing points, he writhed, tormented. Suddenly he was aware of himself again. Frodo, neither the Voice nor the Eye: free to choose and with one remaining instant to do so. He took the Ring off his finger. (I, 417)

This is a scene which has puzzled and irritated critics. Dr C. N. Manlove writes 'the Voice' off as 'providential', and clearly thinks it one more example of the 'biased fortune' which in his opinion makes it impossible to take the story seriously. Actually the Voice is Gandalf's, as we might have guessed from its asperity, and as is anyway confirmed at II, 99: it may seem fair enough to let a wizard oppose a necromancer. More remarkable is the opposition between *Never!* and *I come to you.* Is this a struggle inside Frodo's soul, between his conscious will and his unconscious wickedness (the sort of wickedness which might earlier have made him reluctant to hand over the Ring to Gandalf)? Or is *I come to you* just a projection from the voice of the Enemy, saying to Frodo what he wants to hear, putting words in the mouth but not in the heart, creating ugly fictions as he does later with the phantasmal corpses of the Dead Marshes? Either view is possible. Both are suggested. Evil may accordingly be an inner temptation or an external power.

Similar uncertainty dramatises other scenes when Frodo puts on the

Ring, or tries to, or is ordered to. In the valley of Minas Morgul the Ringwraith sends out a command for him to put it on, but Frodo finds no response to it in his own will, feeling only 'the beating upon him of a great power from outside'. The power moves his hand, as if by magnetism, but he forces it back, to touch the phial of Galadriel and be momentarily relieved. Perhaps the same thing happened to him on Weathertop, where he put the Ring on as the Ringwraiths closed in, but the words used there are 'temptation' and 'desire' – 'his terror was swallowed up in a sudden temptation to put on the Ring. The desire to do this laid hold of him, and he could think of nothing else.' He had felt a similar urge in the Barrow, as the wight's fingers came towards him, and there the temptation offered was to abandon his friends and use the Ring to escape. On Weathertop we are told he had no such conscious and immoral thought. Nevertheless it seems that there the external power is abetted by some inner weakness, some potentially wicked impulse towards the wrong side. In the chambers of Sammath Naur one's judgement must also be suspended. Frodo makes a clear and active statement of his own evil intention: 'I will not do this deed. The Ring is mine!' But at the same time we have been told that even the phial of Galadriel loses its virtue on Mount Doom, for there Frodo is at 'the heart of the realm of Sauron . . . all other powers were here subdued'. Are Frodo's will, and his virtue, among those powers? To say so would be Manichaean. It would deny that men are responsible for their actions, make evil into a positive force. On the other hand to put the whole blame on Frodo would seem (to use a distinctively English ethical term) 'unfair'; if he had been an entirely wicked person he would never have reached the Sammath Naur in the first place. There seems to be a mixed judgement on him. Frodo is saved from his sin by his own earlier repeated acts of forgiveness to Gollum, but in a sense punished by the loss of his finger. 'If thine eye offend thee, pluck it out . . .' As it happens the quotation that ran in Tolkien's mind when he considered this scene very much implies the dual nature of wickedness, but comes from the Lord's Prayer: 'And lead us not into temptation; but deliver us from evil.'†
Succumbing to temptation is our business, one might paraphrase, but delivering us from evil is God's. As for the questions of how far responsi-

---

† Tolkien wrote this in a letter of 12 December 1955 to Mr David I. Masson, who kindly showed it to me and has given me permission to quote from it here. Irritated evidently by the *TLS* review of 25 November 1955 (to which Mr Masson had written a reply, published *TLS* 9 December 1955), Tolkien remarked that the reviewer should not have made such a fuss over giving quarter to orcs. 'Surely how often "quarter" is given is off the point in a book that breathes Mercy from start to finish: in which the central hero is at last divested of all arms, except his will? "Forgive us our trespasses as we forgive them that trespass against us. Lead us not into temptation, but deliver us from evil", are words that occur to me, and of which the scene in the Sammath Naur was meant to be a "fairy-story" exemplum . . .' See also *Letters*, p. 252.

bility is to be allocated between us and our tempters, how much temptation human beings can 'reasonably' be expected to stand – these are obviously not to be answered by mere mortals. Tolkien saw the problem of evil in books as in realities, and he told his story at least in part to dramatise that problem; he did not however claim to know the answer to it.

One can see, then, a philosophical crux in the very nature of the Ring, one that was certainly apparent and deeply interesting to Tolkien, and one which he furthermore expressed with great care and deliberation. This is not important just for Frodo. The uncertainty over evil in a way dominates the entire structure of *The Lord of the Rings*. All the characters would find decisions much easier if evil were unquestionably either just Boethian or else just Manichaean. If evil were only the absence of good, for instance, then the Ring could never be anything other than a psychic amplifier; it would not 'betray' its possessors, and all they would need do is put it aside and think pure thoughts. In Middle-earth we are assured that would be fatal. However if evil were merely a hateful and external power without echo in the hearts of the good, then someone might have to take the Ring to the Cracks of Doom, but it need not be Frodo: Gandalf could be trusted with it, while whoever went would have only to distrust his enemies, not his friends and not himself. As it is the nature of the Ring is integral to the story.

The story also repeatedly reflects back on the nature of temptation and of the Ring. When Gandalf says to Frodo of his wound on Weathertop, 'your heart was not touched, and only your shoulder was pierced; and that was because you resisted to the last', he may be making a moral statement (Frodo was rewarded) or a practical one (he dodged, called out, struck back, put off the Ringwraith's aim). When he says of Bilbo that he gave up the Ring 'of his own accord: an important point', he may be saying only that Bilbo can't have become too badly addicted, or more moralistically that Bilbo's good impulse will help his cure. When Glóin describes the dwarves' urge to revisit Moria we cannot be sure whether this is the prompting of Sauron from outside or dwarvish greed and ambition from inside. All one need say is that this is how things often are. Maybe all sins need some combination of external prompting and inner weakness. At any rate, on the level of narrative one can say that *The Lord of the Rings* is neither a saint's life, all about temptation, nor a complicated wargame, all about tactics. It would be a much lesser work if it had swerved towards either extreme.

Elementary conceptions: luck and the shadow

The word which for Tolkien expressed this distinctive image of evil was 'shadow'. Do shadows exist or not? It is an ancient opinion that they do and they don't. In the Old English poem *Solomon and Saturn II*† the pagan Saturn asks the Christian Solomon (he *is* a Christian in this text) 'what things were that were not?' The answer is oblique, but it contains the word *besceadeð*, 'shadows'. Shadows are the absence of light and so don't exist in themselves, but they are still visible and palpable just as if they did. That is exactly Tolkien's view of evil. Accordingly Mordor is 'Black-Land', 'where the shadows lie', or even more ominously 'where the shadows *are*' (my italics), Aragorn reports that 'Gandalf the Grey fell into shadow', Gandalf himself says that if his side loses 'many lands will pass under the shadow'. At times 'the Shadow' becomes a personification of Sauron, as in Frodo's remark about mocking and making quoted earlier, at times it seems no more than cloud and mirk, as when the Riders' hearts 'quailed under the shadow'. At times one does not know what to think: Balin goes off to Moria and disaster after 'a shadow of disquiet' fell upon the dwarves, and when Glóin says this it appears only a metaphor for mundane discontent. It is an ominous metaphor, though. Maybe the 'shadow' was a Mordor-spell, maybe Balin simultaneously fell and was pushed. In such phrases one sees a characteristic Tolkienian strength: his ideas were often paradoxical and had deep intellectual roots, but they appealed at the same time to simple things and to everyday experience. Tolkien could be learned and practical at once, a style common enough in Old English but (he probably reflected) less and less so as the Norman Conquest and the Renaissance wore on, seeing to it that 'education' meant increasingly 'education in Latin' and the creation of a distinctive literary caste.

Tolkien's other main source for his image of 'the shadow' was probably *Beowulf*, lines 705–7. Here Beowulf and his men are waiting (the latter without hope) for the appearance of Grendel the man-eater. They did not expect to get home, says the poet; still, they went to sleep. Then he adds with sudden confidence, 'It was known to men that the demon-enemy could not draw them under shadow (*under sceadu bregdan*), as long as God did not wish it.' This is a tough thought, for all its confidence. 'Draw them under shadow' may mean no more than 'pull them out of the hall and into the dark', but it implies also 'going we know not where', dying and being handed over for ever to the powers of evil. As for the phrase about God not wishing it, that seems on the whole a benevolent assertion of divine power. But what if God *does* wish it? Notoriously He does sometimes wish things like that, for even in *Beowulf* they have happened

† There is a text and translation of this poem, and an introduction to it, in my *Poems of Wisdom and Learning in Old English* (Cambridge and Totowa, N.J.: D. S. Brewer Press and Rowman and Littlefield, 1976). Tolkien certainly studied the poem, for it is the best riddle-contest in Old English, and most like the Old Norse ones from the *Elder Edda* and *The Saga of King Heidrek*. Gollum's 'Time' riddle in *The Hobbit* is based on Saturn's 'Old Age' one.

before. Tolkien was perhaps attracted by the phrase *under sceadu*, and also by the tableau of silent, rather sullen Anglo-Saxon courage. He would not have disagreed either with the implications about the unfairness of Providence; we should note that a recurrent prospect in *The Lord of the Rings* is for Frodo to be taken by Sauron and tormented till he too goes 'under the shadow', becomes a petty 'wraith' himself, worn out by addiction and privation and torture and fear to a state of nothingness like that of 'the haggard king' of Minas Morgul.[5] This doesn't happen, but no one says it can't. However having spent so long on Tolkien's powerful and complex image of evil, it is time to turn to his portrayal of the (in appearance) often weaker and much more limited power of good.

Once more Tolkien pulled a hint for this from an ancient Beowulfian mystery. That poem opens with the funeral of the ancestor of one of its characters – Scyld, the king of the Danes, who according to legend came drifting to land as a baby, naked on a wooden shield. Now at the end of his life the Danes send him back to the sea in an unmanned funeral barge laden with treasure. 'By no means did [the Danes] provide him with less gifts, less national treasure', says the poet with proud understatement, 'than those did (*þonne þá dydon*) who sent him out at his beginning, alone over the waves, being a child.' Who are 'those'? The line is a very odd one, both technically† and ideologically. The *Beowulf*-poet was a Christian. There should have been no room in his universe for sub-divine but superhuman powers, other than devils or angels; however the senders of Scyld seem supernatural in knowledge and purpose, while showing no interest in the inhabitants of Denmark's souls. One might put Scyld down to divine Providence, except that the word is *þá*, 'those', not *hé*, 'He'. In *Beowulf* the matter is then dropped for good, but it leaves behind the implication that there are powers at work in the world, possibly beneficent ones, which human beings are not equipped to understand.

The same is true of *The Lord of the Rings*, though there as in *Beowulf* the lurking powers are never allowed to intervene openly. From *The Silmarillion* we can infer that Gandalf is a Maia, a spiritual creature in human shape sent for the relief of humanity; much later than he finished the trilogy Tolkien indeed reportedly said 'Gandalf is an angel'.[6] During the action of *The Lord of the Rings*, though, Gandalf never looks very much like an angel, or at least not one of the normal iconographic kind. He is too short-tempered, for one thing, and also capable of doubt, anxiety, weariness, fear. Obviously too strong a flurry of angelic wings, too ready recourse to miracles or to Omnipotence, would instantly diminish the stature of the characters, devalue their decisions and their courage. How then does beneficence operate; and has Gandalf superiors? 'Naked I was

† It is the only instance, out of 63 occurrences in the poem, where the word *þá* as an unsupported demonstrative takes alliteration and stress, so gaining unusual if not unnatural prominence.

sent back', he says at one point (recalling the story of Scyld), but he does
not say who sent him. 'May the Valar turn him aside!' shout the Gondorians as the 'oliphaunt' charges. But the Valar don't. Or perhaps they do,
for the beast does swerve aside, though this could be only chance. Can
'chance' and 'the Valar' be equated? Is 'chance' the word which people use
for their perception of the operations of 'those', the mysterious senders of
Scyld and of Gandalf too?

Tolkien had, probably, been developing some such thought as this for
many years. He uses the word 'chance' quite often in a suggestive way in
The Lord of the Rings. 'Just chance brought me then, if chance you call it',
says Tom Bombadil when he rescues the hobbits from Willow-man; ruin
was averted in the Northlands, says Gandalf in Appendix AIII, 'because
I met Thorin Oakenshield one evening on the edge of spring in Bree. A
chance-meeting, as we say in Middle-earth.' Obviously chance is sometimes meant, as Gandalf says of Bilbo's finding of the Ring, though
even Gandalf can only recognise such 'meanings' retrospectively.
However 'chance' was not the word which for Tolkien best expressed
his feelings about randomness and design. The word that did is probably
'luck'.

This is, of course, an extremely common English word. It is also rather
odd, in that no etymology of it is known. The OED suggests, without
conviction, that it might come from words like Old English (ge)lingan, 'to
happen', giving then a basic meaning of 'happenstance, whatever turns
up'. Tolkien would have liked that, for it would make 'luck' a close modern
equivalent of the Old English word usually translated 'fate' and derived
in exactly the same way from the verb (ge)weorþan, 'to become, to happen'.
The Beowulf-poet often ascribes events to wyrd, and treats it in a way as
a supernatural force. King Alfred brought it into his translation of Boethius
too, to explain why divine Providence does not affect free will: 'What we
call God's fore-thought and his Providence', he wrote, 'is while it is there
in His mind, before it gets done, while it's still being thought; but once
it's done, then we call it wyrd. This way anyone can tell that there are
two things and two names, forethought and wyrd.'⁷ A highly important
corollary is that people are not under the domination of wyrd, which is
why 'fate' is not a good translation of it. People can 'change their luck',
and can in a way say 'No' to divine Providence, though of course if they
do they have to stand by the consequences of their decision. In Middle-
earth, one may say, Providence or the Valar sent the dream that took
Boromir to Rivendell (I, 259). But they sent it first and most often to
Faramir, who would no doubt have been a better choice. It was human
decision, or human perversity, which led to Boromir claiming the journey,
with what chain of ill-effects and casualties no one can tell. 'Luck', then,
is a continuous interplay of providence and free will, a blending of so
many factors that the mind cannot disentangle them, a word encapsulating

ancient philosophical problems over which wars have been fought and men burnt alive.

As important to Tolkien, though, was that it is a word (like 'shadow') which people use every day, and with exactly the right shade of uncertainty over whether they mean something completely humdrum and practical or something mysterious and supernatural. When Farmer Giles of Ham fires his blunderbuss at the giant he hits him 'by luck', indeed 'by chance and no choice of the farmer's': thoughts of the Valar enter no one's mind. On the other hand his advantageous position at the rear of the knightly column which Chrysophlax decimates came about when his grey mare went lame, 'As luck (or the grey mare herself) would have it'. It is not providence, but it may have been *meant* just the same. The browbeating of the dragon outside its den, however, is something even the grey mare's prudence would not stretch to. 'Farmer Giles was backing his luck', as people often do; and it is common knowledge that while this is irrational it works much more often than mere 'chance' would dictate. People in short do in sober reality recognise a strongly patterning force in the world around them, and both in modern and in Old English have a word to express their recognition. This force, however, does not affect free will and cannot be distinguished from the ordinary operations of nature. Most of all it does not decrease in the slightest the need for heroic endeavour. 'God helps those who help themselves', says the proverb. 'Luck often spares the man who isn't doomed, as long as his courage holds', agrees Beowulf. 'Luck served you there,' says Gimli to Merry and Pippin (II, 169); 'but you seized your chance with both hands, one might say.' If they hadn't, 'luck' would no doubt by that time have looked very different.

In Middle-earth, then, both good and evil function as external powers and as inner impulses from the psyche. It is perhaps fair to say that while the balances are maintained, we are on the whole more conscious of evil as an objective power and of good as a subjective impulse; Mordor and 'the Shadow' are nearer and more visible than the Valar or 'luck'. This lack of symmetry is moreover part of a basic denial of security throughout *The Lord of the Rings*. Repeatedly we are told that if its characters fail to resist the Shadow, they will be taken over, but if they do resist they may get killed; similarly if they reject the vagaries of chance (if Frodo for instance had refused to leave the Shire with the Ring), it's likely something highly unpleasant will happen, but if they accept and obey things could grow even worse. The benevolent powers offer no guarantees. The best recommendation Gandalf can make is not to think about such things. 'But let us not darken our hearts by imagining the trial of their gentle loyalty in the Dark Tower. For the Enemy has failed – so far' (II, 100). Since it hasn't happened, in other words, it isn't *wyrd*, and so need not be explained. Still, it is essential to the story that such thoughts be entertained, as indeed Gandalf also says to Pippin: 'If you will meddle in the affairs of Wizards, you must be prepared to think of such things' (II, 199). Without them the characters' courage would look smaller; and courage is perhaps the strongest element in the Tolkienian synthesis of virtue.

Apparent paradoxes: happy sadness and hopeless cheer

This has been both resented and denied: resented, simply because courage is no longer a very fashionable part of virtue; denied, in that some have said things are too easy for Frodo and his companions all through. They do escape, after all. Only Boromir of the Nine dies during the course of the action, and he deserves it. Gandalf is resurrected. Pathos is created only by the sacrifice of a few members of the virtuous side, mostly old ones like Théoden or Dáin, or peripheral ones like Háma and Halbarad and the list of mere names in the Rohan dirge after the Pelennor Fields. In a review in the *Observer* (27 November 1955) – one which Tolkien very much resented, see *Biography*, p. 223 – Edwin Muir propounded a thesis that the non-adulthood of the romance was shown by its painlessness: 'The good boys, having fought a deadly battle, emerge at the end of it well, triumphant and happy, as boys would naturally expect to do. There are only one or two minor casualties.' In this there is a kind of truth (for Tolkien was kind-hearted about things like the 'evacuation' of Minas Tirith and the survival of Bill the pony), but also an evident falsehood. When all is over Frodo for one is neither 'well', 'triumphant' nor even 'happy'. And he only exemplifies a much stronger theme in the work as a whole: the failure of the good, one might even say a sense of 'defeatism'.

In the strict or dictionary sense *The Lord of the Rings* evades that concept totally, for according to the *OED* 'defeatism' is a straight borrowing from French *défaitisme*, recorded in English for the first time in 1918 and meaning 'Conduct tending to bring about acceptance of defeat, esp. by action on civilian opinion'. With his best friends dead in Flanders Tolkien had cause to hate that idea like poison, and indeed no one in Middle-earth is allowed to voice it. Even Denethor's reaction to defeat is to commit ceremonial suicide, not negotiate for some 'Vichy' status – though that is what Sauron's mouthpiece offers at III, 166, in a speech full of the Middle-earth analogues of 'reparations', 'demilitarised zones' and 'puppet governments'. Gandalf rejects that proposal with particular violence, and at all times discussion of odds or probabilities turns him hard and obstinate: ' "Still," he said, standing suddenly up and sticking out his chin, while his beard went stiff and straight like bristling wire, "we must keep up our courage. You will soon be well, if I do not talk you to death. You are in Rivendell, and you need not worry about anything for the present." ' 'Sufficient unto the day is the evil thereof' seems to be his motto. Yet Gandalf also on occasion, together with the other wise men and women of the story, accepts defeat as a long-term prospect, a prospect which *The Lord of the Rings* as a whole does not deny.

Thus Galadriel says of her life, 'Through ages of the world we have fought the long defeat'. Elrond agrees, 'I have seen three ages in the West of the world, and many defeats and many fruitless victories'. Later he queries his own adjective 'fruitless', but still repeats that the victory long ago in which Sauron was overthrown but not destroyed 'did not achieve its end'. The whole history of Middle-earth seems to show that good is attained only at vast expense while evil recuperates almost at will. Thangorodrim is broken without evil being at all 'broken for ever', as the elves had thought. Númenor is drowned without getting rid of Sauron. Sauron is defeated and his Ring taken by Isildur, only to set in motion the crisis at the end of the Third Age. And even if that crisis is surmounted, it is made extremely clear that this success too will conform to the general pattern of 'fruitlessness' – or maybe one should say its fruit will be bitter. Destruction of the Ring, says Galadriel, will mean that her ring and Gandalf's and Elrond's will also lose their power, so that Lothlórien 'fades' and the elves 'dwindle'. Along with them will go the ents and the dwarves, indeed the whole imagined world of Middle-earth, to be replaced by modernity and the domination of men; all the characters and their story, one might say, will shrink to poetic 'rigmaroles' and misunderstood snatches in plays and ballads. Beauty especially will be a casualty. 'However the fortunes of war shall go ...', asks Théoden, 'may it not so end that much that was fair and wonderful shall pass for ever out of Middle-earth?' 'The evil of Sauron cannot be wholly cured', replies Gandalf, 'nor made as if it had not been.' Fangorn agrees when he says of his own dying species, 'songs like trees bear fruit only in their own time and their own way, and sometimes they are withered untimely'. The collective opinion of Middle-earth is summed up in Gandalf's aphoristic statement: 'I am Gandalf, Gandalf the White, but Black is mightier still.'

The implications of that *could* be alarming. It sounds Manichaean. However as has already been seen Tolkien was careful to voice rebuttals of Manichaeanism and assertions of the nonentity of evil many times throughout. Why then the continuing pessimistic expectations of defeat? The answer, obviously enough, is that a major goal of *The Lord of the Rings* was to dramatise that 'theory of courage' which Tolkien had said in his British Academy lecture was the 'great contribution' to humanity of the old literature of the North. The central pillar of that theory was Ragnarǫk – the day when gods and men would fight evil and the giants, and inevitably be defeated. Its great statement was that defeat is no refutation. The right side remains right even if it has no ultimate hope at all. In a sense this Northern mythology asks more of men, even makes more of them, than does Christianity, for it offers them no heaven, no salvation, no reward for virtue except the sombre satisfaction of having done what is right. Tolkien wanted his characters in *The Lord of the Rings* to live up to the same high standard. He was careful therefore to remove easy hope from them, even to make them conscious of long-term defeat and doom.

Nevertheless Tolkien was himself a Christian, and he faced a problem in the 'theory of courage' he so much admired: its mainspring is despair, its spirit often heathen ferocity. One can see him grappling with the difficulty in his poem-cum-essay 'The Homecoming of Beorhtnoth Beorhthelm's Son', published in 1953, the year before *The Fellowship of the Ring*. This is a coda to the Old English poem *The Battle of Maldon*, which commemorates an English defeat by the Vikings in AD 991, and celebrates especially the unyielding courage of the English bodyguard who refused to retreat when their leader was killed, but fought round his body till all were dead. The very core of the sentiment is expressed by an old retainer called Beorhtwold: 'Heart shall be bolder, harder be purpose,/ more proud the spirit, as our power lessens . . .' These lines, said Tolkien, 'have been held to be the finest expression of the northern heroic spirit, Norse or English; the clearest statement of the doctrine of uttermost endurance in the service of indomitable will'. Nevertheless he felt uneasy about them. He thought they were old already in 991; he saw they could be said as well by a heathen as a Christian; he thought the fierce spirit they expressed was one of the reasons for Beorhtnoth's rash decision to let the Vikings cross the river and fight on level ground; they had led to defeat and the death of the innocent.

In Tolkien's poem, accordingly, the words are not given to Beorhtwold but form part of a dream dreamt by the poet Torhthelm:

> 'It's dark! It's dark   and doom coming!
> Is no light left us?   A light kindle,
> and fan the flame!   Lo! Fire now wakens,
> hearth is burning,   house is lighted,
> men there gather.   Out of the mists they come
> through darkling doors   whereat doom waiteth.
> Hark! I hear them   in the hall chanting:
> stern words they sing   with strong voices.
> (*He chants*)   "Heart shall be bolder,   harder be purpose,
> more proud the spirit   as our power lessens!
> Mind shall not falter   nor mood waver,
> though doom shall come   and dark conquer." '

Tolkien himself did not think the dark *would* conquer. The voices Torhthelm hears are those of his pagan ancestors, no better than the Vikings 'lying off London in their long vessels,/while they drink to Thor and drown the sorrow/of hell's children'. They are as wrong as Gandalf, or even more so; Tídwald rebukes Torhthelm for being 'heathenish' when he wakes up, and the poem ends with the monks of Ely singing the *Dirige* or 'dirge' from the Office of the Dead. However Tolkien admired the aesthetic impulse towards good beneath the pride and sorrow. In Middle-earth he wanted a similar ultimate courage undiluted by confidence – but at the same time untainted by rage and despair. One may say that the wise characters in *The Lord of the Rings* are often without hope and so near the edge of despair, but they do not succumb. That is left to Denethor, who will not fight to the last, but turns like a heathen to suicide and the sacrifice of his kin.

Tolkien needed a new image for ultimate bravery, one milder but not weaker than Beorhtwold's. He centred it, oddly enough, on laughter, cheerfulness, refusal to look into the future at all. There are hints of this in Middle English – the critical moment in *Sir Orfeo* comes when the king in his madness sees ladies at falconry, and laughs – while there is a modern analogue in Joseph Conrad's *The Shadow-Line* (1917), where laughter is an exorcising force. In *The Lord of the Rings* it can be expressed by such high-status characters as Faramir, who says at one point that he does not hope to see Frodo ever again, but nevertheless invents a picture of them in an unknown future 'sitting by a wall in the sun, laughing at grief'. However the true vehicle of the 'theory of laughter' is the hobbits; their behaviour is calqued on the traditional English humour in adversity, but has deeper semantic roots.

Thus it is Pippin who looks up at the sun and the banners and offers comfort to Beregond, and Merry who never loses heart when even Théoden appears prey to 'horror and doubt'. But Sam on the road to Mordor goes beyond both. He has less hope even than Faramir. Indeed, we are told, he had:

> never had any real hope in the affair from the beginning; but being a cheerful hobbit he had not needed hope, as long as despair could be postponed. Now they had come to the bitter end. But he had stuck to his master all the way; that was what he had chiefly come for, and he would still stick to him. (II, 246)

Is it possible, one might wonder, to be 'cheerful' without any hope at all? Certainly it seems hardly sensible, but the idea rings true – it is corroborated by several first-hand accounts of the First World War, perhaps especially by Frank Richards's *Old Soldiers Never Die* (published 1933, and written significantly enough by a ranker, not an officer). Sam's twist on semantics is repeated by Pippin. He describes Fangorn and the last march of the Ents: was it 'fruitless'? Evidently not, in the short term, but in the long term Fangorn knows his race and story are sterile. The realisation makes him, according to Pippin, 'sad but not unhappy', and to modern English semantics the phrase makes almost no sense, like hopeless cheer. However an early meaning of 'sad' is 'settled, determined';

'cheer' comes from Old French *chair*, 'face'. The paradoxes put forward Tolkien's theses that determination should survive the worst that can happen, that a stout pretence is more valuable than sincere despair.

However the best delineation of Tolkien's new model of courage is perhaps at the end of Book IV chapter 8, 'The Stairs of Cirith Ungol'. Here Sam and Frodo, like Faramir, have little hope but still think of others in the future maybe 'laughing at grief'. Frodo indeed laughs himself: 'Such a sound had not been heard in those places since Sauron came to Middle-earth. To Sam suddenly it seemed as if all the stones were listening and the tall rocks leaning over them.' But then they fall asleep, and Gollum returns, to see and for a moment to love and aspire to the 'peace' he sees in their faces. It is characteristic of a kind of hardness in the fable that on this one occasion when Gollum's heart is stirred and he makes a gesture of penitence, Sam should wake up, misunderstand, and accuse Gollum of 'pawing' and 'sneaking'. Gollum gets no credit for his minor decency. But then he gave Frodo no credit earlier for *his* decency in saving Gollum from Faramir and the archers, preferring to spit, bear malice, and complain about 'nice Master's little trickses'. This is no excuse for Sam, but it shows maybe where criticisms like Edwin Muir's break down. The good side in *The Lord of the Rings* does win, but its casualties include, besides Théoden and Boromir, beauty, Lothlórien, Middle-earth and even Gollum. Furthermore the characters are aware of their losses all the time, and bear a burden of regret. They just have to make the best of things and not confuse 'sorrow' with 'despair';[8] even the hobbits' schoolboy humour has a point. Tolkien after all put forward his theses about courage and about laughter fairly clearly. The critical inability to see them comes partly from mere ideological reluctance; partly, though, from unfamiliarity with the basic structural mode of *The Lord of the Rings*, the ancient and pre-novelistic device of *entrelacement*.

The ethics of interlace

There is a minor mystery about this mode, for Tolkien might have been expected not to like it. Its greatest literary monuments are the sequence of French prose tales from the thirteenth century about King Arthur, known as the Vulgate Cycle and transposed into English only in highly compressed form by Sir Thomas Malory; and the later Italian epics about the knights of Charlemagne, Boiardo's *Orlando Innamorato*, 'Roland in Love', and Ariosto's *Orlando Furioso*, 'Roland Run Mad', imitated in English by Spenser's *The Faerie Queene*. Hence, no doubt, the early reviewers' comparisons of Tolkien with Malory, Spenser, Ariosto. However Tolkien disobligingly remarked that he hadn't read Ariosto and wouldn't have liked him if he had (*Biography*, p. 218), while Spenser exemplified much that he hated (see pp. 42–3 above). As for King Arthur, Tolkien might well have seen him as a symptom of English vagueness. Why should Englishmen take interest in a Welsh hero committed to their destruction, and known anyway via a French rehash? Still, the fact remains that Tolkien did produce a narrative of *entrelacement*. He had read a good deal of French romance for his *Sir Gawain* edition, and may have reflected further that even *Beowulf* has a kind of 'interlace' technique. He knew also that the Icelandic word for 'short story' is *þáttr*, 'a thread'; sagas often consist of several *þættir*, strands woven together. The image is in Gandalf's mind when he says to Théoden, 'There are children in your land who, out of the twisted threads of story, could pick the answer to your question.' To unravel *entrelacement* – that is at least one route to wisdom.[9]

The narrative of the great 'interlaced' romances is, however, by no means famous for wisdom. Malory's editor, Eugene Vinaver, comments:

> Adventures were piled up one upon the other without any apparent sequence or design, and innumerable personages, mostly anonymous, were introduced in a wild succession . . . The purpose of their encounters and pursuits was vague, and their tasks were seldom fulfilled: they met and parted and met again, each intent at first on following his particular 'quest', and yet prepared at any time to be diverted from it to other adventures and undertakings.[10]

The result was meaningless confusion. This is very much not the case with Tolkien. The basic pattern of the centre of *The Lord of the Rings* is separations and encounters and wanderings, but these are controlled first by a map (something no Arthurian narrative possesses), and second by an extremely tight chronology of days and dates. Along with this goes a deliberate chronological 'leapfrogging'.

To particularise: the narrative of *The Fellowship of the Ring* is single-stranded, following Frodo, with the exceptions of the 'flashback' narratives embedded in 'The Shadow of the Past' and 'The Council of Elrond'. The Nine Walkers themselves stick together from the leaving of Rivendell to the end of the volume, apart from losing Gandalf in Moria. But on Amon Hen, on the 26th February, the fellowship is dispersed. Boromir is killed. Frodo and Sam canoe away by themselves. Pippin and Merry are kidnapped by the Uruk-hai. Aragorn, left to choose between chasing the latter or following the Ring, decides to pursue the orcs, along with Legolas and Gimli. The fates of these three parties are then followed separately. Briefly, what happens is that chapters 1 and 2 of Book III take Aragorn, Legolas and Gimli from the 26th to the 28th February; chapters 3 and 4 lead Pippin and Merry from the 26th February to the 2nd March; chapters 5–7 return to Aragorn and his companions and 'leapfrog' them past Merry and Pippin again to the 4th March; while in chapter 8 these two subgroups of the fellowship meet again on the 5th, for Merry and Pippin to bring their story up-to-date again in recounted narrative. By chapter 11 they are splitting up again, Gandalf (who had returned from Moria in chapter 5) riding off with Pippin, Merry setting off with Théoden, Aragorn, Legolas and Gimli going together once more towards the Paths of the Dead. They will not gather again till chapter 6 of Book V, 'The Battle of the Pelennor Fields'. These, however, are not the only strands. All the time Frodo and Sam are spinning another, and doing it with the same chronological overlapping. They too depart on the 26th February, and have reached the 28th by the start of Book IV. By the end of that book, though, they have got to the 13th March, some eight days later than the last events of which we are told in Book III. Gandalf and the others do not 'catch up' with Frodo and Sam till chapter 5 of Book V, but then they continue once again to the 25th March, which the two hobbits do not reach for another three chapters.

Now this unnatural form of presentation works well for surprise and suspense. It is a shock to have the battle of Helm's Deep decided by the Ents and Huorns, who were last seen marching on Isengard, but whose powers have never come out in the open before. It is a good 'cliffhanger' scene at the end of Book V, as Pippin falls in the black blood of the troll, to have his fate decided by events of which we have no knowledge. But Tolkien meant more by *entrelacement* than that.

One example of a retrospective connection has already been given. As Frodo feels the pressure of the Eye on Amon Hen, a Voice speaks to him and gives him a moment of freedom to act. This voice is Gandalf's, though Frodo thinks he is dead and the reader does too. Gandalf says as much at II, 99, though he is laconic about it – 'I sat in a high place [the great tree in Lothlórien?], and I strove with the Dark Tower' – since Aragorn and the others he is addressing can have no idea what is being referred to. Gandalf remarks at the same time that he sent Gwaihir the eagle to watch the River; presumably he was the eagle Aragorn saw, but thought nothing of, as he stared out from Amon Hen on the first page of *The Two Towers*. Other cross-connections are frequent. Fangorn looks long at the two hobbits when they tell him Gandalf is dead; he does so because he doesn't believe them, having seen Gandalf himself a couple of days before. But we do not realise this till Gandalf remarks on their near-meeting some thirty pages later. Across the whole breadth of the story, meanwhile, fly the Nazgûl. Frodo and Sam feel their presence three times as they wander across the Emyn Muil and the Dead Marshes, at II, 213, 237, and 242, i.e. on the 29th February, 1st March and 4th March. Gollum feels sure this is no coincidence. ' "Three times!" he whimpered. "Three times is a threat. They feel us here, they feel the Precious. The Precious is their master. We cannot go any further this way, no. It's no use, no use!" ' What he says sounds plausible enough, but it's wrong. Three times *is* a coincidence, and actually we can guess each time what the Nazgûl are doing. The first was coming back from a fruitless wait for Gríshnakh the orc, dead and burnt that same day, with the smoke from his burning 'seen by many watchful eyes'. The second was probing towards Rohan and Saruman. The third was heading for Isengard, to alarm Pippin on its way with the thought that it had somehow been despatched for him (II, 204). Meanwhile the body of Boromir establishes a similar transverse thread as it drifts down the Great River, to be seen by Faramir, to have the workmanship on its belt noted and compared with the brooches of Sam and Frodo eight days later. These references and allusions tie the story together, we would say, or to use Gandalf's image show one thread twisting over another. They prove the author has the story under control, and are significant to any reader who has grasped the entire plot. However that is not how they appear to the characters, or to the reader whose attention has lapsed (as whose does not?). In this contrast between half- and full-perception lies the point of interlacings.

For to the characters the story appears, to repeat a term used already, as a 'bewilderment'. They are lost in the woods and plains of Middle-earth. They also do not know what is going on or what to do next. Aragorn has to choose between going to Mordor or to Minas Tirith; delays, and then finds himself choosing between Sam and Frodo or Merry and Pippin; picks one quest, and then has to decide whether to rest or pursue by night. Neither decision nor delay seems to pay off. 'All that I have done today has gone amiss', he says (II, 17); 'Since we passed through the Argonath my choices have gone amiss' (II, 28); 'And now may I make a right choice, and change the evil fate of this unhappy day!' (II, 21). Éomer's intervention does not help him much, for he and his companions cannot decide at the end of chapter 2 whether they have seen Saruman or not. It appears they did (we learn later, II, 102), but the next time they think someone is Saruman it is Gandalf. Furthermore the appearance of Saruman to drive off the borrowed horses is coincidental with the arrival of Shadowfax – the note of joy in their whinnyings puzzles Legolas, though their eventual return with Shadowfax provides an equine equivalent for the unexpected return of Gandalf. Simultaneously, in Fangorn Forest, Gandalf, Saruman and Treebeard himself are wandering, meeting or not meeting seemingly at random. The effect as a whole is like that of *A Midsummer Night's Dream*, where pairs of lovers wander in another enchanted wood, their paths crossed and tangled by Puck, Oberon, Titania and the infatuating Bully Bottom. 'Infatuation' is indeed a word one might use as well as 'bewilderment'. It means following the *ignis fatuus*, the 'will o' the wisp' that traditionally leads travellers into bog or quicksand; an analogue to the multiple wanderings of Book III is Frodo staring at the corpse-candles in chapter 2 of Book IV, to be warned by Gollum not to heed them, or the dead, rotten, phantasmal faces in the marshes below: 'Or hobbits go down to join the Dead ones and light little candles. Follow Sméagol! Don't look at lights!'

Even though it comes from Gollum, this is good advice. For of course Aragorn and the others, including Frodo, are in their feelings of confusion and meaninglessness absolutely wrong – 'infatuated', 'bewildered', drowning in a bog of mere events, caught in a strangler's net of *wyrd*. They have good apparent grounds for despair. But as it turns out (as it happens, as 'chance' or 'luck' would have it) there are things in the web of story to refute those grounds. As Gandalf points out, all Sauron and Saruman and the orcs have done between them is 'bring Pippin and Merry with marvellous speed, and in the nick of time, to Fangorn, where otherwise they would never have come at all!' – and so, one might say, though it is beyond Gandalf's knowledge at the time, to rouse the Ents, overthrow Saruman, save Rohan, and free Théoden to make his decisive intervention at Minas Tirith. There are still several things one can *not* say: for instance, that Saruman's treachery was accordingly a Good Thing, or that the rescue of Minas Tirith is a reward for Aragorn's persistence. After all, if Saruman had stayed loyal things might have ended better; if Aragorn had abandoned the chase Merry and Pippin would have stirred up Fangorn just the same. What one can be absolutely sure about is that giving up does the other side's work for them, and ruins all your own possible futures and other people's as well. The despair of Denethor killed Théoden, Gandalf surmises at II, 132. While persistence offers no guarantees, it does give 'luck' a chance to operate, through unknown allies or unknown weaknesses in the opposition.

As a working theory this is impregnable, whether considered sceptically or superstitiously. To it the *entrelacements* contribute a recognisable attitude towards reality. Events in the world, they say, appear chaotic and unplanned, appear so all but unmistakably. But however strong that impression is, it is a subjective one founded on the inevitably limited view of any individual. If individuals could see more widely – as we can, by virtue of the narrative structure of The Lord of the Rings – they would realise that events have a cause-and-effect logic, though there are so many causes that perhaps no one but God can ever see them all at once. The world is a Persian carpet, then, and we are ants lumbering from one thread to the other and observing that there is no pattern in the colours. That is why one of Gandalf's favourite sayings is 'Even the wise cannot see all ends', and why he often demonstrates its truth himself. Thus it is ironic that he more than once offers a cold-hearted appraisal of the junior hobbits' utility. 'If these hobbits understood the danger', he says to Elrond, 'they would not dare to go.' But they would still *want* to, he concludes, and their wish should outweigh their ignorance. He says to Pippin later, 'Generous deed should not be outweighed by cold counsel'. In the end he is proved both right and wrong: Merry and Pippin between them rouse the Ents, save Faramir, kill the Ringwraith. The last deed is caused by the sheer chance of finding a dagger 'bound round with spells for the destruction of Mordor' in the wight's barrow. 'Glad would he have been to know its fate who wrought it slowly long ago', comments the narrator; and his comment shows that the ancient smith was not glad, did not know, was condemned to defeat and death and oblivion in the barrows. Still, even after thousands of years hope should not be lost: nor relied on.

It is Pippin too who looks in the *palantír* and so misleads Sauron into thinking Saruman may have the Ring. This may have helped draw on the Enemy's hasty stroke, thinks Gandalf at III, 88. More important is the fact that Aragorn has the stone available to him, and that Sauron (having seen a hobbit in the same stone) thinks Aragorn *also has the Ring*: it is because Aragorn showed himself to Sauron in the palantír that Sauron neglects his guard. 'The Eye turned inward, pondering tidings of doubt and danger: a bright sword, and a stern and kingly face it saw' (III, 200). But once more ironically, it is what the Eye does *not* see that matters. The bright sword and kingly face turn out not to be critical. It is the two ants creeping along the Ephel Dúath who are going to change reality. Indeed Frodo and Sam provide perhaps the strongest effects of the *entrelacement*. Their bewilderments, infatuations, sense of being lost and abandoned, are much stronger than those of Aragorn or Gimli or anyone else in the more active half of the story. But by the time we come to following their strand along we know that these are not *true*. 'All my choices have proved ill', says Frodo within a couple of pages of the start of his quest. But his words echo unmistakably those of Aragorn nearly two hundred pages earlier; and we know Aragorn was wrong. What counts, then, is that Frodo should go on choosing. We perceive his doubt and weariness simultaneously as a natural reaction to circumstances, and as a temptation, even a phantasm or illusion of the Dark Tower. Evil works, we realise, by sapping the will with over-complication. Like 'the Shadow', this is in fiction an external force with physical effects of which sensitive characters like Legolas can be aware; it appeals to a recognition of truth outside fiction, however, in its buried statements that clouds have silver linings, that fortune favours the brave, that even in reality things are not always as they seem.

There is indeed a corpus of proverbs scattered through *The Lord of the Rings*, which add weight to the implications of interlace. 'Oft the unbidden guest proves the best company', says Éomer, and later 'Twice blessed is hope unlooked-for'. 'Where will wants not, a way opens', says his sister, more solemnly but also more familiarly. 'Oft hope is born, when all is forlorn', says Legolas. He, Aragorn and Théoden also state proverbs about freshness, with respectively 'Rede oft is found at the rising of the sun', 'None knows what the new day shall bring him', and 'In the morning counsels are best . . .' Legolas adds a spatial metaphor with his 'Few can foresee whither their road will lead them . . .' It should be noted that most

of these are neutral on the optimism/pessimism scale, while some of the
characters' proverbs approach the meaningless. 'Strange are the turns of
fortune', says Gandalf (which could be good or bad depending on context),
and 'Hope oft deceives', says Éomer (also so true as to be non-predictive).
Still, most of those quoted so far are real proverbs as the place-names of
the Shire are real place-names, and they have a similar function: to draw
us in, to make connections between experience inside and outside the
story. Within this continuum, however, other proverbs are planted,
sounding much the same as the others but more original and so closer to
Tolkien's own intention. 'Often does hatred hurt itself', says Gandalf;
'Oft evil will shall evil mar', says Théoden; 'The hasty stroke goes oft
astray', says Aragorn; 'A traitor may betray himself', Gandalf again. It
takes the action of the whole of *The Lord of the Rings* to make these ring
true and there is a vein of proverbial wisdom (about God being on the
side of the big battalions) which would utterly deny them. These invented
sayings show in miniature the 'contrivance' of which the trilogy has often
been accused. Only a fool, though, would deny that the contrivances have
a point; only a very careless reader would think that the *entrelacements* of
this romance are purely for variety, and have nothing to say about 'the
fundamental character of reality' at all.

Just allegory and large symbolism

Tolkien's proverbs edge, on the whole, towards the archaic. So does his
use of omens and prophecies – a feature of *The Lord of the Rings* which
may furthermore seem to deny the idea of free will being left intact by the
forces of providence. Galadriel seems to know in advance that Aragorn
will take the Paths of the Dead, Aragorn to know that he and Éomer will
meet again, 'though all the hosts of Mordor should stand between'.
Someone (or something) foreknew that the Ringwraith would not fall 'by
the hand of man'. These cross-temporal flashes suggest, perhaps, that
some things are bound to happen regardless of what people do or choose.
Yet that would clearly be a false conclusion. The words of prophecies could
be fulfilled after all in many different ways. We are left always at liberty
to suppose that Aragorn and Éomer could have met once more as prisoners,
say, that the Grey Company could have quailed and turned back. If Merry
had failed to stab the Ringwraith, it might have died aeons later at the
hands of some other woman, hobbit, elf-hero. As Galadriel says of her
Mirror (I, 378): it 'shows many things, and not all have yet to come to pass.
Some never come to be, unless those that behold the visions turn aside
from their path to prevent them.' She articulates a theory of compromise
between fate and free will once more at least a millennium old: in the
Solomon and Saturn poem Saturn asks which will be the stronger, *wyrd ðe*

warnung, 'fated events or foresight', and Solomon tells him that 'Fate is hard to alter . . . And nevertheless an intelligent man can moderate all the things that fate causes, as long as he is clear in his mind'. It is important to realise though, that antiquarian as Tolkien's motives often were,[11] and 'pre-scientific' as the opinions of Galadriel and Solomon seem, what Tolkien was writing about is still in a way a live issue. 'Every bullet has his billet' is a distinctively modern saying, first recorded in that form in 1765, and in use up to the present day to indicate that sometimes no precautions work; yet saying the proverb, and believing it, probably never stopped anyone taking cover. 'God helps those who help themselves', to repeat a proverb mentioned earlier. Tolkien in other words never lost his belief in the reality and continuity, not only of language and of history, but of human nature and of some intellectual problems.

This should be kept in mind when considering the much vexed question of allegory, or symbolism, in *The Lord of the Rings*. Tolkien's opinions here are clear only up to a point. As is well known, he wrote in the 'Foreword' to the second edition: 'I cordially dislike allegory in all its manifestations, and always have done so since I grew old and wary enough to detect its presence.' He went on, though: 'I much prefer history, true or feigned, with its varied applicability to the thought and experience of readers. I think that many confuse "applicability" with "allegory"; but the one resides in the freedom of the reader, and the other in the purposed domination of the author.' Some relation between fiction and fact might be perceived, then; and 'The Scouring of the Shire' had 'some basis in experience' though no 'contemporary political reference whatsoever', not even to Britain's Socialist 'austerity' government of 1945–50. As Tolkien wrote of *Beowulf*, it was important to preserve a balance, to see that the 'large symbolism is near the surface, but . . . does not break through, nor become allegory'. 'Allegory' would after all imply, to Tolkien (see pp. 33–7 above), that *The Lord of the Rings* had only one meaning, which would have to remain constant all the way through; he toyed contemptuously with the notion in the 'Foreword' as he sketched out a plan for his work as a *real* allegory with the Ring itself as President Truman's atomic bomb.[12] 'Large symbolism', however, should not be a matter of one imposed diagram, but of repeated offered hints. The hints would work only if they were true both in fact and in fiction. History, thought Tolkien, was varied in its applicability. But if you understood it properly, you saw it repeating itself.

Some of Tolkien's hints have been glanced at already. The Riders of Rohan, and the Rangers of Gondor, will not offer the excuse that they were 'only obeying orders'; one cannot avoid the contrast with the Nazis. When Gandalf tells Frodo about the Ring, Frodo replies 'I wish it need not have happened in my time', but Gandalf reproves him: 'So do I . . . and so do all who live to see such times. But that is not for them to decide'

(I, 60). The rebuke is deserved by Frodo, but also by Neville Chamberlain with his now infamous promise that he brought 'peace in our time'. Elrond, at I, 256, has learnt better. He remembers a moment when 'the Elves deemed that evil was ended for ever' but knows that 'it was not so'. Tolkien himself fought in 'the war to end all wars', but saw his sons fighting in the one after that. Other ironies are not hard to discover. As Gandalf and Pippin ride from the Anórien towards Minas Tirith, they find their way blocked by men building a wall (III, 20). It is Denethor's insistence on defending this (III, 89) that nearly kills Faramir, and all it does in practice is to obstruct the arrival of the Rohirrim (III, 111) by which time it is already a 'ruin', for all the 'labour' wasted on it at the start. Men of Tolkien's generation could hardly avoid thinking of the Maginot line. Gandalf's advice, 'But leave your trowels and sharpen your swords!', has more than an immediate relevance. The hint is unmistakable, as are others in the trilogy, of Vichyism and quislings, of puppet governments and demilitarised zones. How well do they hang together, though? Did Tolkien go on from the exploitation of occasional scenes to the manipulation of plot, the creation of recognisably symbolic characters, the thing the *TLS* reviewer asked for so plaintively, 'a clear message for the modern world'? Of course Tolkien would have scorned 'message' as much as 'modern'. Still, he created two characters in *The Lord of the Rings* of particular suggestiveness, both of them originally on the right side but seduced or corroded by evil, and so especially likely to have analogues in the real world: these are Denethor and Saruman, each of them seen faintly satirically, almost politically.

To take the more obvious example first, Saruman shows many signs of being equatable with industrialism, or technology. His very name means something of the sort. *Searu* in Old English (the West Saxon form of Mercian *saru) means 'Device, design, contrivance, art'. Bosworth-Toller's *Dictionary* says cautiously that often you cannot tell 'whether the word is used with a good or with a bad meaning'. When Beowulf walks into Hrothgar's hall the poet says appreciatively that 'on him his armour shone, the cunning net (*searo-net*) sewed by the crafts (*orþancum*) of the smith'. Jewellers are *searo-cræftig*, and wizards *snottor searu-þancum*, 'wise in cunning thoughts'. The word stretches from wisdom to plot and treachery, though. Beowulf denies he ever sought out *searo-nîþas*, 'cunning malices', Grendel's corpse-holding glove is *searo-bendum fæst*, 'fixed with cunning bands'. The word implies cleverness, but is nearly always linked with metal: iron in armour and clasps, but also silver and gold. The dragon's treasure is a *searu-gimma geþræc*, 'a heap of cunning jewels', in the *Riming Poem* the poet says obscurely *sinc searwade*, 'treasure played the traitor'. That means 'left its possessor', suggest Messrs Bosworth and Toller. To Tolkien, with his theory of dragonish 'bewilderment', it meant more likely 'stayed with its possessor', driving him insidiously to greed and cunning.

These cruxes all form part of Saruman's character. He is learned, but his learning tends to the practical. 'He has a mind of metal and wheels', says Fangorn. His orcs use a kind of gunpowder at Helm's Deep (II, 142); thirty pages later the Ents meet at Isengard, or 'Irontown', a kind of napalm – perhaps one should say with closer reference to Tolkien's own experience, a *Flammenwerfer*. The implication is that Saruman has been led from ethically neutral researches into the kind of wanton pollution and love of dirt we see in 'The Scouring of the Shire' by something corrupting in the love of machines or in the very desire for control over the natural world. It is interesting, too, that Saruman's Orc-men call him 'Sharkey' or 'Old Man'. To a medievalist the name might well suggest the 'Old Man of the Mountains' or leader of the Assassins as described in *Mandeville's Travels*. 'Old Man' is simply Arabic *shaikh* (cp. Orkish *sharkû*). And Mandeville's Old Man ruled, of course, by feeding his followers *hashish* and deluding them with dreams of paradise. So, we might think, 'cunning man', or 'machine man', or 'technological man', keeps a Utopian carrot dangling in front of our noses, of a world of leisure and convenience where each new mill grinds faster than the one before. But as Ted Sandyman ought to have realised, 'you've got to have grist before you can grind'; machine-masters end up machine-minders, and all for nothing, or rather for an insidious logic of expansion.

This may not be a totally convincing critique of modern society, but it has clear modern relevance and is more than mere dislike. There is something suggestive also in Saruman's notorious 'voice', which always seems 'wise and reasonable', and wakes desire in others 'by swift agreement to seem wise themselves'. Gandalf's harshness represents denial of Utopias and insistence that nothing comes free. Even Lotho 'Pimple', Frodo's relative, has a place in the argument because he is such an obvious Gradgrind – greedy and bossy to begin with, but staying within the law till his manipulators take over, to jail his mother, kill him and eat him too (if we can believe the hints about Gríma Wormtongue). Jeremy Bentham to Victorian capitalists? Old Bolshevik to new Stalinist? The progression is familiar enough, and it adds another modern dimension to Middle-earth – or rather a timeless one, for though in the modern age we give Saruman a modern 'applicability', his name, and the evident uncertainty even in Anglo-Saxon times over mechanical cleverness and 'machinations', shows that his meaning was ancient too.

Saruman nevertheless does have one distinctively modern trait, which is his association with Socialism. His men *say* they are gathering things 'for fair distribution', though nobody believes them – a particularly strange compromise of evil with morality, for Middle-earth, where vice rarely troubles to be hypocritical. It is worth saying accordingly that Denethor, contrasted with Saruman as he is in other ways with Théoden, is an arch-conservative. In almost his last speech he declares:

'I would have things as they were in all the days of my life . . . and in the days of my longfathers before me . . . But if doom denies this to me, then I will have *naught*: neither life diminished, nor love halved, nor honour abated.' (III, 130)

'I will have *naught*' is a particularly ominous expression. As *The Lord of the Rings* was coming to the end of its gestation it became possible for the first time for political leaders to say they wanted nothing *and make it come true*. Denethor clearly will not submit to the Enemy, as Saruman did, but he also cares nothing in the end for his subjects, while his love even for his sons would take them both to death with him. 'The West has failed', he says. 'It shall all go up in a great fire, and all shall be ended! Ash! Ash and smoke blown away on the wind!' He does not say 'nuclear fire', but the thought fits. Denethor breaks his own staff of office as Saruman does not. He mingles an excess of heroic temper – the ancient Ragnarǫk spirit, one might say, which Tolkien with significant anachronism twice calls 'heathen'[13] – with a mean concern for his own sovereignty and his own boundaries: a combination that unusually and in this one particular case makes no sense at all before 1945 and the invention of the 'great deterrent'.

It is a risky business finally to draw a Tolkienian 'inner meaning' from these various 'applicabilities'. Tolkien himself insisted that he had not intended one; and finding one need not be the ultimate necessity for the critic, since after all political messages add nothing to Tom Bombadil, or the Ents, or the Riders of Rohan, or the *entrelacements*, or most of the things discussed in this chapter and the ones around it. The real point is that Tolkien's theories about nature, evil, luck and our perception of the world generated as a sort of by-product modern applications and political ones. His attachment to the 'theory of courage' made him believe that the Western world in his lifetime had been short not of wit or of strength, but of will. His readings of heroic poems made him especially scornful of the notion that to say 'evil must be fought' is the same as saying 'might is right'.[14] He thought that England, in forgetting her early literature, had fallen into liberal self-delusions. Naturally all these 'morals' or 'meanings' can in themselves be accepted or rejected, depending very much on the varied experience of readers. What cannot be denied is that they emerge from much experience in the author, and much original thought, that they are moreover integrated in a fiction which has a power independent of them. Tolkien was not writing to a thesis. A good deal of what he wrote may be taken as a rejection of the 'liberal interpretation of history', and indeed of the 'liberal humanist tradition' in literature;[15] nevertheless the centre of his story is the Ring and the maxim that 'power corrupts', a concept unimpeachably modern, democratic, anti- though not un-heroic.

Eucatastrophe, realism, and romance

It should be clear by this time that if there is one critical statement entirely and absolutely wrong, it is the one quoted at the start of this chapter, about *The Lord of the Rings* not being 'moulded by some controlling vision of things which is at the same time its *raison d'être*'. The 'vision of things' is there in the Ring, in the scenes of conflict and temptation, in the characters' words and attitudes, in proverbs and in prophecies and in the very narrative mode itself. Naturally this 'understanding of reality' can be 'denied': so can they all. But not to see that it exists shows a surprising (and therefore interesting) blindness. It is matched only by the insistence of the anonymous reviewer of the *TLS* that in *The Lord of the Rings* all the good and bad sides do is try to kill each other, so that they cannot be told apart: 'Morally there seems nothing to choose between them.'[16] The difference is at the very heart of the plot. As W. H. Auden saw, in his piece for *The New York Review of Books* (22 January 1956), it is vital that Sauron does not guard the Cracks of Doom and discover Frodo because he is sure Aragorn will take the Ring:

> Evil, that is, has every advantage but one – it is inferior in imagination. Good can imagine the possibility of becoming evil – hence the refusal of Gandalf and Aragorn to use the Ring – but Evil, defiantly chosen, can no longer imagine anything but itself.

Not to see points like that (and there are more obvious ones) is in a way shameful. The repeated blindnesses of critics can only be explained by a deep dissatisfaction in them with the very data of 'fairy-story', an inhibition against accepting the conventions of romance.

Of these the greatest must be the 'happy ending' (one brought about, more often than not, by 'hap' or 'chance' or 'luck'). Tolkien, of course, being a Christian, did in absolute fact believe that in the end all things would end happily, that in a sense they already had – a belief he shared with Dante, and a matter of faith beyond argument. It needs to be said though that he was capable of envisaging a different belief and even bringing it into his story. Frodo and Sam debate it after they have destroyed the Ring and are caught in the fall of the Dark Tower:

> 'I don't want to give up yet' [said Sam]. 'It's not like me, somehow, if you understand.'
> 'Maybe not, Sam,' said Frodo; 'but it's like things are in the world. Hopes fail. An end comes. We have only a little time to wait now. We are lost in ruin and downfall, and there is no escape.' (III, 228)

He does not change his mind, nor his perception of how 'things are in the world'. They are changed for him by the eagles who come and take him in his sleep to a new world – which Sam, with a resurrected Gandalf in front of him, very nearly perceives as Heaven. The difference between Earth and Middle-earth, one might say, is that in the latter faith can, just sometimes, be perceived as fact. And while this is an enormous difference, it is not the same as that between the adult and the child.

It cannot be denied that there *is* a streak of 'wish-fulfilment' in *The Lord of the Rings*. Tolkien would have liked to hear the horns of Rohan blow, and watch the Black Breath of inertia dissolve from his own country. If his work has an image inside itself, it is I think the horn that Éomer gives to Merry, only a small one, but one from the hoard of Scatha the Worm and brought from the North by Eorl the Young. It is a magic one, though only modestly so: 'He that blows it at need shall set fear in the hearts of his enemies and joy in the hearts of his friends, and they shall hear him and come to him.' When Merry blows it in the Shire the revolution against sloth and shabbiness and Saruman–'Sharkey' is on: no doubt Tolkien would have liked to be able in his own person to do the same. He got closer to his goal than many, however, at least when it came to bringing 'joy'. At the same time his portrayal of Frodo quietly sliding down to sleep, dismissal and an oblivion which would include ents, elves, dwarves and the whole of Middle-earth, shows that he recognised the limits of his own wishes and their non-correspondence with reality. The last word on the relationship between his literary mode and that of realism may perhaps go to Professor Frank Kermode, who wrote:

> Romance could be defined as a means of exhibiting the action of magical and moral laws in a version of human life so selective as to obscure, for the special purpose of concentrating attention on these laws, the fact that in reality their force is intermittent and only fitfully glimpsed.

Professor Kermode made those remarks however *à propos* of Shakespeare's *Tempest*.[17] And one has to say that while both Prospero and Gandalf are old men with staffs, Prospero brushes aside the oppositions of reality with an ease which Gandalf is never allowed to aspire to.

Chapter 6

'WHEN ALL OUR FATHERS WORSHIPPED STOCKS AND STONES'

Stylistic theories: Tolkien and Shakespeare

Mentioning Tolkien in the same breath with Shakespeare will seem to many rash, even perverse. If there is one image which biographical criticism has projected powerfully, it is that of Tolkien the Philistine, hater of literary mainstreams. He read little modern poetry and little modern fiction, taking 'no serious notice' even of what he read. He liked as much as anything the works of John Buchan. In 1931 he succeeded in eliminating Shakespeare from his part of the Oxford English syllabus. In childhood he found that he 'disliked cordially' Shakespeare's plays, remembering especially an early 'bitter disappointment and disgust . . . with the shabby use made in Shakespeare of the coming of "Great Birnam Wood to high Dunsinane hill" '.[1] Many critics have felt that these strongly anti-literary or anti-poetic attitudes have found suitable reflection in Tolkien's own style, described variously as 'Brewer's Biblical', 'Boy's Own', irresistibly reminiscent of 'the work of Mr Frank Richards' (the creator of Billy Bunter). It is a common critical stance to praise Tolkien's conception, often somewhat vaguely, or with even more vagueness his 'mythological' or 'mythopoeic' powers; but then to declare that the words do not live up to the things, the style 'is quite inadequate to the theme'.[2] There are however immediate reasons for thinking that this stance is imperceptive. Tolkien said that he 'disliked' Shakespeare 'cordially', but he used exactly the same phrase of allegory too, where it concealed an opinion of some subtlety. On a larger scale one might observe that his lifelong preoccupation with words gave him a *kind* of sensitivity to them, even if it was an unorthodox one; and further that it is strange that a myth should so make its way if enshrined and embodied in words as inappropriate as critics have made out. 'Style' and 'mythology' are in fact not to be separated, though they may be disentangled. A concept which helps one to see Tolkien's view of both is that of 'loose' or 'tight' semantic and dramatic 'fit'.

The beginnings of this idea emerge well from a passage in *The Lord of the Rings* which has been singled out for especially ferocious criticism: the parting of Treebeard from Celeborn and Galadriel in *The Return of the King*, p. 259:

Then Treebeard said farewell to each of them in turn, and he bowed three times slowly and with great reverence to Celeborn and Galadriel. 'It is long, long since we met by stock or by stone, *A vanimar, vanimálion nostari!*' he said. 'It is sad that we should meet only thus at the ending. For the world is changing: I feel it in the water, I feel it in the earth, and I smell it in the air. I do not think we shall meet again.'

And Celeborn said: 'I do not know, Eldest.' But Galadriel said: 'Not in Middle-earth, nor until the lands that lie under the wave are lifted up again. Then in the willow-meads of Tasarinan we may meet in the Spring. Farewell!'

These two paragraphs are quoted in his book *Modern Fantasy* by Dr C. N. Manlove, who then goes straight on as usual to spearhead the critical assault and declare:

The overworked cadences, the droning, monotonous pitch, the sheer sense of hearts charged not with lead but gas, can offer only nervous sentimental indulgence or plain embarrassment to the reader.
    Compare this with, say, Ector's lament over Arthur in Malory, or the 'Survivor's Lament' in *Beowulf*, or this from 'The Wanderer' . . .

and Dr Manlove goes on to cite a well-known *Ubi sunt* passage from the Old English poem and to observe that 'This is real elegy, for it has something to be elegiac about'.[3] Considered as criticism, much of this is mere rudeness, but it does have the merit of introducing medieval comparisons: not on the whole good ground for a Manlove to fight a Tolkien on.
    Exactly that passage from *The Wanderer*, for instance, is paraphrased by Aragorn in chapter 6 of *The Two Towers*: a candid mind might have looked to see what Tolkien could make of it. As for Ector's lament, it was in fact over Lancelot, not Arthur. If one reads even more attentively, one cannot help noting a curious stylistic feature not entirely dissociated from Treebeard. What Malory actually wrote was:

'And now I dare say,' sayd syr Ector, 'thou sir Launcelot, there thou lyest, that thou were never matched of erthely knyghtes hande. And thou were the curtest [i.e. most courteous] knyght that ever bare shelde! And thou were the truest frende to thy lovar that ever bestrade hors, and thou were the trewest lover of a synful man that ever loved woman, and thou were the kyndest man that ever strake with swerde.'[4]

The kindest man that ever struck with sword?, modern readers reflect. The truest lover that ever bestrode a horse? In modern contexts phrases like this could only be funny. Strong belief in the virtues of stylistic and semantic consistency urge us to keep kindness and sword-strokes, loved women and bestridden horses, in separate mental compartments. But clearly Malory did not feel this urge towards exactness at all. Did Tolkien? Tolkien furthermore no doubt noted that Malory's insensitivity in this respect (a common thing in medieval writers) had not led necessarily to failure. His emulation of 'loose semantic fit' does however puzzle many modern readers – those especially who have been sophisticated by modern literary practice.

To go back to Dr Manlove and Treebeard: it is actually hard to make out what bits of the text have caused the irritation. It could be the boldly untranslated fragment of Quenya,[5] or the triple repetition of 'feel . . . feel . . . smell', or the sudden change to less plain language in Galadriel's speech, with its elvish place-name (and also its typical echo of wartime English popular song).[6] However all these are easily defensible. If the paragraphs quoted do contain anything to gripe at seriously, it must be Treebeard's opening sentence, with its oddly redundant phrase, 'by stock or by stone'. What have stocks and stones got to do with the matter? Isn't the phrase just meaningless, flung in for the rhythm, meaning no more than 'by pillar or by post', 'by night or by day', 'by hook or by crook'? So one might feel. But it is exactly in phrases like this that one sees Tolkien playing with medieval notions of style, with 'loose semantic fit', with a personal view of poetry.

'By stock or by stone' is certainly a deliberate echo of the fourteenth century poem *Pearl*, written by the author of *Sir Gawain and the Green Knight*, and probably the most powerful of all medieval elegies. Under its image of the jeweller who has lost his pearl in an orchard, this describes a father lamenting his dead infant daughter in the graveyard where she is buried. He falls asleep with his head on her grave mound, to be taken away in spirit to a strange land where all his grief suddenly fades – and where to his utter delight he sees his lost child facing him, on the other side of a river. But she has grown up strangely, and she treats him with a cold formality, calling him 'Sir' but correcting him almost every time he speaks. How sad he has been, he says; he had no need to be, she replies. Quite right, he agrees, for (praise God) he has found her and will live with her in joy from now on; no, she says, she is not there, he cannot join her, he cannot cross the river. Don't send me away again, he pleads, to 'durande doel'. Why are you always talking about sorrow? she asks fiercely. At that the father gives up his attempt to take an active role, humbles himself, but repeats his grief in his apology:

> 'My blysse, my bale, ye han ben bothe,
> Bot much the bygger yet watz my mon;
> Fro thou watz wroken fro vch a wothe,
> I wyste neuer quere my perle watz gon.
> Now I hit se, now lethez my lothe.

> And, quen we departed, we wern at on;
> God forbede we be now wrothe,
> We meten so selden by stok other ston . . .'

The quotation here is based on the edition of *Pearl* by E. V. Gordon (Oxford: Clarendon Press, 1953), originally meant to be a co-operative venture with Tolkien; and I would translate it as follows:

> 'You have been both joy and grief to me, but so far sorrow has been much the greater; I never knew, once you were removed from earthly dangers, where my pearl had gone. But now I see it, my sadness is assuaged. And when we were separated, there was no strife between us. God forbid we should now be angry with each other – we meet so seldom by stock or by stone . . .'

In his version of *Pearl* published in 1975 Tolkien translated that last line as 'We meet on our roads by chance so rare', but probably 'We meet so seldom by stock or by stone' is better. The pathos lies in the characteristic early English understatement – 'so seldom' means 'never' or worse still 'just this once' – and also in the last phrase's suspense between precision and vagueness. 'Stok other ston' could mean nothing, be just a line-filler, like 'erly and late' a few lines afterwards. On the other hand it implies very strongly 'on earth', 'in reality', 'in flesh and blood'. Where *is* the dreamer-father? At the end of the poem he will realise that the water was Death, his daughter in Heaven, the strange land a premonition of Paradise. If at the moment he speaks he thinks he is meeting his child in a land of real stones and tree-stumps, he is sadly mistaken; if he realises he is not, then already a touch of grief is creeping back into consolation.

'By stok other ston' is great poetry, one should see; not a great *phrase*, but great poetry, in its context. Could the same effect be reached in modern English, with its much fiercer attitude towards phrasal looseness? Tolkien tried the experiment in Treebeard's farewell, and maybe he failed; though one might say that the image behind the phrase works well for Fangorn, whose sense of ultimate loss naturally centres on felled trees and barren ground. However the real point is that Tolkien was trying continually to extend the frontiers of style beyond the barbed wire of modern opinion. In this endeavour he thought he had the backing of the great poets and romancers, like Sir Thomas Malory or the anonymous authors of *Pearl* and *Beowulf* and *The Wanderer*. It was true that they had mostly been forgotten, left unappreciated. The tradition they stood for, though, had not. You could see it, thought Tolkien, even in Shakespeare, here and there.

It is thus quite clear that whatever he said about Shakespeare's plays, Tolkien read some of them with keen attention: most of all, *Macbeth*. Motifs from this play are repeated prominently in *The Lord of the Rings*.

The march of the Ents to Isengard makes true the report of the frightened messenger to the incredulous Macbeth in Act V Scene 5: 'As I did stand my watch upon the hill/I looked toward Birnam and anon methought/The wood began to move.' The prophecy that the chief Ringwraith will not fall 'by the hand of man', and his check when he realises Dernhelm is a woman, similarly parallels the Witches' assurance to Macbeth and his disconcertment when told 'Macduff was from his mother's womb/Untimely ripped.' There is a more complicated echo of Shakespeare in the scene when Aragorn, as the true king, revives the sick in the Houses of Healing with his touch and the herb *athelas*. In *Macbeth* too there is a healing king, but offstage – it is Edward the Confessor, the last legitimate Anglo-Saxon king, who sends Siward Earl of Northumbria to assist the rebels. This seems to be a deliberate compliment by Shakespeare to James the First (of England) and Sixth (of Scotland), who had begun to touch for the 'king's evil' or scrofula by 1606. Tolkien probably did not approve, thinking this mere flattery. After all James was of the Stewart dynasty, so called because his ancestor Robert had been High Steward of Scotland, and had succeeded to the throne on the death of David II in 1371. When Denethor says that stewards do not come to be kings by the lapse of a few centuries in Gondor, but only 'in other places of less royalty', the remark is true of Scotland, and of Britain – though not of Anglo-Saxon England, ruled from the legendary past of King Cerdic to 1065 by kings descended in paternal line from one ancestor. *The Return of the King* is in a way a parallel, in another a reproach, to *Macbeth*.

Tolkien however used the play for both more and less than motifs. There is a flash of minute observation in chapter 6 of *The Two Towers*. What shall we do about Saruman, asks Théoden. 'Do the deed at hand', replies Gandalf, send every man against him at once. 'If we fail, we fall. If we succeed – then we will face the next task.' The jingle of 'fail-fall' echoes a famous crux in *Macbeth*, where the hero falters in front of his wife. 'If we should fail?', he asks. 'We fail?' replies she – in the Folio punctuation. Actresses have tried the line different ways: as a sarcastic question, a flat dismissal, a verbal slap. They were all wrong, implies Tolkien; it was a misprint, the word was 'fall' meaning 'die' and is a straight answer to a straight question. The reading might not seem very good, except for one thing. 'Alliterative assonances' such as 'fail' and 'fall' are very common in Old English poetry, and indeed in Middle English in the tradition which includes *Pearl*. *Macbeth* is the only one of Shakespeare's plays to include Anglo-Saxon characters; and by some odd stylistic response it too is full of this ancient (but still popular) rhetorical device. 'My way of *life*/Is fallen into the sere, the yellow *leaf*', says Macbeth; 'why do you start, and seem to *fear*/Things that do sound so *fair*?' asks Banquo; 'I see thee still', says Macbeth to the imaginary dagger, 'And on thy *blade* and dudgeon gouts of *blood*,/Which was not so before.'

'Fail' and 'fall' would then be one in a set of nearly forty – a part of the play's poetic texture. How strange that critics should not have remarked the possibility! Or how typical, thought Tolkien. Modern critics were not good at Anglo-Saxon echoes, especially at ones which hung on into modern times in phrases like 'mock' and 'make', 'chance' and 'choice', 'bullet' and 'billet', all mentioned already in this study.

Gandalf's adaptation of *Macbeth* also, of course, restates the idea of aggressive courage, a quality very strong in the play and expressed very much in Tolkienian style by Old Siward, 'Why then, God's soldier be he ... And so his knell is knolled'; by Malcolm, 'The night is long that never finds the day'; by Macbeth himself, 'Send out more horses, skirr the country round,/Hang those that talk of fear.' To this Tolkien could not remain immune. However the final and strongest influence of *Macbeth* on *The Lord of the Rings* is quite obviously in theme. If there is one moral in the interlacements of the latter it is that you must do your duty regardless of what you think is going to happen. This is exactly what Macbeth does not realise. He believes the Witches' prophecy about his own kingship, and tries to fulfil it; he believes their warning about Macduff and tries to cancel it. If he had not tried to cancel it (and so murdered Macduff's family), Macduff might not have killed him; if he had not killed Duncan, he might conceivably have become king some other way. Macbeth is a classic case of a man who does not understand about the co-operation between free will and luck. Galadriel's warning about the events in her mirror, 'Some never come to be, unless those that behold the visions turn aside from their path to prevent them', would have been well said to him. But he had no Galadriel. The only mirror he sees is controlled (Act IV Scene 1) by the Witches.

Tolkien was trying, then, to make Shakespeare more positive – a bold venture, but based on a clear insight itself based on very minute reading. If he disliked Shakespeare, other than in joke, it was because he thought Shakespeare (a true poet with a deep tap-root into old English stories and traditions) had too often neglected that root for later and sillier interests. *King Lear* stems from the gaudy fictions of Geoffrey of Monmouth, laughed at in *Farmer Giles*, and yet it contains one ancient and resonant line in the mad scene of 'poor Tom':

'Child Roland to the Dark Tower came.'

The line obviously comes from some lost ballad telling the story of how Child Roland went to Elfland to rescue his sister from the wicked King, a monster-legend, a Theodoric-story.[7] Now why couldn't Shakespeare have told *that*, Tolkien must have reflected, instead of bothering with *King Lear*! As things were, Tolkien had to tell the 'Dark Tower' story himself. Still, there was no doubt that Shakespeare knew something.

Besides *Macbeth* and *Lear* Tolkien was probably struck by *The Tempest* and *A Midsummer Night's Dream* (the two 'fairy' plays and the two whose plots were not borrowed but made up by Shakespeare). But he remembered less likely plays too. As the Fellowship leaves Rivendell Bilbo says:

> 'When winter first begins to bite
> and stones crack in the frosty night,
> when pools are black and trees are bare,
> 'tis evil in the Wild to fare.'

In rhythm and theme he echoes the magnificent coda to *Love's Labour's Lost*:

> When icicles hang by the wall,
> And Dick the shepherd blows his nail,
> And Tom bears logs into the hall,
> And milk comes frozen home in pail,
> When blood is nipped, and ways be foul,
> Then nightly sings the staring owl,
>   Tu-who . . .

Shakespeare's piece is better, but Bilbo's is good enough. Remarkably, every single word in both is ordinary if colloquial English; every single word is also (with the doubtful exceptions of 'logs' and 'nipped') rooted in Old English. Both poems would require little change to make sense at any time between AD 600 and now. Yet they are representatives of a tradition Tolkien thought, if not too short, very much too scanty.

The poetry of the Shire

One can see Tolkien's attempt to extend that tradition in the hobbit-poems scattered through *The Lord of the Rings* – or to be more accurate, in the *new* hobbit-poems. Near the start there are a couple of pieces which Tolkien had written up to thirty years before, both rewritten a little for their new context: Frodo's 'Man in the Moon' song in the *Prancing Pony*, Sam's 'Rhyme of the Troll' near Weathertop. Take these away and one is left with a little body of poems from the Shire, mostly in quatrains with alternate lines rhyming, in plain language and metre and with for the most part a gently proverbial quality. They look unambitious. They were all written for *The Lord of the Rings* alone. It is tempting to say that they have no function besides advancing the story or embellishing the characters, no value outside their immediate context. However one check to this theory should be that, although the poems all do fit their settings in the story very tightly, there is a strong sense even so that the same words can mean different things in different places. As in *Pearl*, a stock phrase or cliché can at any moment be given new point.

Bilbo's 'Old Walking Song', for instance, is repeated three times in different versions. The first or basic text is this, sung by Bilbo as he leaves Bag End for the last time:

> 'The Road goes ever on and on
>   Down from the door where it began.
> Now far ahead the Road has gone,
>   And I must follow, if I can,
> Pursuing it with eager feet,
>   Until it joins some larger way
> Where many paths and errands meet.
>   And whither then? I cannot say.'   (I, 44)

Many years later, as *The Return of the King* draws to an end, Bilbo gives a markedly different version sitting in Rivendell, having heard Frodo tell the story of the destruction of the Ring and, in his advanced old age, having failed to understand most of it:

> 'The Road goes ever on and on
>   Out from the door where it began.
> Now far ahead the Road has gone,
>   Let others follow it who can!
> Let them a journey new begin.
>   But I at last with weary feet
> Will turn towards the lighted inn,
>   My evening rest and sleep to meet.'   (III, 266)

And with these words, we are told, 'his head dropped on his chest and he slept soundly'. This seems to be an obvious case of context determining words. The first time he sang the poem Bilbo had just handed over the Ring and was off to Rivendell; the words accordingly express a sense of abdication, of having been left behind, along with determination to accept this and make a new life somewhere as yet unknown. 'I must subordinate my own wishes to the larger world' would be a fair summary, highly appropriate to Bilbo at that time. By contrast the second version – almost a mirror-image of the first – expresses only justified weariness. Bilbo is no longer even interested in the Ring. He thinks the 'lighted inn' is Rivendell, as indeed it is in immediate context. All readers however perceive that it could as easily mean death.

In between these two variants Frodo has sung the song (I, 82–3). His version is identical with Bilbo's first one, except that it makes the significant change, in line 5, of 'weary feet' for 'eager feet'. 'That sounds like a bit of old Bilbo's rhyming', says Pippin. 'Or is it one of your imitations? It does not sound altogether encouraging.' Frodo says he doesn't know. He thinks he was 'making it up', but 'may have heard it long ago'. This uncertainty (over an issue to which the reader knows the answer) points to the great difference between Bilbo's position and Frodo's. Both are leaving Bag End, but the former cheerfully, without the Ring, without responsibility, for Rivendell, the latter with a growing sense of unwished involvement, carrying the Ring and heading in the end for Mordor. Naturally the poem does not mean the same thing for him as for Bilbo. But can the same words carry different meanings?

It depends on how one sees 'the Road'. The most obvious thought is that if the 'lighted inn' means death, then 'the Road' must mean life. It need not be individual life, since in Bilbo's second version others can take it up and follow it in their turn; however in Frodo's and Bilbo's first version the image of the traveller pursuing the Road looks very like a symbol of the individual pursuing his moment of consciousness down the unknown road which is everyone's future life, to an end which no one can predict. There is a further point to add, made by Frodo but repeating Bilbo:

'He used often to say there was only one Road; that it was like a great river: its springs were at every doorstep, and every path was its tributary. "It's a dangerous business, Frodo, going out of your door," he used to say. "You step into the Road, and if you don't keep your feet, there is no knowing where you might be swept off to. Do you realize that this is the very path that goes through Mirkwood, and that if you let it, it might take you to the Lonely Mountain or even further and to worse places?"' (I, 83)

In context this is just a reply to Pippin's remark that the song 'does not sound altogether encouraging'. Frodo does not know he is going to Mordor yet, and Pippin shrugs the whole thing off. However, looking back, and especially looking back after all the interlacements of Volumes Two and Three, one might well think that besides an image of life 'the Road' has crept up to being an image of Providence. After all Bilbo is right about the road outside Bag End leading all the way to Mordor. On the other hand there are on that road, which Frodo takes, thousands of intersections, as also thousands of choices to be made or rejected. The traveller can always stop or turn aside. Only will-power makes the road seem straight. Accordingly when Bilbo and Frodo say they will pursue it, eagerly or wearily, till it is intersected by other roads, lives, wishes, *and will then continue into the unknown, if they can*, they are expressing a mixture of doubt and determination – exactly the qualities Gandalf so often recommends. This has become much stronger and clearer with Frodo. Indeed it is not too much to say that the traveller walking down the branching road becomes in the end an image of 'the Good' in Tolkien, and one opposed to the endless self-regarding circuits of the Ring. By the time one comes to that opinion the immediate dramatic contexts of the poem – leaving Bag End, leaving the Shire – have not been dropped, any more than 'the Road' has lost its obvious literal quality, but they have come to seem only particular instances of a much more general truth.

The 'tight fit' of poems to characters and situations is accordingly illusory. There is a sense that the lines mean more than their composers know, may indeed not be their personal compositions at all; they may also be brooded upon, to be repeated with new understanding much later. Thus at the very end of Volume Three Frodo sings again 'the old walking-song, but the words were not quite the same'; he says not 'we may . . . take the hidden paths that run,/Towards the Moon or to the Sun', but 'I shall'.[8] And he does, leaving Middle-earth the next day. The song he is refashioning is another of Bilbo's, though it is 'to a tune that was as old as the hills'. Even in its innocent context near the start of Volume One, when the hobbits are using it only to help themselves along, it has an odd ring. 'Upon the hearth the fire is red,' they sing, 'But not yet weary are our feet'. If one goes by the 'inn and weariness' symbolism of Bilbo's Rivendell song, that means they still have a zest for life. Still, what the song celebrates are 'hidden paths', 'sudden tree[s]', 'A new road on a secret gate' – things which seem to be or to lead out of this world. The refrain of each stanza addresses the familiar sights of the landscape, the little homely trees of English hedgerows, but bids farewell to them:

> 'Apple, thorn, and nut and sloe,
> Let them go! Let them go!
> Sand and stone and pool and dell,
> Fare you well! Fare you well!'   (I, 87)

Are the hobbits, even in their good humour, 'half in love with easeful death'? A better answer perhaps is that in some inherited way they carry the 'tune' of an ancient grief, lulled by earthly beauty but capable of being woken in Frodo in the end, as in Legolas by the cry of the gulls.

The elvish song which follows immediately on the 'Walking Song' indeed says just that, though probably few readers make the connection straight away. All it contains, apart from its invocations to 'Elbereth', are the two opposed images of the stars, seen as the flowers of the 'Queen beyond the Western Seas', and the wood in which the elves 'wander'. Of course the elves *are* in a wood at that moment, and they *are* looking at the early evening stars, but that is not what they mean. Their song is of regret and exile, its core the oxymoron of 'this far land' – 'this' land is the real land, Middle-earth, 'far land' ought to be the one Elbereth is in beyond the Seas. But the elves refuse to accept the fact, seeing themselves as strangers whose highest function is memory:

> 'We still remember, we who dwell
> In this far land beneath the trees,
> Thy starlight on the Western Seas.'

As for the wood, its beauty is a net and a barrier; starlight and memory alone pierce through 'to us that wander here/Amid the world of woven trees'.

The myth behind the song remains obscure in *The Lord of the Rings*, just as the Sindarin song of Rivendell remains untranslated, merging only with the Quenya one just quoted in the story's last few pages (III, 308). However the image of the Wood of Life breaks through to hobbit-consciousness with increasing clarity. Frodo uses it in the Old Forest:

> 'O! Wanderers in the shadowed land
> despair not! For though dark they stand,
> all woods there be must end at last,
> and see the open sun go past:
> the setting sun, the rising sun,
> the day's end, or the day begun.
> For east or west all woods must fail . . .'   (I, 123)

As usual we take the immediate point – Frodo and the others want to get out of the forest – while reading through to a kind of universality: the 'shadowed land' is life, life's delusions of despair are the 'woods', despair will end in some vision of cosmic order which can only be hinted at in stars or 'sun'. What does Frodo mean by the repeated contrasts of setting/rising, west/east, day's end/day begun? They can hardly avoid suggesting death and life; in that case his song says there can be no defeat – even if the wanderers die in the dark wood, the real Old Forest, they will in death break through to sunlight and out of a hampering shade. 'East or west all woods must fail' is then a statement of exactly the same class as 'The Road goes ever on and on': literally true, literally unhelpful or even banal, but in its literal truth making a symbolic promise. Sam Gamgee hits on the same thought when he takes up the 'Blondin' role of faithful minstrel in Minas Morgul, and sings 'words of his own' fitted to another old Shire tune:

> 'Though here at journey's end I lie
> in darkness buried deep,
> beyond all towers strong and high
> beyond all mountains steep,
> above all shadows rides the Sun
> and Stars for ever dwell:
> I will not say the Day is done,
> nor bid the Stars farewell.'   (III, 185)

'Day is done' is of course another Shakespearean echo, like the Dark
Tower: 'The bright day is done', says Iras to Cleopatra, 'and we are for
the dark'. But Tolkien would no doubt instantly have felt that Shakespeare
had no copyright on the phrase, which must be of immemorial antiquity
in English, 'as old as the hills'. Sam's song is simple and obvious, coming
from 'the voice of a forlorn and weary hobbit that no listening orc could
possibly have mistaken for the clear song of an Elven-lord'. Still, it has
the characteristic qualities of the Shire's 'high style': plain language,
proverbial sentiment, a closeness to immediate context reaching out
simultaneously to myth, a brave suggestiveness at once hopeful and sad.

As has been said, the Shire is a calque on England. Where then is the
source in English poetry for the poetry of the Shire? One might point to
Spenser, whose *Faerie Queene* (regarded by Tolkien with disapproving
interest) often uses the image of the wandering knight lost in trackless
woods, and whose Merlin-vision of Britain reviving underlies Bilbo's
'Riddle of Strider'.[9] An even closer parallel is John Milton's masque of
Comus, which Tolkien must have admired partly for its theme – it is an
analogue of 'Childe Rowland', a tale of a maiden lost in a dark wood and
imprisoned by a wizard, till her brothers and her guardian angel come to
the rescue – but even more for its hovering between fact and symbol. A
herb will protect them, says the disguised angel to the brothers; a shepherd
gave it to him:

> 'The leaf was darkish, and had prickles on it,
> But in another country, as he said,
> Bore a bright golden flower, but not in this soil;
> Unknown, and like esteemed, and the dull swain
> Treads on it daily with his clouted shoon ...'

Ugly, prickly, much-trampled, flowering only in 'another country': it
sounds like Virtue. Maybe the shepherd lad was the Good Shepherd
himself. As for the wood, the Younger Brother wishes he could hear
something from outside it, bleat or whistle or cockcrow:

> ' 'Twould be some solace yet, some little cheering
> In this close dungeon of innumerous boughs.'

His Elder Brother would prefer a glimmer from moon or lamp or candle,
to 'visit us/With thy long levelled rule of streaming light'. Again the wood
sounds like life, the 'levelled rule' from the world outside like Conscience.
But as Tolkien said of *Beowulf*, the 'large symbolism ... does not break
through, nor become allegory'. The plain, even rustic language appeals to
everyday experience. Everyone has been lost and found again, everyone *is*
lost, *will* be found again. The maiden who is the soul will be taken in the
end from 'the perplexed paths of this drear wood ... the blind mazes of

this tangled wood . . . this close dungeon of innumerous boughs', or as the elves would say *galadhremmin ennorath*, 'the world of woven trees'.

The elvish tradition

Shakespeare, Spenser, Milton: the list could be spun out, to include for instance Yeats, whose poem 'The Man Who Dreamed of Faeryland' could stand as a Tolkienian epigraph. However the point should be clear. Tolkien was not by any means cut off from the mainstream of English poetry, though the qualities he valued were not surprise, the *mot juste*, verbal complexity, but rather a slow probing of the familiar. That was not, however, the end of his ambition or of his thoughts on style: there is an elvish streak too in the poetry of *The Lord of the Rings*, signalled in complete contrast by barely-precedented intricacies of line and stanza.

The best example of this is the 'Song of Eärendil' composed and sung in Rivendell by Bilbo (I, 246–9). What the song means and what story lies behind it are typically not explained in *The Lord of the Rings*, but remain in suggestiveness till *The Silmarillion*. That suggestiveness, though, is much aided by devices not of sense but of sound. Bilbo uses some five of these: one is rhyme, which everyone recognises, but the others are less familiar – internal half-rhyme, alliteration (i.e. beginning words with the same sound or letter), alliterative assonance (the *Macbeth* device), and a frequent if irregular variation of syntax. All appear in the first eight lines:

> 'Eärendil was a mariner
> that tarried in Arvernien;
> he built a boat of timber felled
> In Nimbrethil to journey in;
> her sails he wove of silver fair,
> of silver were her lanterns made,
> her prow was fashioned like a swan,
> and light upon her banners laid.'

The rhymes are obvious, on lines 2 and 4, 6 and 8 – '-nien/-ney in', 'made/laid'. The internal rhymes however operate not between even lines but between odd and even, 1 and 2, 3 and 4, and so on. They are furthermore not on the ends of words but in the middle: '*ma*ri*ner/tarri*ed *in*', '*timber fell*ed/*Nimbrethil*', '*silver fair/silver were*', '*like a swan/light upon*'. Nor are they always complete. One might note that the full rhymes are similarly not always exact, some of them being 'masculine', i.e. on one syllable only, but some 'feminine', on more than one syllable, and tending towards similarity rather than identity, as in 'Arvernien/journey in', 'armoured him/harm from him', 'helmet tall/emerald', etc. These are too common to be the result of incapacity, and they are furthermore reinforced by the unpredictable but frequent use of the other devices of sound: alliteration in '*l*ight *l*aid', '*sh*ining *sh*ield', '*w*ard all *w*ounds', etc., alliterative assonance in '*sails* of *silver*', '*Night* of *Naught*', '*sight* . . . he *sought*' and '*boat* it bore with *bit*ing breath'. Typically, in between there are such doubtful cases as '*bui*l*t* a *boat*' – just alliteration, or assonance as well? – while over the whole poem there lies a web of grammatical repetitions and variations, also never quite exact – '*her sails* (he wove) *of silver* fair,/*of silver* (were) *her lanterns* (made), or later '*his sword* (of steel) was *valiant*,/(of adamant) *his helmet tall*'.

Describing the technique is difficult, but its result is obvious: rich and continuous uncertainty, a pattern forever being glimpsed but never quite grasped. In this way sound very clearly echoes or perhaps rather gives the lead to sense. Just as the rhymes, assonances and phrasal structures hover at the edge of identification, so the poem as a whole offers romantic glimpses of 'old unhappy far-off things' (to cite Wordsworth), or 'magic casements opening on the foam/Of perilous seas, in f*aery* l*ands* f*or lorn*' (to remember Keats). Frodo indeed finds himself listening in highly Keatsian style:

> Almost it seemed that the words took shape, and visions of far lands and bright things that he had never yet imagined opened out before him; and the firelit hall became like a golden mist above seas of foam that sighed upon the margins of the world. Then the enchantment became more and more dreamlike, until he felt that an endless river of gold and silver was flowing over him, too multitudinous for its pattern to be comprehended . . . (I, 245–6)

Romanticism, multitudinousness, imperfect comprehension: these are the poem's goals, achieved stylistically much more than semantically.

Yet the 'Song of Eärendil' does of course tell a story as well: how Eärendil tried to sail out of this world to a kind of Paradise, how he succeeded in the end by virtue of the 'Silmaril', how this in turn led to his becoming a star, or rather the helmsman of a celestial boat in which the burning Silmaril appears to Middle-earth as a star. Still, more questions are raised than answered. Why did Eärendil go, why was he kept, what is a Silmaril? More acutely, what is the relationship in the story between success and failure? Eärendil's star appears to be a victory-emblem, 'the Flammifer of Westernesse', and yet is associated with loss and homelessness, with the weeping of women on the 'Hither Shore'. The 'paths that seldom mortal goes' may recall fleetingly the 'hidden paths' of the hobbits' walking-song, and its similar oscillation between adventure and homesickness; in this sense the two stylistically quite different poems relate to each other like elvish assonances, hinting at a pattern but stressing change as much as identity. The overall effect of the song in Rivendell is perhaps to show Bilbo approaching a body of lore and of poetry higher than the normal hobbitic vein, higher indeed than mortals can normally comprehend. Aragorn sings his song of Beren and Lúthien some fifty pages earlier with a certain reluctance, explaining that it is 'in the mode that is called *ann-thennath* among the Elves, but is hard to render in our Common Speech, and this is but a rough echo of it'. 'Echo' is a useful word, for that in a way is what the poem's metric is based on; there is no immediate similarity of stanza-form to Bilbo's song, but once again the 'elvish' idea of poetry comes through in an unexpected subtlety.

Briefly, one can say that each stanza is in eight lines, rhyming abac/babc; and that the fourth and eighth lines at once interrupt the flow of each stanza and hold the two halves together by their strong 'feminine' three-syllable rhymes, on 'glimmering/shimmering', 'sorrowing/following', etc. More significant is the fact that the actual rhyming *words* in each first half are repeated once or more in each second half, as for instance 'seen' in the first stanza, 'leaves' in the second, 'feet' and 'roam' in the third, and so on. The device is somehow congruous with the repeated images of hair like a shadow, beauty flying, leaves and years falling, through it all the hemlock-leaves of death. But the last stanza of nine breaks the pattern. Its rhyme words are all different: 'bare/grey/door/morrowless//lay/more/away/sorrowless'. What does this fact mean? All one can say is that the story being told (or hinted at) is also one of gloom, death and parting, like that between Eärendil and Elwing, the mariner and the weeping women of Middle-earth. The last words of the song, 'singing sorrowless', stand out against this current, but still wherever the lovers go it is 'away', 'in the forest', maybe the forest of mortality and final death. Aragorn indeed confirms this thought with his gloss that not only has Lúthien died (as many elves do), but 'died indeed and left the world'. Further explanation has to wait till *The Silmarillion*, but in a sense is not needed. A point has been made by a sudden (if barely perceptible) breaking of pattern, an absence of echoes. Perhaps that is the essence of *ann-thennath*.

Further stylistic and thematic variations could easily be listed. Gimli's 'Song of Durin' at I 329–30 is dwarvishly plain and active, but still carries on the sense of decay in Middle-earth opposed to ultimate hope; Legolas's 'Song of Nimrodel' a little later makes similar oppositions but ends on an opposite note, of faltering and ultimate defeat on the 'Hither Shore'. Frodo's elegy for Gandalf ends on the word 'died'; but Sam's coda prefers 'flowers', and turns out to be truer in the end. Galadriel's song in the Common Speech ends with regret and a question, 'What ship would ever bear me back across so wide a Sea?', but her Quenya one on hope and an assertion, 'Maybe thou shalt find Valinor. Maybe even thou shalt find it.'[10] As with the hobbit-songs, behind all these there lies some story of a Sentence and a Great Escape, but an escape forever hindered by loving involvement with Middle-earth itself; that is the root of the disagreement between Fangorn, Celeborn and Galadriel when the Ent half-voices his lament for the stocks and the stones. However the surprise in this 'elvish tradition' of mythic poetry is how much of its stories is conveyed by purely formal devices, by verbal patterns with meaning as apparently inherent in them as elsewhere in place-names, in untranslated fragments, or in Bombadil. Tolkien's idea of poetry mirrored his ideas on language; in neither did he think sound should be divorced from sense.

In reality this 'elvish tradition' was an English tradition too. The ultimate source for much that has been discussed must certainly be *Pearl*, with its story of the (failed) escape from mortality, its heavily traditional phrasing, and its fantastically complex metrical scheme, of twelve-line cross-rhymed stanzas with alliteration, assonance, syntax-variation and (even Tolkien did not attempt this) stanza-linking and refrains.[11] However the *Pearl* tradition did not last till Shakespeare and Milton and the Romantics, who are accordingly and to that extent impoverished. Tolkien obviously hoped in one way to recreate it. More generally, the link between the last three sections of this book is Tolkien's perception, from *Pearl* and from poems like it, that poetry does not reduce to plain sense (so far most critics would agree with him), but furthermore that this is because words have over the centuries acquired meanings not easily traced in dictionaries, available however to many native speakers, and (this is where many critics part company) at times breaking through the immediate intentions of even poetic users. 'Loose fit', in a word, works better in poetry than 'tight fit'; there are roads to wisdom besides the painstaking perverse originality of twentieth-century writers.

Middle-earth and Limbo: mythic analogues

What has been said about Tolkien's poetry has an immediate bearing on that most attractive but least tractable subject, 'Tolkien's mythology'. In a sense the problems and intentions were the same. Tolkien wanted his poems to make good sense in their dramatic context, as part of the story of *The Lord of the Rings*; he also wanted them to suggest a truth independent of their context. 'East or west all woods must fail' therefore applies *both* to the Old Forest *and* to the symbolic woods of Life and Error. In the same way his legends of Eärendil and Lúthien, his central fable of Frodo and the Ring, must firstly and continually work as fiction, but also reach out towards non-fictional truths about humanity – and perhaps about salvation. Yet in this latter ambition there lies a danger. If *The Lord of the Rings* should approach too close to 'Gospel-truth', to the Christian myth in which Tolkien himself believed, it might forfeit its status as a story and become at worst a blasphemy, an 'Apocryphal gospel', at best a dull allegory rehearsing in admittedly novel form what everyone ought to know already. In that case *The Lord of the Rings* would look like one of Bilbo's poems removed from context and put without explanation in *The Oxford Book of English Verse* – fictionless and unhappy. Tolkien had to take a rather strict line over 'myth'.

One reason, no doubt, was that he had little tolerance for real pagan myths or for naïve mythicizers. In his *YWES* chapter for 1924 (p. 58), he remarked that 'it will be a grievous shock to many an innocent sentimentalist, accustomed to see the one-eyed and red-bearded deities everywhere, to learn that *Þórr* and *Óðin* cannot be found in any Scandinavian place-name in England'.† Tolkien did not believe in 'old religions' or 'witch-cults'; C. S. Lewis wrote a paper called 'The Anthropological Approach' which damned the learned variety of that error beyond redemption. Probably a major cause for their intolerance was that both, but especially Tolkien, had some idea of what genuine old paganism was like. The earliest account of the English (Tacitus's *Germania*, AD 97–8) remarks on their habit of drowning sacrificial victims in bogs. Many such have been recovered from the preserving peat of Denmark and of 'the Angle'. It would be surprising if Tolkien had not looked at the calm face of Tollund Man, or the hideously frightened one of 'Queen Gunhild' (all too obviously still struggling as she was pinned down alive), and reflected that *these* were the true lineaments of his pagan ancestors.[12] 'There, but for the grace of God, go I.' No statement could be more apposite. Tolkien had grounds to suspect simple views of 'the noble pagan'.

Virtuous pagans, however, were quite another matter. Indeed it is not too much to say that the Inklings were preoccupied with them. C. S. Lewis offered the most daring statement in the final volume of the 'Narnia' series, *The Last Battle* (1956), in which we come across a young (dead) virtuous pagan, Emeth, who explains that all his life he has served Tash and scorned Aslan the Lion – earlier on it has been made clear that Tash is a bloody demon, Aslan, one might as well say, the 'Narnian' Christ. But once he is dead Emeth meets Aslan and falls at his feet in instinctive adoration, as in terror, 'for the Lion . . . will know that I have served Tash all my days and not him'. But Emeth is saved, for good deeds done for Tash belong to Aslan, and bad deeds for Aslan to Tash; as if to say that God and Allah are different, but yet that virtuous Mohammedans will be saved rather than murderous Christians. Later on each of the souls pouring out of Narnia on Doomsday looks at Aslan as it comes through the Door-way of Death – to be saved if it loves, destroyed if it hates. Lewis here repeats the belief of the fourteenth-century friar Uhtred of Boldon, that

† Here, as a matter of fact, Tolkien was wrong. 'Roseberry Topping' in North Yorkshire preserves beneath pastoral euphemism the Viking name *Othinesbeorg*, 'Odin's mountain'. But Tolkien could have replied that this name had been so sharply changed as to suggest a deliberate de-mythicizing policy in the Middle Ages, which would support his general point.

each dying person has a 'clear vision' or *clara visio* of God, on his reaction
to which depends his ultimate fate.[13] Uhtred's opinion was denounced as
heretical at Oxford in 1367 – it tends to suggest no man needs the Christian
Church to be saved. But Lewis, a Protestant, might have agreed with that.

Tolkien, a determined Catholic, would not. Still, he was doubtless
interested. Uhtred after all was an Englishman, only one of a list of would-
be savers of righteous pagans from the British Isles. Pelagius, the great
opponent of St Augustine, was a Welshman, his real name probably
'Morgan'. The story of the salvation of Trajan, the virtuous pagan
Emperor, was first told by an Anglo-Saxon from Whitby about the year
710. The poem *St Erkenwald* is a variant of that tale; some people have
argued it is by the author of *Sir Gawain* and *Pearl*. Above all, to Tolkien's
mind, there must have been present the problem of *Beowulf*. This is
certainly the work of a Christian writing after the conversion of England.
However the author got through 3182 lines without mentioning Christ,
or salvation, and yet without saying specifically that his heroes, including
the kind and honest figure of Beowulf himself, were damned – though he
must have known that historically and in reality they were all pagans,
ignorant even of the name of Christ. Could the Christian author have
thought his pagan heroes were saved? He had the opinion of the Church
against him if he did. Could he on the other hand have borne to consign
them all to Hell for ever, like Alcuin, the deacon of York, in a now notorious
letter to the abbot of Lindisfarne, written about AD 797: 'What has Ingeld
to do with Christ?' he asked scornfully – Ingeld being a minor character
in *Beowulf*. 'The King of Heaven wishes to have no fellowship with lost
and pagan so-called Kings; for the eternal King reigns in Heaven, the
lost pagan laments in Hell'.[14] The *Beowulf*-poet's dilemma was also
Tolkien's. His whole professional life brought him into contact with the
stories of pagan heroes, Englishmen or Norsemen or Goths; more than
anyone he could appreciate their sterling qualities. At the same time he
had no doubt that paganism itself was weak and cruel. Uhtred's and
Lewis's individualistic beliefs did not appeal to him, any more than
Alcuin's smugly intolerant one. If there was anyone in the twentieth
century to resolve the dilemma, repeat the *Beowulf*-poet's masterpiece of
compromise, and preserve 'the permanent value of that *pietas* which
treasures the memory of man's struggles in the dark past, man fallen and
not yet saved, disgraced but not dethroned' ('Monsters', p. 266), Tolkien
must have thought it should be himself. Such activity was for one thing
'part of the English temper'. *The Lord of the Rings* is quite clearly, then,
a story of virtuous pagans in the darkest of dark pasts, before all but the
faintest premonitions of dawn and revelation.

Yet there is at least one moment at which Revelation seems very close
and allegory does all but break through – naturally enough, a moment of
'eucatastrophe', to use Tolkien's term for sudden moments of fairy-tale

salvation. This appears to different characters in different ways. As has been said, Sam and Frodo experience it as thinking for a moment they have died and gone to Heaven, when they wake up on the field of Cormallen. Faramir, however, in the next chapter feels it more physically. He and Éowyn sense the earthquake that is the fall of Barad-dûr, and for a moment Faramir thinks of Númenor drowning. But then like the father in *Pearl* an irrational joy comes over him, to be explained by the eagle-messenger in a song:

> 'Sing now, ye people of the Tower of Anor,
> for the Realm of Sauron is ended for ever,
>   and the Dark Tower is thrown down.
>
> Sing and rejoice, ye people of the Tower of Guard,
> for your watch hath not been in vain,
> and the Black Gate is broken,
> and your King hath passed through,
>   and he is victorious.
>
> Sing and be glad, all ye children of the West,
> for your King shall come again,
> and he shall dwell among you
>   all the days of your life.'   (III, 241)

There is no doubt here about Tolkien's stylistic model, which is the Bible and particularly the Psalms. The use of 'ye' and 'hath' is enough to indicate that to most English readers, familiar with those words only from the Authorised Version. But 'Sing and rejoice' echoes Psalm 33, 'Rejoice in the Lord', while the whole of the poem is strongly reminiscent of Psalm 24, 'Lift up your heads, O ye gates, and be ye lift up, ye everlasting doors, for the King of glory shall come in.' 'Who is the King of glory?' asks the Psalm, and one traditional answer is Christ, crucified but not yet ascended, come to the city of Hell to rescue from it those especially virtuous pre-Christians, Moses and Isaiah and the patriarchs and prophets. Of course the eagle's song is *not about that*. When it says 'the Black Gate is broken' it means the Morannon, a place in Middle-earth described at II, 244–5; when it says 'your King shall come again', it means Aragorn. Yet the first statement could very *easily* apply to Death and Hell (Matthew xvi, 18, 'and the gates of hell shall not prevail'), the second to Christ and the Second Coming. This is a layer of double meaning beyond that even of 'East or west all woods must fail' or 'The Road goes ever on and on'.

Approach to the edge of Christian reference was here deliberate, as one can tell from the date Gandalf so carefully gives for the fall of Sauron (III, 230), 'the twenty-fifth of March'. In Anglo-Saxon belief, and in European popular tradition both before and after that, 25 March is the date of the Crucifixion; also of the Annunciation (nine months before Christmas); also of the last day of Creation.[15] By mentioning the date Tolkien was presenting his 'eucatastrophe' as a forerunner or 'type' of the greater one of Christian myth. It is possible to doubt whether this was a good idea. Almost no one notices the significance of 25 March; the high style of the eagle's song has not had much appeal; though Tolkien himself wept over the grandeur of the Field of Cormallen (*Letters*, p. 321), many other readers have found the delight, tears and laughter (of Sam especially) unconvincing. Tolkien did right normally to avoid such allusions, to keep like the author of *Beowulf* to a middle path between Ingeld and Christ, between the Bible and pagan myth. The care with which he maintained this position (highly artificial, though usually passed over without mention) is evident, with hindsight, on practically every page of *The Lord of the Rings*.

Consider for instance the Riders. As has been said, they resemble the ancient English down to minute detail – with the admitted partial exception of their devotion to horses. However the real ancient English had some belief in divine beings, the **ósas* or 'gods' analogous to the Norse *æsir*, Gothic **ansós*, whose names survive in our days of the week (Tíw's day, Wóden's day, Thunor's day, Fríge day). To this the Riders have no counterpart, or almost none. Their place-names sometimes suggest ancient belief *in something or other*: thus 'Dunharrow' in Common Speech presumably represents Rohirric *dún-harg*, 'the dark sanctuary', just as 'Halifirien' on the borders of Gondor must be *hálig-fyrgen*, 'the holy mountain'. In 'Drúadan Forest' the second element is Gondorian -*adan*, 'man', the first probably *drú-*, 'magic'. In the same way the Anglo-Saxons borrowed the Celtic element of 'Druid' to create the term *drý-cræft*, 'magic art'. The Riders, one may say, have a sense of awe or of the supernatural; but they do nothing about it. No religious rites are performed at Théoden's burial. His followers sing a dirge and ride round his barrow, as indeed do Beowulf's. The only real-life burial where this combination of song and cavalcade is reported is that of Attila the Hun, in Jordanes' *Gothic History*. But there the mourners also gash their faces so their king will be lamented properly in human blood, and when he is in his tomb they murder (or sacrifice) the slaves who dug it. That kind of thing seems very out of place in Middle-earth. The Riders, like most of the characters of *Beowulf* but unlike all we can guess of the real pre-Christian English, do not worship pagan gods; they also do not hold slaves, commit incest, practise polygamy.[16] Their society has in a word been bowdlerised. They are so virtuous that one can hardly call them pagans at all.

Certainly Tolkien never does. As has been noted before, he followed the *Beowulf*-poet in being very loath to use the word 'heathen', reserving it twice for Denethor and by implication the Black Númenoreans. Nevertheless his characters *are* heathens, strictly speaking, and Tolkien, having pondered for so long on the *Beowulf*-poet's careful balances, was as aware of this fact as he was aware of the opposing images of open Christianity poised at many moments to take over his story. The pagan counterpart of the eagle's song may be the death of Aragorn, relegated as it is to an Appendix. Aragorn is a remarkably virtuous character, without even the faults of Théoden, and he foreknows his death like a saint. Nevertheless he is not a Christian and nor is Arwen. He has to say then to her, 'I speak no comfort to you, for there is no comfort for such pain within the circles of the world' (III, 343). When she still laments her fate he can only add 'We are not bound for ever to the circles of the world, and beyond them is more than memory. Farewell!' Arwen is not comforted. She dies under the 'fading trees' of a Lórien gone 'silent', and the end of her tale is oblivion, 'and elanor and niphredil bloom no more east of the Sea'. Aragorn, then, has some hope of the future and of something *outside* the 'circles of the world' that may come to heal their sorrow, but he does not know what it is. This is a deathbed strikingly devoid of the sacraments, of Extreme Unction, of 'the consolations of religion'. It is impossible to think of Aragorn as irretrievably damned for his ignorance of Christianity (though it is a view some have tried to foist on Beowulf). Still, he has not fulfilled the requirements for salvation either. Perhaps the best one can say is that when such heroes die they go, in Tolkien's opinion, neither to Hell nor Heaven, but to Limbo: 'to my fathers', as Théoden says, 'to sit beside my fathers, until the world is renewed', to quote Thorin Oakenshield from *The Hobbit*, perhaps at worst to wait with the barrow-wight 'Where gates stand for ever shut, till the world is mended'. The whole of Middle-earth, in a sense, is Limbo: there the innocent unbaptised wait for Doomsday (when, we may hope, they will join their saved and baptised descendants).

Tolkien took different views of his own work's religious content at different times. In 1953 he wrote to a Jesuit friend:

> *The Lord of the Rings* is of course a fundamentally religious and Catholic work; unconsciously so at first, but consciously in the revision. That is why I have not put in, or have cut out, practically all references to anything like 'religion', to cults or practices, in the imaginary world. For the religious element is absorbed into the story and the symbolism. (*Letters*, p. 172)

Tolkien perhaps found difficulty in explaining to a Jesuit why a 'fundamentally' Catholic work should *cut out* references to religion, but the reason is clear: he thought, or hoped, that God had a plan for pre-Catholics too. Later in life Tolkien may have become more uncertain about his own originality, and wrote that the elvish song of Rivendell was a 'hymn', that 'these [invocations of Elbereth] and other references to religion in *The Lord of the Rings* are frequently overlooked' (*Road*, p. 65). On the whole the earlier statement that references have been cut out seems truer than the later one that they are in but 'overlooked'. The elvish song is only analogous to a hymn as Gandalf is analogous to an angel; Elbereth too is unlike (say) the Holy Ghost in remaining visible, to elves, and remember-able as a being by those elves like Galadriel who have been across the Sea and met her. Tolkien did best when he kept mythic invention on the borderline between literal story and a wider suggestiveness (Fangorn, Bombadil, Lúthien, Roads and Rings); too conscious an approach to 'mythopoeia' would have ended only in allegory. To repeat a philological point made already in this study, the Old English translation of Greek *euangelion* was *gód spell*, modern 'Gospel', the 'good news' of salvation. Besides 'news', however, *spell* meant 'spell' and also 'story'. The foundation of Gospel lies then in 'good story', though 'good story' ought to generate a spell (or glamour) of its own.

Fróda and Frodo: a myth reconstructed

If one thinks that a 'myth' is an 'old story containing within itself vestiges of some earlier state of religious belief' – like the Grail-legend with its hints of sacrificed kings and vegetation-rituals – then *The Lord of the Rings* definitely is not one. Tolkien was alert to all such echoes and did his best to eradicate them. If one thinks that a 'myth' should be a 'story repeating in veiled form the truth of Christ Crucified', then *The Lord of the Rings* does not qualify either. There is an evil Power in both stories, and a glorious Tree, but Frodo, to make only three of the most obvious points, is not sacrificed, is not the Son of God, and buys for his people only a limited, worldly and temporary happiness. Nevertheless there is at least one sense in which *The Lord of the Rings* can claim 'mythic' status, which is as 'a story embodying the deepest feelings of a particular society at a particular time'. If one can speak of *Robinson Crusoe* as a 'myth of capital-ism' and of *Frankenstein* or *Dr Faustus* as 'myths of scientific man', then *The Lord of the Rings* could be claimed as a 'myth against discouragement', a 'myth of the Deconversion'. In 1936 Tolkien had warned the British Academy that the Ragnarǫk spirit had survived Thórr and Óthinn, could revive 'even in our own times . . . martial heroism as its own end'. He was quite literally correct in this, as he was also in his further prophecy that it would not succeed, since 'the wages of heroism is death'. Still, he wanted to keep something of that spirit, if only its dauntlessness in what looked like a hopeless future; for similarly contemporary reasons he wanted to offer his readers a model of elementary virtue existing without the support of religion. Perhaps most of all he wanted to answer Alcuin's scornful question, relevant again after 1150 years: 'What *has* Ingeld to do with Christ?'

To his intentions here Tolkien left two very strong clues. One is the name of the 'hero' of *The Lord of the Rings*, Frodo. The other is the note in Appendix F, which says that some hobbit-names have been retained by Tolkien without translation, 'though I have usually anglicized them by altering their endings, since in Hobbit-names *a* was a masculine ending, and *o* and *e* were feminine.' (III, 413). 'Frodo', in other words, is an English form of original 'Froda'. But what kind of a name is that? Most readers probably take it as explained by Tolkien's preceding remark, "To their man-children [hobbits] usually gave names that had no meaning at all in their daily language . . . Of this kind are Bilbo, Bungo, Polo, Lotho . . . and so on. There are many inevitable but accidental resemblances to names that we now have or know . . .' If 'Frodo' strikes any chords, then, it could be accident. On the other hand 'Frodo', surprisingly, is never mentioned in the name-discussion of that Appendix. Maybe his name is not a Bilbo-type, but a Meriadoc–Peregrin–Fredegar-type. As Tolkien goes on to say:

> In some old families . . . it was, however, the custom to give high-sounding first-names. Since most of these seem to have been drawn from legends of the past, of Men as well as of Hobbits, and many while now meaningless to Hobbits closely resembled the names of Men in the Vale of Anduin, or in Dale, or in the Mark, I have turned them into those old names, largely of Frankish and Gothic origin, that are still used by us or are met in our histories.

'Frodo' could be one of these, like 'Peregrin'. It could still and at the same time be an anglicisation of 'Froda', a name 'meaningless' to hobbits by the time of the War of the Ring, and accepted by them as just another chance disyllable like 'Bilba, Bunga, Pola', but actually preserving in oblivion the name of an ancient hero from the Dale or the Mark. That would make Frodo's name something of a freak in hobbit-nomenclature. However this seems only appropriate for the central figure, especially since his name is so strikingly left uncategorised.

'Froda' actually *is* a name from the dimmest reaches of Northern legend. It is mentioned once in *Beowulf* (not in the main story), when the hero, discussing politics, says that the king of the Danes means to marry his daughter *glædum suna Fródan*, 'to the fortunate son of Fróda'. By this means he hopes to heal the feud between the Danes and the 'Bards' over whom Fróda once ruled. His idea won't work, says Beowulf, for the pressure on heroes to take blood-revenge is too strong – it seems, though this is speculation from other sources, that Ingeld's father Fróda was killed by the Danish king who now wants to make alliance with his son. The likelihood is that in this as in other matters Beowulf is meant to appear a good prophet, since the unsuccessful, possibly treacherous, but in heroic terms entirely praiseworthy attack which Ingeld made on his father-in-law is repeatedly mentioned in Northern story. Probably it was the subject of the Northumbrian songs which so scandalised Alcuin. When he asked, then, 'What has Ingeld to do with Christ?', he was using Ingeld as an example of the most extreme gap between good 'heroic' behaviour and good Christian behaviour; Ingeld took unforgivingness as far as it could go. There is no need, however, to think the son was exactly like the father.

Nothing else is ever heard of Fróda in Old English, but the Norse form of the word – it means literally 'the wise one' – is Fróthi, and round this there are several stories. The most persistent is that Fróthi was a contemporary of Christ, alleged by both Saxo Grammaticus (c. AD 1200) and Snorri Sturluson (c. 1230). During his reign there were no murders, no wars, no robberies, and gold rings lay untouched in the open, so that everyone referred to his age as the *Frótha-frith*, the 'peace of Fróthi'. But it came to an end because of greed, or maybe over-altruism. The peace really came from Fróthi's magic mill, turned eternally by two giantesses to grind out gold and peace and prosperity. Fróthi (perhaps fearing for his subjects' security) would never let them rest – and so one day they ground out an army to kill Fróthi and take his gold. The viking army also would not let the giantesses rest, but sailed away with them and set them to grinding salt; they ground so much that the boat sank and the mill with it, though still (adds folk-tradition) in the Maelstrom the giantesses grind their magic quern. And that is why the sea is salt.

This is a story, one can see, about the incurability of evil. Has it anything to do with *Beowulf*? There is no overt connection, but Tolkien was used to 'reconstructing' stories. The point that seems to have struck him is the total *opposition* between son and father, Ingeld/Ingjaldr and Fróda/Fróthi. The one is an example of the Ragnarǫk-spirit undiluted, of heroic conventionality at its worst; in the *Beowulf* lecture Tolkien called Ingeld 'thrice faithless and easily persuaded'. The other has about him a ring of nostalgic failure; in his time everything was good, but it ended in failure both personally (for Fróthi was killed) and ideologically (for Fróda's son returned to the bad old ways of revenge and hatred, scorning peace-initiatives and even apparently his own desires). Of course the *Frótha-frith* could have been just an accident, a result of the Incarnation which not even virtuous pagans knew about. For all these reasons the composite figure of Fróda/Fróthi became to Tolkien an image of the sad truth behind heroic illusions, a kind of ember glowing in the dark sorrow of heathen ages. In 'The Homecoming of Beorhtnoth' Tídwald says reprovingly to Torhthelm – who has just discovered his master's headless body:

> 'Aye, that's battle for you,
> and no worse today   than wars you sing of,

> when Fróda fell,   and Finn was slain.
> The world wept then,   as it weeps today:
> you can hear the tears   through the harp's twanging.'

There is something grimly appropriate, further, in the fact that 'Ingjaldr' remained a common Norse name for centuries. 'Fróthi' however was quickly forgotten.

All this sounds very much like Tolkien's 'Frodo'. He is a peacemaker, indeed in the end a pacifist. One can trace his progress from I, 339, when he stabs the Moria troll, to II, 221, when he threatens to but does not stab Gollum. At II, 294–6 he saves Gollum's life from the archers, against Sam's strong inclination to keep quiet and let him die. He gives Sting away at III, 204, keeping an orc-blade but saying 'I do not think it will be my part to strike any blow again.' He throws even that away ten pages later, saying 'I'll bear no weapon, fair or foul'. In 'The Scouring of the Shire' his role is to forbid killing (III, 285 and 289), and later, after a battle in which he has not 'drawn sword', to protect prisoners. He will not kill Saruman even after his *mithril*-coat has turned a treacherous stab. His self-control has been learnt, of course, while carrying the Ring; but there is a touch of witheredness about it. ' "All the same," said Frodo to all those who stood near, "I wish for no killing..." ' 'Those who stood near'? One might have hoped Frodo would get up on a block and speak to everybody, impose his will. But Wit is the opposite of Will, and as a figure of increasing wisdom, Frodo ('the wise one') seems to lose all desire, even for good. Merry puts forward his plans for dealing with the ruffians by force. ' "Very good," said Frodo. "You make the arrangements." '

This sense of age perhaps motivates the general unconcern for Frodo shown by the Shire, his unfair though unintended supplanting by the large and 'lordly' hobbits Merry and Pippin, the rudeness or much-qualified respect shown to him by Sharkey's men and Gaffer Gamgee too. Saruman knows better, and so do some others, but 'Sam was pained to notice how little honour [Frodo] had in his own country'. It is prophets who proverbially have no honour in their own country, and Frodo is increasingly a prophet or a seer. However even in other countries the honour he gets is the wrong sort. One may remember Ioreth repeating to her cousin in Gondor that Frodo 'went with only his esquire into the Black Country and fought with the Dark Lord all by himself, and set fire to his Tower, if you can believe it. At least that is the tale in the City.' A wrong tale, naturally, but a *heroic* tale. In Gondor as in the Shire one sees how all achievement is assimilated to essentially active, violent, military patterns – 'the better fortitude', as Milton said in *Paradise Lost*, 'Of patience and heroic martyrdom/Unsung'. The end of Frodo's quest, in the memory of Middle-earth, is nothing. Bilbo turns into a figure of folklore ('mad Baggins'), the elves and dwarves percolate through to our world as time-

shifters and ring-makers, even 'the Dark Tower' remains as an image for
'poor Tom' in *King Lear*. Of Frodo, though, not a trace: except hints of
an unlucky, well-meaning king eclipsed on the one hand by the fame of
his vengeful son, on the other by the Coming of the true hero Christ.

What has Ingeld to do with Christ? Nothing. But Fróda had something
to do with both. He was a hinge, a mediation, like *The Lord of the Rings*
in its suspension between pagan myth and Christian truth. He stood, in
Tolkien's view, for all that was good in the Dark Ages – for the heroic
awareness of heroic fallibility which Tolkien thought he could detect in
Beowulf and in *Maldon*, for the spark of virtue which had made Anglo-
Saxon England ripe for conversion (a process carried out without a single
martyrdom). Maybe his story had been, in God's plan, an *evangelica
praeparatio*: a clearing of the ground for the good seed of the Gospel. It
is possible that Tolkien thought of *The Lord of the Rings* in the same way.
He knew his own country was falling back to heathenism again (if only
on the model of Saruman, not Sauron), and while mere professorial
preaching would make no difference, a story might. Frodo presents then
an image of natural man in native decency, trying to find his way from
inertia (the Shire) past mere furious dauntlessness (Boromir) to some
limited success, and doing so without the inherited resources of the heroes
and *longaevi* like Aragorn, Gandalf, Legolas, Gimli. He has to do so
furthermore by destroying the Ring, which is merely-secular power and
ambition, and with no certain faith in rescue from outside the *géara
hwyrftum*, 'the circles of the world'. 'Myth is alive at once and in all its
parts, and dies before it can be dissected', declared Tolkien,[17] and his
statement is more than usually true of *The Lord of the Rings*, as I have said
on p. 100 above. Something like the last few sentences must however have
been at least a part of Tolkien's intention.

The styles of romance

One can see that ancient story is used very differently in *The Lord of the
Rings* from the way it is in, say, James Joyce's *Ulysses*. Not only is the
relation in the latter between Homeric 'myth' and modern novel one of
irony and transformation; in it the 'myth', oddly enough, is given a higher
and more assured status as something less sophisticated, more archetypal,
closer to the holy and the divine. Tolkien by contrast was pre-eminently
aware of *his* source-texts, like *Beowulf*, or Snorri's *Edda*, or Laȝamon's
Brut, as the works of individuals like himself, who used old stories for
contemporary purposes just as he did. In his view *The Lord of the Rings*
was not a derivative or a metamorphosis of them and *Pearl* and *Comus* and
Macbeth and all the other works I have mentioned of 'mythic' or near-
'mythic' status: instead all of them, including *The Lord of the Rings*, were

splinters of a truth, transformations *on the same level* of something never clearly expressed, not even (in entirety) in the Gospels.[18] Human awareness of this truth, he may have concluded, was passed on with just the same loose and haunting persistence as the rhythms and phrases of English poetry, surviving from Anglo-Saxon times to Middle English and 'The Man in the Moon', and on again to Shakespeare and Milton and Yeats and nursery-rhyme, without intention as without a break. Middle-earth itself survived in song even after people had forgotten what it meant: 'O cocks are crowing a merry midd-larf,/A wat the wilde foule boded day.'[19] Should that ballad of 1776 be classified as a 'myth'? It has old roots and is about a supra-rational world; but it was also sung for immediate pleasure without claims to any specially transmitted truth. In all these ways 'Sweet William's Ghost' is analogous to *The Lord of the Rings*, and even more so to its embedded songs and verses.

There is another way of approaching the question of the trilogy's literary status, which has the further merit of concentrating attention on its prose style as well as on poetry. This is via Northrop Frye's now-famous book, the *Anatomy of Criticism* (1957), a work which never mentions *The Lord of the Rings*, but nevertheless creates a literary place for it with Sibylline accuracy. Mr Frye's theory, in essence, is that there are five 'modes' of literature, all defined by the relationship between heroes, environments, and humanity. 'If superior in *kind* both to other men and to the environment of other men', declares Mr Frye, 'the hero is a divine being and the story about him will be a *myth*.'[20] One sees immediately that this does not apply to Gandalf or Aragorn, still less to Frodo: Gandalf can feel fear and cold, Aragorn age and discouragement, Frodo pain and weakness. Two steps down from 'myth', according to the *Anatomy*, we find 'high mimesis', the level of most epic and tragedy, in which heroes are 'superior in degree to other men but not to [their] natural environment'. This looks more like *The Lord of the Rings*, where many of the characters – Éomer, Faramir, Aragorn again – are very much of the stamp of old Siward or Coriolanus or other Shakespearean heroes. But are they on a par with their natural environment? Aragorn can run 135 miles in three days; he lives in full vigour for 210 years, dying on his birthday. Around him cluster characters who are immortal, like Elrond or Legolas, who can make fire or ride on eagles, while he himself can summon the dead. Clearly the mode intended is the one below 'myth' but above 'high mimesis', the world of 'romance' whose heroes are characteristically 'superior in *degree* [not *kind*] to other men *and* to [their] environments'.

The main points of this mode are then displayed by Mr Frye in ways immediately applicable to *The Lord of the Rings*. In it, we are told, 'the hero's death or isolation has the effect of a spirit passing out of nature, and evokes a mood best described as elegiac'; 'passing out of nature' is of course the main theme of hobbit-poetry. Elegy is further accompanied 'by a diffused, resigned, melancholy sense of the passing of time, of the old order changing and yielding to a new one'; while true of *Beowulf* and *The Idylls of the King* this is conspicuously truer of *The Return of the King* and its dissolution of the Third Age. However the main merit of Mr Frye's analysis, at this moment, is that besides describing Tolkien's literary category so well it further indicates, first, an inevitable problem associated with that category, and then, more indirectly, the terms in which to express a solution.

To take the problem first: it is caused by the fact that there are literary modes beneath romance and beneath epic or tragedy, i.e. 'low mimesis' – this being the mode of most novels, in which the hero is much on a level with us – and lower still 'irony', where heroes turn into anti-heroes like Sancho Panza or Good Soldier Schweik or Leopold Bloom. 'Looking over this table', Mr Frye observes, 'we can see that European fiction, during the last fifteen centuries, has steadily moved its center of gravity down the list' – so much so that, as has been remarked of *The Hobbit*, the co-existence of 'romance' characters like Thorin Oakenshield with 'ironic heroes' like Bilbo Baggins is immediately comic and only after many adventures rises to gravity. Tolkien's problem all through his career lay in his readership's 'low mimetic' or 'ironic' expectations. How could he present heroes to an audience trained to reject their very style?

His immediate solution was to present in *The Lord of the Rings* a whole hierarchy of styles. In this the hobbits are, orcs apart, at the bottom. Their very pronouns are against them, for the Shire version of Common Speech, like English but unlike all other major European languages, fails to distinguish polite from familiar forms of 'you'; Pippin, Merry and the others accordingly talk in a style which appears to Gondorians as unnaturally assured (though it is in fact almost 'democratic', see III, 411). In a more obvious way they are prone to compulsive banter. Merry, in the Houses of Healing, asks immediately after his recall from death by the sacral king for 'supper first, and after that a pipe'. The resultant memory of Théoden is dissolved by jokes about tobacco, about his pack, and by friendly abuse from Pippin. 'It is the way of my people to use light words at such times', says Merry apologetically, but just the same he cannot stop. One sees what causes the unkind critical remarks about *Boy's Own* and Billy Bunter. However the emergence of anti-heroes like Billy Bunter, the demotion of romance to children's literature, are obvious consequences of the Western world's fifteen-hundred-year long climb down the ladder of literary modes. All the hobbitic jokes are doing, then, is to reflect and by intention deflect the modern inhibition over high styles which we and they share; if we were not embarrassed by the hobbits, in other words, we would be by the heroes.

Many people indeed manage to be embarrassed by both, and for the latter reaction there is more excuse. As he climbed to the top of his stylistic hierarchy Tolkien on occasion *wrote in* the responses he wanted instead of evoking them. High style is accompanied by characters stepping back, swelling, shining. Aragorn puts down Andúril at the gate of the Golden Hall, and declares its name: 'The guard stepped back and looked with amazement'. A few lines earlier 'wonder' has come into his eyes at the mention of Lothlórien. In the same way the guards at the Great Gate of Gondor 'fell back before the command of [Gandalf's] voice', while at the last embassy near the Morannon 'before his upraised hand the foul Messenger recoiled'. At that moment 'a white light shone forth like a sword' from Gandalf, as many people see 'the light that shone' round Éowyn and Faramir as they come down to the Houses of Healing. Galadriel is 'illuminated' by 'a great light' when Frodo offers her the Ring, and seems 'tall beyond measurement'. All these images together are used when Aragorn draws Andúril and declares himself to Éomer (II, 36):

> Gimli and Legolas looked at their companion in amazement, for they had not seen him in this mood before. He seemed to have grown in stature while Éomer had shrunk; and in his living face they caught a brief vision of the power and majesty of the kings of stone. For a moment it seemed to the eyes of Legolas that a white flame flickered on the brows of Aragorn like a shining crown.
> Éomer stepped back . . .

Obviously his reaction is meant to be ours. Equally obviously that reaction cannot be counted on, because of the surly distrust engendered in us (as in Éomer) by generations of realistic fiction. Nevertheless it is a mistake to think that the only literary modes which exist are those one period is familiar with. By his continual switching from one level of style to another, and his equally continual use of characters as 'internal reflectors' of embarrassment or suspicion, Tolkien showed at least that he was aware of that very predictable mistake, and ready to do what he could to help his readers round it. The worst one can fairly say is that in some scenes – the Andúril ones, the Field of Cormallen, the eagle's song – Tolkien underestimated his audience's resistance and reached too hastily for the sublime or the impressive. The real difficulty, though, is not his but ours: in ordinary modern 'low mimetic' novels such qualities are simply not allowed.

In fact one can often feel Tolkien, between these 'low' and 'high' stylistic poles, breaking with complete success out of all the categories into which he should have been put, rising again from the edge of romance to what almost anyone might call 'myth'. Perhaps the best example occurs at the end of Volume V, chapter 4, 'The Siege of Gondor'. Here many of the story's threads are about to intersect. Faramir lies critically ill within the walls. Pippin is rushing to fetch Gandalf to save him, while Merry

and Théoden are simultaneously approaching from Anórien; but at the
Great Gate the chief Nazgûl, the 'haggard king' himself to whom Frodo
had almost surrendered in the vale of Minas Morgul, leads the assault.
All this is presented simply as story, even as history, but supra-realistic
suggestions keep crowding in. The battering-ram of Mordor has a 'hideous
head, founded of black steel . . . shaped in the likeness of a ravening wolf;
on it spells of ruin lay. Grond they called it, in memory of the Hammer
of the Underworld of old' – as if to recreate some earlier unstated triumph
of the chthonic powers. Meanwhile the Nazgûl himself goes even more
than usual beyond the boundaries of even 'romantic' humanity: he *looks*
like a man, and carries a sword, but it is a 'pale' or insubstantial one; he
bursts the Gate not only by Grond but by a projection of fear and dread,
'words of power and terror to rend both heart and stone', which work like
'searing lightning'. On the one hand he turns almost to abstraction, 'a vast
menace of despair', as also to an image of the un-existence of evil, a 'huge
shadow' which Gandalf tries to send back to 'nothingness'. But though the
Nazgûl ironically proves Boethius right by throwing back his hood – 'and
behold! he had a kingly crown; and yet upon no head visible was it set' –
his deadly laughter shows that 'nothingness' can still have power and
control. At this moment he calls himself Death:

> 'Old fool!' he said. 'Old fool! This is my hour. Do you not know
> Death when you see it? Die now and curse in vain!' And with that he
> lifted high his sword and flames ran down the blade.
> Gandalf did not move. And in that very moment, away behind in
> some courtyard of the City, a cock crowed. Shrill and clear he crowed,
> recking nothing of wizardry or war, welcoming only the morning that
> in the sky far above the shadows of death was coming with the dawn.
> And as if in answer there came from far away another note. Horns,
> horns, horns. In dark Mindolluin's sides they dimly echoed. Great
> horns of the North wildly blowing. Rohan had come at last.

In this passage the key words are perhaps 'as if'. Within the world of
romance everything that happens here is literally 'co-incidence'. The cock
means nothing by crowing, that he crows at this moment is mere
happenstance. Nor are the horns replying – they only seem to. Nevertheless no reader takes the passage like that. The cockcrow itself is too laden
with old significance to be just a motif. In a Christian society one cannot
avoid the memory of the cock that crowed to Simon Peter just as he denied
Christ the third time. What did *that* cockcrow mean? Surely, that there was
a Resurrection, that from now on Simon's despair and fear of death would
be overcome. But then again, what of *Comus* and the cockcrow the Younger
Brother wishes for? ' 'Twould be some solace yet, some little cheering/In
this close dungeon of innumerous boughs.' It would show there is a world

elsewhere. Tolkien too might think of the Norse legend of the 'Undying Lands', the *Ódáinsakr*: when King Hadding reached its boundary the witch who guided him killed a cock and threw it over the wall – a moment later he heard the cock crow before he himself had to turn away and go back to mortality.[21] Cockcrow means dawn, means day after night, life after death; it asserts a greater cycle above a lesser one.

And what of the horns? They too are just the horns the Riders happen to be blowing, but they carry meaning in a more complicated way as well. Their meaning is bravado and recklessness. When he sets out from Rivendell Boromir blows his horn, the family heirloom, and is rebuked by Elrond for doing so; but he takes no notice. 'Always I have let my horn cry at setting forth, and though thereafter we may walk in the shadows, I will not go forth as a thief in the night.' He means that good is stronger than evil, and even if it is not, that makes no difference to him. Challenging horns echo through Northern stories, from the trumpets of Hygelác, Beowulf's uncle, coming to rescue his dispirited compatriots from death by torture, to the war-horns of the 'Forest Cantons', the 'Bull' of Uri and the 'Cow' of Unterwalden, lowing to each other across the field of Marignano, as the Swiss pikemen rallied in the night for a second suicidal assault on overwhelming numbers of French cavalry and cannon. Horns go back to an older world where surrenders were not accepted, to the dead defiant Roland rather than the brave, polite, compromise-creating Sir Gawain, whose dinner is served to 'nwe nakryn noyse' – the sound of chivalric kettledrums. Nor are these the 'horns of Elfland dimly blowing' of late Romanticism; their echoes may be 'dim', but they themselves are 'wild', uncontrolled, immune to the fear and calculation on which the Nazgûl is counting. The combination of horncall and cockcrow means, if one listens, that he who fears for his life shall lose it, but that dying undaunted is no defeat; furthermore that this was true before the Christian myth that came to explain why.

The implications of that scene are more than realistic, and more than romantic. Nevertheless the style of the passage is deliberately neutral. There are touches of alliteration in 'wizardry' and 'war', 'death' and 'dawn', 'dark' and 'dim', while the verb 'recking' is old-fashioned. However the vocabulary as a whole could hardly be simpler, largely monosyllabic, mostly words from Old English or Old Norse, but with an admixture of French words taken into the language many centuries ago, and even one Classical one in 'echoed'. Like Bilbo's and Shakespeare's winter songs, the 'breaking of the Gate' would take little rewriting to seem comprehensible and even colloquial at any time over the last half-millennium. The power of the passage lies not in *mots justes* but in the evocation of ideas at once old and new, familiar in outline but strongly redefined in context: like 'stocks and stones'.

The way this works has been once more illuminated by Mr Frye, who notes that though the line from Charles Kingsley's ballad about the 'cruel, crawling foam' (which swallows a girl drowned by accident) could be censured by rationalistic critics as the 'pathetic fallacy' – thinking nature is alive – what the phrase actually does is to let realism aspire for a second to higher modes, to give to the drowned Mary 'a faint coloring of the myth of Andromeda'. That aspiration is true of Tolkien in many places. It seems only apposite that he should hover so often on the edge of the 'pathetic fallacy', as for instance in the assault on Caradhras, where Aragorn and Boromir insist the wind has 'fell voices' and that stone-slips are aimed, or on the bridge at Khazad-dûm, where Gandalf is 'like a wizened tree', but the Balrog a mixture of fire and shadow, a 'flame of Udûn' – checked only for a moment by Boromir's horn. A good example of open discussion of such ambiguities *within* the trilogy is Frodo's passage of the Dead Marshes in II, 233–6. It is Sam who falls with his face to the mud and cries out 'There are dead things, dead faces in the water'. Gollum explains them as materialistically as possible. The dead are from the great battle long ago; the marsh-lights are exhalations from rotting corpses; he dug down once to eat them, though he found them beyond reach. Frodo sees more in them than that, though he cannot explain what:

> 'They lie in all the pools, deep deep under the dark water. I saw them: grim faces and evil, and noble faces and sad. Many faces proud and fair, and weeds in their silver hair. But all foul, all rotting, all dead. A fell light is in them.'

He does not say that 'fair is foul', like the witches in *Macbeth*. But the fear of the vision comes from the way that all, elves and orcs, evil and noble, are reduced to weeds and foulness in the end. The image picks up Merry's awakening from the barrow pages earlier, with its unexplained juxtaposition of the noble dead in the barrow with the wight itself. Does all glory decompose? That is what makes Frodo stand 'lost in thought'. Later on Faramir is to dismiss the whole thing as a sending of the Enemy. But there remains a feeling that the Enemy is not telling *absolute* untruth, even so. The landscape itself reinforces that belief. 'Far above the rot and vapours of the world the sun was riding high and golden', but all the hobbits can see and hear is 'the faint quiver of empty seed-plumes, and broken grass-blades trembling in small air-movements that they could not feel'. The discharged seed, the breathless air, are images of the discouragement and sterility the Enemy projects. Mordor-flies have red eyes on them; all Mordor-bushes have thorns.

Both characters and readers become aware of the extent and nature of Tolkien's moralisations from landscape in such passages. In the thematic opposite to Mordor and the Marshes, however, in and around Lothlórien, old poems, old beliefs, and fictional geography are much more closely intertwined, with the combination much less readily identified as fallacious. The word associated with Lórien most often is 'stain' – an odd word, both French and Norse in origin, with an early meaning of 'to lose lustre' as well as 'to discolour'. Frodo perceives the colours of Cerin Amroth accordingly as at once 'fresh' and familiar, with a light on them he cannot identify: 'On the land of Lórien there was no stain.' A few pages earlier he had felt that 'on the land of Lórien no shadow lay'. Much later Gandalf in the 'Song of Lórien' confirms, 'Unmarred, unstained is leaf and land'. With this mysterious absence of 'stain' goes a forgetting of grief; though the Fellowship has just lost Gandalf in Moria, the fact is not mentioned for some twenty pages (I, 350–70), and indeed we are told that 'In winter here no heart could mourn for summer or for spring'. This is very like *Pearl*, where the visionary landscape he wakes in makes the dreamer-father forget even his bereavement, 'Garten my goste al greffe forȝete'. It should be noted though that *he* crosses one boundary, from graveyard to dream, but not the next; when he tries to swim the river to Heaven at the end of the poem he is halted and woken before he reaches the water. Frodo and the Fellowship, however, cross two rivers, deliberately described and distinguished. One is the Nimrodel, which consoles their grief and promises them partial security; as Frodo wades it 'he felt that the stain of travel and all weariness was washed from his limbs'. The next is Celebrant, the Silverlode which they cannot ford but have to cross on ropes. Here they are totally secure, for though the orcs can splash across the Nimrodel – 'curse their foul feet in its clean water!' says Haldir – it seems they cannot wade or swim the Silverlode. Even Gollum, though seen by the elves, vanishes 'down the Silverlode southward', i.e. on the far bank, and according to Aragorn has followed the Fellowship only 'right down to Nimrodel'.

With *Pearl* in mind, one might easily conclude that the stretch between the two rivers is a sort of 'earthly Paradise' for Frodo and the others, though one still capable of violation and invasion from the outside world. The 'Naith' of Lórien, though, across the second river, is Heaven; the company undergoes a kind of death in getting there, while there is a feeling of significance in the fact that they may not touch the water, not even to have their 'stains' washed away. A determined allegorist (or mythiciser) might go on to identify the Nimrodel with baptism, the Silverlode with death. A force which holds one powerfully *back* from such opinions is however Sam Gamgee, who counterpoints the most solemn moments of crossing with banalities like 'Live and learn!' and chatter about his uncle Andy (who used to have a rope-walk at Tighfield). He, and Gimli and Gollum and Haldir, keep even Lórien tied down to the level of story, in which rivers are tactical obstacles and not symbols for something else. Nevertheless, even though the *Pearl* analogue may occur to few, the references to absence of 'stain' and grief and blemish, the assertion that Lórien is a place apart, have their effect and keep one finally uncertain about the section's proper mode. The best one can say is that in those chapters, as in *The Lord of the Rings* more generally, a work essentially of 'romance' manages to rise at times towards 'myth', and also to sink towards 'high' or even 'low mimesis'.

Even 'irony' is not always out of place, though it is beneficent. As Sam and Frodo struggle on in Mordor, they come on a streamlet, 'the last remains, maybe, of some sweet rain gathered from sunlit seas, but ill-fated to fall at last upon the walls of the Black Land and wander fruitless down into the dust'. 'Fruitless' (a significant adjective elsewhere)? The water seemed so, but turns out not to be. By refreshing the Ringbearer it does the best that any water could. The 'streamlet', in its apparent failure and eventual success, becomes a kind of analogue to Frodo's pity for Gollum, say, to all appearances useless, in the end decisive. It is hard to say what mode such scenes are in. They could be (by themselves) anywhere in Northrop Frye's stylistic hierarchy. This resonance of passages which can be read with different levels of suggestion at once, with 'myth' and 'low mimesis' and 'irony' all embedded deeply in 'romance', is perhaps the major and least-considered cause for the appeal of *The Lord of the Rings*.

Some contradictions mediated

If the three volumes had a thematic heart (in fact their whole method defies centralisation) one might like to see it in the dialogue of Legolas and Gimli, walking through Minas Tirith at III, 149, and looking at the masonry. Gimli is critical:

> 'It is ever so with the things that Men begin: there is a frost in Spring, or a blight in Summer, and they fail of their promise.'
> 'Yet seldom do they fail of their seed,' said Legolas. 'And that will lie in the dust and rot to spring up again in times and places unlooked-for. The deeds of Men will outlast us, Gimli.'
> 'And yet come to naught in the end but might-have-beens, I guess,' said the Dwarf.
> 'To that the Elves know not the answer,' said Legolas.

The exchange makes a point about Gondorian history. It also brings out further one character's *idée fixe* (stonework), and develops the theme of racial tension/personal harmony which has been a feature of this relationship in the story for some time. Yet the characters' speech here reaches out from its immediate context to timelessness and universality. Their sentences sound like proverbs. The idea of seed lying in the dust is furthermore likely to arouse memory of the parable (Matthew xiii, 18–23) of the seed that fell on stony ground. With a shock one may wonder whether these proverbially soulless creatures, Elf and Dwarf, are here – *all unwittingly* – talking about the Son of Man. It would be like the elves to know a Saviour would come to men, without having the slightest or remotest idea of the mingled horror and beauty with which that event would come about. We get a glimpse of how history might seem to the most virtuous, and most pagan, of virtuous pagans – an odd effect in, but not at all a contradiction to 'a fundamentally religious and Catholic work'. In this way *The Lord of the Rings* can be seen mediating between Christian and pagan, Christ and Ingeld and Frodo, as between myth and romance, large pattern and immediate context.

It is at the same time hovering between styles. There is no archaic word in the passage, except perhaps 'naught'. Nevertheless a strong archaic effect is produced, by inversion of nouns and adjectives, careful selection of adverbs of time like 'yet' and 'seldom', and other less obvious linguistic features. Tolkien could have given a lecture about all these at any time. It would have been no trouble to him to write the exchange in modern English: 'It's always like that with the things men start off on . . . But they don't often fail to propagate . . . They'll still come to nothing in the end . . . The elves don't know the answer to that one . . .' *The Lord of the Rings* would have offered fewer hostages to criticism if it had been written like that. But would it have been better? It seems very unlikely. The discrepancy between modern usage and archaic thought would simply have sounded bogus, leading to a deep 'disunion of word and meaning' (as Tolkien showed by rewriting a similar passage, see *Letters*, pp. 225–6). His prose style was carefully calculated, and had its proper effect, in the long run, and for those not too provoked to read carefully. One might say, in Aristotelian terms, that the trilogy succeeded in harmonising its *ethos*, its *mythos*, and its *lexis* – the subjects, roughly speaking, of the last three chapters respectively.

By those three words Aristotle would have meant 'setting', 'plot' and 'style', all meanings intended in the sentence above. However semantic change often gives an unexpected bonus, which one should accept in this case as in others. The sentence above would still be true if the Greek words meant 'ethics', 'myth' and 'lexis' (the technical term for what one gets from dictionaries or lexicons). Tolkien thought there was a truth in the vagaries of words independent of their users. He probably did not, for instance, personally admire either Milton or Wordsworth: the one was a Protestant, a divorcer, and a spokesman for regicides, the other a tinkerer with medievalism and a linguistic critic of the most ignorant type. But both were English poets, and the language spoke through them. How nearly Wordsworth echoed *Pearl* in his famous elegy on 'Lucy':

> No motion has she now, no force,
>   She neither hears nor sees,
> Roll'd round in earth's diurnal course
>   With rocks, and stones, and trees!

He should have written 'stocks', not 'rocks'. But he preferred the *r* alliteration (and the tautology). Milton meanwhile got the phrase right in his sonnet 'On the Late Massacre in Piedmont':

> Avenge, O Lord, Thy slaughtered saints, whose bones
> Lie scattered on the Alpine mountains cold,
> Ev'n them who kept Thy truth so pure of old,
> When all our fathers worshipped stocks and stones . . .

However in Tolkien's view everything else in the poem would be wrong: its ferocity, its equation of God's truth with Protestantism, most especially its contempt for 'our fathers' before they were converted, for the Anglo-Saxons indeed. Milton knew very little about them, and his contempt was based on ignorance. Yet poetry which uses old phrases is not always bound down to its creator's intention. Reading that line, and adding to it his memories of Finn and Fróda, of Beowulf and Hróthgár and the other pagan heroes from the darkness before the English dawn, Tolkien may have felt that Milton was more accurate than he knew. Perhaps 'our fathers' *did* worship 'stocks and stones'. But perhaps they were not so very bad in doing so. After all if they had not Christ to worship, there were worse things, many worse things for them to reverence than 'stocks and stones', rocks and trees, 'merry Middle-earth' itself.

Chapter 7

VISIONS AND REVISIONS

The Dangers of Going On

Both *The Hobbit* and *The Lord of the Rings* can be seen as primarily works of mediation. In the former Bilbo acts as the link between modern times and the archaic world of dwarves and dragons. In the latter Frodo and his Shire companions play a similar part, though the world they move in has also and in more complex ways been 'mediated', turned into a Limbo. Outside these works, though, hobbits are not to be met with. And in the books published after Tolkien's death, *The Silmarillion* and the *Unfinished Tales*, mediation is very much less apparent. That is the main reason for deciding to treat them here, instead of where (some would say) they belong, before *The Hobbit* and along with the 'Philological Inquiries' of Chapter 2. For *The Silmarillion* at least, though not published till 1977, four years after its author's death, was in existence as a 'narrative structure' not long after the First World War, while a version of it was submitted to George Allen & Unwin for publication forty years before it eventually came out. A 'very high proportion' even of the detailed wording of this 1937 text remains in the published version.[1] Much of *The Silmarillion*, then, could be seen as chronologically pre-*Hobbit*, while the *Unfinished Tales* (though much more varied in date and nature) at least contain a good deal of material whose composition preceded the appearance of *The Lord of the Rings*.

That, though, is not how most readers experience them. Probably ninety-nine people out of a hundred come to *The Silmarillion* and the *Unfinished Tales* only after reading *The Lord of the Rings*. Furthermore, because of the uncompromising nature of the posthumously-published works, it will probably always be hard for most readers to understand them *except* after reading *The Lord of the Rings*. In that work Tolkien had set himself to write a romance for an audience brought up on novels. In the others, whether we consider them as earlier or later, we are left with far less guidance. It is accordingly the main aim of this chapter to indicate as far as possible how *The Silmarillion* in particular should be read. Subsidiary to that, though still important, are the issues of what it has to say and how it came to be: 'sources' and 'designs' once more, both things Tolkien disliked, but useful if not essential to a proper reading.

Before considering even those issues, however, there is one more very obvious question to ask: which is why Tolkien never saw *The Silmarillion* into print himself, and why the *Unfinished Tales* remained unfinished. There were, after all, nearly eighteen years between the appearance of *The Return of the King* and Tolkien's death on 2 September 1973 – as long an interval as that between *The Hobbit* and *The Fellowship of the Ring*. During most of that period Tolkien was furthermore relieved of distracting academic duties, while he was not putting his energies into other creative work: almost all the sixteen poems in *The Adventures of Tom Bombadil* had seen print before, his contribution to *The Road Goes Ever On* consisted mostly of explanation and footnote, and *Smith of Wootton Major* is of no higher a degree of importance than 'Leaf by Niggle'. Besides, to repeat the point, *The Silmarillion* was very largely in existence from 1937 on; was also known to be in existence, and very much in demand! Why, then, could Tolkien not finish his legends of the First Age off?

An answer to this, of a personal kind, has been given by Humphrey Carpenter on pp. 239–41 of his *Biography*. There was in Tolkien's later life, he notes, 'a perpetual discontinuity, a breaking of threads which delayed achievement and frustrated him more and more'. Partly the causes were external – loss of friends, hosts of visitors – but partly temperamental: Tolkien could not 'discipline himself into adopting regular working methods' (a fault of which he had been aware since the time of 'Leaf by Niggle'). *The Silmarillion* was accordingly held up to a great extent, in Mr Carpenter's view, by procrastination and bother over inessentials, by crosswords and games of Patience, by drawing heraldic doodles and answering readers' letters – all compounded, one might add, by the failing energies of age (see *Letters*, p. 228). This is a convincing picture, and no doubt partly true. Yet it is not a picture of someone taking things easy: rather of continual, if misdirected, intellectual effort. One may remark that it is common experience to find that conscientious people who have a job to do that is too much for them (like writing a book) turn in their uncertainty to doing a succession of easier jobs instead (like answering their mail, drawing up syllabuses, or rationalising office organisation). Something like this seems to have been the case with Tolkien. He may have frittered his time away in constructing etymologies and writing kindly letters to strangers. But these activities occupied him, one may well think, because he could see he had painted himself into a corner: the purely *literary* reason for not finishing *The Silmarillion* is deducible not only from that work itself, but from almost the whole of Tolkien's professional career.

To go back to '*Beowulf*: the Monsters and the Critics': if this makes one thing clear it is that the literary quality Tolkien valued above all was the 'impression of depth . . . effect of antiquity . . . illusion of historical truth and perspective' which he found in *Beowulf*, in the *Aeneid*, or for that matter in *Macbeth*, *Sir Orfeo*, or the Grimms' *Fairy Tales*. In all these works there was a sense that the author knew more than he was telling, that behind his immediate story there was a coherent, consistent, deeply fascinating world about which he had no time (then) to speak. Of course this sense, as Tolkien kept repeating, was largely an illusion, even a provocation to which a wise man should not respond. The 'heroic lays' which the *Beowulf*-poet knew and alluded to sound very fine from his allusions, but if we had them we might discover that the fascination came from his art, not theirs. 'Alas for the lost lore, the annals and old poets that Virgil knew, and only used in the making of a new thing!', wrote Tolkien, and he meant it. However he also meant everyone to realise that the 'new thing' was worth more than the 'lost lore'.

The application of this to his own career must (once *The Lord of the Rings* was published) have seemed all too obvious. One quality which that work has in abundance is the Beowulfian 'impression of depth', created just as in the old epic by songs and digressions like Aragorn's lay of Tinúviel, Sam Gamgee's allusions to the Silmaril and the Iron Crown, Elrond's account of Celebrimbor, and dozens more. This, however, is a quality of *The Lord of the Rings*, not of the inset stories. To tell these in their own right and expect them to retain the charm they got from their larger setting would be a terrible error, an error to which Tolkien would be more sensitive than any man alive. As he wrote in a revealing letter dated 20 September 1963:

> I am doubtful myself about the undertaking [to write *The Silmarillion*]. Part of the attraction of The L.R. is, I think, due to the glimpses of a large history in the background: an attraction like that of viewing far off an unvisited island, or seeing the towers of a distant city gleaming in a sunlit mist. To go there is to destroy the magic, unless new unattainable vistas are again revealed. (*Letters*, p. 333)

To go there is to destroy the magic. As for the revealing of 'new unattainable vistas', the problem there – as Tolkien must have thought many times – was that in *The Lord of the Rings* Middle-earth was already old, with a vast weight of history behind it. *The Silmarillion*, though, in its longer form, was bound to begin at the beginning. How could 'depth' be created when you had nothing to reach further back to?

The problem was not absolutely insoluble: Milton, after all, had managed to begin *his* epic very near the beginnings of time, in *Paradise Lost*. Furthermore one can perhaps see the solution to which Tolkien, in his philological way, was drawn, namely to present the First Age as 'a complex of divergent texts interlinked by commentary' (*UT*, p. 1), the texts themselves being supposedly written by Men, of different periods, looking back across the ages to vast rumours of whose truth they knew only part. *The Silmarillion* might then have come to look like (for example)

The Saga of King Heidrek the Wise, written late but preserving intensely moving fragments of verse from some much older time now lost; even the editorial matter would then reinforce the effect of age and darkness (a device Tolkien used on a much smaller scale for *The Adventures of Tom Bombadil*). However that avenue was never explored to its end; and if it *had* been, one may doubt whether many readers would have grasped the total effect. A *Silmarillion* on that plan could have ended as merely a pastime for scholars. It is better, no doubt, to see it as it is now, 'a completed and cohesive entity' (*UT*, p. 1 again). But in any case *The Lord of the Rings* had created other problems for its author besides the issue of 'depth': these affected *The Silmarillion*, but show up more strongly in the *Unfinished Tales*.

One was the strong temptation towards explicitness and over-clarity. In *Letters*, p. 348, Tolkien noted the comic case of a Mr Shorthouse, who produced by accident a strange, queer, debatable book called *John Inglesant*. Slowly it caught on, became a best-seller, 'the subject of public discussion from the Prime Minister downwards'. Success, however, ruined its author, who took to strange clothes and beliefs and 'never wrote any more, but wasted the rest of his time trying to explain what he had and what he had not meant in *John Inglesant*'. 'I have always tried to take him as a melancholy warning' (wrote Tolkien in 1964), so the danger was seen. Still, it was there.

It emerges, for instance, if one considers water. No scene, perhaps, in *The Lord of the Rings* is more moving or more suggestive than the one in which Sam and Frodo, in Mordor, see the wind changing and the darkness driven back, and then as if in answer to prayer come upon a trickle of water: 'ill-fated' and 'fruitless' in appearance, but at that moment seemingly a message from the world outside, beyond the Shadow. In *The Silmarillion* we learn that water is the province of the Vala Ulmo, and that from it (sea or river) there often comes assistance; the incident with Sam and Frodo begins to seem less and less like chance, more and more of a 'sending'. If this went too far, of course, the sense of supernatural assistance would destroy one's awareness of the companions' courage, as also the deeply-felt implicit moral that this is the way to behave. None of *us* can expect assistance from a Vala; nevertheless in any kind of Mordor it is one's duty to go on. By the time *The Lord of the Rings* was finished, Tolkien *was* beginning to think of taking matters further. He had shown inspiration coming from Ulmo to Tuor, as the hero sat by a trickling stream, both in *The Silmarillion* (p. 238), and in 'Of Tuor and his Coming to Gondolin' (written *c.* 1951),[2] in the *Unfinished Tales*, p. 20. Clearly the idea of water as a sanctity and an unfailing refuge from the Dark Lord had started to appeal to him; and in 'The Hunt for the Ring', accordingly, a sort of coda to *The Lord of the Rings* written *c.* 1955, he wrote that all the Nazgûl save their chief 'feared water, and were unwilling, except in dire need, to enter it or to cross streams unless dryshod by a bridge' (*UT*, p. 343). How then had they crossed Wilderland to the Shire? Christopher Tolkien notes that his father saw 'the idea was difficult to sustain'. Besides that, it would have brought the Valar too far forward; at many points it would have destroyed the hobbits' highly realistic sense of loneliness and confusion.

One may think that Tolkien was rightly pushing towards a clarification of his 'mythology'.[3] Yet at the same time he was edging back from his long concern with heroic valour, or hobbitic moral courage. It has been remarked already (p. 116 above) that he was in minor matters soft-hearted. As *The Lord of the Rings* came to an end this temptation, too, grew upon him. Bill the pony is saved in *The Return of the King*. In the unpublished 'Epilogue' to that work,[4] we learn that Shadowfax will be saved too, to be taken on the last ship from the Havens to Aman, simply because Gandalf could not bear the parting. This would be a failure of nerve in a work which had sacrificed Lórien, and Tolkien, having written it, wisely decided to leave it out. Still, the second edition of *The Lord of the Rings* cuts out some minor, but convincing, asperity on the part of a strained Aragorn; it seemed too tough.[5] More seriously, in the 'late' narrative of 'The Disaster of the Gladden Fields' (*UT*, pp. 271–87), one can see Tolkien reconsidering Isildur. His use of the ominous word 'precious' in *The Fellowship of the Ring* (p. 266) had been quite enough to suggest that he was already becoming 'addicted', that his death was in a way a mercy. In the later narrative, though, Isildur uses the Ring painfully and reluctantly, with much excuse and apology. The Ring seems to find no answer in him to its call. But this again is running against a crucial point in *The Lord of the Rings*, namely that no one can be trusted, not even 'the Keepers of the Three'. Tolkien, no doubt, would have seen this point and dealt with it somehow if he had published a full account. Still, one can see him becoming more loath to accept the evil in the good: and while this is charitable, it does not make for powerful story.

A final straw in the wind may be Tolkien's increasing desire to pull strands together. The Middle-earth of *The Hobbit* and *The Lord of the Rings* is full of chaotic half-glimpsed independent lives, ears in the forest, fell voices on the wind, enemy powers older than Sauron and unconnected with him. In a letter of 1955 Tolkien had rather laughed at the idea that Willow-man and the wights were agents of the Dark Lord: 'Cannot people imagine things hostile to men and hobbits who prey on them without being in league with the Devil!' (*Letters*, p. 278). But in manuscript B of 'The Hunt for the Ring' (written at much the same time) just this idea is being entertained. The Chief Ringwraith stays on the Barrow-downs for some while before Frodo sets out, 'and the Barrow-wights were roused, and all things of evil spirit, hostile to Elves and Men, were on the watch with malice in the Old Forest and on the Barrow-downs' (*UT*, p. 348).

None of the points just mentioned is of any great significance in itself. As a whole, though, they do suggest an author looking back over his own work *and trying to reduce it to order*. The menace in that, as everyone knows, is that with system comes rationalisation and loss of vitality. There are moments when one fears that Tolkien, in the *Unfinished Tales* – and in fairness one must repeat that they *are* unfinished, were never finally 'passed' by their author – was turning against the sources of his inspiration. He tried to realign retrospectively things he had written many years before, for what at the time had been entirely adequate reasons. The point of making Bilbo both 'bourgeois' and 'burglar' has been explained above, see pp. 55–6; and the scene in Bag End in chapter 1 of *The Hobbit* is completely successful as comedy. But by the time he wrote 'The Quest of Erebor' (perhaps around 1950), Tolkien had come to think it undignified. In repeated versions he explains laboriously that Gandalf forced Bilbo on Thorin out of some Valinorean 'foresight'; or because he knew hobbits were stealthy; or because he thought Bilbo had the right 'mix' of Took and Baggins; while as for the word 'burglar', it was all a dwarvish misunderstanding. The very multiplicity of reasons suggests doubt; and in romance it is a good rule that not everything should be explained.

In any case one may well think that the sheer effort of dotting 'i's and crossing 't's was draining. On one issue – the nature of the orcs – Tolkien seems very nearly to have arrived at a solution without quite being able to grasp it, a sign, perhaps, of exhaustion. There can be little doubt that the orcs entered Middle-earth originally just because the story needed a continual supply of enemies over whom one need feel no compunction – 'the infantry of the old war', to use Tolkien's phrase from 'Monsters' (p. 264). But several readers had pointed out that if evil could not create, was only good perverted, then presumably the orcs had been by nature good and might in some way be saved; Tolkien certainly balked at calling them 'irredeemable', see *Letters*, pp. 195, 355. *The Silmarillion* accordingly expresses more than once the theory that orcs were in fact captured elves 'by slow acts of cruelty . . . corrupted and enslaved' (*S*, p. 50). One can only say that in that case there are an awful lot of them – 'the pits of Angband seemed to hold store inexhaustible and ever-renewed' (*S*, p. 157). They must have been bred, one thinks, and indeed we are told they multiplied 'after the manner of the children of Ilúvatar', i.e. sexually. But in *that* case one wonders (a) why what we would call 'brainwashed' creatures should breed true, and (b) why we never come upon female orcs. Tolkien shrank from that last, and recorded (*UT*, p. 385) a rival theory that the orcs were bred from something like the Drúedain, the Púkel-men. I suspect that at the back of his mind there lurked a phrase from *Beowulf*, about those very similar monsters Grendel and his mother: *no hie fæder cunnon*, 'men know of no father for them'. It would be a good solution to

see the orcs as multiplying 'like flies', i.e. non-sexually, in hatcheries in
Barad-dûr or Moria or the pits of Angband. Such beings would be
'creatures' of evil in a special sense, made and animated by their master
in a way which falls just short of the heresy that evil can itself create. As
Ilúvatar says of Aulë's dwarves, they would have no being of their own,
'moving when [he thinks] to move them, and if [his] thought is elsewhere,
standing idle'. Tolkien saw the problem, and collected the parts of a
solution. He did not however assemble the parts – perhaps because it
would have involved, to be consistent, a complete revision of all his earlier
work.

The word underlying these last few pages is 'thrift'. All minds possess
a drive towards consistency, towards reducing data, events, characters to
some smaller set of principles or categories. Much of Tolkien's writing in
Silmarillion and *Unfinished Tales* shows that urge, a strong and honourable
one. It is fair to say, though, that against this basic drive all minds also
possess a wish to ignore principles and concentrate instead on single
entities regardless of their place in larger systems, to appreciate them
simply for themselves. For most of his career Tolkien was a most extreme
example of a man with this second urge strongly developed: he was
fascinated by names, to give only one example, part of whose nature is
that they are for one thing and one thing alone, very hard to reduce to
system! Hence the supreme lavishness of Middle-earth in *The Lord of the
Rings*, with its vast store of plants and races, names and languages and
individuals and landscapes. As he turned towards thrift, consistency,
classification, Tolkien forfeited much of what he had valued before; he
was contracting, not expanding. In a way the very success of *The Lord of
the Rings*, founded on its immense solidity and scope, made life difficult
for him afterwards. Not only would *The Silmarillion* have to achieve the
'depth' it had already been used to create, it would have to do so without
contradicting, and while if possible reinforcing, all the millions of
details Tolkien had handed over to his readership already. For these
two reasons it is hardly any wonder that Tolkien balked, and that the
Unfinished Tales in particular show a mind searching in different directions. After 1955 many ways forward were blocked. The question was,
whether the vitality of his original conceptions and compositions of
the period before *The Lord of the Rings*, indeed from 1914 on, could
survive.

Here one must concentrate, not on those explanations of the Second
and Third Ages which Tolkien wrote as background for *The Lord of the
Rings*, but on his labour and preoccupation for nearly sixty years, the
legends of the First Age: Tuor and Túrin in the *Unfinished Tales*, but
beyond and around them the whole 'narrative structure' of *The Silmarillion*.
To repeat questions posed earlier: what have these to say, and how did
they come to be?

Philosophical Inquiries

The most obvious fact about the design of *The Silmarillion* is that, like the Shire, it is a 'calque', though on the history of *Genesis* rather than the history of England. In chapter X of *A Preface to Paradise Lost* (London: Oxford University Press, 1942), C. S. Lewis gave a summary list of doctrines of the Fall of Man common to Milton, to St Augustine, and to 'the Church as a whole'. Most of them reappear with little change in the 'Ainulindalë' or 'Valaquenta'. Thus Lewis asserts that 'God created all things without exception good'; in Tolkien even Melkor begins with good intentions (p. 18). 'What we call bad things are good things perverted . . . This perversion arises when a conscious creature becomes more interested in itself than in God . . . the sin of Pride'; compare Melkor in the music of the Ainur seeking 'to increase the power and glory of the part assigned to himself'. Lewis again, 'whoever tries to rebel against God produces the result opposite to his intention . . . Those who will not be God's sons become his tools'; and Ilúvatar to Melkor, 'no theme may be played that hath not its uttermost source in me . . . he that attempteth this shall prove but mine *instrument* in the devising of things more wonderful, which he himself hath not imagined' (my italics). It seems very likely that Lewis and Tolkien collaborated in their analysis of Christian essentials; *The Silmarillion*, with its exile from paradise, its ages of misery, and its Intercessor, is a calque on Christian story, an answer to *Paradise Lost* and *Paradise Regained*.

Is it a *rival* to Christian story? The thought clearly occurred to Tolkien, if only to be repudiated. Significantly he left a gap in *The Silmarillion*, or designed a dovetail, for the Fall of Man as described in the Old Testament. In his work the human race does not originate 'on stage' in Beleriand, but drifts into it, already sundered in speech, from the East. There something terrible has happened to them of which they will not speak: 'A darkness lies behind us . . . and we have turned our backs on it' (p. 141). Furthermore they have met 'the Lord of the Dark' before they meet the Elves; Morgoth went to them as soon as they were created, to 'corrupt or destroy'. Clearly one can, if one wishes, assume that the exploit of Morgoth of which the Eldar never learnt was the traditional seduction of Adam and Eve by the serpent, while the incoming Édain and Easterlings are all sons of Adam flying from Eden and subject to the curse of Babel. *The Silmarillion*, then, tells the story of the fall and partial redemption of the elves, without contradicting the story of the Fall and Redemption of Man.

There is no point, though, in merely repeating a known pattern. Tolkien, in his history of the elves, would not wish to go against what he accepted as doctrine universally true. He did however want to say something different: as with a linguistic 'calque', familiar structure has to join with strange or novel material. The alienness of Tolkien's elves, the thing which makes their whole history different from that of humanity, is obviously that (in the natural course of things) they *do not die*. Accordingly they do not have to be rescued from death by a Saviour; nor from Hell, for they are not judged at death to Hell or Heaven, but sent to 'the halls of Mandos', from which they may in time return. Orthodox correspondents of Tolkien worried about this, and thought he was overstepping the mark (see especially *Letters* no. 153). To their doubts Tolkien could only reply that he was writing fiction, he had a right to use his imagination, and that after all his elves were only 'certain aspects of Men and their talents and desires, incarnated in my little world'. Romance, as Professor Kermode said (see p. 132 above), is a stripped-down form which enables one to concentrate.

What Tolkien wanted to concentrate on, obviously, was death: more precisely perhaps on why people love this world and want so strongly to stay in it when it is an inescapable part of their nature 'to die and go we know not where'. His imagination centred again on a kind of calque, a diagrammatic reversal. Since we die, he invented a race which did not. Since our 'fairy-stories' are full of the escape from death (as he remarked near the end of 'On Fairy-Stories', *TL*, p. 59), 'the Human-stories of the elves are doubtless full of the Escape from Deathlessness'. Certainly one was, his own tale of Beren and Lúthien as embodied in his 'Lay of Leithian, Release from Bondage', in which Lúthien alone of the elves is *allowed* as a favour to 'die indeed' and leave the world like a mortal. *Paradise Lost*, one might say, exists to tell us that death is a just punishment, and anyway (see *Paradise Regained*) not final. *The Silmarillion* by contrast seems to be trying to persuade us to see death potentially as a gift or reward – an attitude to which other authors in this sceptical age have felt drawn.[6] While the legends of the First Age are a 'calque', then, their resemblance to a known pattern directs us primarily to difference from that pattern; the elvishness of the elves is meant to reflect back on the humanity of man.

That seems, anyway, to be what Tolkien came to think. There must however be at least a suspicion that – as with the languages of Middle-earth – he created a structure of thought to justify a more primary urge, delight in language, delight in ancient story. Elves, like dragons, are embedded deeply in several different traditions of North-West Europe, and the inconsistencies of those traditions may only have made Tolkien itch to create a *Zusammenhang*. Did elves have souls, for instance? Could they be saved? Anyone who had read Hans Christian Andersen's 'The Little Mermaid' would know that they did not and could not – not unless they married a mortal, as with Lúthien. Tolkien did know 'The Little Mermaid', though he did not like it (*Letters*, p. 311), probably because he thought it too sentimental. Older and tougher belief on the same issue is embodied in another tale Tolkien had probably read, the Scottish story of 'The Woman of Peace and the Bible Reader'[7]: in this an elf-woman approaches an old man reading his Bible and asks 'if there was any hope given in holy Scripture for such as she'. The old man replies kindly, but says there is no mention of salvation in the Good Book 'for any but the sinful sons of Adam' – at which the lady gives a cry of despair and hurls herself into the sea. The old man's answer is strict and orthodox but (as with the view that pre-conversion heroes like Beowulf or Aragorn could not be saved) hardly seems fair. Why should only the 'sinful' be saved? However it was not Tolkien's way to deny orthodoxy: nor to abjure equally old and traditional belief in the allure of elves and their separation from evil. He looked for a middle path. And in this activity he had at least one model.

This is not, for once, the *Beowulf*-poet, who took a strong line on *ylfe* or elves, putting them into a list with 'ettens' and indeed with 'orcs' – a very stern view of all non-human and un-Christian species. But at least one other English poet preceded Tolkien in being less sure, the author of the legend of St Michael in *The Early South English Legendary*, written about 1250. Tolkien never mentions reading this, but it is unlikely that as a medievalist he did not. What the Middle English poet has to say, in essence, is that in the war between God and Satan for men's souls, there may perhaps be *neutrals*. In the War in Heaven not all the angels were whole-heartedly for God or for Lucifer. The ones who inclined toward the devils without actually joining them are accordingly confined in tempests till Doomsday, when they will go to Hell. Correspondingly, those who wavered towards God have been sent from Heaven to Earth, where 'they will be in a certain pain up to the end of the world, but at Doomsday they shall return to Heaven. Others are still in the Earthly Paradise, and in other places on Earth, doing their penance.' Both good and evil spirits come to Earth to protect or corrupt men, but these neutrals can be seen too:

> And ofte in fourme of wommane: In many derne weye
> grete compaygnie men i-seoth of heom: boþe hoppie and pleiȝe,
> þat Eluene beoth i-cleopede: and ofte heo comiez to toune,
> And bi daye muche in wodes heo beoth: and bi niȝte ope heiȝe dounes.
> Þat beoth þe wrechche gostes: þat out of heuene weren i-nome,
> And manie of heom a-domesday: ȝeot schullen to reste come.

> And often men see great numbers of them, shaped like women, dancing and sporting on many dark paths. *These are called Elves* (my italics), and often they come to town, and by day they are usually in the woods, by night on high hills. Those are the wretched spirits that were taken from Heaven. And at Doomsday many of them shall still come to rest.[8]

It is surprising how much of these few lines finds an echo in *The Silmarillion*. Of course Tolkien could not accept the basic postulate that elves were angels; like the story of the fairy and the Bible-reader, that is the product of a strict Christianity with very little space for outsiders.

However, his elves are very *like* fallen angels, quite similar enough for confusion in the minds of fallible men. They seem part of a hierarchy which goes from Valar (good and bad) to Maiar (good and bad) to Eldar; they are 'like in nature to the Ainur, though less in might and stature', close enough in one case (Melian and Elwë Thingol) to intermarry. For a man to say that Galadriel was an angel, for instance, might then seem natural enough.[9] Would she be a *fallen* angel? In a way the answer is 'No', for certainly the elves play no part in Tolkien's War in Heaven, when Melkor is shut out. On the other hand Galadriel has been expelled from a kind of Heaven, the Deathless land of Valinor, and has been forbidden to return.[10] One can imagine the expulsion to Earth (of Melkor) and the expulsion to Middle-earth (of Galadriel) coming, in a mind like Éomer's, to seem much the same thing. Furthermore one notes the *South English Legendary*'s interesting conviction that some 'neutrals', or elves, are still on Earth, and others in the 'Earthly Paradise'. In a way this too is made true by *The Silmarillion* and *The Lord of the Rings* combined; for the latter predicts that some elves will refuse to leave Middle-earth, however much they may 'dwindle', while the former shows that others remain in Valinor, once part of the Earth, though now in some mysterious way sundered from it. What Tolkien took from that passage (and others) was, in short, the ideas that elves were like angels; that they had however been involved in a 'Fall'; that their fate at Doomsday is not clear (for men 'shall join in the Second Music of the Ainur', elves perhaps not, *S*, p. 42), that they are associated with the Earthly Paradise, and cannot die till the end of the world. No earlier source puts forward the idea of the Halls of Mandos, but that half-way house, like Limbo, seems almost to be demanded by the terms of the problem. Have elves souls? No, in that they are not free to leave the world; so far the Ross-shire Bible reader was right. Yes, in that they do not go out like a candle on death; so far natural justice is satisfied. One sees that, as well as *Genesis*, Northern folk-tradition has helped to frame *The Silmarillion*. Its story has a root in the puzzles of ancient texts.

Pride and Possessiveness: another view

None of the foregoing says anything about the 'Silmarils' themselves, the jewels which give their name to *The Silmarillion*, and whose fate determines its plot. However they do in a way fit the scheme already outlined. *The Silmarillion* was based on the Christian story of Fall and Redemption, whether one took it from *Genesis* or *Paradise Lost*. It was different from the Christian story in being about a race which had not been punished by death, rather by weariness of life (see especially *Letters*, p. 236). A natural question is, what was their sin? To keep the pattern consistent, it ought not to be the same as that of Adam and Eve, by tradition Pride, the moment when, as Lewis said, 'a conscious creature' became 'more interested in itself than in God'. In fact the elves seem much more suscept-ible to a specialised variety of pride not at all present in *Paradise Lost*, not quite Avarice or 'possessiveness' or wanting to own things (as has been suggested),[11] but rather a restless desire to *make* things which will forever reflect or incarnate their own personality. So Melkor has the desire 'to bring into Being things of his own'; Aulë, though subjecting himself to Ilúvatar, creates the dwarves without authority; Fëanor forges the Silmarils. One might rewrite Lewis's phrase to say that in Valinor, as opposed to Eden, the Fall came when conscious creatures became 'more interested in their own creations than in God's'. The aspect of humanity which the elves represent most fully – both for good and ill – is the creative one.

There could be several reasons why Tolkien chose to write about fascination with the artefact (a theme present in his work since chapter 1 of *The Hobbit*). The most obvious is that he felt it himself: to him his fictions were what the Silmarils were to Fëanor or their ships to the Teleri, 'the work of our hearts, whose like we shall not make again'. Significantly Fëanor learns not from Manwë, nor Ulmo, but from Aulë, the smith of the Valar and the most similar of them to Melkor; Aulë too is responsible for the despatch of Saruman to Middle-earth, see *UT*, p. 393; Aulë is the patron of all craftsmen, including 'those that make not, but seek only for the understanding of what is' – the philologists, one might say, but also the *scopas*, the 'makars', the *fabbri*, the poets. Tolkien could not help seeing a part of himself in Fëanor and Saruman, sharing their perhaps licit, perhaps illicit desire to 'sub-create'. He wrote about his own temp-tations, and came close to presenting the revolt of the Noldor as a *felix culpa*, a 'fortunate sin', when Manwë accepts that their deeds will live in song, so that 'beauty not before conceived [shall] be brought into Eä'; fiction, poetry, craftsmanship are seen as carrying their own justification and as all being much the same thing. Rightly, Tolkien must have thought, did the poet of *Pearl* call himself a 'jeweller'.

A more wide-ranging reason is that love of things, especially artificial things, could be seen as the besetting sin of modern civilisation, and in a way a new one, not quite Avarice and not quite Pride, but somehow attached to both (see pp. 68, 128 above). In that view *The Silmarillion* would have something like the distinctively modern 'applicability' of *The Lord of the Rings* and *The Hobbit*, for all its archaic setting. Yet Tolkien believed, to repeat a point made already, that modern sins had ancient origins. The fall of the Noldor (*S*, p. 69) repeats a phrase from the Old English poem *Maxims I* about 'inventing and tempering wounding swords': the Anglo-Saxon poet seems to have looked back to Cain and Abel for the origin of evil, rather than Adam and Eve, and to have seen evil's symptom in metallurgy. More deeply the Silmarils themselves seem to stem from yet one more philological crux, this time from Finnish.

The influence of that language and literature on *The Silmarillion* is undoubted. Finnish was 'the original germ of *The Silmarillion*', Tolkien wrote in 1944 (*Letters*, p. 87), and he repeated the assertion twenty years later (*Letters*, p. 345). Quenya itself is similar to Finnish in linguistic 'style'; names like Ilúvatar and Ulmo recall the Ilmatar and Ilmo of the *Kalevala*; the Valar are the powers who have agreed to be 'bounded in the world', and *vala* in Finnish means 'bond'; many more connections can be made.†

It is therefore almost inevitable that the great mystery of the epic of Finland, the *Kalevala*, should irresistibly recall the Silmarils: it is the riddle of the *sampo*, or *tsampo*. This object is described repeatedly in the *Kalevala* as the work of the master-smith Ilmarinen, handed over as payment for a bride, but then stolen back, broken in the pursuit, surviving only in fragments; yet no one knows what it is – or rather, what it was, for its loss is irrevocable. The singers themselves are uncertain, often replacing *sampo* (a word without a referent) by some other nonsense-word like *sammas*. Meanwhile the philologists, putting together the various clues inside the *Kalevala* – it is bright, it was forged, it is a kind of mill, it brings luck, it made the sea salt – have come up with innumerable solutions, at once vague and pedantic: the *sampo* was the Golden Fleece, some fertility-cult object, a Lappish pillar-idol, an allegory of the sky. In recent years, despondently, they have concluded 'that questions about what the *sampo* was can never be satisfactorily answered and that even if they could, an answer would probably make little contribution to the understanding of the poems'.[12] Nothing could be more provocative to Tolkien than a word without a referent (*emnet*, *wodwos*, *Gandálfr*, *ent*), except perhaps an ancient poem written off by modern scholars as hopelessly irrational. In this case he clearly decided that the *sampo* was at once a thing and an allegory, like the Silmarils: a jewel, bright, hypnotic, intrinsically valuable, but also the quintessence of the creative powers, provoking both good and evil, the maker's personality itself. Some Finnish singers thought the *sampo* was their own poetry; all agreed that its fragments were the true prosperity of Suomi.

If only the Silmarils could inspire a true prosperity for England! As is well known, Tolkien's grand design, or desire, was to give back to his own country the legends that had been taken from it in the Dark Ages after the Conquest, when elves and woodwoses and *sigelhearwan* too had all been forced into oblivion. For that to be possible, the Silmarils and their chain

† The point is made much more explicitly in Jim Allan's *An Introduction to Elvish* (Hayes: Bran's Head, 1978): Quenya resembles Finnish in 'style', especially in its complex noun-declensions, Sindarin is close to Welsh in for instance its sound-changes. A philological point not made by Allan is that Finnish preserves several words borrowed from Early Germanic in their early (or *) form: *kuningas* for 'king', *var(k)as* for 'warg', *jetanas* for 'etten' or 'giant'. Tulkas, the warlike Vala of *The Silmarillion* seems a similar formation, cp. the Norse word *tulkr* ('tolke' in *Sir Gawain*), 'man, fighting man'.

of stories would have to be multi-faceted indeed, leaving scope for 'other minds and hands' to add their own significances. Certainly Tolkien's own efforts to say what *The Silmarillion* was 'about' were never completely illuminating. Still, his borrowings and his changes do at least define his area of interest. In *The Silmarillion* Tolkien played through once more the drama of 'paradise lost'; but he added to it a hint of 'paradise well lost' (for many of the elves preferred Middle-earth even to immortal life, like Arwen); and through the story there runs a delight in mutability, as languages change and treasures pass from hand to hand; the deepest fable is of beauty forged, stolen, and lost forever in recovery. Though springing from *Genesis*, this is at once more ambiguous, more heroic, and more humane.

Eärendil: a Lyric Core

The preceding section (as Tolkien would have been the first to declare) probably falls into the perennial academic vice of neatness, over-valuing system and 'invention' instead of 'inspiration'. To redress the balance, it is worth noting that Tolkien was capable of working in quite a different way. He said repeatedly and consistently (*Letters*, pp. 221, 345, 420) that the 'kernel' of his mythology in the story of Beren and Lúthien was not a thought, not a principle, not a calque, but the vision of 'a small woodland glade filled with hemlocks at Roos in Yorkshire', where he saw his wife dancing. Everything else might be changed by the demands of story and of ratiocination – there are clear differences, for instance, between the accounts of that scene in the 1925 poem 'Light as Leaf on Lindentree' and in Aragorn's song on Weathertop – but to the vision itself he remained true, working out from it as from the detailed paintings of Lake Mithrim, Nargothrond, Gondolin, etc., which he made in the 1920s (see *Pictures* 32–6). Probably Tolkien would have accepted the thesis (not unfamiliar to medievalists) that all great works of fiction should contain a kernel scene or a 'lyric core': to use the terminology of Marie de France, whose 'Breton lays' Tolkien imitated in 'Aotrou and Itroun', 1945, every *conte* or story comes from a *lai* or song. There is one very striking example in the *Unfinished Tales*, namely the tale of 'Aldarion and Erendis: the Mariner's Wife'. This may have some root in Tolkien's own experience, for it stresses the unwisdom of fathers leaving their children – Tolkien hardly knew his own father – and seems to be groping towards a statement about the incompatibility of men and women, users and providers, wasters and winners. However as a story it reaches no conclusion. What it does is to create an image of total separation expressed in understatement. Having been left by her husband in his urge for voyages abroad, Erendis retreats to the centre of Númenor, away from the sea, where she hears only the bleating of sheep. ' "Sweeter it is to my ears than the mewing of gulls", she said.' Tolkien must have been thinking of Njǫrthr the sea-god and Skathi, daughter of the mountain-giant, in Snorri Sturluson's *Prose Edda*. Obliged to marry, these two tried taking turns to live in each other's homes. But the marriage was a failure, marked in Snorri's account by sudden quotation from yet one more lost poem:

'Leið erumk fjǫll,   vaska lengi á,
    nætr einar niu;
ulfa þytr   þóttumk illr vesa
    hjá sǫngvi svana.'

'Hateful to me were the mountains, I was there no longer than nine nights; the howling of wolves seemed ugly to me against the song of the swans.'

So Njǫrthr; his wife replies with a complaint about the noise of the sea-mews. Wolves and swans, gulls and sheep: the contrasts generate the Norse poem and Tolkien's story by themselves.

Other tales in *The Silmarillion* are better worked up into narrative, and yet seem to spring likewise from single scenes, single outcries. An obvious case is that of Eärendil, the first character to take shape in Tolkien's mythology. His 'invention', like that of hobbits, has been well-chronicled by Humphrey Carpenter (*Biography*, pp. 64 and 172); the two cases are in several ways similar. With Eärendil, what happened is that Tolkien was initially struck by several lines from an Old English poem in the *Exeter Book*, now known as *Christ I* or *The Advent Lyrics*:

Eala earendel,   engla beorhtast,
ofer middangeard   monnum sended . . .

'Oh, Earendel, brightest of angels, sent to men above Middle-earth . . .'

These form the start of a speech by the prophets and patriachs in Hell, who appeal for an Ambassador – this is before Christ's Advent – to bring them rescue from the *deorc déapes sceadu*, the 'dark shadow of death'. But the word *earendel* is strange, not ordinary Old English, and evidently pre-dating its context; Tolkien was caught by a difference of texture, prompting his own verses on 'The Voyage of Earendel', in 1914, and the reply to G. B. Smith's question as to what they were about, 'I don't know. I'll try to find out.'

But actually Tolkien had no doubt already started finding out, taking the two obvious courses of looking up 'Earendel' in A. S. Cook's 1900 edition of *Christ* and in the index of Jacob Grimm's *Teutonic Mythology*. From the latter he would have learnt that Earendel-references appear in several Germanic languages. In the *Prose Edda*, for instance, Aurvandill is a companion of the god Thórr, who loses a toe to frostbite only to have it thrown into the sky to become a star; as one might have guessed from

Christ, 'Earendel' is the old name of a star or planet. Grimm also referred though to the German poem of *Orendel*, written about 1200. In this Orendel is a king's son shipwrecked in the Holy Land, but rescued naked by a fisherman. He retrieves a grey robe from a whale they catch, and in it returns to his own land to convert his heathen countrymen. The *grâwe roc* he wears is the seamless robe Christ wore to the Crucifixion; in the end Orendel becomes *der Graurock*, 'Greycloak', is identified with his garment. What this may have suggested to Tolkien is that if the Old English and Old Norse sources agreed that 'Earendel' was a star, the Old English and medieval German ones agreed he was a messenger of hope to the heathens. Perhaps the hope-association was as old as the star one; perhaps 'Earendel' had contained a presentiment of salvation even for the old heroes (like Beowulf) who lived before Christianity was brought to them. The notes in Cook's edition would meanwhile have told Tolkien that the Old English lines were based on a Latin antiphon, '*O Oriens...*' ('O Rising Light, splendour of eternal light and sun of justice: come and shine on those who sit in darkness and the shadow of death'). In a Christian context this appeal is to Christ; in a pre-Christian context they could be a pagan's appeal, to a forerunner of Christ, to a Saviour whose nature he did not know.

These thoughts frame both the poem of 1914 and the *Silmarillion* account written many years later. In the latter Eärendil is, not a Redeemer, but an Intercessor, unlike the true Messiah in that it is not his own sacrifice which persuades the Valar to change the sad history of Middle-earth, but still 'a man of sorrows, and acquainted with grief', hailed by Eönwë with eagle-like ambiguity (see p. 151 above) as 'the looked for that cometh at unawares, the longed for that cometh beyond hope'. In the former, it is perhaps the inadequacy of Earendel that is more prominent than his partial success; at the end of the poem his light is blotted out by the greater light of dawn. However one image is common to all Tolkien's versions and to the Old English poem too. This, one might say, is the 'lyric core', the flashpoint of the imagination. It is the vision of people looking up from the depths, *de profundis*, from the 'dark shadow of death' and of despair, and seeing a new light: 'unlooked for, glittering and bright; and the people of Middle-earth beheld it from afar and wondered, and they took it for a sign, and called it Gil-Estel, the Star of High Hope'. What the star was, how it was connected to Eärendil, how the name could cover both star and man, from what danger it signalled deliverance, whether that deliverance was final for the soulless elves... all these questions, and others, could find answers in the inventions of later narrative, in the different viewpoints of *The Silmarillion* or Bilbo's song in *The Fellowship of the Ring*. However the image and the emotions associated with it did not change. They were central; part of Tolkien's 'data'; of the same order of importance as those other early captured scenes of Tinúviel dancing in the woods, Túrin answered by the 'cold voice' of his own sword, Valinor beyond the 'sunless lands' and 'dangerous seas'. If 'philosophical inquiries' provided material for Tolkien to brood on, these 'lyric cores' gave him the stimulus to go on brooding, to keep philosophy from aridness.

Characters and Cobwebs

Aridness is, however, a vice of which *The Silmarillion* stands accused: partly, no doubt, from a (mistaken) disappointment in those who wanted a second *Lord of the Rings*, but largely, as was said at the start of this chapter, because of the absence from it of 'mediators' like the hobbits and a generally novelistic mode of presentation. Much can be said about the 'meaning' of *The Silmarillion*, and more about its 'origins'. But it is more important in the end to get some idea of how to read it. And there are ways to appreciate *The Silmarillion* better, always provided that one is prepared to make certain basic assumptions.

One of these is that 'character' is in a sense fixed, static, even diagrammatic. Such was the common assumption of earlier times; as has been noted above, the modern saying that 'all power tends to corrupt' (with its assumption that character changes) is prefigured in Old English only by the saying that 'a man shows what he's like when he can do what he wants' (which assumes that changes are only apparent). The convention of Norse saga, then, is to say what a man is like as soon as he comes into the story: 'He was very hard to manage as he grew up, taciturn and unaffectionate, quarrelsome both in words and deeds' (Grettir, in *Grettir's saga*), or 'he had a crooked nose and teeth which stuck out, looked rather ugly in the mouth and yet extremely warlike' (Skarphethinn, in *Njáll's saga*). These statements are always true, though there is still an interest, and a suspense, in seeing how events will prove them so. In *The Silmarillion* Tolkien follows this convention closely: Fëanor 'was tall, and fair of face, and masterful, his eyes piercingly bright and his hair raven-dark; in the pursuit of all his purposes eager and steadfast. Few ever changed his courses by counsel, none by force'; or, later, 'Húrin was of less stature than his fathers, or his son after him; but he was tireless and enduring in body, lithe and swift after the manner of his mother's kin, Hareth of the Haladin'.

This second 'character-sketch' furthermore introduces another point in which *The Silmarillion* follows Norse belief, if not Norse convention: this is the conviction, shared also by the *Beowulf*-poet, that people are their heredity. Sagas commonly introduce characters with a list of their ancestors, often significant in their distinction, wisdom, ferocity, or unreliability. Tolkien did not trespass so far on the short patience of modern times, but he did supply diagrams and family-trees: it is essential that these should be borne in mind. Thus one could easily say that the central tragedy of the Noldor is one between *sámmoeðri* and *sundrmoeðri*,[13] between full-brothers, half-brothers and cousins, a tragedy of mixed blood. The 'Elves of the Light' are divided into three groups, in order of seniority, or wisdom, or attachment to the Valar: the Vanyar, Noldor, Teleri. Fëanor is pure Noldor on both sides, as are his sons. After the death of his mother, though, his father marries again, so that Fëanor has two half-brothers (Fingolfin, Finarfin). It is vital to remember that *their* mother is not of the Noldor, but of the 'senior' race of the Vanyar. While junior to Fëanor in birth and even in talent, therefore, his two half-brothers are marked from the beginning as superior to him in restraint and generosity. Their children are then again differentiated by a further 'out-breeding', in that Finarfin, of mixed descent himself, marries a wife from the 'junior' elvish branch, the Teleri; *his* sons and daughters, who are only a quarter Noldor, are more sympathetic than their uncle's children (mixed Noldor/Vanyar), and markedly more so than their other, pure-blooded cousins, the sons of Fëanor. One needs, perhaps, to ponder the diagram on p. 305 of *The Silmarillion* to see this clear. However once the picture *is* clear one can appreciate the significance of some of Tolkien's oppositions, between Galadriel and Aredhel, for instance (bold as against rash), or between Finrod and Turgon (both founders of Hidden Kingdoms, but the latter retaining a connection with the higher wisdom of the Valar which the former, related to elves who refused the crossing to Aman, has given up). Nor do the oppositions stay on the level of diagram; they go on to shape narratives, and individual scenes.

The whole story of the ruin of Doriath, for instance, might be said to run from the moment when Caranthir, fourth son of Fëanor, reacts angrily to the fact that his Teleri-descended cousins have been talking to their maternal great-uncle Elwë Thingol (or 'Greycloak'), to whom he is not related at all. He says (p. 112):

'Let not the sons of Finarfin run hither and thither with their tales to this Dark Elf in his caves! Who made them our spokesman to deal with him? And though they be come indeed to Beleriand, let them not so swiftly forget that their father is a lord of the Noldor, though their mother be of other kin.'

The last clause is weighted with contempt – an improper contempt, if one remembers that the 'sons of Finarfin' have both 'junior' Teleri and 'senior' Vanyar blood from their mother and grandmother. There is a further irony in the phrase 'this Dark Elf in his caves', for though Elwë is king of the Dark Elves, he himself is not one, since he was one of the three original ambassadors to the light of Valinor, though his love for Melian kept him from returning to it. Fifty-six pages earlier we were told that he alone of his people had seen 'the Trees in the day of their flowering, and king though he was of Úmanyar, he was not accounted among the Moriquendi, but with the Elves of the Light . . .' The reader who has forgotten his genealogies, or forgotten the original embassy to Valinor, or never realised the equation of 'Dark Elves' and 'Moriquendi', is left at a loss. The tension of the moment, the skewed relation between truth and whole truth, pass him by. And once the thread is lost, the bitter resentment of Angrod seventeen pages later, the cold mood in which Nargothrond is founded, the whole structure indeed of *The Silmarillion* lose their connections and begin to seem mere happenstance.

An underlying stasis has to be picked out from genealogies, positions on the order of march to and from Valinor, relationships of all kinds. Yet once that has been done, it is possible to see a kind of dynamism in *The Silmarillion*, a chain of causes and effects. As often with Norse saga, a good question to keep asking is, with each disaster, 'who is to blame?' Answers are never simple. Take, for instance, the fall of Gondolin, the 'Hidden City' of which Tolkien had written as far back as *The Hobbit*. It was founded by Turgon under the direct guidance of the Valar, and from it comes in the end the stock of Eärendil, the Intercessor. How was it betrayed to Morgoth? Unfolding the answer takes in much of *The Silmarillion*, but one can say that again it turns on a 'lyric core', and a conflict of kinship.

The 'lyric core' is the single scene in which Húrin, 'mightiest of the warriors of mortal Men', having sat twenty-eight years as Morgoth's prisoner observing the torments of his race, is released to wander. Neither elves nor men will take him in. He remembers his boyhood stay in Gondolin, as also the fact that he was captured, and his house destroyed, while covering the retreat of Turgon at the Fen of Serech. He goes therefore towards Gondolin, hoping the eagles will carry him to it. But though the eagles see him and tell Turgon, the king of Gondolin refuses to trust the man who saved him once; and when he changes his mind, after sitting 'long in thought', it is too late:

For Húrin stood in despair before the silent cliffs of the Echoriath, and the westering sun, piercing the clouds, stained his white hair with red. Then he cried aloud in the wilderness, heedless of any ears, and he cursed the pitiless land; and standing at last upon a high rock he looked towards Gondolin and called in a great voice: 'Turgon, Turgon, remember the Fen of Serech! O Turgon, will you not hear in your hidden halls?' But there was no sound save the wind in the dry grasses. 'Even so they hissed in Serech at the sunset', he said; and as he spoke the sun went behind the Mountains of Shadow, and a darkness fell about him, and the wind ceased, and there was silence in the waste.

Yet there were ears that heard the words that Húrin spoke, and report

of all came soon to the Dark Throne in the north; and Morgoth smiled
... (p. 228)

Obviously, everything in this scene is emblematic. Even narrative almost
disappears, for the 'long' and thoughtful delay of Turgon seems to take
no time at all. Húrin is in the same place, listening to the same 'hissing'
wind, after the delay as before. In fact Turgon's pause is there only to
allow him to make a fateful decision and then regret it – or, one might say,
to prove the adjective 'pitiless' in the passage quoted. It is not the land
which has no pity, but Turgon, and the elves and men who rejected Húrin
earlier. By similar transference cliffs are 'silent', grasses 'dry', the red
sunset and white hair stand for future catastrophe and present despair,
while the sun behind 'Shadow' marks the beginning of the end for
Gondolin, as it revives the memory of a past sunset of defeat. Over all
hangs the implication that the real sunset is in Húrin's heart, a loss of hope
to elvish, and natural, indifference. And yet the indifference is an illusion,
the silence full of ears, the despair a fatal mistake . . .

The scene is a picture, a posed *tableau*. Yet it centres on an outcry of
spontaneous passion (like so many scenes of medieval romance). Dynamism
is generated from it as soon as one asks the question, 'whose fault?'
Húrin's, for despair? Turgon's, for suspicion? One could even blame the
rulers of Doriath, for the true embitterment of Húrin's heart lies in the
death of Túrin his son, in which many were involved. A full answer
would consist of the whole unhappy history of Middle-earth. Yet that
general answer still has to be reinforced by individual weakness, which is
the true irony and wretchedness of the single scene. And still this is only
a part of the fall of Gondolin. A second strand leads from Maeglin, spun
once more from the strains of mixed blood.

Maeglin is the son of Turgon's sister Aredhel, carried off by Eöl, 'Dark
Elf' *par excellence*, one of those who never went to Valinor and saw all the
elves who returned as dispossessors. In a sense that dispossession is the
ultimate source of all Maeglin's treachery, and yet it too has to be magnified
by a chain of individual sins or errors. One is the forced detention of
Aredhel by Eöl; this means that father is resented by son, son in the end
cursed prophetically by father. Another, though, is the pride of the sons
of Fëanor, who (as with Thingol) will not recognise kinship except by
blood. Eöl's relationship to them by marriage is ignored. Curufin tells
him, 'You have my leave but not my love . . . The sooner you depart from
my land the better will it please me' (p. 135). The *Macbeth*-style play on
words is returned by Eöl (with a memory indeed of *Hamlet*), 'It is good,
Lord Curufin, to find a *kins*man thus *kind*ly at need' (my italics). But the
sarcasm only provokes outright disclaimer: 'those who steal the daughters
of the Noldor . . . do not gain kinship with their kin.' It is significant that
Turgon, though more injured than Curufin, does not make the same

mistake and opens his speech, 'Welcome, kinsman, for so I hold you . . .'
But by this time Eöl is embittered and refuses the relationship in his turn.
He was at fault to begin with; Curufin has made matters worse; finally one
could simply put the blame on Aredhel. She left Gondolin pridefully,
against advice, and turned away from her wiser brothers to her more
dangerous cousins, prompted by desire in the heart (p. 131), the evil
attraction of Fëanorian fieriness. Her breach of the orders of Turgon is
echoed by her son Maeglin 111 pages later, when he too goes illegally
beyond 'the leaguer of the hills', to be caught by Morgoth and made a
traitor. Even his motivation is multiple: fear, but also jealousy of Tuor the
mortal, imperfect loyalty to a grandfather who killed his father, the
ambitious desire for Idril which seems a last reflection of the Sindar
desire to get their lands back from their supplanters. Húrin, Maeglin,
Aredhel, Eöl, Curufin, Turgon: all interact to create the fall of Gondolin.
In each case, one may say, character remains fixed, but its flaws (or
strengths) are brought to light by the strains of action.

The Silmarillion is even more tightly constructed than *The Lord of the
Rings*, and it would be easy to trace its *entrelacements* further: Gondolin,
for instance, is only one of three Hidden Kingdoms, Gondolin, Nargothrond, Doriath, each ruined and betrayed, each penetrated by a mortal
(Tuor, Túrin, Beren), well-meaning but carrying a seed of destruction,
and all three mortals related by blood and with their fates to some degree
intertwined. The book is in fact a 'web'. But that word does not so readily
take the meaning of 'woven tapestry' as it did in *The Lord of the Rings*
(see p. 99 above). Rather it keeps its familiar sense of 'cobweb', a trap
spun by a great spider. In spite of Eärendil the later-published work feels
blacker and grimmer than the earlier, the sense that 'chance' or 'luck' may
contain a providential element is not so strong. Much of Tolkien's tonal
intention for *The Silmarillion* can indeed be deduced by looking through
its threads at his archaic alternatives for 'luck', the words 'fate' and 'doom'.

Etymologies and ambiguities

Neither of these words is used in modern English any more, though
phrases like 'fatal accident' or 'doomed to disaster' survive. The reason
for their unpopularity lies in their etymology. 'Fate' is derived, as the
OED says, from Latin *fari*, 'to speak', and means originally 'that which
has been spoken', i.e. spoken by the gods. It has never been anything but
a literary word in English. 'Doom' by contrast is native, the modern
pronunciation of Old English *dóm*, a noun related to the verb *déman*, 'to
judge'. It too meant in early times what was spoken, what people said about
you (especially once you were dead), but it had also the meaning of a
judicial sentence, a law or a decision. Judgement Day, the day at the end

of the world when all souls will be tried and sentenced, was accordingly in Old English *dómesdæg*, 'Doomsday'. A sense of 'future disaster' was soon attached to the word as a result. However, common to both words is the idea of a Power sitting above mortals and ruling their lives by its sentence or by its speech alone. This sense is completely absent from 'luck' or 'chance'; and with the waning of belief in superior Powers the more neutral words have become the common ones.

In *The Silmarillion*, though (unlike *The Lord of the Rings*) the influence of the Valar for good or ill is prominent, so that 'fate' and 'doom' become once again etymologically appropriate words, to be used frequently and with a complexity which determines the tone of several of its component stories. To take the simplest example, 'fate' in the story 'Of Beren and Lúthien' seems to have two meanings, related but separable even by grammar. On the one hand fate is an external force, which could without difficulty be capitalised: 'fate drove' Carcharoth the wolf through the protecting spells of Melian, and Beren managed the same feat because he was 'defended by fate'. There are many more occasions, though, when 'fate' does not seem a proper name, a word for some external Power, but rather the personal possession of someone or something: to it must be attached *either* a personal pronoun ('my fate', 'his fate', 'your fate') *or* another noun in the genitive case ('the fate of Arda', 'the fate of a mightier realm', 'the fates of Beren and Lúthien') *or else* an identifying relative clause ('the fate that was laid on him', 'the fate that lies before you'). What all these uses suggest is that fate is not something external and organising, like Providence, but something individual, like 'life' – something however, unlike 'life', which *has been organised*. The very use of the word thus brings up a question of free will.

The word 'doom', in *The Silmarillion*, is more complicated. It too can appear as an overmastering Power: when Lúthien first sees Beren 'doom fell upon her', a phrase also found in Aragorn's 'Lay of Tinúviel' in *The Lord of the Rings*. However it can be something much more elementary, retaining its basic meaning of a sentence or a decision: in the *Narn i Hîn Húrin* in the *Unfinished Tales* we find Thingol holding 'a court of doom', waiting 'to pronounce his doom', and saying 'otherwise shall my doom now be', or to paraphrase 'I am now going to change my sentence'. Much more often, though, the reader cannot make a clear decision as to the word's meaning. The sense of 'future disaster' is present: when Thingol challenges Beren to recover a Silmaril, the narrator says 'Thus he wrought the doom of Doriath', and means that Doriath will be ruined by Thingol's words. So, when Melian says to him a few lines later (p. 168), 'you have doomed either your daughter, or yourself', she could mean either that he has given a judicial decision on Lúthien (old sense), or condemned himself to death (modern sense), or of course both, since both are true. There is a sense also in which 'doom' is a personal attribute, like 'my fate' or 'my life', but blacker and more hostile: 'So their doom willed it', says the narrator, as Beren and Lúthien make the fatal decision to go home, and Thingol recognises when he sees them that 'their doom might not be withstood by any power of the world'. What does it mean, then, when Beren says 'Now is the Quest achieved . . . and my doom full-wrought'? That sentence on him has finally been executed? Or that disaster has come at last? Or that his life has now reached a proper close, with all debts paid, promises and curses fulfilled? All these meanings are present, as they are in many instances in *The Silmarillion*; 'doom' and 'fate' determine the tone especially of the stories of Beren and of Túrin Turambar.

What these words imply is in a sense illogical or self-contradictory. They indicate the presence of controlling powers, in whose toils the heroes are 'caught', 'meshed', 'ensnared'; yet people can be told, as Túrin is, 'the doom lies in yourself'. 'Fate' and 'doom' may be 'wrought' or 'devised' by people, and yet can take on a volition of their own; they 'lie' on characters, 'fall' on them, 'lead' them, but can at least in thought be 'turned from' or 'denied'. Túrin calls himself 'Turambar', 'Master of Doom', only to have the boast thrown back in his epitaph *A Túrin Turambar turún' ambartanen*, 'Master of Doom, by doom mastered'. Are people free to determine their own fate, one might ask, or are they 'the stars' tennis-balls, struck and bandied/Which way please them'? To accept the second alternative would have been, for Tolkien, to go against an orthodox Christian doctrine; to state the first positively would have lost for him that sense of interlacing, of things working themselves out, of a poetic justice seen only in the large scale, to which he had been attached from near the start of his career.

The denial of logic, it may be added, is an ancient one, found in Old English, but part of the fibre of the Norse 'family sagas', which Tolkien had imitated in other ways. In the *Saga of Gísli Súrsson*, Gísli sends a warning to his brother-in-law Vesteinn to say if he comes home he will be killed. But the messengers ride along the top of a sandhill while he rides below it, and so miss him. When they catch up he says: 'I would have turned back if you had met me earlier, but now all the streams run towards Dýrafjord and I shall ride there. And in any case I want to.' He goes on, and is killed. In his decision there is a strand of volition, for he says he wants to; one of pride, for he would not like to be seen turning back; one of chance in the way the messengers miss him. However the centre of his speech is the remark about watersheds, and while this could be taken as merely practical, expressing the difficulty of travel in mountainous Iceland, all readers automatically take it as a sign of surrender to some superior force of embroilment. 'The words of fate will be said by someone', Gísli had remarked earlier. Individual will and external force, in other words, notoriously co-operate.

One sees in all this an echo of that dualism which had produced the

Ring as hostile presence and psychic amplifier, or Sauron as enemy and as tempter. However it is enough to say that in his tales of heroes in *The Silmarillion* (and the *Unfinished Tales*), Tolkien was aiming at a tone, or perhaps better a 'taste' which he knew well but which had fallen outside the range of modern literature: a tone of stoicism, regret, inquiry, above all of awe moderated by complete refusal to be intimidated. The complexities of 'fate' and 'doom' show us the intention clearly enough. But, one must ask, how far is that intention realised: especially in those early and central tales of heroic mortals, 'Of Beren and Lúthien' and (in its two main versions) 'Of Túrin Turambar'?

The Tale of Beren

Opinions here may vary: and I come now to one place where I feel that Tolkien would *not* have agreed with the opinions I express. He clearly valued 'Of Beren and Lúthien' in some ways above anything else he wrote. It was one of his first inspirations, based (see *Biography*, p. 97) on a vision of his own wife; to that vision he remained loyal all his life, for though he reworked his 1925 poem extensively in 1954, and kept rehandling both till his death in 1973, he never changed its essential features; he remained loyal to it even after death, for his tombstone and his wife's read only 'Beren' and 'Lúthien', a striking identification. Yet the tale itself has faults.

It contains, to begin with, a strong element of duplication. Thus Beren, once he knows he has to win a Silmaril from the Iron Crown, goes to get help, only to fail, to be captured with Finrod, and to be rescued from the 'Isle of the Werewolves' by Lúthien and the hound Huan. He goes into the woods to spend an idyllic season with Lúthien. But then the pattern repeats itself. He leaves Lúthien again, to go into the enemy's country, but is overtaken by her and Huan once more. They gain the Silmaril, lose it to the wolf, and then retire again to the woods and 'houseless lands', still with survival but without victory. The pattern is completed when Huan fights Carcharoth to recover the Silmaril, repeating his earlier battle against Carcharoth's sire Draugluin. Two wolf-fights, three scenes of the power of song (including Sauron's defeat of Finrod), three woodland idylls, two pursuits and rescues by Lúthien ... Beren meanwhile is wounded three times, twice by Carcharoth, once by Celegorm, and interposes himself twice between dart and Lúthien, wolf's teeth and Thingol. Three times Huan speaks, to advise Lúthien, to advise Beren, to bid farewell. Simultaneously the plot is traversed by the evil sons of Fëanor, Celegorm and Curufin: they capture Lúthien by coincidence on p. 173, and meet her and Beren by coincidence once again, after the rescue from Tol-in-Gaurhoth. Though they provide the knife Angrist that would cleave iron 'as if it were green wood', the scenes they contribute cost a good deal in contrivance. In 'Beren and Lúthien' as a whole there is too much plot.

The other side of that criticism is that on occasion Tolkien has to be rather brisk with his own inventions. Celegorm wounds Beren, and the hound Huan turns on his master and pursues him: 'returning he brought to Lúthien a herb out of the forest. With that leaf she staunched Beren's wound, and by her arts and her love she healed him . . .' The motif of the healing herb is a common one, the centre for instance of the Breton *lai* of *Eliduc* (turned into *conte* by Marie de France). But in that it occupies a whole scene, if not a whole poem. In *The Silmarillion* it appears only to be dismissed in two lines, while Beren's wound is inflicted and healed in five. Repeatedly one has this sense of summary, and even (for a gloomy tale) of easy victory. Carcharoth is the Red Maw and the Jaws of Thirst, but when Lúthien stands before him her inner power fells him 'as though lightning had smitten him'. The blindness, anxiety and dark dreams of Morgoth are built up better, as is the thawing of Thingol's heart when he sees Beren's mutilation. However the scene in the Halls of Mandos, when Lúthien moves the Lord of the Dead to pity, was beyond attempting, as Tolkien realised. One might say that this tale, more than any other of *The Silmarillion*, depends for success on its 'lyric core', the songs of Finrod, Sauron, Beren, and of Lúthien before Morgoth and before Mandos. However these could not be provided. One has to take the will for the deed.

A further criticism, and perhaps a connected one, is that in 'Beren and Lúthien' Tolkien had not yet freed himself from his many sources – as if trying to bring in all the bits of older literature that he liked instead of forging a story with an impetus of its own. The framework of the tale is the legend of Orpheus, the singer who challenges the power of the Underworld to rescue his wife. To this the Middle English 'lay' of *Sir Orfeo* had added the motif of the Rash Promise, by which the king of the Underworld – in *Sir Orfeo* the elf-king – has to stand by an undertaking carelessly worded. Tolkien picked this up too, converting it into the oath of Thingol (which provokes a corresponding oath from Beren). But around this we have the wizards' singing-contests (from the *Kalevala*), the were-wolves devouring bound men in the dark (from the *Vǫlsunga saga*), the rope of hair let down from a window (the Grimms' 'Rapunzel'), the 'shadowy cloak' of sleep and invisibility which recalls the *heoloðhelm of the Old English *Genesis B*. The hunting of the great wolf recalls the chase of the boar Twrch Trwyth in the Welsh *Mabinogion*, while the motif of 'the hand in the wolf's mouth' is one of the most famous parts of the *Prose Edda*, told of Fenris Wolf and the god Týr; Huan recalls several faithful hounds of legend, Garm, Gelert, Cafall. Of course old motifs often do their work, as when the Iron Crown rolls on the silent floor of

Thangorodrim, or Lúthien's rope of hair sways with more-than-elvish 'glamour' above the heads of her guards. However some of them could have been omitted. The effect is garish where it ought to be spare.

The strength of the tale lies perhaps in its interweavings *around* the central fable. Its heart is the 'rash promise' of Thingol, 'Bring to me in your hand a Silmaril from Morgoth's crown; and then, if she will, Lúthien may set her hand in yours', with the countervailing promise by Beren, to be fulfilled in letter only and not spirit, 'when we meet again my hand shall hold a Silmaril'. The tale works through to the ironic fulfilment of both. However, as it works other strands are drawn in, to raise, increasingly, retrospective questions. Oaths are commonly regretted in this story. Finrod's oath 'of abiding friendship and aid in every need to Barahir and all his kin' was made in gratitude and affection, but when it comes to redeeming it he is sad for others rather than himself. What makes matters worse is that he had foreseen his own rashness long before, saying to Galadriel, 'An oath I too shall swear, and must be free to fulfil it, and go into darkness. Nor shall anything of my realm endure that a son should inherit.' How great the gratitude to overcome that foreboding; how much greater the disaster to quench that gratitude! Spontaneous motivations come to seem weak, and by reflection from the case of Finrod one may begin to wonder about others. The reaction of the sons of Fëanor against Beren seems spontaneous, but the narrator adds as gloss, 'the curse of Mandos came upon [them]'. If one looks back one sees that that curse dictates failure 'by treason of kin unto kin', and the sons of Fëanor plot treason against their cousin, grandson of another mother. They remember also that since the rescue of Maedhros they have been 'the Dispossessed'. Jealousy of Finrod, then, creeps into their contempt for Beren. From that jealousy Doriath will fall, and the sons of Fëanor themselves die.

But since motivations are so opaque one may look back at the offer of Thingol, the very heart of the story. To demand a Silmaril for Lúthien could be a fair offer: so Beren pretends to take it, calling it a 'little price'. In fact, as everyone sees, it is an attempt to commit murder in circumvention of the earlier, regretted oath not to kill Beren himself. Beneath that, though, there may be a yet worse motive; the sudden 'desire' for a Silmaril could contain a genuine impulse of greed beneath a calculated impulse of hatred. In that case Beren's insulting suggestion that Thingol values his daughter no more than a 'thing made by craft' would be true, if unconscious. The end of that strand is 65 pages later, when the dwarves in their turn seek 'a pretext and fair cloak for their true intent' in 'desiring' the Silmaril, and Thingol, like Beren before him, answers scornfully. His desire is like theirs, though, not like Beren's. So his death 'in the deep places of Menegroth', far from the light which he alone of his kingdom had seen, becomes an analogue of his descent to greed and cunning.

Words overpower intentions. In any case intentions are not always known to the intenders. This is the sense of 'doom' which Tolkien strives to create from oaths and curses and bargains, and from the interweaving of the fates of objects, people and kingdoms. At moments in the tale 'Of Beren and Lúthien' it comes through strongly.

Túrin Turambar turún' ambartanen

For a successful striking of the note, however, one has to wait for the story 'Of Túrin Turambar' in *The Silmarillion*, or better still, for the longer version of it in the *Unfinished Tales*, the *Narn i Hîn Húrin*. The existence of these two variants immediately makes several points about Tolkien's way of working. One is that 'Of Túrin' has been selectively compressed with regard to its major features; the interest in 'doom' is proclaimed by Túrin's final nickname 'Master of Doom', yet in the *Silmarillion* version the word is used only some ten times in 29 pages, considerably less than in the slightly shorter chapter 'Of Beren and Lúthien'. The *Narn* adds many more references, some of them prominent. It makes one wonder what the tale of Beren would be like if we had a full or final version. A second point is that both accounts of Túrin seem to have digested their source much more fully than the *Silmarillion* account of Beren. The basic outline of the tale owes much to the 'Story of Kullervo' in the *Kalevala*, which Tolkien had versified as early as 1914. In both a hero survives the ruin of his family to grow up with a cruel, wayward streak in fosterage; in both he marries (or seduces) a lost maiden, only for her to discover she is his sister and drown herself; in both the hero returns from his exploits to find his mother gone and home laid waste, and to be condemned by his own associates. Kullervo's dog leads him only to the place where he met his sister, and like Túrin, when he asks his sword if it will drink his blood, it agrees scornfully:

'Wherefore at thy heart's desire
Should I not thy flesh devour,
And drink up thy blood so evil?
I who guiltless flesh have eaten,
Drank the blood of those who sinned not?'[14]

But for all these points of derivation, 'Túrin' goes beyond 'Beren' in neatness of structure. It is striking, though, that its true point becomes clear (to all but extremely perceptive eyes) only in the *Narn*.

The *Narn i Hîn Húrin* centres on Tolkien's favourite question of how corruption worked, how far evil had power over the resisting mind. Possibly the most important scene added to the *Narn*, and not present in *The Silmarillion*, is the one in which Morgoth debates with his captive

Húrin on top of the 'Hill of Tears', looking out over the kingdoms of the world like Christ and Satan in *Paradise Regained*. Morgoth's temptation is perfunctory, however. His *threat* is that he will ruin Húrin's family and break them on his will 'though you all were made of steel'. He cannot do it, says Húrin, having no power to 'govern them from afar'. He has a power of clouds and shadows, asserts Morgoth: 'upon all whom you love my thought shall weigh as a cloud of Doom'. Húrin refuses to accept this last intangible, and claims that whatever happens Morgoth cannot pursue men beyond death and beyond 'the Circles of the World'. This is not denied, any more than it is denied that Húrin's family are free to resist. However the scene leaves a feeling that Morgoth is not entirely a liar, and that when he says Húrin does not understand the power of the Valar (including himself) he may be telling the truth. The power of the Valar, however, as one may remember from the 'oliphaunt' scene, is to be equated with 'chance'.

Chance indeed seems to control the tragedy of Túrin. He takes the seat of Saeros (in the *Narn*) 'by ill-luck'. This leads to Saeros's taunting, Túrin's violent reply, the death of Saeros and expulsion of Túrin; so, stage by stage, to the fall of Nargothrond and ruin of Doriath. It is likewise a coincidence that orcs come on Nienor as she is led back from meeting the dragon; 'Ill chance', says Melian. It is a further ill chance that Nienor meets her brother exactly on the spot where his sentiments are most stirred, the grave of the woman he betrayed. At the same place Túrin meets Mablung, the one person who can confirm the secret he has been told. 'What a sweet grace of fortune!' he cries, with hysterical irony. 'Some strange and dreadful thing has chanced', says Mablung. The plot of the *Narn* seems to work on coincidence.

But what *is* a coincidence (a question traditional in Oxford philosophy examinations)? Throughout the *Narn* there is a strong tendency to give double explanations of what happens. Thus Túrin's boyhood friend Sador Lobadal has been lamed 'by ill-luck or the mishandling of his axe'. It might seem hardly material which it was; but if it were the latter one might say his pain was his own fault, as Túrin's mother Morwen claims: 'He is self-maimed by his own want of skill, and he is slow with his tasks, for he spends much time on trifles unbidden.' Túrin's father puts in a plea for good intentions, 'An honest hand and a true heart may hew amiss'. Character is fate, says one; accidents will happen, says the other. The narrator keeps on expressing no opinion. Túrin escapes from Dor-lómin 'by fate and courage', Túrin and Hunthor cross the Teiglin 'by skill and hardihood, or by fate', Túrin survives the illness that killed his sister, for 'such was his fate and the strength of life that was in him'. 'Fate' can always be offered as an explanation, it seems; but the word may mean nothing, be just what people say when they cannot find a better one.

There is a third possibility, which is that Morgoth was what he said, 'master of the fates of Arda'. *He* could have turned Sador's axe; he *did* send the plague that carried off Lalaith. He could have had *something* to do with Saeros. The latter's motivation is clearly his own, based on pride, jealousy, resentment of Beren and consequently all Beren's kin. However after he has spoken the words that provoke Túrin's outburst Mablung says, 'I think that some shadow of the North has reached out to touch us tonight. Take heed, Saeros son of Ithilbor, lest you do the will of Morgoth in your pride'. The 'shadow' is not the jealousy, but Saeros's accidental (?) touching on Túrin's sorest spot, his sense of having deserted mother and sister. 'If the Men of Hithlum are so wild and fell, of what sort are the women of that land? Do they run like deer clad only in their hair?' Being hunted with hounds was Sador's explanation to Túrin of what it might be to be a thrall. It remains a possibility for Morwen and Nienor. The hunted woman with her clothes torn instantly sends Túrin into a fury among the Gaurwaith. And before the end Nienor *does* appear as a quarry, flying naked 'as a beast that is hunted to heart-bursting' – perhaps that is what stirs Túrin's pity into love. One might say that this image, this fear, haunts the whole tale. For Saeros to pick on it unwittingly seems indeed more than chance. Morgoth put the words in his mouth; they are 'the words of fate'.

Responsibility for *saying* them, however, remains on Saeros, and Túrin's reaction too is largely his own fault. There is a cruel and morbid streak in the stripping and hunting of his enemy, even if it was meant to end short of death. Túrin repeatedly strikes too soon, at Saeros, Forweg, Beleg, Brandir, in the end himself. Where does this element come from? The *Narn* offers two answers, one reaching towards a kind of 'character-isation', the other more simply genetic. Like so many others in *The Silmarillion*, Túrin is a hybrid, his father of the house of Hador – fair, masterful, 'quick to anger and to laughter' – his mother of the house of Bëor, dark, clever, inveterate, 'moved sooner to pity than to laughter ... most like to the Noldor and most loved by them'. One might use an ancient racial stereotype and say that the one line seems 'Germanic', the other 'Celtic'. Túrin, dark, taciturn and slow to forget, clearly takes after his mother, though he has his father's soft-heartedness. In a way his life is a struggle between two sets of impulses; and another fact clearer in *Narn* than *Silmarillion* is that the impulses that come from Morwen are wrong. If one starts to disentangle the threads of blame for the fate of Túrin, Morwen holds a considerable share. Her husband's advice to her was '*Do not wait!*' She remembers this after his defeat, but does not obey – partly from fear for her unborn child, partly from hope that Húrin will come back, but largely from pride: 'she would not yet humble her pride to be an alms-guest, not even of a king. Therefore the voice of Húrin ... was denied, and the first strand of the fate of Túrin was woven.'

So mother and son are separated. Pride keeps up the separation, and separation generates the fear that turns Túrin savage. The pride which Túrin inherits from his mother also makes him refuse pardon; and with it comes, not cowardice, but something less than the dauntlessness of his father. 'My father is not afraid', says Túrin, 'and I will not be; or at least, as my mother, I will be afraid and not show it.' But he does show it. Glaurung the dragon, like Saeros, strikes the hidden fear when he calls Túrin 'deserter of thy kin'; and so Túrin abandons Finduilas to save Morwen, comes too late to do anything but doom Aerin, and then falls into despair, rejecting the obvious solution of following his mother and sister to safety. 'I cast a shadow wherever I dwell. Let Melian keep them! And I will leave them in peace unshadowed for a while.' 'Shadow' is an ominous word; it may not come from Túrin. Similarly Morwen falls into despair and rushes from security to her own death and her daughter's abandonment. Pride and fear, then, combine in mother and son to separate them and keep them apart. The 'thought of Morgoth' may influence their 'fates' and 'dooms', but also they take after each other, they co-operate.

The other fatal element in Túrin's character centres on the perception that in him something is missing: he is only half a man. This idea Tolkien clearly took from Norse sources, for instance from the famous *Saga of Egill Skallagrímsson*. In that saga Egill's grandfather is Kveld-Úlfr ('Evening-Wolf'), not entirely human, 'a great shape-changer', very like Beorn in *The Hobbit*. Kveld-Úlfr has two sons, Thórólfr and Skalla-Grímr ('Bald-Grim'), and the latter has two sons as well, Thórólfr junior and Egill himself. In each generation there is one fair, handsome, cheerful brother – these are the two Thórólfs – and one like Egill or Grímr who is big, bald, ugly, overbearing and greedy. As long as the handsome brother is alive the other can be kept in check, but when his own magnanimity kills him the brother who carries the marks of ogre descent becomes worse. So, in the *Egill's saga*, Egill sits silent and morose at the feast after Thórólfr's death, half-drawing his sword and then slamming it back, alternately raising and lowering his eyebrows; his mood remains dangerous till the king of England quietly begins to load him with gold and silver. Túrin, admittedly, is not as bad as that. Nevertheless he has lost something – his sister Urwen or Lalaith, an analogue of Thórólfr, an image of Túrin's paternal side in her fairness, her merriment, her ability to charm. Lalaith, we are told, means 'laughter'. When she dies of the Evil Breath his nurse tells Túrin, 'Speak no more of Lalaith . . . of your sister Urwen you must ask tidings of your mother'. Obviously the capital letter could be removed, and in that sense the sentence would still be true, and be obeyed. Túrin hardly ever laughs, and when he does it is 'bitter' or 'shrill': he is a fraction of a personality, bereft of 'fairness' or ability to see 'the bright side' (which is why his second sister Nienor, also golden-haired, has such fatal attraction for him). Filling out this sense of an imperfect humanity is Túrin's affinity with evil, made concrete in his weapons – the Black Sword of Beleg, which kills him in the end, and even more the Dragon-helm of Dor-lómin.

This too is clearly based on a Norse idea, or word. In the Eddic poem *Fáfnismál* the dragon boasts of bearing an *ægishjálmr*, a 'helmet of fear', over all the race of men. Is this a word for something intangible, awe or horror, or for some object that produces that effect, perhaps the 'dragon-mask' itself, the sight of the dragon's face?† Certainly both Nienor and Túrin are bespelled when they stare into the dragon's eyes and feel his 'fell spirit'; it seems that Túrin's heirloom is designed to counterfeit this effect, its image of Glaurung striking 'fear into the hearts of all beholders'. But is it right for heroes to use an *ægishjálmr*? Sigurthr in the Norse poem had thought not, insisting that one would be no protection against true courage. Húrin seems to agree, declaring 'I would rather look on my foes with my true face'. Túrin, however, is prepared to use the tactics of the enemy, fear and 'terrorism', and by doing so plays into Morgoth's hands. It seems clear (from p. 153 of the *Unfinished Tales*) that Tolkien meant the acceptance of the name Gorthol, 'Dread Helm', to mark a stage in Túrin's corruption. Certainly the decision to reveal himself seems the last stage in a progress from pity to fear, to despair, to a compensating rashness and that 'Ragnarǫk-spirit' which Tolkien had condemned else-where, a sign of courage without self-confidence or that ultimate hope Húrin had expressed on top of the 'Hill of Tears'.

Túrin's tragedy is silently opposed by the actions and fate of his cousin Tuor, whose path intersects with Túrin's at one point (see p. 239 of *The Silmarillion*, and pp. 37–8 of *Unfinished Tales*). The one relies on himself, the other on the Valar, the one brings hope to Middle-earth by his descendant Eärendil, the other leaves nothing behind. Yet the moral of the tale of Túrin remains uncertain in all versions: much is his fault, much the fault of the 'malice' that emanates from Morgoth – a word used repeatedly in the *Narn*, a word which the *OED* interestingly notes as having a sense in English law as 'That kind of evil intent which constitutes the aggravation of guilt distinctive of certain offences'. Malice turns man-slaughter into murder, turns accident into crime; in the same way one feels that the circumstances of Túrin's life would have been similar in any case, but that his resentful attitude makes matters qualitatively worse. Had he any right to call himself *Turambar*, 'Master of Doom'? In the sense that he had free will, that he could have changed his attitudes, Yes. How-ever 'Doom' is equated in the *Narn* with 'the Dark Shadow', and that Shadow knows how to turn strength to weakness. That is why the 'Master

† For some reason, several medieval words mean both 'mask' and 'ghost': Latin *mascha*, *larva*, but also the Old English word *gríma* (as in Gríma Wormtongue). *Gríma*, however, is also applied to helmets; the Anglo-Saxon helmet found at Sutton Hoo is a mask as well. In conjunctions the words suggest a buried memory of a fearsome, uncanny war-mask, linked with belief in dragons. See also the Nazgûl in *The Two Towers*, p. 315, 'helmed and crowned with fear', and note 5 to chapter 5 above.

of Doom' ends 'by doom mastered'; it is an inextricably blended process of temptation and assault. The ironies of the tale of Túrin, one is meant to see, are constructed by Morgoth.

In places in this tale Tolkien comes close to supersitition – unlucky objects, inherited failings, changing one's name to change one's luck, and so on. To that extent the *Narn i Hín Húrin*, like *The Lord of the Rings*, approaches fairy-tale. At the same time one ought to recognise that it is capable, in its most fully worked-up passages, of exposing exactly the type of subtle internal treachery which has been the staple of the English novel since its inception. 'What is fate?' asks Túrin as a child. He might as well have asked 'How are the heroes betrayed?', a question as applicable to him as to that other victim of 'dark imaginings', Othello. Finally one should note that, just as *Hamlet* peeped out of the tale of Eöl, so *Macbeth* was once more in Tolkien's mind with Túrin. At the end Túrin comes to the gorge of Cabed-en-Anas, and sees 'that all the trees near and far were withered, and their sere leaves fell mournfully' (*UT*, p. 145, cp. *S*, p. 225). He might well have said, 'My way of life/Is fall'n into the sere, the yellow leaf'. Like Macbeth, he has been caught in a web of prophecy and inner weakness, has slid down the scale from 'man' to 'monster', and to murderer. The best epitaph he might have chosen for himself is Macbeth's vaunt:

> 'The mind I sway by, and the heart I bear,
> Shall never sag with doubt nor shake with fear.'

Both tales are about the hardening of the heart.

Some Conclusions

The Silmarillion as a whole (and by this I mean as well those variants of its component parts printed in the *Unfinished Tales*) shows two of Tolkien's great strengths. One is 'inspiration': he was capable of producing, from some recess of the mind, images, words, phrases, scenes in themselves irresistibly compelling – Lúthien watched among the hemlocks by Beren, Húrin calling to the cliffs, Thingol's death in the dark while he looks at the captured Light. The other is 'invention': having seen the vision Tolkien was capable of brooding over it for decades, not altering it but making sense of it, fitting it into more and more extraordinary sequences of explanation. So the boat of Eärendil generates a disaster, a rescue, an explanation of why the rescue has had to be so long delayed. The processes are exactly the same as the generation of Bilbo Baggins from 'In a hole in the ground there lived a hobbit . . .', and the expansion of his story all the way to the last explanation of *holbytla* seventeen years and 1500 pages later. Where *The Silmarillion* differs from Tolkien's earlier works is in its refusal to accept novelistic convention. Most novels (including *The Hobbit* and *The Lord of the Rings*) pick a character to put in the foreground, like Frodo and Bilbo, and then tell the story as it happens to him. The novelist of course is inventing the story, and so retains omniscience: he can explain, or show, what is 'really' happening and contrast it with the limited perception of his character, as Tolkien does with Frodo lamenting his ill-choices in *The Two Towers* (we have seen that Aragorn's similar laments were unfounded), or as Joseph Conrad does when his Dr Monygham tells Nostromo if he had the treasure he would give it to their enemies (we know Nostromo has the treasure, but is bitterly offended to have his efforts made vain). Novels work on a mixture of suspense and special knowledge: there is about them, one may as well say, something wildly unrealistic.

Against this *The Silmarillion* tries to preserve something much closer to the texture of reality, namely, that the full meaning of events can only ever be perceived retrospectively. Its stories are full of ironies only grasped on second reading. 'False hopes are more dangerous than fears', says Sador in the *Narn*. Once we have realised how Morwen ruined her life and her son's by waiting for Húrin we see that Sador is, unwittingly, a 'soothsayer', and read all his remarks with much greater attention. At first reading, though, that point is invisible. So are most of the moments that lead to future disaster, like Aredhel's turn southward outside Gondolin, or Finrod's ignorance of the Noegyth Nibin (on *S*, p. 114). 'Ominous' statements are common enough – 'Their swords and their counsels shall have two edges' (Melian, *S*, p. 128), or 'Not the first' (Mandos, fifty pages before) – but for their immediate meaning one has to wait, and their full meaning often depends on unravelling the entire book. *The Silmarillion* could never be anything but hard to read: it is arguably trying to say something about the relationship between events and their actors which could not be said through the omniscient selectiveness of the ordinary novel.

None of this, however, waves away the very nearly prophetic remark by Frodo sitting on 'The Stairs of Cirith Ungol' in *The Two Towers*. Sam Gamgee has just given a summary of the tale of Beren and Lúthien, and remarked that he and Frodo appear to be in the same tale: perhaps some hobbit-child in the future will demand the story of 'Frodo and the Ring'. Yes, says Frodo, and he will demand 'Samwise the stouthearted' too: 'I want to hear more about Sam, dad. Why didn't they put in more of his talk, dad? That's what I like, it makes me laugh.' This embryonic piece of literary criticism does make a point about *The Silmarillion*, which is that it is all on the level of 'high mimesis' or 'romance', with no Gamgees in it. Not only children find that a lack. There is a reason for the decision once more, in that Tolkien was quite clearly, in the *Silmarillion* stories, recommending virtues to which most moderns no longer dare aspire: stoicism, nonchalance, piety, fidelity. In *The Lord of the Rings* he had learnt – by mixing hobbits in with heroes – to present them relatively unprovocatively. In *The Silmarillion* feelings of antagonism or doubt are often accidentally triggered, as when Fingon 'dared a deed which is justly renowned' or we are told the same of 'the Leap of Beren'. 'Don't tell us, show us', is the reply. 'We are not impressed by scale so much as by effort – by Bilbo going on alone in the dark.'

But the debate between ancient and modern modes of presentation, and between ancient and modern theories of virtue, need not be protracted. In his maturity, from the scenes at the end of *The Hobbit* almost all the way through *The Lord of the Rings*, Tolkien was able to hold a balance between them. In youth he had not learnt it, and in his later years he was unable to recover it – especially as recovering that balance would have meant what is notoriously one of the hardest jobs in the literary world, namely making a radical revision of something which has already taken a fixed shape of its own. Tolkien did not solve the problem of 'depth'; nor of 'novelising' romance; and in ignoring the one, as in brooding over the other, he showed himself out of step with his time, and exposed himself even more to lack of sympathy and careless reading. His decision to bring back the modes of the past was, however, not indefensible (as this chapter ought to show). It was also his last and boldest defiance of all the practitioners of 'lit.'.

Chapter 8

'ON THE COLD HILL'S SIDE'

Of Birch Hats and Cold Potions

There is, in a way, no more of 'Middle-earth' to consider. However something may still be said of 'the road to Middle-earth', or Tolkien's own attitudes to his work, as they emerge especially from the short pieces and poems of his later years. Tolkien might not have approved of such a study, for he valued his privacy. Still, the inquiry has much to do with the major theme of this book, namely the interlocking of philology and fiction. Here one cannot help looking at the third in Tolkien's triad of short stories about the sources of his invention, *Farmer Giles* (written 1938), 'Leaf by Niggle' (a few years later), and finally, written in 1965, *Smith of Wootton Major*.

This is not a difficult piece. Like 'Leaf by Niggle' (and possibly *Farmer Giles*), its mode is allegorical, and its subject is the author himself, especially the relations between his job and his private sources of 'inspiration'. To make the point about the job: the name of the foolish Master Cook in *Smith* is Nokes; the central character's name, Smith, is actually a description, like Harper or Prentice, but his wife is Nell, his daughter Nan, his son Ned. Nokes, Nell, Nan, Ned are all names marked by ancient English linguistic error. Noke – a town in Oxfordshire not far from Brill – is derived from Old English *æt þæm ácum*, 'at the oaks'. This became in Middle English **atten okes*, and in Modern English, by mistake, 'at Nokes'. Similar confusion lies behind Ned for Edward, and the others.[1] One could say summarily that its very nomenclature shows that 'Wootton Major', like the Shire and like modern England, is careless and oblivious of its past; yet it *has* a past, and the roots to it remain, even if people like Nokes never notice.

That professional joke (written off as 'unimportant' in 'Guide', p. 170) nevertheless encourages one to see a professional element in the fable's allegory. Tolkien liked to bring 'philologist-figures' into his fiction: the parson of Farmer Giles, the Master of the Houses of Healing, even Gollum as Sméagol with his head turned down and his fascination with 'roots and beginnings'. There is then something faintly recognisable in the first Master Cook, whose retirement prompts the rest of the story: 'He had been a kind man who liked to see other people enjoying themselves, but he was himself serious, and said very little'. His sojourn in Faërie made

him merrier. Nevertheless one might say that the man who knows a lot,
but does not communicate it, and gives a false and unfortunate impression
of gravity, is a good image of the nineteenth-century philologist – the type
of man who turned the subject into a bogy. By contrast Nokes seems an
unsympathetic picture of the propounders of 'lit.'. He has no idea of the
charms of fantasy. He equates the supernatural with the childish, and both
with what is sweet and sticky. His idea of elvish allure has dwindled to a
doll with a wand, labelled 'Fairy Queen'. As for what he has to offer, his
Great Cake is good enough, with no particular faults, 'except that it was no
bigger than was needed . . . nothing left over: no coming again'. Not much
food for the imagination, one might paraphrase. In any case much of the
cake's goodness seems derived from the sly watch Nokes keeps on Alf
Prentice, and from the 'old books of recipes left behind by previous cooks',
which Nokes cannot understand, but from which he scrapes a few ideas.
Literary criticism in England (one might translate) leapt forward from a
springboard of old philology, without which even readings of Shakespeare
would not get very far. But once it took over the Mastership from the old
serious philologists it refused to give credit; this thwarted its own development and left great areas of its proper subject misunderstood.

Nokes has other faults too: his blunt rationalism makes him disbelieve
the supernatural quality of his own cure even after he has been cured, he
is a foe to all that is 'nimble' (a word which once meant 'quick to learn' as
well as 'quick to move'). All this makes it especially surprising that the
successor to Smith and to Alf Prentice is one of Nokes's family, not
Smith's. Is this an admission of defeat – or maybe one of hope? Tolkien
played for his own side all his life, but in spite of his praise of 'lang.' he
was no real enemy to 'lit.'. He thought only that it had fallen into the
wrong hands; maybe in the right hands even the least linguistic of studies
could prosper. His last word on the animosities of his profession, then,
was fairly benign.

One may say that the Master Cook is a philologist-figure (like the parson
in *Farmer Giles*), and that Nokes is a critic-figure (like the tyrant Ambrosius
Aurelianus in *Farmer Giles*). In *Farmer Giles*, though, we were left with
the farmer, that image of vulgar imaginative vitality blessed with the
discarded heirloom Caudimordax. One of the odd things about *Smith* is
that it contains not a single farmer, but a split or double hero: Smith
himself at the centre of the story, but abetted by Alf Prentice, with this
story's heirloom, the star, passed from one to the other and back again.
Alf Prentice is anyway a 'split character' himself. Prentice is his 'trade-
name', like Smith, but while Alf is common English short-for-Alfred (and
so looks like Ned or Nan or Tim) it is also the modern spelling of Old
English *ælf*, 'elf', which is what Alf is. He disguises himself as an ordinary
person, but is revealed at the end as King of Faërie, to whom the Queen
sends her cryptic message, '*The time has come. Let him choose.*' Alf/

Prentice, Smith/Prentice: what did Tolkien mean by this (for him) novel double duality?

If the old Cook is a philologist-figure, and Nokes a critic-figure, the suspicion must be that Smith is a Tolkien-figure. Smith himself never becomes Cook, never bakes a Great Cake. It is perhaps fair to remark that Tolkien never produced a major full-length work on medieval literature. Against that Smith's life is one of useful activity: pots, pans, bars, bolts, hinges, fire-dogs – or, one might say, lectures, tutorials, scripts, pupils. Furthermore Smith has the ability to pass into Faërie, and the mark of his strangeness is not only on his brow but in his song: he brings back visions for others. These visions furthermore expand. The doll 'on one foot like a snow-maiden dancing', the maiden 'with flowing hair and kilted skirt' who drags Smith into the dance, the Queen 'in her majesty and her glory' – all three are avatars of the Queen of Faërie, representing successively the tawdry images of former fantasy which are all the modern world has left, Tolkien's own first attempts to produce something truer and better, his final awareness that what he had attempted had grown under his hand, from *Hobbit* to *Silmarillion*. The image of Smith apologising for his people, and being forgiven – 'Better a little doll, maybe, than no memory of Faery at all. For some the only glimpse. For some the awaking' – might be taken without too much strain as Tolkien forgiving himself for 'Goblin Feet'. But still one is left with Alf.

He, perhaps, is born of a kind of weakness. Defeat hangs heavy in *Smith of Wootton Major*. Smith has to hand over his star, and return to Faërie no more; though he gains the right to say who shall have the star, his choice falls on Nokes's blood, not his own. These points are hard to read except as a kind of valedictory, an admission of retirement – Smith is 'An old man's book', as Tolkien said in *Letters*, p. 389. But Alf is there *to put Smith into a longer history*. There were men who wore the star of inspiration before Smith; in a later age there will be others; in any case that star, that inspiration, is only a fragment of a greater world, a forest in which the world of men is only a little clearing (for 'Wootton' comes from *wudu-tún*, 'the hamlet in the wood'). Alf is there to reassure. His 'message', to put it with deliberate bathos, is that if stories have a particular quality of conviction or 'inner consistency', then they must (as Tolkien had said before) in some sense be true. The star on Smith's brow that makes him sing is a guarantee of the existence of Faërie; by the same reasoning Tolkien's drive to create a world came not from within him but from some world outside.

Of course Tolkien had no 'Alf' to reassure him or to ease his retirement. No doubt he wished very much that he had. Yet there is one further oddity to keep *Smith of Wootton Major* from being just a fable of self-justification. This comes from the story's centre, i.e. the sequence of Smith's Faërie visions. First he sees the great warship returning from the

Dark Marches; then the Great Tree; then the lake of glass and fire-creatures; then the maidens dancing; finally the Faërie Queen. In the third of these visions, though, we find an odd sequence of events. When Smith touches the lake he falls, while a great 'boom' raises a wild wind to sweep him away. He is saved by clinging to a birch:

> and the Wind wrestled fiercely with them, trying to tear him away; but the birch was bent down to the ground by the blast and enclosed him in its branches. When at last the Wind passed on he rose and saw that the birch was naked. It was stripped of every leaf, and it wept, and tears fell from its branches like rain. He set his hand upon its white bark saying: 'Blessed be the birch! What can I do to make amends, or give thanks?' He felt the answer of the tree pass up from his hand: 'Nothing', it said. 'Go away! The Wind is hunting you. You do not belong here. Go away and never return!' (pp. 29–30)

What is the birch that saves, the wind that threatens?

Tolkien had written poems about birches before, in the 1936 *Songs for the Philologists*. One is in Gothic, 'Bagme Bloma', or 'Flower of the Trees': this hails the birch as defier of wind and lightning, *bandwa bairhta, runa goda,/þiuda meina þiuþjandei*, 'bright token, good mystery, blessing my people'. The other is in Old English, 'Éadig béo þu' or 'Blessed be you'. Its last stanza, in translation, reads: 'Let us sing a cheerful song, praise the birch and birch's race, the teacher, the student and the subject – may we all have health, joy and happiness. The oak shall fall into the fire, losing joy and life and leaf. The birch shall keep its glory long, shine splendidly over the bright plain.' The birch, it seems, represents learning, severe learning, even discipline. But those who subject themselves to serious study are under its protection.

And the birch has one further association Tolkien did not miss. He respected the *English and Scottish Popular Ballads* collected by F. J. Child as being (see p. 41 above) the last living relic of Northern tradition; in what is perhaps the most famous ballad of all the birch takes on a special role. 'The Wife of Usher's Well' is about a widow who calls her drowned sons back from the dead:

> It fell about the Martinmass,
>   When nights are lang and mirk,
> The carlin wife's three sons came hame,
>   And their hats were o the birk.
>
> It neither grew in syke nor ditch,
>   Nor yet in any sheugh,
> But at the gates o Paradise,
>   That birk grew fair eneugh.

The 'birk' is the birch; its wearers come to Middle-earth from another world; but they are not allowed to remain past dawn. In Lowry C. Wimberly's *Folklore in the English and Scottish Ballads* (Chicago: University of Chicago Press, 1928), Sir Walter Scott is quoted as having found a story of an apparition who wore the birch 'to the end the wind of the world may not have power over me'. Smith's Wind, then, could be the world; the birch is its traditional opponent, scholarly study; but that study, like the birch hats of the drowned sons, also acts as a passport, into and out of Middle-earth. It is a kind of Golden Bough; not between Earth and Hell, like Aeneas's bough, but between Earth and Paradise.

All this has a bearing on Tolkien's fable, and on his state of mind. The birch protects Smith, but is left naked and weeping. Did Tolkien feel he had *exploited* philology for his fiction? It also tells Smith to 'go away and never return', a command he cannot obey. Why should he have included this embargo, from within Faërie, against revisiting it? Did he feel, perhaps, that in writing his fiction he was trespassing in a 'perilous country' against some unstated law? The *Songs for the Philologists* again contain two poems (in Old English) about mortals who trespass in the Other World and suffer for it, 'Ides Ælfscýne', about the 'elf-fair maiden' who lures the young man away only to return him to a land where he is a stranger, and 'Ofer Wídne Gársecg', where a young man is lured away by a mermaid, to the sea-bottom and (traditional motif) the forfeit of his soul. It seems that at times, at least, Tolkien thought that getting involved with Faërie was deeply dangerous. Though *Smith of Wootton Major* offers a reassurance that imaginative visions are true, it also declares, in a concealed way, in private images, that mortal men cannot wander in these visions all the time, without danger. They must give up and make their peace with the world.

This thought is strengthened, if not confirmed, by Tolkien's longest published poem, 'The Lay of Aotrou and Itroun' of 1945. Its kernel, interestingly, is also in Wimberly, who quotes the Breton song of 'Le Seigneur Nann et la Fée', about a childless lord who gets a fertility potion from a witch and promises her her own reward; later she leads him into the woods in the shape of a white hart, only to reveal herself and demand his love as payment. He refuses (unlike the young men in 'Ides Ælfscýne' and 'Ofer Wídne Gársecg'), preferring death. To this story Tolkien has added a heavy weight of faith. The lord's defiance of the Korrigan is associated explicitly with home and Christendom; but his sin has been to despair of Christianity in his childlessness, and take 'cold counsel', the grey and frozen potion of the witch. He would have done better to trust in 'hope and prayer', even if the prayer were unanswered. As an anonymous voice comments, when the potion brings Aotrou twins:

> 'Would every prayer were answered twice!
> the half or nought must oft suffice

> for humbler men, who wear their knees
> more bare than lords, as oft one sees.'

The Tolkienian moral of the story is: be content; be resigned; we can't all have everything. One might note, coincidentally, that in the *OED*'s 1972 Supplement, 'escapism' is defined for the first time as 'the practice of seeking distraction *from what normally has to be endured*' (my italics). A fear of barrenness, of leaving no descendants, and with it a fear that the escape from forge or castle into fantasy may not be permitted – these are the themes of 'Aotrou' and of *Smith*, like goblin doubts padding through Tolkien's mind.

An End to 'Glamour'

The Adventures of Tom Bombadil, which Tolkien put together with unusual speed in 1961–2, may seem to have little connection with the foregoing. It is one of his more light-hearted books, centring on a character essentially fearless and self-confident, and a good deal of it is evidently old material from a more cheerful period (poems 1, 3, 5–7 and 9–10), while more is in a similar mode and probably of similar age (poems 4, 8, 11–12). The collection did not however escape Tolkien's ponderings over 'depth'. A letter to Rayner Unwin (*Letters*, p. 315) shows him wondering how to create a 'fiction' which would enable him to draw early works into the world of *The Lord of the Rings*, and deciding to do it by means of a comic 'editorial' preface. He carried this out with great *finesse*, explaining for instance that the poem 'Errantry' (which he had really written in 1933, when he had no need to harmonise his rhymes with Quenya) was actually written by Bilbo after he had returned from the Lonely Mountain – and so had learnt something of elves – but before he retired to Rivendell and began to learn Elvish properly. Other poems are ascribed to Sam, or (no. 14, reworked from 1937) given a link with the still unpublished *Silmarillion*. But the collection also contains both old and new work which hints at a deep sadness in Tolkien, and at an old but growing uncertainty.

The most obvious case is no. 16, the last poem, called 'The Last Ship'. In this Fíriel – once more a name which is really a description, 'mortal woman', Everywoman – gets up in the morning to go to the river, hears 'A sudden music', and sees the vision of the last elvish ship leaving Gondor. Where are they going, she asks, to Arnor, to Númenor? No, the elves reply, they are leaving Middle-earth for ever to go to the Undying Lands. Come with them, they call, escape from the world:

> 'One more only we may bear.
>   Come! For your days are speeding.
> Come! Earth-maiden elven-fair,
>   Our last call heeding.'

She takes a step towards them, but her feet sink 'deep in clay'; she takes this as a sign.

> 'I cannot come!' they heard her cry.
> 'I was born Earth's daughter!'

She turns back to her home, but the life of the morning – cockcrow, sunlight, jewels of dew on her gown – has gone. She goes through the 'dark door,/under the house-shadow', puts on dull clothes, starts work. The last word of both the two last stanzas is 'faded', and in the last stanza Fíriel herself has disappeared. Clearly she is dead, and she condemned herself to it when she stopped with her feet in the clay. 'Earth to earth, ashes to ashes', says the Funeral Service, and in this poem 'Earth-maiden', 'Middle-earth' and death are all equated. The poem takes on even more point if one remembers the ballad-genre which Tolkien knew so well and imitated in his two early *Songs* just mentioned – the one in which the elves steal away a human man or woman to live with them in delight in 'elf-hill'. 'The Last Ship' is an unprecedented reversal of that genre, in which the maiden refuses to go. It is true that she then avoids the risk of returning 'disenchanted' like Keats's lover from 'La Belle Dame Sans Merci'. She also turns from glamour to dullness and oblivion. The cockcrow at the start of the poem may hint at resurrection, but it does not carry the bravura of the cockcrow and the horns of Rohan in *The Return of the King*.[2]

Other poems in the *Bombadil* collection also end with emptiness. No. 2, 'Tom Bombadil Goes Boating' (written 1962), seems to have very much the same outline as no. 1, 'The Adventures of Tom Bombadil' (rewritten with only minor changes from the version of 1934): in it Tom good-humouredly browbeats a succession of creatures, wren, kingfisher, otter, swan, hobbits and finally Farmer Maggot. In the end all help him, with a central scene of merry-making. Just the same, there is a suggestion that the whole thing is a dream:

> Ere dawn Tom was gone: as dreams one half remembers,
> some merry, some sad, and some of hidden warning.

Even his footprints are washed away, his boat vanishes, and all that is left is a pair of forgotten oars, which by themselves mean nothing. It is as if Tom has gone back to his natural world, leaving Maggot and his mortal friends to meet their own fate, separate from his. Certainly 'Long they lay at Grindwall hythe for Tom to come and find them' is a more 'downbeat' ending than 'While fair Goldberry combed her tresses yellow'. *Grindr* is used in the *Poetic Edda* for the gate that separates the living from the dead.

An even more striking revision comes in poem 15, titled 'The Sea-Bell', but in the editorial 'fiction' at the start given another title and a highly suggestive placing within the world of *The Lord of the Rings*. 'It is the latest piece [in the collection]', surmises Tolkien's imaginary 'editor':

> and belongs to the Fourth Age; but it is included here, because a hand has scrawled at its head *Frodos Dreme*. That is remarkable, and though the piece is most unlikely to have been written by Frodo himself, the title shows that it was associated with the dark and despairing dreams which visited him in March and October during his last three years. But there were certainly other traditions concerning Hobbits that were taken by the 'wandering-madness', and if they ever returned, were afterwards queer and uncommunicable. The thought of the Sea was ever-present in the background of hobbit imagination; but fear of it and distrust of all Elvish lore, was the prevailing mood in the Shire at the end of the Third Age, and that mood was certainly not entirely dispelled by the events and changes with which that Age ended. (*TB*, p. 9)

So the hobbits, like Fíriel, turned Earth-fast and Sea-shy. Meanwhile the remark that the piece could not have been by or about Frodo, but was about some other hobbit, is Tolkien's bow to the fact that 'The Sea-Bell' is a thorough reworking of a piece he had written and published in 1934, before Frodo was thought of, called 'Looney'.

Close comparison of the two shows an increasing darkness. Both are poems of 'disenchantment' (as 'The Last Ship' was not), and in both the speaker, who has been in a magic boat to a far land, finds himself hunted out of it by a 'dark cloud', and returned to lonely and ragged craziness, scorned by others. In 'The Sea-Bell', though, a whole series of significant changes has been made. For one thing the boat is much more like the boat of Fíriel, the *last* boat; when he sees it the voyager calls out 'It is later than late!', and leaps into it with a new haste. For another the menacing elements in the far country have been much expanded, with 'glooming caves' seen beneath the cliffs as soon as the speaker lands; in 'Looney' the impression of paradise lasted for a couple of stanzas. The 'Sea-Bell' landscape also includes 'gladdon-swords' (i.e. of wild iris) and 'puffballs' in the mould. One may remember that it was in the Gladden Fields that Isildur died, and that 'puffballs' were associated by Tolkien – since his 'Preface' to Walter Haigh's *Huddersfield Glossary* of 1928, p. xviii – with 'Dead Sea apples' and the bitter fruit of the Cities of the Plain.

A more important change, though, is that in the later version the speaker seems in a way guilty, as 'Looney' did not. In both poems the 'black cloud' comes, but in the earlier it is for no reason, while in the later it appears to be called, or provoked, by the speaker presumptuously naming himself 'king'. It casts him down, turns him into a kind of Orfeo-in-the-wilderness, till eventually he realises he must find the sea: 'I have lost myself, and I

know not the way,/but let me be gone!' And seemingly as a result of that
guilt the end is different. In 'Looney' the man returned from Paradise still
had a shell in which he could hear the voice of the sea, as a kind of witness
to what he had seen. In 'The Sea-Bell' the shell is there at the beginning,
and it contains a call from across the seas; but at the end it is 'silent and
dead':

> Never will my ear that bell hear,
>   never my feet that shore tread,
> never again, as in sad lane,
>   in blind alley and in long street
> ragged I walk. To myself I talk;
>   for still they speak not, men that I meet.

In the later poem – as in *Smith* – the return to Faërie, even in memory,
is banned. As for the mistaken title *Frodos Dreme*, what it suggests with
great economy is first of all an age in which only the sacrifices of the War
of the Ring are remembered (for some scribe has associated gloom with
Frodo), and second, more indirectly, a sense of ultimate defeat and loss
in the hero of *The Lord of the Rings*. Frodo doubted his own salvation. This
could be seen as a dark illusion born of losing the 'addictive' Ring, but one
senses that Tolkien was doubtful too: not of salvation, but of the legitimacy
of his own mental wanderings. For many years he had held to his theory
of 'sub-creation', which declared that since the human imagination came
from God, then its products must come from God too, must be fragments
of some genuine if other-worldly truth, guaranteed by their own 'inner
consistency' and no more the artist's own property than the star from
Elfland was Smith's.[3] But by the 1960s he was not so sure. It is hard not
to think that by then he saw himself (perhaps only at times) as Fíriel,
Farmer Maggot, Frodo, 'Looney' and eventually Smith – a mortal deserted
by the immortals and barred from their company. He no longer imagined
himself rejoining his own creations after death, like Niggle; he felt they
were lost, like the Silmarils.

The Lost Straight Road

Tolkien of course asked more than he had a right to. No one can expect
fantasy to turn real, and all hopes for a star or shell or supernatural
guarantee are bound to be disappointed. In any case these late and gloomy
reactions have no bearing on *The Hobbit*, *The Lord of the Rings* or *The
Silmarillion*, which keep their own purely literary justification; the theory
of 'sub-creation' is not needed. If it is the function of works of literature
to enlarge their readers' sympathies and help them understand what their
own experience may not have taught them, then Tolkien's fictions qualify

on all counts. Certainly they are about 'creatures who never existed'. Most novels are about 'people who never existed'. The cry that fantasy is 'escapist' compared to the novel is only an echo of the older cry that novels are 'escapist' compared with biography, and to both cries one should make the same answer: that freedom to invent outweighs loyalty to mere happenstance, the accidents of history; and good readers should know how to filter a general applicability from a particular story. So Tolkien need not have yearned so much for a justification in fact and truth, nor felt such a sense of loss as 'inspiration' receded. Nevertheless the burden of his loss becomes greater if one realises how consistent and long-lasting Tolkien's visions had been, especially his visions of that 'earthly Paradise' from which 'Looney' is returned and which Fíriel never reaches.

He remarked in later life (*Letters*, pp. 213, 347) that he had a 'terrible recurrent dream' of Atlantis and 'the Great Wave, towering up, and coming in ineluctably over the trees and green fields'. He seems to have been haunted also by other visions which had to be expressed in narrative: of cities sculptured in lifeless stone (see the poem 'The City of the Gods', 1923, a forerunner of Pippin's sight of Gondor in *LOTR* III, 23), of towers overlooking the sea (everywhere from 'Monsters' to the Tower Hills), most of all of beautiful unreachable countries across the ocean. Fascination with this may explain why the poem *Pearl* so appealed to him: it contains a land where grief is washed away, and in his poem of 1927, 'The Nameless Land', Tolkien wrote 60 lines in the complex *Pearl*-stanza describing a country further 'Than Paradise', and fairer 'Than Tir-nan-Og', the Irish land of the deathless. In 'The Happy Mariners' seven years before – also translated into Old English as 'Tha Éadigan Sǽlidan' – he saw himself looking out from 'a western tower' to the sea and the 'fairy boats' going through 'the shadows and the dangerous seas' to 'islands blest', from which a wind returns to murmur of 'golden rains'. The longing for a Paradise on Earth, a paradise of natural beauty, was compelling and repeated and there before Tolkien took to fiction. But in the last poems the murmuring wind has ceased, and the sense of a barrier is much stronger.

There is a resolution of hope and prohibition, finally, in an extremely private poem by Tolkien, 'Imram', from 1955. This is based on the famous voyage by St Brendan ('the Navigator') from Ireland to the unknown countries of the West, found in many medieval versions and related to a whole Irish genre of *imrama* which includes the famous *Imram Brain mac Febail* or 'Voyage of Bran son of Febal to the Land of the Living'. In the heavily Christianised Brendan-story, the saint hears of a Land of Promise in the West, and sets sail, to find islands of sheep and birds, a whale-island (like 'Fastitocalon', poem 11 in *TB*), islands of monks and sinners, till in the end they reach the Land of Promise – from which Brendan is sent back, to lay his bones in Ireland. In 'Imram' Tolkien assimilates this story very closely to his own fiction. His St Brendan can remember only three things from his journeys, a Cloud over 'the foundered land' (of Númenor), a Tree (full of voices neither human nor angelic but of a third 'fair kindred'), and a Star, which marks the 'old road' leading out of Middle-earth 'as an unseen bridge that on arches runs/to coasts that no man knows'. Brendan says he can remember these things, but never reach them; at the end of the poem he is dead, like Fíriel.

However there is in this poem an image of possible escape, drawn out further in *The Silmarillion*. There, at the end of 'Akallabêth', Tolkien records the Númenorean belief that once mariners had been able to sail from Middle-earth to Aman, but that with the drowning of Númenor the deathless lands were removed and the earth made round; though since ships still came and went from the Grey Havens:

the loremasters of Men said that a Straight Road must still be, for those that were permitted to find it. And they taught that, while the new world fell away, the old road and the path of the memory of the West still went on, as it were a mighty bridge invisible that passed through the air of breath and of flight (which were bent now as the world was bent), and traversed Ilmen which flesh unaided cannot endure, until it came to Tol Eressëa, the Lonely Isle, and maybe even beyond, to Valinor, where the Valar still dwell and watch the unfolding of the story of the world. And tales and rumours arose along the shores of the sea concerning mariners and men forlorn upon the water who, by some fate or grace or favour of the Valar, had entered in upon the Straight Way and seen the face of the world sink below them, and so had come to the lamplit quays of Avallónë, or verily to the last beaches on the margin of Aman, and there had looked upon the White Mountain, dreadful and beautiful, before they died.

For those that were permitted . . . by some fate or grace or favour. Tolkien was deeply attached to Middle-earth, and knew that his bones must lie in England as St Brendan's in Ireland. His last works are full of resignation and bereavement. Still, if he had an inner hope, it might possibly have been that he too could take 'the secret gate', 'the hidden paths', 'the Lost Straight Road', and find the Land of Promise which was still within 'the circles of the world'. It had happened to others. In the *South English Legendary* version of the 'Life of St Brendan', a maiden tells Abbot Beryn that he ought to thank Jesus Christ for leading him to the Paradise in the West, for:

'Þis is þat lond þat he wole: ȝuyt are þe worldes ende
his dernelinges an erþe ȝyue: ȝ hyder heo schulle wende.'

'This is the country that [Christ] will give, before the end of the world, to his secret favourites on earth, and this is where they will come.'[4]

That land would be both sanctified *and* earthly, an ideal 'mediation' for Tolkien. It must have increased his hope and longing to observe that the last line, about the 'dernelinges', is not in the text but (like 'Frodos Dreme') has been added in the margin by a later hand – as if some early but forgotten scribe had received a mysterious promise of his own. The promise lay in the philological detail; and the philology was true, even if the promise could not be expected to 'come true'.

AFTERWORD

This book's main purpose has been to provide the material for a more thorough and appreciative reading of Tolkien. Closely associated with that, however, has been a desire to broaden the scope of criticism. Several writers have suggested recently that the toolkit of the professional critic at this time is too small: it does not work at all on whole genres of fiction (especially fantasy and science fiction, but including also the bulk of 'entertainment' fiction, i.e. what people most commonly read). Furthermore it has a strong tendency to falsify much of what it *does* attempt to explain by assimilating it, often unconsciously, to more acceptable models.[1] Tolkien may be a peripheral writer for the theory of fiction. However it seems time to pay more attention to the peripheries, and less to the well-trodden centre. If that extroversion were to encourage a greater interest in pre-novelistic fiction and in 'philology' as a whole, I am sure that both 'lit.' and 'lang.' would be the gainers.

There are still several reasons for thinking that happy issue unlikely, all of which have become clearer and clearer to me during the writing of this book. If one reads very much at all of what has been written on Tolkien, one cannot help concluding that there is an enormous 'culture-gap' between him and his critics, which they cannot bridge and usually have not noticed. The gap seems to yawn most widely not between Tolkien and his detractors, but between him and his admirers, at least when these happen to be professors of English at American universities: in some ways it looks like one not only of culture but also of temperament. Reference has been made above (p. 175) to two opposing human urges: one towards comprehension of wholes and classification of data under principles and categories, the other towards a grasp of single items, careless of their context or meaning as long as they are there to be fully seen, explored, felt, tasted. The distinction aimed at is the famous one of William James between 'tender-mindedness' (interest in abstract schemes) and 'tough-mindedness' (interest in concrete particulars).[2] In this Jamesian sense Tolkien was almost excessively 'tough-minded': his temperament, his philological training, and, it may be, something in the 'pragmatic' Anglo-Saxon tradition, all drove him to work out from single words, or cruxes, or kernels, or nuggets. There is a perfect example of this 'tough-mindedness' – though it is not tough in any aggressive sense at all – in *Letter* no. 312, which Tolkien wrote in 1969. This ponders mutation in flowers, and remarks that just occasionally one can see a plant which proves the taxonomies of scientists by not fitting into them, by being (he mentions a

particular example) 'foxglove' and 'figwort' at once. He goes on to trace
the history of a patch of garden daisies, in his flower-bed, then on the lawn,
finally on a patch of bonfire ash. The same seed, he observes, came up
different every time; and it was difference that intrigued and delighted
him, not similarity.

Tolkien's professional admirers do not write like that at all. Most of
them seem 'tender-minded' excessively and without qualification. The real
horror for Tolkien would probably have come when he realised that there
were people writing about him who could not tell Old English from Old
Norse, and genuinely thought the difference didn't matter. If he got past
that, he would have discovered writers contentedly using those cribs and
'substitutes for proper food' he had excoriated in his 1940 'Preface',
tracing his thoughts through flattening, second-hand, language-less and
usually wildly incorrect 'Encyclopaedias of Mythology'. The end-product
of book after book, meanwhile, is a scheme: *The Lord of the Rings* reduced
to 'archetypes', related to solemn trudging plots of 'departure and return',
'initiation, donor and trial', hutching out banalities like 'for every good . . .
there is a corresponding evil'. '*Every* good', Tolkien would no doubt have
replied, his mind already turning to a list, 'maybe to beer there is alcoholism
and to pipeweed lung cancer. But what about hot baths? starlight seen in
a wood? the Eucharist? a round of hot buttered scones?' As for the other
theses, he observed of W. P. Ker ('Monsters', p. 250) that if you read
enough plot-summaries everything got to seem similar; but this told you
nothing about any particular work. The critical remark for which Tolkien
would have had least sympathy is finally Anne C. Petty's 'the mythogenetic
zone for our times is the individual heart and psyche'. 'Blast our times!'
(I can imagine Tolkien replying), 'and if that sentence means we should
all try to get in touch with our insides isn't it obvious myths need to come
from *outside*?' As for 'mythogenetic zone', it sounds like Saruman: vague
beneath a claim to precision.[3]

'Tough-minded' literature is as legitimate as 'tender-minded', and
students of literature ought to have better ways of dealing with it. But
even those who appreciate this quality, or say they do, have found Tolkien
difficult. I cannot forbear from quoting once more the statement of
Professor Mark Roberts (pp. 103, 131 above) that *The Lord of the Rings*
'is not moulded by some controlling vision of things which is at the same
time its *raison d'être*'. Had Professor Roberts searched high and low for a
work in which world-view and narrative were identical, he could not have
found a clearer example! But Tolkien's detractors repeatedly seem blind
to exactly those qualities in him which they had always said they were
looking for. Thus Philip Toynbee – whose disobliging remarks on Tolkien
were quoted at the start of this study – had preceded them only a little
before (*Observer*, 23 April 1961) by a definition of 'the Good Writer'.
'The Good Writer', he declared, is a private and lonely creature who takes

no heed of his public. He can write about anything, even 'incestuous dukes in Tierra del Fuego', and make it relevant. He 'creates an artifact which satisfies him' and 'can do no other', he takes 'certain perceptions to what would normally be regarded as excess', he 'knows much more about certain things than other people do', and when as a result his work appears it will be 'shocking and amazing . . . unexpected by the public mind. It is for the public to adjust'. This self-motivated and daemon-driven perfectionist sounds exactly like Tolkien – 'as easy to influence as a bandersnatch', said Lewis. And when one adds to it all Mr Toynbee's *sine qua non*, number 1 on his list of qualities, the assertion that 'the Good Writer is not directly concerned with communication, *but with a personal struggle against the intractable medium of modern English*' (my italics), all one can say is that it is a mystery how the critic failed to match such a clear blueprint to such a clear example in the flesh! 'It is for the public to adjust.' *But not too far.* Incestuous dukes in Tierra del Fuego, evidently, were much more acceptable as centrally humane than Sam Gamgee, or Théoden King, or Barad-dûr.

It was no doubt partly Tolkien's generation which acted as a bar. Not that he was so much older than (the late) Mr Toynbee; rather that, unlike many men of his age, he had not been alienated even by the Great War from the traditions in which he had been brought up. Unlike Robert Graves, his near-contemporary and fellow-Fusilier, he never said 'Goodbye to All That'. As a result his elementary decencies – over patriotism, over euphemism, perhaps especially over sex and marriage – soon become an object of satire, provoking automatic derision from much of the literary world and preventing a fair reading. Once again the thought stirs, naturally, that if Tolkien got through to so many people who would find no 'relevance' in 'incestuous dukes' at all, then possibly the preoccupation with licence and self-gratification which that example suggests is not a universal instinct, and no more broadly based than Tolkien's Victorian pieties. One of his correspondents told him she had found in *The Lord of the Rings* 'a sanity and sanctity', and he prized the compliment perhaps more than any – though he replied that the 'sanctity' was not his, while 'of his own sanity no man may securely judge' (*Letters*, p. 413). He can judge others' sanity more fairly, though, and Tolkien thought (with good reason) that his reviewers' nausea and contempt for what he had done was so violent as to be proof of an unnatural one-sidedness: 'Lembas – dust and ashes, we don't eat that'.

Such ideological differences are even harder to bridge than the gap between 'tough' and 'tender' minds. There may be something more hopeful, though, in Mr Toynbee's remarks about 'modern English', that 'intractable medium' against which 'the Good Writer' is supposed to struggle. Finding English 'intractable' is certainly a common opinion, its *locus classicus* in recent times probably the passage from T. S. Eliot's *Four Quartets* (1944) about:

> Trying to learn to use words, and every attempt
> Is a wholly new start, and a different kind of failure
> Because one has only learnt to get the better of words
> For the thing one no longer has to say, or the way in which
> One is no longer disposed to say it. And so each venture
> Is a new beginning, a raid on the inarticulate
> With shabby equipment always deteriorating
> In the general mess of imprecision of feeling . . .

With this one might compare Edmund Wilson's opinion in *Axel's Castle* (op. cit., p. 245) that the meaning of words depends on 'a web of associations as intricate and in the last analysis as mysterious as our minds and bodies themselves', while using words inevitably involves 'pouring them full of suggestion by our inflections, our pauses, our tones'. Wholly new, shabby equipment, mystery, suggestion, empty words being topped up by individual will-power: what these passages share is a conviction that since language is very complicated it is beyond the reach of reason. Inflections are private and personal; what one person means can never be fully understood by another; as in the paradox of 'Achilles and the Tortoise', you can only get closer and closer to what you want to say, but never be exactly *there.*

I do not think Tolkien would have agreed with this. He knew better than Edmund Wilson how hard words were to trace, but he also knew there were techniques for doing so; at the foundation of his art there was the perception of Grimm and Verner and Saussure and all the other old philologists, that in matters of phonology at least people were strictly controlled by laws of which they were not conscious. T. S. Eliot might not know *why* he said 'whole', 'heal', 'old', 'elder', but he *did*, and there was a reason for it which could be rendered (see p. 11 above). Semantic associations, too, could be traced, used, and communicated: see 'glamour', 'spell', 'bewilderment', 'panache', 'worship', 'luck', 'doom', and all the rest.[5] Where 'lit.' quailed before English or felt discontented with it, in other words, 'lang.' could at least feel at home. Tolkien did not think his equipment was 'shabby', nor the Tree of language leafless. As for modern English being 'intractable', that was a failure of education which had left its products historically deaf, deafer even than those uncorrupted ears which might be able to say – not knowing why – 'Garstang sounds northern' or 'Bree-hill and Chetwood have the same "style" '. All one can say is that this failure at least could be corrected. If there were a will, there would be a way.[6]

The problem remains 'misology', hatred of words, the opposite of philology. Tolkien used 'misology' and gave it this sense – it is in the *OED* under other senses – in his 'Valedictory Address to the University of Oxford': a technical piece, and addressed to a limited audience, but one which summed up much of his career experience. In 1959 he was looking back over thirty-nine years as a university teacher, all of it marked by the feuding between 'lang.' and 'lit.' which he had hoped to resolve, and his mood was not with a certain bitterness. He did not mind 'misologists' being dull or ignorant, he said, but he did feel:

a grievance that certain professional persons should suppose their dullness and ignorance to be a human norm, the measure of what is good; and anger when they have sought to impose the limitations of their minds upon younger minds, dissuading those with philological curiosity from their bent, encouraging those without this interest to believe that their lack marked them as minds of a superior order.[7]

Philology, in short, was a natural state; but where the Powers That Be were 'misologists', putting forward the views of Eliot or Toynbee or Wilson with the authority and prestige of 'modern literature' behind them, nature could be deformed. From this both sides lost, falling into a state Tolkien labelled bluntly as *'apartheid'*. All he could do was go outside 'proper channels' and try to reach an unspoilt audience reading just to suit itself.

He did that successfully; his success goes far to proving his point about the naturalness of philology and the appeal of names, words and linguistic 'styles'; and in the wider sense of philology as that branch of learning which 'presented to lovers of poetry and history fragments of a noble past that without it would have remained for ever dead and dark' ('Valedictory', p. 28), he showed that its appeal too was not confined to antiquity. I do not see how Tolkien can be denied the tribute of having enlarged his readers' apprehensions (of language), or their human sympathies (with the disciplined, or the heroic, or the addicted, or the self-sacrificing). But most of all I think his utility for the lover of literature lies in the way he showed creativity arising from the ramifications of words: unpredictable certainly, but not chaotic or senseless, and carrying within themselves very strong suggestions of 'the reality of history' and 'the reality of human nature', and how people react to their world. Fawler, *saru-man*, fallow, Quickbeam: in each of these a word created a concept, and the concept helped to generate its own story.[8] In *The Road to Xanadu*, John Livingston Lowes's 1927 study of Coleridge and 'the ways of the imagination' (a book of a kind we need only one of, said T. S. Eliot stuffily), Lowes wrote that the 'hooks and eyes' of the memory 'will lead us to the very alembic of the creative energy'.[9] If he was wrong it was because he thought too passively. Words, ancient words, do not have to be hooked together to make something. They have their own energy and struggle towards their own connections. Observing this impulse and co-operating with it is as good a guide for the artist as turning within oneself to the inarticulate.

Appendix A

TOLKIEN'S SOURCES: THE TRUE TRADITION

Tolkien himself did not approve of the academic search for 'sources'. He thought it tended to distract attention from the work of art itself, and to undervalue the artist by the suggestion that he had 'got it all' from somewhere else. This appendix accordingly does not attempt to match 'source' to 'passage' in Tolkien. It does however offer a brief guide to the works which nourished Tolkien's imagination and to which he returned again and again; since many of them are not well known, this may give many people who have enjoyed Tolkien something else to enjoy. Whether that changes their reading of *The Lord of the Rings* or *The Silmarillion* is less important: though in fact comparison with 'the sources', in my experience, almost always brings out Tolkien's extremely keen eye for the vital detail.

He was also very quick to detect the bogus and the anachronistic, which is why I use the phrase '*true* tradition'. Tolkien was irritated all his life by modern attempts to rewrite or interpret old material, almost all of which he thought led to failures of tone and spirit. Wagner is the most obvious example. People were always connecting *The Lord of the Rings* with *Der Ring des Nibelungen*, and Tolkien did not like it. 'Both rings were round', he snarled, 'and there the resemblance ceases' (*Letters*, p. 306). This is not entirely true. The motifs of the riddle-contest, the cleansing fire, the broken weapon preserved for an heir, all occur in both works, as of course does the theme of 'the lord of the Ring as the slave of the Ring', *des Ringes Herr als des Ringes Knecht*. But what upset Tolkien was the fact that Wagner was working, at second-hand, from material which *he* knew at first-hand, primarily the heroic poems of the *Elder Edda* and the later Middle High German *Nibelungenlied*. Once again he saw difference where other people saw similarity. Wagner was one of several authors with whom Tolkien had a relationship of intimate dislike: Shakespeare, Spenser, George MacDonald, Hans Christian Andersen. All, he thought, had got something very important not quite right. It is especially necessary, then, for followers of Tolkien to pick out the true from the heretical, and to avoid snatching at surface similarities.

The single work which influenced Tolkien most was obviously the Old English poem *Beowulf*, written in Tolkien's opinion somewhere round the year 700. The best edition of this is by F. Klaeber (Boston: D. C. Heath, 1922, 3rd ed. 1950). There are many translations of it, including the one by J. R. Clark Hall and C. L. Wrenn to which Tolkien wrote the 'Preface' in 1940. The reasons for its appeal to him, however, seem to me to be expressed best in R. W. Chambers, *Beowulf: an Introduction* (Cambridge: Cambridge University Press, 1921, 3rd ed. with supplement by C. L. Wrenn, 1959). The first two chapters of this show with particular force and charm the way in which history and fairy-tale are in *Beowulf* intertwined. Other Old English poems which Tolkien used include *The Ruin*, *The Wanderer* and *The Battle of Maldon*, all conveniently edited and translated in Richard Hamer's *A Choice of Anglo-Saxon Verse* (London: Faber and Faber, 1970), and the 'Treebeard-style' gnomic poems *Maxims I* and *II*, edited and translated, along with *Solomon and Saturn II*, in my *Poems of Wisdom and Learning in Old English* (Cambridge: D. S. Brewer and Totowa, N.J.: Rowman and Littlefield, 1976). Tolkien's own edition and translation of the poem *Exodus*, prepared for publication by Joan Turville-Petre, is to be published by Oxford University Press in 1982. Significantly enough, Tolkien valued the work as an example of Christian material treated in an old-fashioned or heroic style; his own fiction, one might argue, was a similar mixture but the other way round.

The poem of *Solomon and Saturn* just referred to centres on a riddle-contest, a form with two other prominent examples, both in Old Norse. One is the *Vafðrúðnismál*, one of twenty-nine poems in the *Elder* or *Poetic Edda*, a collection made in Iceland perhaps about AD 1200. Tolkien knew this well, drawing on the poem *Vǫluspá* for the names of the dwarves in *The Hobbit*, on the *Fáfnismál* for the conversation with Smaug, and on the *Skírnismál* for the 'tribes of orcs' and the 'Misty Mountains'. More generally the whole collection gives a sharper edge than *Beowulf* to the ideal of heroism, and a stronger sense of a tumultuous history filtering down to echo and hearsay. Both points are well brought out in the old, now-superseded edition of the *Corpus Poeticum Boreale*, by Gudbrand Vigfusson and F. York Powell (2 vols., Oxford: Clarendon Press, 1883), as also in Ursula Dronke's much later edition of four poems, *The Poetic Edda, Volume I: Heroic Poems* (Oxford: Clarendon Press, 1969). There is an old-fashioned translation of the whole of *The Poetic Edda* by Lee M. Hollander (Austin: University of Texas Press, revised ed. 1962); a much better one has recently appeared, *Norse Poems*, by Paul B. Taylor and W. H. Auden (London: Athlone Press, 1981). An earlier version of this last was dedicated to Tolkien.

The other major riddle-contest in Old Norse appears in *The Saga of King Heidrek the Wise*, edited and translated by Christopher Tolkien (London: Nelson, 1960). The relevance of this to all Tolkien's work, including *The Silmarillion*, should be obvious; the combination of pride, ferocity and sadness in the older poem of 'The Battle of the Goths and Huns' which has found its way into the saga seems to be the note that Tolkien often aimed at, and as often disapproved. Another *fornaldarsaga* or 'saga of old times' of much interest to Tolkien readers is the *Vǫlsunga Saga*; William Morris's translation of it in 1870 was reprinted with an introduction by Robert W. Putnam (London and New York: Collier–Macmillan, 1962) and it has also been edited and translated by R. G. Finch in the same series as Christopher Tolkien's *Heidrek* (London: Nelson, 1965). Meanwhile the other great work of Old Norse mythology, later and more 'novelistic' in tone than the poems, is the *Prose Edda* of Snorri Sturluson, written in Iceland between 1225 and 1241. This too is a work of 'mediation', like Tolkien's; Snorri was a Christian trying to preserve pagan material for his countrymen and for the cause of poetry. In several ways, especially its combination of respect for antiquity with a certain detached humour, Snorri prefigures Tolkien. One of the 'lost' poems known only by its quotations was a model for 'Aldarion and Erendis', see pp. 182–3 above; another poem added to a manuscript of Snorri's *Edda* by some well-wisher is the *Rígsþula*, for the relevance of which see note 8 to chapter 4 above. There is a good translation of most of Snorri's work in *The Prose Edda*, trans. Jean I. Young (Berkeley and Los Angeles: University of California Press, 1966).

It is a jump of many centuries to the great 'fairy-tale' collections of the nineteenth, but, as mentioned above (p. 48), Jacob Grimm at least thought the similarity between German fairy-tale and Scandinavian 'Edda' striking enough to prove that both were the debris of a greater unity. Whether this is so or not, the folk-tales of North-West Europe affected Tolkien profoundly. The three major collections (from his point of view) were probably those by the brothers Grimm, printed first in 1812, but expanded, revised and translated ever since: I have used *The Complete Grimm's Fairy Tales*, no translator named, published in London by Routledge and Kegan Paul in 1975, but Tolkien certainly read them in German – he relished the dialect forms of 'Von dem Machandelboom', quoting it in the original in 'On Fairy-Stories' (*TL*, p. 32). Another work he refers to is *Popular Tales from the Norse*, collected by P. C. Asbjörnsen and J. I. Moe and translated by Sir George Dasent, published first in English in Edinburgh, 1859, but reprinted in London by The Bodley Head, 1969. In the same modern series (1968) is *English Fairy Tales* by Joseph Jacobs, a reprint from 1890; No. 21, 'Childe Rowland' is a 'Dark Tower' story, see p. 138 above. Tolkien also quoted from J. F. Campbell's *Popular Tales of the Western Highlands* (4 vols., Paisley and London: Alexander Gardner, 1890–3).

Parallel to the fairy-tale tradition collected by the Grimms and others is the ballad tradition, also preserved by collectors of the nineteenth century and containing much similar, and similarly archaic material. The greatest collection of these is certainly F. J. Child's *The English and Scottish Popular Ballads*, first published in five volumes by Houghton Mifflin, Boston, 1882–98, and reprinted by Dover Publications, New York, 1965.

Particularly vital to this are the philological introductions to each ballad, see especially no. 19, 'King Orfeo', no. 60, 'King Estmere', and others; while Tolkien also almost certainly read Lowry C. Wimberly's commentary *Folklore in the English and Scottish Ballads* (Chicago: University of Chicago Press, 1928). Tolkien probably also knew the Danish collection begun by Svend Grundtvig, *Danmarks gamle Folkeviser*, out in 12 volumes from 1853 onwards, and partly available to English readers in *A Book of Danish Ballads*, ed. Axel Olrik, trans. E. M. Smith-Dampier (Princeton: Princeton University Press, 1939). The collection includes several elf-and-mortal or mermaid-and-mortal ballads like Tolkien's own poems mentioned on p. 207 above. The collector's father, Nicolai Grundtvig, was in my opinion the 'Beowulfian' whom Tolkien most respected – he appears in 'Monsters' as one of the 'very old voices' calling ' "it is a mythical allegory" . . . generally shouted down, but not so far out as some of the newer cries'. Grundtvig senior was also remarkable for his efforts to reconcile his studies in pagan antiquity with his position as evangelistic reformer and 'apostle of the North', arguing for Óthinn as a 'forerunner', Earendel-like, of the Messiah, both 'sons of the Universal Father'.

But Tolkien was also interested in later traditions, and even in American traditions: anyone who reads the 'Introduction' to *English Folk-Songs from the Southern Appalachians* (collected by Olive D. Campbell and Cecil J. Sharp, New York and London: G. P. Putnam's Sons, 1917) will be struck by the strange resemblance of the mountain country of North Carolina before the First World War to 'the Shire' as Tolkien described it. Nor is this accident. A piece by Mr Guy Davenport in the *New York Times* (23 February 1979) records Tolkien grilling an American classmate of his for 'tales of Kentucky folk . . . family names like Barefoot and Boffin and Baggins and good country names like that'. *Old* country names, one might add: in Kentucky and its neighbours, Tolkien obviously thought, there had for a time been a place where English people and English traditions could flourish by themselves free of the chronic imperialism of Latin, Celtic and French. In the same way Fenimore Cooper's hero Natty Bumppo prides himself on being 'a man whose blood is without a cross'; and Tolkien recorded an early devotion to Red Indians, bows and arrows and forests ('OF-S' in *TL*, p. 39). The journey of the Fellowship from Lórien to Tol Brandir, with its canoes and portages, often recalls *The Last of the Mohicans*, and as the travellers move from forest to prairie, like the American pioneers, Aragorn and Éomer for a moment preserve faint traces of 'the Deerslayer' and the Sioux, see p. 97 above. The complaint in one of the sillier reviews of *The Lord of the Rings*, that none of its characters (except Gimli) had 'an even faintly American temperament', is as imperceptive as irrelevant. Once upon a time all Americans were English: *caelum non animam mutant qui trans mare currunt*.

The medieval or middle period between the high vernacular culture of

North-West Europe and the collecting or 'reconstructing' era of Child and the Grimms was in several ways a disappointment to Tolkien, though of course he found much in its more traditional poems such as *Pearl*, *Sir Gawain* and *Sir Orfeo*. His translations of these must be recommended (see 'Abbreviations' under *SGPO*), as also the edition of *Sir Gawain* by himself and E. V. Gordon (*SGGK*), and of *Pearl* by E. V. Gordon alone (Oxford: Clarendon Press, 1953). Tolkien's assistance to the latter is acknowledged. Tolkien also lived for many years with the *Ancrene Riwle*, or *Ancrene Wisse*, and those concerned to seek out an influence on him might read *The Ancrene Riwle*, translated by Mary Salu, a pupil of his (London: Burns & Oates, 1955). That work was written *c.* 1225, in Herefordshire. Close in both place and time was the *Brut*, an Arthurian Chronicle-epic by one Laȝamon. Tolkien certainly valued this as a repository of past tradition, borrowing from it, for instance, Éowyn's word 'dwimmerlaik'. At some stage he must also have noted that the stream by which the poet lived – it is a tributary of the Severn – was the River Gladdon. Part of the poem can be found in *Selections from Laȝamon's Brut*, ed. G. L. Brook with preface by C. S. Lewis (Oxford: Clarendon Press, 1963). I am also persuaded that Tolkien found stimulus in the slightly later legends of St Michael and St Brendan in *The Early South English Legendary*, edited by C. Horstmann for the Early English Text Society (London: Trübner, 1887).

Two other clear medieval English influences on Tolkien are *Mandeville's Travels*, written about 1375, and available in a modern translation by M. C. Seymour (London: Oxford University Press, 1968); and the *Lais* of Marie de France, also available in translation by Eugene Mason (London and New York: Dent and Dutton, 1911). The latter is a clear source for 'Aotrou and Itroun', the former perhaps the best guide to Tolkien's notions of the trees of Sun and Moon, the *Paradis terrestre*, and the road to it encumbered by enchantments like those of the Dead Marshes. Many phrases from this book seem to have stayed in Tolkien's mind. One should add that for all their names and preferred languages, both 'Sir John Mandeville' and Marie de France were certainly English by nationality.

Dealing with Tolkien's knowledge of other languages could protract this essay interminably, but a source of the highest importance was clearly the Finnish epic *Kalevala*, which Tolkien knew in the translation of W. F. Kirby (London and New York: Dent and Dutton, 1907). For a more modern and scholarly treatment, see note 12 to chapter 7 above. Also recommendable is the Irish *imram*, *The Voyage of Bran Son of Febal*, ed. Kuno Meyer (2 vols., London: David Nutt, 1895–7). Tolkien's wanderings in German romance, though probably considerable – see the remarks on *Orendel* and others on pp. 17 and 184 above – are too complex for me to trace. Some guides through the wilderness of heroic legend can be found, however, in the philologists: and when it comes to it these were the men whom Tolkien probably followed with the keenest and most professional interest. Three major works may be cited, though they give the interested reader no more than a taste: *Grimm's Teutonic Mythology*, trans. J. S. Stallybrass (4 vols., London: George Bell, 1882–8); R. W. Chambers, *Widsith, A Study in Old English Heroic Legend* (Cambridge: Cambridge University Press, 1912); and R. M. Wilson, *The Lost Literature of Medieval England* (London: Methuen, 1952). It should be noted that a vital part of this latter came out as early as 1941, in plenty of time for Tolkien to recall it in *The Lord of the Rings*, see note 11 to chapter 5 above.

The last major 'old' source for Tolkien which need be mentioned lies in history and chronicle. Gibbon's *Decline and Fall of the Roman Empire* certainly stayed in Tolkien's mind, though probably in the same compartment as Wagner; 'Radagaisus' may be found in its 'Index', if not 'Radagast', as also 'Fredegarius', though not 'Frodo'. Of the Latin histories which Gibbon used the most interesting for Tolkien were probably Saxo Grammaticus's *History of the Danes*, of which Books 1–9 were translated by Oliver Elton, with an introduction by F. York Powell (London: David Nutt, 1894); and *The Gothic History of Jordanes* translated by C. C. Mierow (Princeton: Princeton University Press, 2nd edition 1915). One has to add that Mr Mierow's grasp of Gothic, unlike his Latin, is feeble. The true opinions of Jordanes lie buried in Karl Müllenhoff's notes to Mommsen's edition of 1882. A final note on the Germanic tribes as they appealed to Tolkien's imagination may be found in Sir Charles Oman's classic, *A History of the Art of War in the Middle Ages* (London: Methuen, 1898). Its description on pp. 48–51 of the Lombards, that other Germanic 'horse-folk' *par excellence*, strongly recalls the Riders of the Mark.

When it comes to modern writers, Tolkien was notoriously beyond influence (though reports of his skimpy reading have been much exaggerated, see especially the start of Chapter 6 above). Three authors of his youth must remain prominent in any account. One is George MacDonald, whose influence Tolkien both admitted and minimised, see references in the 'Index' to *Letters*: besides *The Princess and the Goblin* of 1872 and *The Princess and Curdie* ten years later one should note especially *Phantastes* (1858) and *Lilith* (1895). Tolkien also read William Morris, probably with more appreciation: Morris after all knew a good deal of Icelandic and had been stirred by heroic story, trying to reproduce its effects in three of the romances of his last years, *The House of the Wolfings* (1888), *The Roots of the Mountains* (1889) and *The Glittering Plain* (1891). The first is clearly about Goths; the second gave a hint for Gollum, as for Brodda the Easterling in *The Silmarillion*; the last is about a quest for the Undying Lands. In my introduction to the World's Classics 1980 reprint of Morris's *The Wood at the World's End* (1894) I suggest a slight connection between that and the bewilderments of Fangorn Forest. Finally – though Tolkien never mentions him in a letter – I cannot help thinking that Tolkien knew

Kipling's stories well, especially the collections *Puck of Pook's Hill* (1906) and *Rewards and Fairies* (1910). In both the theme of an unchanging Englishness is strong, as is that of smithcraft; and Puck's dislike for the word 'fairies' and the 'sugar-and-shake-your-head' Victorian concepts attached is exactly that of Tolkien (see especially the story 'Weland's Sword').

I do not think Tolkien would have had much time for Kipling's 'Indian' works. The centre of all that has been mentioned in this essay is English tradition, though Tolkien was prepared to accept connections by blood with Iceland or Saxony or America, and (in a more gingerly way) by old proximity with the Irish or even the Finns. However he was in some ways what would now be called an 'ethnic' writer, though the rule for 'ethnicity' seems to be that anyone can have it *except Anglo-Saxons* (Tolkien was not quite a WASP). Largely this restriction is a penalty of success; since English is international the language naturally ceases to carry strong national sentiment. Behind that success, though, Tolkien was conscious of many centuries of discouragement which had suppressed native tradition in England more quickly, perhaps, than in any other European country. He valued what was left the more highly. In much of what he wrote and read one can see him trying to return to the time before confusion set in, when the traditions of the Shire and the Mark were uncorrupted.

Appendix B

FOUR 'ASTERISK' POEMS

Tolkien contributed some thirteen poems to *Songs for the Philologists*, according to Humphrey Carpenter in *Biography*, p. 271. Most are *jeux d'esprit*, either mildly satirical like 'Lit. and Lang.' (see p. 5 above), or else remarkable only for their linguistic dexterity (like 'Syx Mynet', an Old English rendering of 'I've Got Sixpence', or 'Ruddoc Hana', which is 'Who Killed Cock Robin?'). Four of them, however, seem to have something more personal to say, and I accordingly reprint them here by kind permission of the executors of Tolkien's estate. At some time after the production of *Songs for the Philologists* all four were furthermore carefully corrected and emended by Tolkien himself; I am grateful to Christopher Tolkien for showing me copies of the corrected texts, and have included, or noted, all such changes in the versions below. Since three of the poems are in Old English and one in Gothic, I have followed each text with a translation.

Two of the four may be described as 'birch' poems: for their relevance see pp. 206–7 above. The other two are poems in which a mortal is trapped in some way by an immortal. They are meant, I think, to appear as 'ancestors' for such ballads as 'Tam Lin' or 'The Queen of Elfan's Nourice' in the Child collection, or 'The Daemon Lover' in Sharp's, or 'Agnes and the Merman' in Svend Grundtvig's (see Appendix A above). The corrected version of 'Ofer Wídne Gársecg' indeed includes the note, in Tolkien's hand, 'An OE version of 'Twas in the broad Atlantic in the equinoctial gales That a young fellow fell overboard among the sharks and whales'.

The Birch Poems

(a)   BAGME BLOMA

> Brunaim bairiþ Bairka bogum
> laubans liubans liudandei,
> gilwagroni, glitmunjandei,
> bagme bloma, blauandei,
> fagrafahsa, liþulinþi,
> fraujinondei fairguni.

Wopjand windos, wagjand lindos,
lutiþ limam laikandei;
slaihta, raihta, hweitarinda,
razda rodeiþ reirandei,
bandwa bairhta, runa goda,
þiuda meina þiuþjandei.

Andanahti milhmam neipiþ,
liuhteiþ liuhmam lauhmuni;
laubos liubai fliugand lausai,
tulgus, triggwa, standandei
Bairka baza beidiþ blaika
fraujinondei fairguni.

(Gothic)

FLOWER OF THE TREES

The birch bears fine leaves on shining boughs, it grows pale green and glittering, the flower of the trees in bloom, fair-haired and supple-limbed, the ruler of the mountain.

The winds call, they shake gently, she bends her boughs low in sport; smooth, straight and white-barked, trembling she speaks a language, a bright token, a good mystery, blessing my people.

Evening grows dark with clouds, the lightning flashes, the fine leaves fly free, but firm and faithful the white birch stands bare and waits, ruling the mountain.

(I am indebted to Miss Rhona Beare of Adelaide University for showing me her translation of this poem.)

(b)   ÉADIG BÉO ÞU

Éadig béo þu, góda mann!
Éadig béo þu, léofe wíf!
Langre lisse ic þe ann –
hafa lof and líþe líf!
Hé þe hér swa sáre swanc,
rúna rædde' and fyrngewrit,
hál beo hé, on sálum wlanc,
healde láre' and wís gewit!

Éadge béo we eft swa nú!
Dréam ne dréose, drync genóg
flówe on fullum síþ swa iú –
fyllaþ wæge, fyllaþ cróg!

Byrla! byrla! medu scenc!
Dóm is feor þeah dóm sie strang.
Swinc forlǽt and géot ús drenc!
Lust is lýtel, earfoþ lang.

Uton singan scírne sang,
herian Beorc and byrcen cynn,
láre' and láreow, leornungmann –
sie ús sǽl and hǽl and wynn!
Ác sceal feallan on þæt fýr
lustes, léafes, lífes wan!
Beorc sceal ágan langne tír,
bréme glǽme glengan wang!

(*Old English*)

GOOD LUCK TO YOU

Good luck to you, good man, and to you, dear woman. I give you lasting joy, have praise and pleasant life. He who worked you here so hard, expounded runes and ancient texts, may he be happy too, merry at his feasts, and keep up good sense and learning.

May we be happy later as we are now, may joy not fail, and drink enough flow in the cups in times to come as times gone by – fill the cups and fill the pitchers! Waiter, waiter, give us mead! Doom is far though doom be strong, give up work and pour us drink.† Joy is little and labour long.

Let's sing a cheerful song, praise the Birch and birch's race, the teacher, the student and the subject, may we all have health and joy and happiness. The oak will fall into the fire, losing joy and leaf and life. The birch shall keep its glory long, shine in splendour over the bright plain.

'Trapped mortal' poems

(a)   IDES ÆLFSCÝNE

Þa ǽr ic wæs cniht, þa cóm ic on pliht:
Sum mægden mé métte ond mǽlde:
'Lá, léofa, wes hál! Sceal uncer gedál
nú nǽfre má weorðan on eorðan!'

† Tolkien wrote three versions of the fifth and seventh lines of this stanza. The printed text of *Songs* reads *Byrla! byrla! medu briht . . . Swinc tomorgen, drinc toniht!*, or 'Waiter! waiter! bright mead . . . work tomorrow, drink tonight!' Tolkien rejected this in his corrected version, writing at the bottom '*briht* is not an OE form'. In the left-hand margin he wrote: *Byrla medu! Byrla wín . . . Scenc nu his and scenc nu mín*, or 'Serve mead! Serve wine! . . . Now give him his and give me mine'. In the right-hand margin, in a more careful hand, he wrote the version used in text and translation above.

Nó má weorðan on eorðan. (*bis*)
Wá! ides ælfscýne, ond wá, wine míne!
Sceal næfre má weorðan on eorðan.

Héo cyste me sóna, þær líxte se móna;
  on clommum me clypte ond sælde;
on ofste me nóm mid hire' under glóm,
  þær sceadugong æfre wæs wæfre,
    wælmist æfre wæs wæfre. (*bis*)
  Wá! ides ælfscýne, ond wá, wine míne!
  Þær sceadugong æfre wæs wæfre.

Hwær wære' hit ic nát: we stigon on bát,
  þær murcnede mere on mealme.
Ofer lagu ic láð, ond módes ic máð,
  ac æfre me strongode longað,
    áwa strongode longað. (*bis*)
  Wá! ides ælfscýne, ond wá, wine míne!
  Þær æfre me strongode longað.

Þær gréne wæs grund, ond hwít hire hund,
  ond gylden wæs hwæte on healme,
on fyrlenum londe, on silfrenum stronde,
  þær darode dweorg under beorgum
    darode dweorg under beorgum. (*bis*)
  Wá! ides ælfscýne, ond wá, wine míne!
  Þær darode dweorg under beorgum.

To Gode' ic gebæd, elþéodunga sæd
  be dimmum ond dréorigum wægum.
Þær sunne ne scán, ac micel ʒimstán
  on lyfte þær gléow mid his léomum,
    léohte gléow mid his léomum. (*bis*)
  Wá! ides ælfscýne, ond wá, wine míne!
  On lyfte þær gléow mid his léomum.

Ofer missera hund ic wædla ond wund
  eft cyrde to mennisce' ond mæʒum:
on moldan wæs nú se ðe cúðe me iú,
  ond hár ic nu wániʒe ána.
    sáre wániʒe ána. (*bis*)
  Wá! ides ælfscýne, ond wá, wine míne!
  Ond hár ic nu wániʒe ána.

(*Old English*)

ELF-FAIR LADY

Before I was so much as a boy, I came into danger; a maiden met me and said: 'Greetings, my darling, from now on the two of us must never be separated on earth'
– never be separated on earth. Alas! elf-fair lady, and my friend, alas! must never more be separated on earth.

She kissed me straight away, where the moon was shining, she embraced me and bound me in her grasp. Quickly she took me with her under the gloom, where the shadow-way always flickered
– where the death-mist always flickered. Alas! elf-fair lady, and my friend, alas! where the shadow-way always flickered.

I don't know where I was, we stepped in a boat, where the sea moaned on the sand. I travelled over the ocean, and hid my thoughts to myself, but always my longing grew stronger
– always longing grew stronger. Alas! elf-fair lady, and my friend, alas! where longing always grew stronger.

There the ground was green, and her hound was white, and the wheat on the stalk was golden – in the far-off land, on the silver strand, where the dwarf lurked under the mountains
– the dwarf lurked under the mountains. Alas! elf-fair lady, and my friend, alas! where the dwarf lurked under the mountains.

I prayed to God, tired of my exile by the dim and dreary waves, where the sun did not shine, but a great gem-stone glowed there in the sky with his beams
– glowed brightly with his beams. Alas! elf-fair lady, and my friend, alas! glowed there in the sky with his beams.

Fifty years later I returned again, poor and hurt, to men and my family. The one who had known me before was now in the mould, and now I dwindle, grey and alone
– dwindle alone and in pain. Alas! elf-fair lady, and my friend, alas! and now I dwindle, grey and alone.

(b)   OFER WÍDNE GÁRSECG

þa ofer wídne gársecg wéow unwidre ceald,
    Sum hagusteald on lagu féoll on nicera geweald.
He legde lást swa fýres gnást, he snude' on sunde fléah,
    Oþþæt he métte meremenn déopan grunde néah.

La! hwæt, ic Gárdena on geárdagum geseah
Þéodcyninga-ninga-ninga þrym and –
   brýdealoþ under brimfaroþ déopan grunde néah!

Þæt merewíf þá of stóle úplang héo gestód,
   Mid fágum fintan fægniende: wæs hire grétung gód.
Héo smearciende smǽre' hie wende, tǽhte hire hand;
   'Nú, wilcuma, lá, hláford mín, on meremenna land!'

   La! hwæt, ic Gárdena on geárdagum onfand
   Þéodcyninga-ninga-ninga þrym and –
      brýdealoþ under brimfaroþ on meremenna land.

'Hér leng ne mót ic bídan, gedǽle' ic nú wiþ þé!'
   Héo cwæþ: 'Ná, ná! ne biþ hit swá! Þu gewífast nu on mé.
Nú eft þu gá, and cweþ: "Nó má fare' ic on sunde héah;
   Gemǽcca mín is meremenn déopan grunde néah." '
                                          (*First refrain*)

On nacan his genéatas hine sohton wíde' ymb sund;
   Hi wéopon and hi hréopon and hi sméadon þone grund.
Þa úp he sprang and hlúde sang, and hearde helman hrand:
   'Gáþ eft ongen! me béodeþ cwén on meremenna land.'
                                          (*Second refrain*)

'Tódǽlaþ nú mín ágen, pannan, páde, préon!
   Gifaþ hrægelciste mínre nifte, méder míne méon!
Se stéorman stód on stefne wód, and he to brime béah;
   Cwæþ: 'Far nu wel! þe hæbbe Hel, déopan grunde néah!'
                                          (*First refrain*)
                                          (*Old English*)

ACROSS THE BROAD OCEAN

When the cold blast was blowing across the broad ocean, a young man fell
into the sea, into the power of the monsters. As fast as fire he made his
way, he swam along so quickly – until he met the mermen near the deep
sea-bottom.
– Listen, I have seen the power of the kings of the people of the Spear-
Danes in days gone by† – and also the bridal beneath the sea, near the
deep sea-bottom!

The mermaid then stood up from her chair, fawning with her shining
tail: her greeting was good. Smirking with her lip she turned and stretched

---

† This is a quotation from the first few words of *Beowulf*. One might paraphrase
the refrain as saying that Tolkien wished for other epics more firmly centred on
monsters.

out her hand. 'Now welcome indeed, my lord, to the mermen's land!'
– Listen, I have discovered the power of the kings of the people of the
Spear-Danes in days gone by – and also the bridal beneath the sea, in the
mermen's land!

'I may not stay here any more, now separate from me!' She said: 'No, no,
it will not be so! Now you will marry me. Now go back again and say:
"I'll go on the high sea no more. My wife is from the mermen near the
deep sea-bottom." '

His companions in the ship sought him far across the sea. They wept and
cried out and scanned the sea-bottom. Then up he sprang and sang aloud
and thrust hard at the rudder: 'Go back again! The queen makes me an
invitation, from the mermen's land!'

'Share out my goods, my pots and coats and brooches, give my clothes-
chest to my niece and my shoes to my mother!' The steersman stood
angrily at the prow, and turned towards the sea, said: 'Fare you well, and
may Hell take you, near the deep sea-bottom.'

NOTES

CHAPTER 1

1 Edmund Wilson, *Axel's Castle* (New York and London: Scribner's, 1931), p. 252.
2 C. N. Manlove, *Modern Fantasy: Five Studies* (Cambridge: Cambridge University Press, 1975), p. 206.
3 Holger Pedersen, *The Discovery of Language: Linguistic Science in the Nineteenth Century*, trans. J. W. Spargo, 1931 (reprinted ed. Bloomington: Indiana University Press, 1962), p. 79.
4 L. Bloomfield, 'Why a Linguistic Society?', *Language* vol. 1 (1925), p. 1.
5 J. C. Collins, *The Study of English Literature*, 1891, but quoted here from D. J. Palmer, *The Rise of English Studies* (London: Oxford University Press, 1965), pp. 83–4.
6 See L. Bloomfield, *Language* (London: George Allen & Unwin, rev. ed. 1935), p. 12 ff.
7 See Pedersen, op. cit., pp. 263–4.
8 See Pedersen, op. cit., especially chapters 1, 2 and 7.
9 Max Müller, 'Comparative Mythology', 1856, in *Chips from a German Workshop* (4 vols., London: Longmans, 1880), vol. 2, p. 26.
10 There is an account of the affair in Peter Ganz's 'Eduard Sievers', *Beiträge zur Geschichte der Deutschen Sprache und Literatur*, vol. 100 (1978), pp. 76–8.
11 See D. J. Palmer, op. cit., p. 97.
12 R. W. Chambers, *Man's Unconquerable Mind* (London: Jonathan Cape, 1939), pp. 342–3.
13 The phrase was coined by Sir Walter Raleigh, Professor of English Literature at Oxford 1904–29 and quoted as evidence in *The Teaching of English in England* (London: HMSO, 1921), p. 218.
14 Pedersen, op. cit., p. 108.
15 *Widsith: a study in Old English Heroic Legend*, ed. R. W. Chambers (Cambridge: Cambridge University Press, 1912), pp. 1–2.
16 *Die beiden ältesten Gedichte aus dem achten Jahrhundert*, ed. W. and J. Grimm (Cassel: Thurneisen, 1812), p. 31.
17 Axel Olrik, *The Heroic Legends of Denmark*, trans. Lee Hollander (New York: American–Scandinavian Foundation, 1919), p. 85.
18 'Monsters', p. 271.
19 *Corpus Poeticum Boreale*, ed. G. Vigfusson and F. York Powell (2 vols., Oxford: Clarendon Press, 1883), vol. 1, p. xcvii.
20 See Pedersen, op. cit., pp. 277–92, and O. Jespersen, *Language* (London: George Allen & Unwin, 1922), pp. 80–3.
21 Text and translation are those of Thomas Jones, 'The Black Book of Carmarthen "Stanzas of the Graves" ', *Proceedings of the British Academy*, vol. 53 (1967), pp. 125–7.
22 See R. M. Wilson, *The Lost Literature of Medieval England* (London: Methuen, 1952), p. 15.
23 Palmer, op. cit., pp. 66–117.
24 Peter Ganz, 'Jacob Grimm's Conception of German Studies', Inaugural Lecture (Oxford: Clarendon Press, 1973), pp. 7–9.

25 J. Grimm, *Teutonic Mythology*, trans. J. S. Stallybrass (4 vols., London: George Bell, 1882–8), vol. 3, p. lv.

26 Remarks quoted in the preceding paragraph come respectively from Edmund Wilson in the review already cited, p. 312; Lin Carter, *Tolkien: A Look Behind The Lord of the Rings* (New York: Ballantine, 1969), pp. 93–4; Neil D. Isaacs, 'On the Possibilities of Writing Tolkien Criticism', in *Tolkien and the Critics*, ed. N. D. Isaacs and Rose A. Zimbardo (Notre Dame: University of Notre Dame Press, 1968), p. 7; and Robert J. Reilly, 'Tolkien and the Fairy Story', Isaacs and Zimbardo anthology, p. 137.

CHAPTER 2

1 J. R. R. Tolkien, 'For W.H.A.', *Shenandoah: The Washington and Lee University Review*, vol. 18 no. 2 (Winter 1967), pp. 96–7.

2 See W. Grimm, *Die deutsche Heldensage*, 3rd ed. (Gutersloh: Bertelmann, 1889), p. 383, and 'O F-S', p. 31.

3 J. R. R. Tolkien, 'Goblin Feet', in *Oxford Poetry 1915*, ed. G. D. H. C[ole] and T. W. E[arp] (Oxford: B. H. Blackwell, 1915), pp. 120–1. I quote from this first published version, which differs slightly from that used by Humphrey Carpenter, *Biography*, pp. 74–5.

4 G. B. Smith, 'Songs on the Downs', *Oxford Poetry 1915*, p. 116.

5 See *Biography*, pp. 71–7, 89–95.

6 A list of published poems appears in *Biography*, p. 268ff., though nothing in print has yet disclosed their serpentine intertwinings. Several poems were clearly rewritten several, or many, times.

7 J. R. R. Tolkien, 'The Name "Nodens"', Appendix 1 to *Report on the Excavation . . . in Lydney Park, Gloucestershire*, Reports of the Research Committee of the Society of Antiquaries, no. 9 (London: Oxford University Press, 1932), pp. 132–7.

8 Since writing this I have noticed that one of the Inklings, the Rev. Adam Fox, actually *did* write a narrative poem on *Old King Coel* (the proper spelling), which Tolkien knew, see *Letters*, p. 36.

9 There is an edition of it, with translation, in *Medieval English Lyrics*, ed. R. T. Davies (London: Faber and Faber, 1963), pp. 71–3.

10 J. R. R. Tolkien, '*Sigelwara Land*: Part II', *Medium Aevum* vol. 3 (1934), pp. 110–11.

11 See *Biography*, pp. 138, 194–5, 239–41.

12 I have to admit no source for this other than Oxford gossip. There is however a highly characteristic anti-Tolkien conversation presented in fictional form in J. I. M. Stewart's *A Memorial Service* (London: Methuen paperback, 1977), p. 176. In this a Regius Professor writes off 'J. B. Timbermill' – evidently Tolkien – as 'A notable scholar' who 'ran off the rails'.

13 For the quotations above, see *The Saga of King Heidrek the Wise*, ed. and trans. C. Tolkien (London: Nelson's, 1960), pp. xxiii and 45.

CHAPTER 3

1 The gloss, to the poem 'June', was not written by Spenser himself, but by a friend known only as 'E.K.' – someone even prouder than Spenser of his Classical learning and so the more likely to make unbelievable errors over non-Classical matters.

2 'Elfin' is in the poem 'Light as Leaf on Lindentree', but has become 'elven'

in the revision given to Aragorn, *LOTR* I 204–5; 'fairy' occurs once in all editions of *The Hobbit*, 'gnome' in the first edition only. 'Goblin', a Latin-derived word, is used throughout but not after *The Hobbit*. For 'dwarfish', see below p. 52 – another printer's correction?

3 This is a modernised form of a ballad recorded in *Danmarks Gamle Folkeviser* (12 vols., Copenhagen: Thiele, 1853–1976) Vol. II, 105–9, by Svend Grundtvig – son of the Beowulfian scholar Nikolai Grundtvig.

4 C. S. Lewis, *The Problem of Pain* (London: Geoffrey Bles, 1940), Fontana Books reprint, 1957, p. 13. This was clearly an 'Inkling' theory, cp. Tolkien's 'supremely convincing tone of Primary Art' (*TL*, p. 63).

5 See the *Prose Edda* of Snorri Sturluson, *Skáldskaparmál* sections 35 and 39. There is a full translation by A. G. Brodeur (New York: American–Scandinavian Foundation, 1916).

6 Preface to J. and W. Grimm, *Haus- und Kindermärchen* (3rd ed., Göttingen: Dieterichische Buchhandlung, 1849), p. xxviii.

7 Snorri, *Prose Edda*, *Skáldskaparmál* section 49.

8 As a youth (by dwarvish reckoning) he kills Azog in revenge for his father, and looks into Moria, *LOTR* III, 356; as an old man he is killed fighting, III, 360. In between he is seen bandying words with Sauron's messenger, *LOTR* I, 254; and sticking to the letter of Thorin's bargain in *The Hobbit*, p. 304.

9 Quoted in Ganz, Inaugural Lecture, p. 5.

10 I am indebted for this point to an article by Jessica Kemball-Cook, in *Amon Hen: the Bulletin of the Tolkien Society of Great Britain*, no. 23 (December 1976), p. 11.

11 See Paul Kocher, *Master of Middle-earth* (Boston: Houghton Mifflin, 1972), Penguin Books edition, 1974, p. 24.

12 C. S. Lewis, *The Problem of Pain* (London: Geoffrey Bles, 1940), Fontana reprint 1957, p. 42.

13 See 'The Wreck of the Birkenhead', *Annual Register* 1852, pp. 470–3.

14 See *The Vinland Sagas*, trans. M. Magnusson and H. Pálsson (Harmondsworth: Penguin Books, 1965), p. 104.

15 Since this is a contentious piece, I have not given my own translation but that of Clark Hall and Wrenn, to which Tolkien wrote the 'Preface' in 1940.

16 Lewis, *The Problem of Pain*, p. 62.

17 'Monsters', pp. 258–9.

CHAPTER 4

1 Paul Kocher, *Master of Middle-Earth*, p. 161, notes that the definition of 'blunderbuss' ascribed in Farmer Giles to 'the Four Wise Clerks of Oxenford' is that of the *OED*, the Four Wise Clerks being the four editors, J. A. H. Murray, H. Bradley, W. A. Craigie and C. T. Onions. Giles's blunderbuss, like Tolkien's dwarves, does not fit the *OED* definition.

2 When I first thought of this, in my article 'Creation from Philology in *The Lord of the Rings*' in *Memoriam Essays*, I wrote it off as 'entirely adventitious'. It has grown on me since, which may be no more than *furor allegoricus* or allegorist's mania. However I did not at that time realise how well *Farmer Giles* fitted the other allegories of 1935–43.

3 This point is also made by Paula Marmor, 'An Etymological Excursion among the Shire-Folk', in *An Introduction to Elvish*, ed. Jim Allan (Hayes: Bran's Head Books, 1978), pp. 181–4.

4 C. S. Lewis's *That Hideous Strength* once again offers a close parallel in the idea of language with meanings 'inherent in [its syllables] as the shape of the great

Sun is inherent in the little waterdrop', p. 281. Later it appears that this is a language even beyond 'Numinor', as Lewis spells it.

5 The two towns from *Giles* and *LOTR* are linked in traditional rhyme: 'Brill on the hill, Oakley in the hole, dirty Ickford and stinking Worminghall.'

6 It is interesting that the first version of this song, 'Light as Leaf on Lindentree' in *The Gryphon* for 1925, does not use the word 'shadow'. Tolkien rewrote it to bring it into line with his developing myth.

7 *Road*, p. 64. Even there it is not entirely clear. Tolkien gave first a word-for-word translation of the Sindarin and then a connected English one, but the two are not altogether consistent with each other. I have combined them.

8 It is perhaps worth noting that *all* the names in Théoden's pedigree from Thengel back to Brego are Old English words for 'king', except for Déor and Gram, for reasons I do not understand, and excepting Eorl the Young, founder of the line, who looks back to a time before kings were created and when all men, as in the Old Norse poem *Rígspula*, were 'earl', 'churl' or 'thrall'.

9 This even has an effect on Merry the hobbit. At III, 77 he begs Théoden to let him come with the Riders: 'I would not have it said of me in song only that I was always left behind!' The phrasing is ironic, but it is an attempt to find an argument that Théoden will accept. For remarks on how styles shape thoughts, see especially *Letters*, pp. 225–6.

10 See N. Barley, 'Old English colour classification: where do matters stand?' *Anglo-Saxon England*, vol. 3 (1974), pp. 15–28.

11 It is mentioned by C. L. Wrenn, 'The Word "Goths"', *Proceedings of the Leeds Philosophical and Literary Society* (Lit.-Hist. Class), vol. 2 (1928–32), pp. 126–8.

12 See Arthur J. Evans, 'The Rollright Stones and their Folk-lore', *Folklore*, vol. 6 (1895), pp. 6–51.

CHAPTER 5

1 These opinions are taken from the anonymous review in the *Times Literary Supplement* (25 November 1955); C. N. Manlove's *Modern Fantasy*, p. 183; an anonymous review in *Punch* (16 November 1966); a review by Mark Roberts in *Essays in Criticism*, vol. 6 (1956), p. 459. But the list could easily be extended.

2 See Louise Creighton, *The Life and Letters of Mandell Creighton* (2 vols., London: Longmans Green & Co., 1904), vol. 1, p. 372.

3 It is no. 14 of *The Durham Proverbs*, ed. O. S. Arngart (Lund: Lunds Universitets Årsskrift, 1956), vol. 52, no. 2.

4 These accusations are made most clearly in C. N. Manlove's *Modern Fantasy*, pp. 173–84 – a book I find often imperceptive and almost always unreflective, but certainly written with energy.

5 It is worth noting that not even the Ringwraiths were originally evil, though they have become absolutely so. The word 'haggard', used at II, 315, implies how this happened. It was first used as a noun, to indicate a hawk caught when fully fledged; later it came to mean 'wild, untamed', and to be applied with special reference to a look in the eyes, 'afterwards to the injurious effect upon the countenance of privation, want of rest, fatigue, anxiety, terror or worry'. At this stage it was influenced by 'hag', an old word for witch, and implied also gaunt or fleshless. The Ringwraiths are fleshless and 'faded' from addiction, and privation, and from being caught by Sauron. They are also witches, simultaneously victims of evil within and agents of evil without. Their leader is 'helmed and crowned with fear', i.e. he wears an *ægishjálmr* or 'fear-helm' like

Fáfnir the dragon; dragons too were in some opinions misers transformed by their own wickedness, see p. 69 above.

6 Edmund Fuller says that Tolkien said this to him in a conversation in June 1962, see 'The Lord of the Hobbits: J. R. R. Tolkien', in *Tolkien and the Critics*, ed. Neil D. Isaacs and Rose A. Zimbardo, p. 35. I am sure Tolkien did say this; but he had perhaps grown accustomed to suiting his conversation to his interviewers' understanding. 'Angel' is anyway derived from Greek *angelos*, 'messenger'; in that (recondite) sense Gandalf is 'an angel'.

7 *King Alfred's Old English Version of Boethius*, ed. W. J. Sedgefield (Oxford: Clarendon Press, 1899), p. 128, my translation.

8 The two concepts are distinguished with special sharpness by Aragorn in his death-scene in Appendix A I, III, 343–4. It is not clear that Arwen appreciates the distinction.

9 Richard C. West, in 'The Interlace Structure of *The Lord of the Rings*', *A Tolkien Compass*, ed. Jared Lobdell (La Salle, Illinois: Open Court, 1975), pp. 77–94, also asks why Tolkien should for once follow Old French models, but gives a more abstract answer.

10 *The Works of Sir Thomas Malory*, ed. E. Vinaver (3 vols., Oxford: Clarendon Press, 2nd ed. 1967), vol. 1, pp. lxiv–lxv. The passage is a description of one 'Vulgate' romance specifically, but can be applied readily to others.

11 Thus Galadriel's piece of advice to Legolas at II, 106, 'Legolas Greenleaf, long under tree/In joy thou hast lived. Beware of the Sea! . . .' echoes in rhythm and syntax one of R. M. Wilson's scraps of *The Lost Literature of Medieval England*, p. 99:

> In clento cou bache   kenelm kynebearn
> lith under [haȝe] thorne   hæuedes bereaved.
> 'In Clent by the cow-stream   Kenelm the king's child
> lies under hawthorn,   robbed of his head.'

I think Tolkien put this in only because the model came from the depths of the Mark, indeed from Clent, five miles from his boyhood home in Rednal. Wilson's book came out in 1952, but the section on Kenelm had come out separately as an article in 1941.

12 If the war of the Ring had been World War II, 'then certainly the Ring would have been seized and used against Sauron; he would not have been annihilated but enslaved, and Barad-dûr would not have been destroyed but occupied. Saruman, failing to get possession of the Ring, would in the confusion and treacheries of the time have found in Mordor the missing links in his own researches into Ring-lore, and before long he would have made a Great Ring of his own with which to challenge the self-styled Ruler of Middle-earth.' One sees that the Ring=the A-bomb; Sauron=the Axis powers; the parties at the Council of Elrond=the Western Allies; Saruman=the U.S.S.R.; 'treacheries' and 'in Mordor'=the role of Anglo-American traitors and of German scientists in creating the Russian A-bomb. This is a proper allegory, exact in all parallels; but it is not *The Lord of the Rings*.

13 See III, 99 and 129. 'Heathen' of course is a word used normally only by Christians and so out of place in Middle-earth. In Appendix (c) to his British Academy lecture Tolkien had remarked on the one place where the *Beowulf*-poet used this word of men, thinking it a mistake or an interpolation. By the 1950s he may have changed his mind, accepting stronger Christian and anti-heroic elements in *Beowulf*, *Maldon* and his own fiction.

14 The *TLS* reviewer was convinced of this, see p. 110 above. But compare Aragorn, III, 53: right does not give might, nor vice versa. The 'theory of courage' and Beorhtwold of course say unmistakably 'right is weak and might is wrong', though Tolkien did not believe that either.

15 Fair and uncommitted views of these concepts may be found in Herbert Butterfield's *The Whig Interpretation of History* (London: George Bell, 1931), and C. B. Cox's *The Free Spirit* (London: Oxford University Press, 1963). The former discusses Lord Acton (and his maxim) in some detail.

16 This comes in a reply to Mr David I. Masson's letter in the *TLS* (9 December 1955), remarking on several factual and thematic inaccuracies in the earlier review. The reviewer flatly denied them all. 'Hoity-toity', observed Tolkien.

17 *The Tempest*, ed. Frank Kermode (Arden edition of the Works of Shakespeare, London: Methuen, 5th ed., 1954), p. liv.

CHAPTER 6

1 See *Biography*, pp. 27–8, 137, 165.

2 The quotations above are taken from reviews in the *Sunday Times* (30 October 1955) and *Daily Telegraph* (27 August 1954), from Mark Roberts's long account already cited in *Essays in Criticism* (1956), and from Edwin Muir's review in the *Observer* (22 August 1954).

3 C. N. Manlove, *Modern Fantasy*, p. 189.

4 *Works of Sir Thomas Malory*, ed. Vinaver, vol. III, p. 1259.

5 In *Letters*, p. 308, Tolkien said the phrase means 'O beautiful ones, parents of beautiful children'. This has a significance in context, for Fangorn's tragedy is to be childless; however even untranslated it attains its main effect, of ceremoniousness.

6 I am thinking of Vera Lynn's famous rendering of 'We'll meet again,/Don't know where, don't know when,/But I know we'll meet again/Some sunny day'. No critic would ever argue that this is a great poem. However in the context of wartime separations it may well have said something, very powerfully, for people ordinarily unaffected by poetry of any description.

7 There is a modern version of it in Joseph Jacobs's collection of *English Fairy Tales*, first published in London by David Nutt, 1890, but reprinted by the Bodley Head Press in 1968. Jacobs's source, however, goes back to 1814 and beyond. The fairy-tale makes it clear that Shakespeare *had* got the story right, and had not confused it, as modern editors usually assert, with 'Jack the Giant-Killer'.

8 There is a confusion here in all indexes to *LOTR*. 'The Old Walking Song' – i.e. the one sung twice by Bilbo and once by Frodo – is at I 44, I 82–3, III 266. Though Frodo *calls* his song at III 308 'the old walking-song' it is in fact a variant of the verse indexed as 'A Walking Song', I 86–7. Fluidity is however an element of all these verses. The elvish song at III 308 is a mixture of English and Sindarin variants from I 89 and I 250.

9 See *The Faerie Queene* Book III canto III stanza 48, 'There shall a sparke of fire, which hath long-while/Bene in his ashes raked up and hid,/Be freshly kindled . . .'. 'From the ashes a fire shall be woken,' says Bilbo.

10 Tolkien's notes on this passage in *Road*, pp. 58–62, make it clear that Galadriel is making a wish for Frodo (one that comes true). Tolkien there refined his translation of the Quenya to 'May it be that' (thou shalt find Valinor) . . .

11 The poem 'The Nameless Land', printed in *Realities*, ed. G. S. Tancred, 1927, is however in a close imitation of the *Pearl* stanza-form.

12 There is an account of the finds, with photographs, in P. V. Glob, *The Bog People* (London: Faber and Faber, 1969).

13 Lewis's attention may have been drawn to Uhtred by M. D. Knowles, 'The Censured Opinions of Uhtred [*sic*] of Boldon', *Proceedings of the British Academy*, vol. 37 (1951), pp. 305–42.

14 The most convenient excerpt from this is in *Beowulf and its Analogues*, trans. G. Garmonsway and J. Simpson (London and New York: Dent and Dutton, 1968).

15 All these are asserted in *Byrhtferth's Manual*, ed. S. J. Crawford, Early English Text Society, Original Series 177 (London: Oxford University Press, 1929), pp. 82–5.

16 There is similarly no reference (or almost none) to any of these things in *Beowulf*. The person who steals the dragon's cup may have been a slave – the word is blurred in the manuscript. Two characters known from other sources to have had incestuous births pass without comment in *Beowulf*. These seem clear cases of the poet saying the best he could, or not saying the worst he could, of characters he knew had been pagan, slave-owning, ignorant of Christian sexual ethics. All this gave a lead to Tolkien.

17 'Monsters', p. 257.

18 There is an extensive 'reconstructed' account of this thesis in Carpenter, *Inklings*, Part One, section 3, especially pp. 42–5.

19 *The English and Scottish Popular Ballads*, ed. F. J. Child (5 vols., Boston: Houghton Mifflin, 1882–98), vol. II, p. 230, 'Sweet William's Ghost'.

20 Northrop Frye, *Anatomy of Criticism: four essays* (Princeton: Princeton University Press, 1957), p. 33. The material cited here is from pp. 33–43 of the first essay, but see also p. 117 (on C. S. Lewis and Charles Williams), p. 186 (on Gothic revivals), p. 187 (on 'middle' worlds); and further N. Frye, *The Secular Scripture: a study of the structure of romance* (Cambridge, Mass.: Harvard University Press, 1976), where some remarks on Tolkien *are* made.

21 See Saxo Grammaticus, *The Danish History, Books I–IX*, trans. O. Elton with intro. by F. York Powell (London: David Nutt, 1894), p. 38.

CHAPTER 7

1 Phrases in quotation marks are from a letter to me by Christopher Tolkien.

2 Dates of parts of the *Unfinished Tales* given here and subsequently are deductions from Christopher Tolkien's notes, *UT*, pp. 4–13.

3 This is the opinion, for instance, of Robert Foster in *The Complete Guide to Middle-Earth* (London: George Allen & Unwin, 2nd ed., 1978), who argues in the 'Introduction' that the human conflicts of *The Lord of the Rings* gain force from their relation to the greater ones of *The Silmarillion*.

4 This 'Epilogue' is to be found in the manuscript copy of *The Lord of the Rings* in the possession of Marquette University. It consists of a scene in which Sam Gamgee answers the questions of his children, and receives an invitation to meet Aragorn at the Brandywine Bridge.

5 In the first version of 'The Passing of the Grey Company' (*LOTR* III, 53), Gimli learns that Aragorn has looked in the palantír, and expresses astonishment. ' "You forget to whom you speak," said Aragorn sternly, and his eyes glinted. "What do you fear that I should say: that I had a rascal of a rebel dwarf here that I would gladly exchange for a serviceable orc?" ' (in the second edition this last sarcastic question is eliminated).

6 I am thinking of Ursula LeGuin's *Earthsea* trilogy, see my article 'The Magic Art and the Evolution of Words' in *Mosaic*, vol. 10, no. 2 (1977), pp. 147–64.

7 See J. F. Campbell's *Popular Tales of the Western Highlands* (4 vols., Paisley and London: Alexander Gardner, 1890–3), vol. 2, p. 75. Tolkien refers to this collection in the notes to 'On Fairy-Stories' (*TL*, pp. 21, 22, 59).

8 This quotation is from the legend of St Michael in *The Early South English*

Legendary, ed. C. Horstmann, Early English Text Society, Original Series 87 (London: Trübner, 1887), lines 253–8.

9 To labour this point further: Gandalf is a Maia, was called by Tolkien 'an angel', yet is perceived by Men – as his name indicates – as some sort of 'elf'. Conversely an ignorant Man, looking at Galadriel (an elf), might well think she was an 'angel', or of the same order as the Maia Melian. Both ladies would be so superior to him as to make fine distinction impossible.

10 Tolkien kept changing his mind about this: the strong implication of *LOTR* I, 394 (confirmed by *Road*, p. 60), is that Galadriel, as last survivor of the leaders of the Noldorian revolt, was banned from returning to Valimar. In *The Silmarillion*, pp. 83–4, Galadriel acquiesces in the revolt out of the motive (surely not entirely a good one) 'to rule a realm [in Middle-earth] at her own will'. There is an echo of this when Frodo offers her the Ring at *LOTR* I, 381, and she sees herself as 'a Queen'. In his later years, however, after 1968, Tolkien suggested that she was not banned, but self-exiled, having refused pardon (*UT*, pp. 230–1). And in 'the last month of his life' he wrote a more complicated account (*UT*, pp. 231–2), exculpating her entirely. This, I feel, was another example of the 'soft-heartedness' discussed on p. 173 above.

11 By Paul H. Kocher, *A Reader's Guide to The Silmarillion* (London and New York: Thames and Hudson, 1980), p. 56.

12 For older theories, see Kaarle Krohn, *Kalevalastudien* (Helsinki: Finnish Academy of Sciences, 1924–5). The modern remark quoted is from *Finnish Folk Poetry, Epic: An Anthology in Finnish and English*, ed. and trans. Matti Kuusi, Keith Bosley and Michael Branch (Helsinki: Finnish Literature Society, 1977), p. 526. This book however gives an excellent introduction to the *sampo* concept.

13 'Having the same mother, having different mothers': the terms are taken from the Eddic poem *Hamðismál* (about the death of the king of the Goths).

14 *Kalevala: the land of the heroes*, trans. W. F. Kirby (London and New York: Dent and Dutton, 1907, repr. 1977), vol. 2, p. 124. This is the translation Tolkien used. He no doubt read on and may have relished the moral at the end of the *runo*, warning men against sending children to be fostered by strangers.

CHAPTER 8

1 Compare 'the skin o' my nuncle Tim' in Sam's 'Rhyme of the Troll', *LOTR* I, 219. Many years before Tolkien had noted 'naunt' for 'aunt' in *Sir Gawain*; and Haigh's Huddersfield glossary of 1928 (see p. 72 above) showed that saying 'aunt' instead of 'nont' was considered affected by his older informants. As often, old English survived only as vulgar modern English.

2 Since writing the paragraph above, I have been informed by Mr John D. Rateliff of Milwaukee, Wisconsin, that 'The Last Ship' was not a new poem in 1962, but a revision of the poem 'Firiel', published first on pp. 30–2 of the 1934 volume (no. 4) of *The Chronicle of the Convents of the Sacred Heart*, produced by the convent at Roehampton. Sister Joan Loveday, the convent's archivist, provided Mr Rateliff with a copy, which he very kindly passed to me. Comparison of the two versions, however, shows substantial changes made between 1934 and 1962. In particular the tone of 'Firiel' is much more optimistic than that of 'The Last Ship'. It is 'a vision' which fades, not 'sunlight'; the last two stanzas are not of resignation but of cheerful activity; the last words are not 'their song has faded' but 'please pass the honey'. 'The Last Ship' relates to 'Firiel', then, much as 'The Sea-Bell' to 'Looney'; it shows increasing darkness, growing uncertainty. I should add that Mr Rateliff is of the opinion that few

of the poems in *TB* are entirely new, though early versions may be in obscure periodicals or hidden under pseudonyms.
3 The best account of this theory is in *Inklings*, pp. 42–5, but see also 'On Fairy-Stories' (*TL*, pp. 43–50, 61–3).
4 *Early South English Legendary*, ed. Horstmann, 'Life of St. Brendan', lines 55–6.

AFTERWORD

1 For thorough analyses of the two deficiencies mentioned, see respectively Darko Suvin, *Metamorphoses of Science Fiction* (New Haven and London: Yale University Press, 1979), and C. S. Ferns, *Aldous Huxley: Novelist* (London: Athlone Press, 1980). Tolkien liked science fiction, and had some (not very obvious) similarities to Huxley.

2 See William James, *The Will to Believe and other essays* (New York: Longmans Green, 1896), pp. 65–6, and further *Pragmatism* (same imprint, 1907), pp. 11–14.

3 I am referring in the paragraph above to such works as Ruth S. Noel, *The Mythology of Middle-Earth* (Boston: Houghton Mifflin, 1977), Timothy R. O'Neill, *The Individuated Hobbit: Jung, Tolkien and the Archetypes of Middle-Earth* (Boston: Houghton Mifflin, 1979), Anne C. Petty, *One Ring to Bind them All: Tolkien's Mythology* (University: University of Alabama Press, 1979), especially p. 103. But see also the books cited in note 26 to chapter 1. For a detailed critique of one particular work, see my review of Jane Chance Nitzsche, *Tolkien's Art: A Mythology for England* (London: Macmillan, 1979), in *Notes and Queries* N.S. vol. 27 (1980), pp. 570-2.

4 *Four Quartets*, 'East Coker', lines 174–81, quoted here from *The Complete Poems and Plays of T. S. Eliot* (London: Faber and Faber, 1969).

5 All of these have been discussed above, except 'worship'. If one re-reads the line from Milton's sonnet quoted on p. 168 above, one can see that Milton *meant* 'worship' to mean 'honour or revere as a supernatural being . . . or as a holy thing'. But that idolatrous sense vanishes if one gives 'worship' its older sense (derived from 'worth') of 'regard . . . with honour or respect'. Tolkien surely appreciated the way an insult to 'our fathers' could be read as a compliment.

6 Tolkien was perhaps amused by the proverb 'Where there's a will there's a way'. It is not recorded till 1822, but would have sounded much the same in Old English. He made it into a line of alliterative poetry, accordingly, in *LOTR* III, 77, 'Where will wants not, a way opens'. 'Where there's a whip there's a will', say the orcs, *LOTR* III, 208. In the Old Norse *Hamðismál* there is a discouraging variant, *Illt er blauðom hal brautir kenna*, 'It is ill luck to show cowards the road', or as I would put it, 'Where there's no will there's no way'. This often seems more appropriate.

7 Tolkien's 'Valedictory Address to the University of Oxford, 5 June 1959', comprises pp. 16–32 of *Memoriam Essays*; this quotation is on p. 18.

8 Two of these have been discussed above; for 'fallow' see *Memoriam Essays*, pp. 299–300; 'Quickbeam' is a dictionary joke. *Cwicbéam*, 'live-tree', is glossed in Anglo-Saxon dictionaries as 'poplar' or 'aspen', a decision Tolkien knew was wrong (a) because poplars were imports, like rabbits, (b) because in England 'quicken' or 'wicken' is still the common word for 'mountain-ash'. Quickbeam accordingly *is* a rowan-Ent (*LOTR* II, 86); but he has become a 'quick-tree' in the modern sense, not the old one.

9 J. L. Lowes, *The Road to Xanadu: A Study in the Ways of the Imagination* (London: Constable, 1927), p. 44.

INDEX

References to characters, places, species etc. in Tolkien's fiction are deliberately selective, as is the indexing of Appendix A, on sources.